CHALLENGING BOUNDARIES

CHALLENGING BOUNDARIES

GENDER AND PERIODIZATION

edited by

Joyce W. Warren and Margaret Dickie

The University of Georgia Press . Athens and London

© 2000 by the University of Georgia Press
Athens, Georgia 30602
All rights reserved
Set in ten on thirteen Electra with Gill Sans
by G & S Typesetters, Inc.
Printed and bound by Maple-Vail
The paper in this book meets the guidelines for
permanence and durability of the Committee on
Production Guidelines for Book Longevity of the
Council on Library Resources.

Printed in the United States of America
04 03 02 01 00   C   5 4 3 2 1
04 03 02 01 00   P   5 4 3 2 1

Library of Congress Cataloging-in-Publication Data

Challenging boundaries : gender and periodization / edited by Joyce W. Warren
and Margaret Dickie.
    p. cm.
    Includes bibliographical references.
    ISBN 0-8203-2123-0 (alk. paper). — ISBN 0-8203-2124-9 (pbk. : alk. paper)
    1. American literature—Women authors—History and criticism.
2. Feminism and literature—United States—History. 3. Women and
literature—United States—History. 4. American literature—Periodization.
5. Feminist literary criticism. 6. Authorship—Sex differences. I. Warren,
Joyce W. II. Dickie, Margaret, 1935–   .
RS147.C48 2000
810.9'9287—dc21   99-32052

British Library Cataloging-in-Publication Data available

In memory of Margaret Dickie—
a scholar of great integrity and penetration,
a respected colleague,
and a beloved friend

CONTENTS

ix   **The Challenge of Women's Periods**
Joyce W. Warren

ONE   CHALLENGING BOUNDARIES

3   **Performativity and the Repositioning of American Literary Realism**
Joyce W. Warren

26   **Women's Masterpieces**
Josephine Donovan

39   **Frances Harper, Charlotte Forten, and African American Literary Reconstruction**
Carla L. Peterson

62   **"A Queer Lot" and the Lesbians of 1914: Amy Lowell, H.D., and Gertrude Stein**
Susan McCabe

91   **Black Women Writers of the Harlem Renaissance**
Crystal J. Lucky

107   **Complications of Feminist and Ethnic Literary Theories in Asian American Literature**
Shirley Geok-lin Lim

TWO   RE(DE)FRAMINGS

137   **"American Puritanism" and Mary White Rowlandson's *Narrative***
Teresa A. Toulouse

159   **Essential, Portable, Mythical Margaret Fuller**
Mary Loeffelholz

185 **Emily Dickinson in History and Literary History**
Margaret Dickie

202 **María Amparo Ruiz de Burton Negotiates American Literary Politics and Culture**
Amelia María de la Luz Montes

226 **Edith Wharton's Ironic Realism**
Carol J. Singley

248 **The "Founding Mother": Gertrude Stein and the Cubist Phenomenon**
Jacqueline Vaught Brogan

267 **The Self-Categorization, Self-Canonization, and Self-Periodization of Adrienne Rich**
Sylvia Henneberg

285 **List of Contributors**

287 **Index**

THE CHALLENGE
OF WOMEN'S PERIODS

Joyce W. Warren

One of the most obdurate institutional restraints in literature is its periodization. Reinforced by the needs of teaching, of criticism, and of professional specialization, established literary periods persist because they serve all of these activities. Originally created by a critical establishment that was male-dominated for a predominantly white male literary tradition and sanctioned by a chronological inevitability, such literary periods have always been fictions, but fictions with the tenacity of convenience and convention. Now, however, as the profession disentangles itself from the white male establishment, it confronts the inadequacy of the old periodization of literature. New historicists, African American specialists, Asian American specialists, literary historians, and feminists who may belong to some of the other categories as well — all have mounted an attack on traditional literary periods. Still, inscribed in anthologies, perpetuated by the college curriculum, and central to most faculty search committees, these periods appear unyielding and their replacements a matter of considerable debate.

The feminist challenges to the periodization of American literature provide the focus of this collection of essays, although, as will become apparent, these concerns intersect with other issues and interests. Although feminist critics have worked successfully to recover neglected women writers and to place them in the canon along with established women writers, generally these critics have not been able to dislodge the periods into which American literature is divided. Typically, women writers are simply wedged into established literary periods that hardly suit them. For example, Emily Dickinson is sometimes located in the so-called American Renaissance, a category of all-male writers that was created by F. O. Matthiessen in the 1940s for his own and the nation's purposes and that, although frequently challenged, still dominates studies of nineteenth-century American literature. Only by being considered a disciple of the much lesser poet Ralph Waldo Emerson can Dickinson be added to this literary period, and even then she is out of place. Or, if located with writers in the last half of the nineteenth century, Dickinson is no more easily accommodated among the prose writers of that era. In the twentieth century, critics have found it difficult to find a place for Gertrude Stein in the literary period of modernism with its present boundaries. Despite the priority of Stein's experimental work, critics continue to begin the period with Ezra Pound. The awkwardness of this situation, the challenge she poses to Pound's supremacy, has perhaps occasioned the creation of the new term "High Modernist" to designate the old guard. The condescending implications of this designation are obvious: if the male writers are "high modernists," does that mean that Stein is a "low modernist"?

But gender is only one factor in the complicated process of questioning established literary periods. Issues of race, ethnicity, class, and sexuality combine with gender to challenge traditional periodization. African American literary critics, for example, have generally approached periodization by separating black literature from the conventional divisions of white writers and identifying African American periods (the Harlem Renaissance, for example, instead of modernism). As Crystal Lucky points out in her essay here, however, those periods are themselves rendered more problematic by the inclusion of African American women writers. Similarly, adding ethnicity to a gendered critique of periodization, as Shirley Geok-lin Lim and Amelia M. de la Luz Montes do here, or addressing issues of class, as Montes and Carol Singley do, further problematizes the question of periodization. Moreover, a consideration of lesbian writers, as, for example, in Susan McCabe's essay, generates an additional challenge to the boundaries of preestablished periods.

In this interrogation of the boundaries and framings set by traditional periodization, certain general questions recur. If women writers break the boundaries of literary periods, can and should other periods be established? Is periodization even a useful organizational concept? More specifically, if some periods, such as realism or modernism, appear to be categories largely gendered as male, can they be expanded to include women writers or should they be abandoned altogether? Are there periods that might be defined by women's work and would such periods then be limited by gender? In other words, should there be separate "women's periods"? Or would the establishment of separate periods for women simply reify socially constructed binaries that support current hegemonies and result in a totalizing appropriation of difference? Instead, should each woman's body of work constitute its own period, without restrictive boundaries or political signifiers? Ultimately, this book asserts that, whether seen individually or in groups, women's periods will subvert or provide a challenge to and displacement and destabilization of what has been for many years perceived as "naturalized" periodization.

The challenge to literary periodization reflects significant developments in literary theory, changes that have led to a rejection of the critical confidence of earlier literary theorists. The New Criticism, which dominated the literary establishment into the 1960s, maintained a faith in universal meaning and the stability of categories. As long as literary critics accepted this stability, they were not tempted to question periodization. René Wellek and Austin Warren established the objectivity of literary categories in *Theory of Literature* in 1949; a period, they wrote, is "a time section defined by a system of norms embedded in the historical process and irremovable from it."[1] It is this concept of periods irremovably "embedded" in literary history that the critics here are questioning.

Although the discussion in these essays focuses on the feminist challenge to literary periodization, it is important to recognize that that challenge is not narrowly confined to questions of literary history and feminist theory. It derives from and affects significant historical, political, and cultural developments. To understand the evolution of the debate over periodization, we need to look at some of these developments. The critical confidence in stability articulated by the New Critics in the 1940s and 1950s was reflected in the political confidence of the postwar years. With fascism defeated and the economy booming, Americans focused on extending and protecting American-style democracy against Communism, while dissent at home was stifled by the McCarthy witch-hunt. If we look at political events in the United States in the next quarter of a century, however, we find much to disturb this confidence: the civil rights movement, the women's movement, the Vietnam War protests, student demonstrations, court decisions, the Watergate scandal. Activities on the campuses, in the streets, and in the courts were operating to create a national skepticism or discontent with authority and a recognition of the existence of multiple points of view.

This change in the political scene corresponded to changes in critical thinking. The first major challenge to the critical confidence in stability began with the introduction of deconstruction theory into the United States in the late 1960s and early 1970s. Particularly important was the Foucauldian concept that what society believes is "true" is instead the result of a discursive power struggle.[2] Added to this challenge to cultural definitions was the poststructuralist insistence on the indeterminacy of the text and the questioning of cultural binaries.[3] Another important development was the challenge to authoritarian systems by Mikhail Bakhtin, whose work began to be translated into English in the late 1960s. Of particular importance was his concept of heteroglossia — the idea that all language is socially determined and reflects the discourse of others.[4] Developing side by side with these theories was feminist criticism. Writing from the point of view of the "other" or the unrepresented in a patriarchal society, feminists approached texts not as truths, but as constructs.[5] French feminists introduced the concept of *l'écriture féminine* and attacked the totalizing dialectic of phallogocentric culture.[6] Anglo-American feminist critics rediscovered and revalued works by women writers which had been devalued by the patriarchal value system, exploring the concept of a female literary tradition and opening up the question of what happens to literary judgements when women are centered.[7] In the United States in the late 1970s and 1980s the feminist approach was itself challenged by African American, Asian American, Native American, and Chicana women writers who criticized feminists as white middle-class women who did not speak for or to women of color or of working-class background.[8] At the same time, lesbian critics questioned the heterosexual bias of most feminist criticism, pointing out that just as white male critics had assumed universality for their own perspective, heterosexual feminists had assumed universality for their perspective.[9]

The question of "universal" became "universal for whom?" This led to the further breakdown of the question of categorization as feminists accused each other of being "essentialist." Even the category of "woman" was not universal: women could be black or white, lesbian or heterosexual, Asian or Chicana, working class or middle class — or various combinations of any of the above. An extension of this critique of essentializing womanhood developed in the 1990s into identity theory, which maintains that there is no innate identity: all identity — racial identity, sexual identity, gender identity — is socially constructed and the result of performance.[10]

In addition to the challenges of deconstruction and feminist theory, belief in the stability of systems was further challenged by developments in such areas as psychology, history, hermeneutics, and anthropology. Of particular importance was the challenge to the "universal truths" of Freudian psychology from a feminist perspective.[11] Another important challenge was the development of the New Historicism, which maintains that history itself is a fiction, that narratives of history, like literary narratives, are written from a particular perspective.[12] Similar conclusions were reached in the study of hermeneutics which emphasized the importance of the situatedness and historicity of both the author and the interpreter of a text.[13] Also significant was the growing awareness of the effect of ethnocentrism on literary and historical perspectives.[14] Finally, anthropological studies of the problem of objective reporting revealed the extent to which a person's cultural background and personal perspective influenced his/her narrative.[15]

Perhaps the best way to understand how these theories have taken hold in

American thought is to look at the concept of postmodernism, the term that has been used to characterize the intellectual and cultural climate of the last forty years. A global movement, postmodernism is characterized by discontinuity and fragmentation, the decentering of the subject, and the effacement of boundaries.[16]

All of these developments have in common three principal factors: they challenge boundaries, they reflect the growing awareness of "otherness," and they question the truth of established systems, pointing out that what has been regarded as "true" is in fact somebody's creation. These three factors are important to the questioning of periodization. If there is no universal person, no essential identity, no category that cannot be questioned, how can there be universal periods in American literature? Moreover, the realization that historical and cultural givens were not objectively true led to a more skeptical view of knowledge and an examination of who "authored" the presumed givens. Applying these concepts to the study of periodization opened up the idea that previously defined periods might not be permanent and true, but rather might be constructs, determined by the dominant culture to serve its own ends. This thinking led to important questions: How do marginalized writers fit into periods that were not designed for them or in their interests? Do we distort the works of such writers when we attempt to accommodate them into existing periods? Should the periods themselves be revised or eliminated altogether? What happens if we redefine or erase boundaries?

Although these questions are important, relevant, and clearly the result of significant cultural developments, little has been written recently on the subject of periodization in American literary history.[17] What discussion there has been has generally come about peripherally in discussions that have questioned the white male character of the American literary canon.[18] Feminist historians, however, have questioned periodization in history. In 1977, for example, Joan Kelly noted that women experienced historical periods differently than men; in fact, periods in history that have been emancipatory for men have often had the opposite effect upon women.[19] But as David Perkins points out in *Is Literary History Possible?* (1992), "despite the importance of the topic, not much critical reflection has been focused recently in the United States on literary classification and its problems."[20]

In the mid-1980s a series of articles appearing in "The Extra" section of *American Literature* focused on the question of rewriting American literary history in view of some of these new ideas and included discussions of the question of periodization. The opening essay by Annette Kolodny, "The Integrity of Memory: Creating a New Literary History of the United States" (May 1985), asserts that as we become aware of previously marginalized writers, we will need to reorder contexts: "Women's writings about the frontier, Afro-American narrative traditions, the song and chant expressions of Native Americans—each, in their way, evade or even defy our inherited categories of discourse and evaluation. They fit neither the periodicity nor the critical frameworks that have informed prior literary histories."[21] As Kolodny notes, other critics, for example, Hortense Spillers in tracing the connections between African-American women writers, find that they will be free to discover such connections only if they defy standard periodicity.[22]

During the next decade literary critics became increasingly aware of the effect of otherness on American literary history. In 1994 *American Literature* printed a series of essays derived from sessions at the Modern Language Association meeting in 1993, "Repositionings: Multiculturalism, American Literary History, and the Curriculcum." Elaine Hedges introduced the essays by describing the questions she had asked the authors: "What, I asked them to consider, begins to happen when we locate a minority or hitherto marginalized text, or group of such texts, at the center of our study? . . . What shifts of emphasis, what new meanings and new alignments emerge? How do such realignments encourage us to reconceptualize the literary categories and terminology, the periodization and the thematization we have traditionally used to interpret and teach American literature?"[23]

Yet even when we know what questions to ask, there are no easy answers. The catch-22 of literary history is that, as David Perkins points out in *Is Literary History Possible?*, "it must be written from a point of view."[24] As the title of his book suggests, Perkins himself is dubious about the possibility of writing literary history and concludes that although literary history is useful to establish "a dialogue with the past," the literary historian must recognize that "the past is necessarily transformed in the effort to represent it discursively."[25] In contrast, Robert Ellrodt, in a 1996 essay, "Literary History and the Search for Certainty," criticizes the use of scientific concepts such as the chaos theory to prove the indeterminacy of writing and concludes that it *is* possible to establish a pattern in literary history. As long as the "general trends of a period are the object of inquiry," he maintains, it is possible for the literary historian to determine "a probabilist explanation of the prevailing themes and forms of expression in a given environment at a stated time."[26]

For Ellrodt, then, although other issues in literary history might be up for question, the "trends of a period" can be established. What he does not discuss, however, is which authors are to be included in those trends. It is the object of this book to analyze what happens to theories of periodization when previously excluded or marginalized writers are factored into the "trends of a period."

We have divided the essays in this book into two sections corresponding to how they address the subject of periodization and women writers. The essays in the first section, "Challenging Boundaries," question the current boundaries of literary periods, asking whether the boundaries should be redrawn or eliminated. In the second section, "Re(De)framings," each essay focuses on an individual writer, asking how or if the writer should be framed and how the current framing affects our reading of the writer's work.

In this book, the critics argue not only that women writers will destabilize the existing literary periods but also that they should. The first section, "Challenging Boundaries," begins with the essay by Joyce Warren, "Performativity and the Repositioning of American Literary Realism." Considering women realists of the antebellum period, Warren points out not only their absence from conventional discussions of realism in American fiction, but also the very fluidity of the term "realism." It has been devalued by New Critical formalists and attacked by Marxist critics who thought that it reified bourgeois capitalism, by feminists for its establishment of a false authenticity of experience, and by poststructuralists for its shaky claim to a mimetic representation of the "real." In her examination of Caroline Kirkland, Fanny Fern, and Harriet Wilson, Warren shows how these early women realists "challenged hegemonic definitions of gender, class, and racial identities," and created a body of work that requires the repositioning of American literary realism. In the second essay, "Women's Masterpieces," Josephine Donovan focuses on nineteenth-century regionalist writers Harriet Beecher Stowe, Rose Terry Cooke, Sarah Orne Jewett, and Mary E. Wilkins Freeman. Donovan argues that if traditional critics have organized literary periods around "masterpieces," then why not designate women's work as major, if not "master," pieces? Such work, if added to our understanding of the period, Donovan says, would require a new definition of nineteenth-century culture, "away from one characterized by dominance, violence, competition, and exploitation toward one governed by a sense of humility, humanity, and compassion."

Carla Peterson's essay, "Frances Harper, Charlotte Forten, and African American Literary Reconstruction," focuses on African American women writers during the period of Reconstruction. Both Harper, who wrote domestic tutelary fiction for a middlebrow African American audience, and Forten, whose increasingly political work was gradually excluded from highbrow white periodicals, were rendered invisible by twentieth-century analyses of the period. Such analyses focused on nonpolitical highbrow periodical literature written for a "new emerging elite," thus excluding African American women writers like Harper and Forten, who "refused to disassociate literary career from political participation."

In "'A Queer Lot' and the Lesbians of 1914: Amy Lowell, H.D., and Gertrude Stein," Susan McCabe seeks to define the lesbian tradition of Modernism, asking if the "lesbians of 1914" as opposed to the "men of 1914" might be seen as writing an entirely different kind of modernist poetry. Foregrounding "desire and embodiment" instead of "an impersonal, antiromantic aesthetic," McCabe interprets the years 1912–19 as a "lesbian period" that shaped modernism; modernist studies, she asserts, have excluded the "lesbian signifier."

The next two essays in this section deal with the question of how race and ethnicity interact with gender in relation to literary boundaries. Arguing for the loosening of boundaries, Crystal Lucky, in "Black Women Writers of the Harlem Renaissance," claims that the borders of the Harlem Renaissance have been drawn so strictly that they exclude women writers. Lucky seeks to reclaim black women writers and reevaluate the period with respect to gender. In the process, the time period will need to be expanded into the 1930s and the geographical location also enlarged both toward the west and the south. As a graduate student studying Alain Locke's *The New Negro*, Lucky found only eight women in his collection of thirty-six contributors. She seeks to correct that situation by offering a fuller understanding of African American women's writing.

Shirley Geok-lin Lim, in "Complications of Feminist and Ethnic Literary Theories in Asian American Literature," studies the evolution of the construction of Asian American literature. In the 1970s, she notes, Asian American critics authorized a male-centered language and culture—omitting women writers from anthologies, denigrating women's writings, and presenting the assertion of manhood as the only "authentic" Asian American literature. In the 1980s the entry of feminist consciousness foregrounded issues of gender identity, resulting in overtly woman-centered texts that took up themes of intergenerational tensions, mother-daughter relations, and culturally specific conflicts, as well as less ethnic-identified and deessentialized materials. Lim concludes that the intersection of feminist and ethnic theories is inadequate to account for the diverse traditions of Asian American literature, for example, South, Southeast, as well as East Asian traditions. Impatient with the idea of an "authentic" Asian American identity, recent writers articulate a postcolonial global consciousness elided by postmodern theory. Periodization, then, is complicated by pluralism: "Antihegemonic and antiauthoritarian, Asian American women's writing cannot be periodized or uniformly classified."

In the second section of the book, "Re(De)framings," the authors challenge the traditional framings of individual writers. The section begins with Teresa Toulouse's essay, "'American Puritanism' and Mary White Rowlandson's *Narrative*." In recovering women writers from seventeenth- and eighteenth-century American literature, feminist critics have not been altogether comfortable with the choices available to them or even the choices they might create. Puritan literature, as defined by Perry Miller at mid-century around the same time that Matthiessen named the American Renaissance, no longer serves as a workable literary period once we consider the need to include women writers. Toulouse points out that contemporary criticism of Rowlandson has challenged the model of the unified "New England mind"; in looking for another location that might suit Rowlandson, however, Toulouse does not opt for another model of unity but rather suggests that there are multiple ways of recasting the notion of "Puritanism," "colonialism," "early American," and even Northeastern "American." And she cautions her colleagues to analyze every new idea of periodization in such a way as to question any notion of stability.

In the nineteenth century, according to Mary Loeffelholz in "Essential, Portable, Mythical Margaret Fuller," the same caution against stability can be made regarding Margaret Fuller. Critiquing critical treatments of Fuller which persist in seeing her as a "marginal" figure whom anthology editors struggle to periodize, Loeffelholz argues that "it could become a positive strength for feminist literary history if Fuller were to continue hovering . . . not batting her wings at the glowing windows of Concord, but ranging, mobile and attentive, over different realms of intellectual territory." In "Emily Dickinson in History and Literary History," Margaret Dickie seeks to rescue both Emily Dickinson, who wrote most of her poetry during the Civil War, and the war itself from a literary history that cannot find a satisfactory place for Dickinson and would relegate the war to the silent space between the conventional two volumes in which textbooks divide American literature.

If literary critics have been baffled by the placement of New England writers Margaret Fuller and Emily Dickinson, they have chosen to ignore rather than address the placement of late-nineteenth-century California writer María Amparo Ruiz de Burton. Amelia M. de la Luz Montes's essay, "María Amparo Ruiz de Burton Negotiates American Literary Politics and Culture," provides a cogent illustration of the problematics of classification when complicated by issues of ethnicity, class, and gender. Ruiz de Burton does not fit easily into any preestablished periods or traditions. She was a novelist of the West whose works cannot be categorized as "Westerns" in the traditional association of the genre with Anglo stories of western exploration; she was an upper-class Mexican American woman whose perspective does not coincide with a tradition of Chicano working-class literature; she was a realist and a muckraker *and* an author of the sentimental romance; and she was a woman writer seeking to establish herself in a male Mexican and Anglo-American culture. As Montes says, we need to examine Ruiz de Burton's work both within and outside of periods and traditions in order to "explode conventions"; Ruiz de Burton "complicates and deepens literary historical discourse."

Bridging the nineteenth and twentieth centuries, Edith Wharton has had a precarious critical position, according to Carol Singley, partly because she does not fit comfortably into any one literary period. In "Edith Wharton's Ironic Realism," Singley introduces the subject of class, in addition to gender, as a complicating factor in periodization. Regarded as either a nineteenth-century local colorist or a novelist of manners, Wharton, Singley maintains, is kept out of the modernist period by critics who have unexamined assumptions about the meaning of art for an upperclass woman. Gertrude Stein has also been hard to place, although she clearly lived and wrote in the modernist period. According to Jacqueline Brogan in "The 'Founding Mother': Gertrude Stein and the Cubist Phenomenon," reinserting Stein into modernism moves the period's dates back a decade, but it also "dismantles the very notions of 'modernism' and 'postmodernism' themselves in a way that allows us to appreciate anew and more accurately Stein's self-proclaimed genius." For Brogan, Stein's work transforms the notion of "modernism" into a "cubist phenomenon" that expands as we approach the next century.

By the late twentieth century, women writers themselves had become increasingly aware of their need to locate themselves and, as a consequence, have come to insist on naming their own place in literature, breaking up the usual divisions and even defining their own periods. Sylvia Henneberg, in "The Self-Categorization, Self-Canonization, and Self-Periodization of Adrienne Rich," writes that Adrienne Rich has consciously manipulated through her essays the periodization and categorization of her poetry. Although Rich herself has demonstrated a remarkable ability to change, remake herself, and explore new ranges of expression, she wants to fix her place in twentieth-century literature rather than to rely on the changing estimate of her work which will come through canon-forming critics or future readers of her poetry.

This collection of essays does not attempt to cover all of American literary history; there are many writers and "periods" that space simply does not allow us to include. No collection can be exhaustive, and our purpose is to question and suggest rather than to define. Moreover, the aim of this collection is not to set new literary periods for women writers but rather to suggest both some of the values and some of the issues that such an enterprise would entail. What benefits would accrue to the teaching, criticism, and professional specialization of American literature, if literary periods were expanded or dismantled consistently to include women writers in the process and to respond to their interests? What questions would result?

Some benefits are already in place, as the contributors to this collection suggest. In their discussions of individual writers, the authors frequently include a survey of anthologies, suggesting that, even when women writers have not made great changes in literary periodization, they are now being more fully represented in the anthologies that are organized by periods. As this process continues, those writers, such as Margaret Fuller and Edith Wharton, who do not fit neatly into existing periods, can perhaps force a reconception of such divisions. Moreover, those women writers who until recently had been excluded from anthologies, such as the early realists and writers like Ruiz de Burton, or who have been included only by minimal representation, such as the local colorists, may be given greater prominence in redefining and reevaluating the concerns of the period.

Because anthologies and course syllabi and even professional specializations express, if only implicitly, an interpretation of our culture, then organizing them by literary periods that include a wide range of women writers will have to spring from as well as encourage a reconsideration of those values. Such a task, however necessary, will not be easy.

In this context, then, we see that the desire of many critics here to expand the borders or keep under constant surveillance any stabilized literary period runs athwart the practical needs of those who serve and preserve the profession. Stable literary periods have been the stock in trade of academe. And anthologies that depend on them enforce such stability. Because they are vast business enterprises, anthologies change slowly, responding to marketing economies as well as to changes in the profession. Although revised editions of the major textbooks appear regularly, major revisions are seldom an easy or economic possibility. As a result of this institutional lag, college teachers are increasingly assembling their own course readings by assigning a collection of single texts or compiling a course book at the local copy shop. Moreover, as the work of women writers becomes more easily available in paperback reprints, instructors can bypass the anthologies and assign their work a central place in the curriculum.

Course curricula, conventionally organized by literary periods, are even more entrenched restraints on change, as anyone who has witnessed faculty discussions about revising the curriculum can attest. But here, too, some faculty are redefining the course offerings, refusing, for example, to teach romantic literature or American realism as a predominantly male production. Finally, although literature faculties themselves divide by periods, and faculty lines have been determined conventionally by literary periods, new specialties are often the occasion for new hirings. If they must find their place in a profession dominated by established periods of specialization, such new positions have the potential for redrawing the map of literary studies.

In confronting the institutional barriers of the anthologies, the curriculum, and the professional specializations, feminist critics have still to articulate an interpretation of American culture that will compete with the democratic nationalism of F. O. Matthiessen or the tradition set out by T. S. Eliot which have structured literary periodization of American literature for half a century. Although she posits some extremely interesting possibilities for reframing Margaret Fuller, Mary Loeffelholz admits that the anthology that would connect Fuller's essay on Bettine Brentano to her "Dialogue" and then her writing to more recent generically, sexually, and linguistically transgressive works "has yet to be imagined—let alone the periods such an anthology might fall into, or how its periods could reshape those of the standard American literature anthology." But the first efforts toward that imagining should be encouraged by these essays.

NOTES

This chapter was written by Joyce Warren and derives from the original concept for the book developed by her and Margaret Dickie before the latter's final illness.

1. René Wellek and Austin Warren, *Theory of Literature* (New York: Harcourt, Brace, 1949), 277–78.

2. In "The Discourse on Language," in *The Archaeology of Knowledge*, trans. A. M. Sheridan Smith (New York: Pantheon Books, 1972), Michel Foucault wrote: "In every society the production of discourse is at once controlled, selected, organised and redistributed according to a certain number of procedures, whose role is to avert its powers and its dangers" (216, 219, 234). Foucault also specifically attacked the concept of classification in his discussion of the problems of taxonomy in *The Order of Things: An Archaeology of the Human Sciences*, translated in 1970 (New York: Pantheon, 1970).

3. The work of French philosopher Jacques Derrida, the central figure in this movement, translated into English in the 1970s, argued that meaning did not derive from a fixed text but involved the free play of signifiers and the impossibility of closure. See, e.g., Derrida, *Of Grammatology*, trans. Gayatri Spivak (Baltimore: Johns Hopkins Uni-

versity Press, 1976). Also undermining the idea of a fixed text were the arguments of some of the proponents of reader-response criticism, for example, Wolfgang Iser, who maintained that a text was not an independent entity: interpretation depended on what the reader brought to the text. See Iser, *The Act of Reading: A Theory of Aesthetic Response* (Baltimore: Johns Hopkins University Press, 1978).

4. See Bakhtin, *Rabelais and His World*, trans. Hélène Iswolsky (Cambridge: MIT Press, 1968), and *The Dialogic Imagination: Four Essays*, ed. Michael Holquist, trans. Caryl Emerson and Michael Holquist (Austin: University of Texas Press, 1981).

5. The first American literary texts on this subject to have an important impact were Mary Ellmann, *Thinking About Women* (New York: Harcourt Brace Jovanovich, 1968); and Kate Millett, *Sexual Politics* (Garden City: Doubleday, 1970). Elaine Showalter asserted in "Women and the Literary Curriculum," *College English* 32 (March 1971), that women students of literature were "expected to identify with a masculine experience and perspective, which is presented as the human one" (856), and Judith Fetterley wrote in *The Resisting Reader: A Feminist Approach to American Fiction* (Bloomington: Indiana University Press, 1978), that women readers had to "identify against themselves" (e.g., xi–xiii). Nina Baym, in "Melodramas of Beset Manhood: How Theories of American Fiction Exclude Women Authors," *American Quarterly* 33 (Summer 1981): 123–39, pointed out that books by white American male writers were not canonized because of their universal truths but because they spoke to white male readers who dominated the cultural and literary establishment.

6. See, e.g., Luce Irigaray, *The Sex Which Is Not One* (1977), trans. Catherine Porter with Carolyn Burke (Ithaca: Cornell University Press, 1985); and Hélène Cixous, "The Laugh of the Medusa," trans. Keith Cohen and Paula Cohen, *Signs* 1 (1976): 875–99.

7. See, e.g., Elaine Showalter, *A Literature of Their Own: British Novelists from Brontë to Lessing* (Princeton: Princeton University Press, 1922); Jane Tompkins, *Sensational Designs: The Cultural Work of American Fiction, 1790–1860* (New York: Oxford University Press, 1985); Nina Baym, *Women's Fiction: A Guide to Novels by and About Women in America* (Ithaca: Cornell University Press, 1978); Sandra M. Gilbert and Susan Gubar, *The Madwoman in the Attic: The Woman Writer and the Nineteenth-Century Literary Imagination* (New Haven: Yale University Press, 1979); Adrienne Rich, "Vesuvius at Home: The Power of Emily Dickinson" (1976) in *On Lies, Secrets, and Silence: Selected Prose, 1966–1978* (New York: Norton, 1979); Patrocinio Schweickart, "Reading Ourselves: Toward a Feminist Theory of Reading," in *Gender and Reading: Essays on Readers, Texts, and Contexts*, ed. Elizabeth Flynn and Patrocinio Schweickart (Baltimore: Johns Hopkins Press, 1986).

8. Barbara Smith expressed her "rage" at the way black women writers were ignored by white feminists in "Toward a Black Feminist Criticism," *Conditions: Two* 1 (October 1977); and Deborah McDowell wrote in "New Directions for Black Feminist Criticism," *Black American Literature Forum* 14 (1980), that white feminists, "wittingly or not, perpetrated against the Black woman writer the same exclusive practices they so vehemently decried in white male scholars." Both articles are reprinted in *The New Feminist Criti-*

cism, ed. Elaine Showalter (New York: Pantheon Books, 1985), 168–99. Not only did women of color resent being ignored by white feminists, but they also pointed out that some of the givens of white feminism did not apply to them. See, for example, Patricia Zavella, "The Problematic Relationship Between Feminism and Chicana Studies," *Women's Studies* 17 (1989): 25–36; reprinted in *Across Cultures: The Spectrum of Women's Lives*, ed. Emily K. Abel and Marjorie L. Pearson (New York: Gordon and Breach, 1989), 25–36. For a good discussion of the problems faced by early Asian American women writers, see Amy Ling, "Chinamerican Women Writers: Four Forerunners of Maxine Hong Kingston," in *Gender/Body/Knowledge/Feminist Reconstructions of Being and Knowing*, ed. Alison M. Jaggar and Susan R. Bordo (New Brunswick: Rutgers University Press, 1989), 309–23.

9. Bonnie Zimmerman wrote in "What Has Never Been: An Overview of Lesbian Feminist Literary Criticism," *Feminist Studies* 7 (1981): 451–75, reprinted in *The New Feminist Criticism*, ed. Elaine Showalter, 200–224, that literary scholarship, even feminist scholarship, served "to obliterate lesbian experience." Zimmerman's essay provides a good survey of lesbian criticism in the 1970s and early 1980s. See also the essays in *Lesbian Texts and Contexts: Radical Revisions*, ed. Karla Jay and Joanne Glasgow (New York: New York University Press, 1990).

10. See, e.g., Judith Butler, *Gender Trouble* (New York: Routledge, 1990). Butler writes: "There is no gender identity behind the expressions of gender; that identity is performatively constituted by the very 'expressions' that are said to be its results" (24–25). For a critique of the social construction of sexual identity inherent in queer theory, see, in additon to Butler, e.g., Eve Kosofsky Sedgwick, *Epistemology of the Closet* (1990).

11. See, for example, Naomi Weisstein, "Psychology Constructs the Female" (1968), reprinted in *Woman in Sexist Society: Studies in Power and Powerlessness*, ed. Vivian Gornick and Barbara K. Moran (New York: Basic Books, 1971), 207–24. Weisstein wrote that psychological theory had erroneously "made the central assumption that human behavior rests on an individual and inner dynamic, perhaps fixed in infancy, perhaps fixed by genitalia . . . . [In actuality] what a person does and who he believes himself to be will in general be a function of what people around him expect him to be, and what the overall situation around him implies that he is." It is interesting that current identity theory derives from these 1960s challenges to psychology's belief in innate identity.

12. See, e.g., Stephen Greenblatt, Introduction to *The Power of Forms in the English Renaissance* (Norman: University of Oklahoma Press, 1982). Greenblatt writes that, whereas earlier historicism did not see that its vision "was the product of the historian's interpretation, nor even of the particular interests of a given social group in conflict with other groups . . . the new historicism erodes the firm ground of both criticism and literature. It tends to ask questions about its own methodological assumptions and those of others." See also Hayden White, *Tropics of Discourse* (Baltimore: Johns Hopkins University Press, 1978).

13. See Hans-Georg Gadamer, *Truth and Method* (original German publication

1960), trans. Sheed and Ward, Ltd. (New York: Seabury Press, 1975): "A person who imagines that he is free of prejudices, basing his knowledge on the objectivity of his procedures and denying that he is himself influenced by historical circumstances, experiences the power of the prejudices that unconsciously dominate him" (324).

14. For example, Edward W. Said, in *Orientalism* (New York: Pantheon Books, 1978), critiques the tendency of one culture to portray another culture as an abstraction (e.g., 23).

15. See, e.g., James Clifford's analysis of ethnography in *The Predicament of Culture: Twentieth-Century Ethnography, Literature, and Art* (Cambridge, Mass.: Harvard University Press, 1988). Clifford asks how any ethnographic account that involves power relations and personal cross-purposes can be said to be an authoritative narrative (25). See also Clifford Geertz, *The Interpretation of Cultures: Selected Essays* (New York: Basic Books, 1973), and *Works and Lives: The Anthropologist as Author* (Stanford: Stanford University Press, 1988).

16. See Fredric Jameson, *Postmodernism or, the Cultural Logic of Late Capitalism* (Durham: Duke University Press, 1991), e.g., 1–2, 14–15, 26, 28, 63.

17. The bibliography for the MLA International Index, 1981–May 1997, lists 192 items under "Periodization"; of these, however, only seven are on American literature. Of these seven, only four are in English: two are on male writers (Nabokov and James); one is on the relationship of periodization to neurosis; and one is the all-male entry on modernism in the 1987–88 edition of the *Columbia Literary History of the United States*. Of the three non-English entries, two are on Latin America and the third is a report of a conference in Germany.

18. See, e.g., Lillian Robinson, "Treason Our Text: Feminist Challenges to the Literary Canon," *Tulsa Studies in Women's Literature* 2 (1983): 83–98; Barbara Herrnstein Smith, "Contingencies of Value: The Task of Feminist Literary Criticism," *Critical Inquiry* 10 (September 1983): 1–35; Paul Lauter, *Canons and Contexts* (New York: Oxford University Press, 1991).

19. Joan Kelly, "Did Women Have a Renaissance?" (1977), reprinted in *Women, History, and Theory* (Chicago: University of Chicago Press, 1984), 19–50.

20. David Perkins, *Is Literary History Possible?* (Baltimore: Johns Hopkins University Press, 1992), 63.

21. Annette Kolodny, "The Integrity of Memory: Creating a New Literary History of the United States," *American Literature* 57 (May 1985): 296. The series also included essays by William Spengemann, "American Things/Literary Things: The Problem of American Literary History," *American Literature* 57 (October 1985): 456–81; Emory Elliott, "New Literary History: Past and Present," *American Literature* 57 (December 1985): 611–21; Sacvan Bercovitch, "America as Canon and Context: Literary History in a Time of Dissensus," *American Literature* 58 (March 1986): 99–107; Lawrence Buell, "Literary History Without Sexism? Feminist Studies and Canonical Reconception," *American Literature* 59 (March 1987): 102–14; and Emory Elliott, "The Politics of Literary History," *American Literature* 59 (May 1987): 268–76.

22. See, e.g., Hortense Spillers, "A Hateful Passion, a Lost Love," *Feminist Studies* 9 (1983): 295.

23. Elaine Hedges, Introduction to the Forum "Repositionings: Multiculturalism, American Literary History, and the Curriculum," *American Literature* 66 (December 1994): 769. The Forum runs from pages 769 to 829.

24. Perkins, *Is Literary History Possible?*, 13.

25. Ibid., 182, 184, 19.

26. Robert Ellrodt, "Literary History and the Search for Certainty," *New Literary History* 27 (Summer 1996): 533.

ONE

CHALLENGING BOUNDARIES

PERFORMATIVITY AND THE REPOSITIONING OF AMERICAN LITERARY REALISM

Joyce W. Warren

> I have seen too much of life to be merry at a wedding.
>
> —Fanny Fern, 1852

Critics who have addressed the question of literary realism have maintained that although the movement began in Europe in the mid–nineteenth century, literary realism did not develop in the United States until the end of that century.[1] In all of the essays and books on American literary realism that have been published since the term became part of our cultural vocabulary, few writers have even considered the work of mid-nineteenth-century American women writers. Feminist critics have noted realistic elements in the work of antebellum women writers,[2] but most critics who have written specifically on American literary realism have begun their discussions with works that were not published until after the Civil War, the authors of which were predominantly male.[3] Although most male writers in the United States did not begin writing "realism" until the late nineteenth century (Howells, James, Crane, Norris) and into the twentieth century (Dreiser, Steinbeck), there were many women writers who were writing realistic fiction in the mid–nineteenth century. That their work has not been considered realism is owing primarily to the gendered construction of the definition of American "realism."

First, it is important to recognize that "realism" is a fluid term: its definition varies depending on the speaker and the historical period. In the medieval period the word "realism" meant the reality of the ideal image. It was not until the eighteenth century that realism was established as the opposite of idealism.[4] Moreover, it is inaccurate to say that literary realism began in the nineteenth century; we can speak of the "realism" of Chaucer or Shakespeare, for example, and the eighteenth-century novel provides many examples of realism.[5] But it was in the nineteenth century that the term was first used in a literary context.[6]

In the twentieth century, literary realism has proved to be a problematic concept from many different perspectives. New Critical formalists in the 1950s and 1960s devalued realism because of its emphasis on social contexts and reinterpreted it in terms of literary form.[7] Marxist critics have criticized realism, maintaining that realist texts have simply reified bourgeois capitalism.[8] Feminists have criticized realism, asserting either that it seeks to establish a false authenticity of experience or that it is a reification of male hegemony and patriarchal language.[9] Advocates of literary modernism have criticized realism, maintaining that it focuses on the external without recognizing the social and psychological forces at work beneath appearances.[10] Poststructuralists have critiqued the realists' assertion of a mimetic representation of the "real" and have insisted that language does not reflect but rather produces and shapes reality.[11] There is overlapping among these critical approaches to realism and there are differences in emphasis, but what is significant is that there are many different responses. Some critics talk about epistemological realism, while others mean only realism as a mode of writing. Others have conflated the two.[12] As Terry Lovell notes, "There is no concept in the history of aesthetics which has generated more confusions."[13]

Considering the instability of the term "realism," one is tempted to say that it might be better to dispense with the category altogether. Certainly there are arguments in favor of such a move: the problems associated with chronological labeling, the confusion regarding the definition of realism, and even the question of the desirability of moving women writers into the category. Nevertheless, the concept of American literary realism exists as a genre and has existed for more than a hundred years. Although we might wish to dissolve the category, we cannot erase its hundred-year history. What we must do instead is rewrite American literary history, making important changes in the category "realism."

In a discussion of realism, what is most important is to recognize that the concept is itself a construct.[14] Ideologically, representations in the name of "realism" constitute one writer's perception; what one perceives as real depends on one's situatedness, and gender as well as race and class are important factors in determining one's perceptions. Postmodernist theory asserts that there is no "reality," only "representations."[15] In the nineteenth century, however, the term "realism" was difficult to challenge because its practitioners maintained that they were writing the "truth,"[16] and it is difficult to argue against what is termed the truth when society's power structure reinforces the discourse as true.[17] If a society supports the definers of truth, how does one whose "truth" differs from the dominant truth assert the *reality* of her very different truth? The perceptions of the dominant strata and the criteria for their fictional representation constitute logocentric constructions that determine power and hierarchical valuations.

The late nineteenth-century movement toward literary realism in the United States was dominated by white male writers; in fact, late nineteenth-century realism was developed specifically as a rejection of the feminine.[18] The realists established themselves in opposition to the feminine and asserted their realism by differentiating it from women's writing, which they characterized as sentimental and soft. In 1894, Charles Dudley Warner asked rhetorically: "Are the women, or are they not, taking all the vitality out of literature?"[19] William Dean Howells repeatedly attacked the sentimental novel, calling it escapist reading that was comparable to "opium-eating."[20] Henry James complained that literature was "becoming feminine," written by "eunuchs and sempstresses."[21] Howells and James were themselves attacked for being too feminine, writing, as Frank Norris said in 1901, of "the drama of a broken teacup."[22] So intense was the animosity toward women writers that some turn-of-the century women writers, for example Edith Wharton and Willa Cather, in an effort to be taken seriously as writers, found it necessary to assert their difference from other women writers.[23] Defensively and in an attempt to protect their own viability as writers, the late nineteenth-century male realists struggled to affirm the virility of realism, and in the process, they scapegoated the women writers, both their predecessors, about whom they betrayed an "anxiety of influence," and their contemporaries, whom they relegated to "minor" status.[24]

Recent critics have identified several reasons for the tendency of male critics to write women out of the canon: fear of competition, fear of women's sexual energy and power, fear that women would tell their own stories, differences in ideology.[25] All of these reasons derive from a fear that women's writing threatens hegemonic structures. With respect to realism in particular, there is an additional reason: the woman's view of reality was deemed unrealistic because it was different from the patriarchal view. Women could not write realism, the male writers insisted, because, as Henry James said, "half of life was a closed book to women" or as Frank Norris put it, women were "shut away from . . . real life."[26] The phallocentric definition of "real life" precluded women from being realists. It is not surprising, then, that the "realism" of women—white women and African American women—which preceded white male realism by at least forty years has been so thoroughly discounted. The established definition of American literary realism denied the authenticity of the woman's point of view.

At the same time, nineteenth-century editors and publishers actively prevented women writers from writing as "realistically" as they wanted to, forcing them to conform to society's image of femininity, and reviewers castigated those who did not conform. Women writers were required to use "feminine" language and subject matter. Rose Terry Cooke, for example, reported that the editors at the *Atlantic Monthly* edited her stories, requiring her to change any words that seemed "vulgar" or unladylike, and rejected stories that the editors regarded as too somber for a lady to write. In 1861 Rebecca Harding Davis's novel *Margret Howth* was rejected by James T. Fields, who said that the publishers would reconsider the novel if she rewrote it to eliminate the realistic scenes of poverty and factory work and made the novel more "cheerful." Fanny Fern was criticized by reviewers for such offenses as using vulgar language (words that were not "ladylike"), portraying improper subjects (for example, a woman's sexual slavery to a brutish husband), and satirizing her male relatives.[27] In general, women were criticized for going out of their "sphere" if they portrayed violence, degradation, or cruelties; if they used "indelicate" language; and if they portrayed femininity that did not conform to the passive, dependent, obedient image of the "true woman." Such proscriptions enforced the binary of gender among writers, ensuring that women writers would remain within the straitjacket of convention and inhibiting their realism.

In spite of these proscriptions, some women writers in mid-nineteenth-century America did not accept the hegemonic system. By freeing themselves of cultural restrictions, they were able to write more frankly, and consequently more "realistically," about life and society. The phenomenon that enabled their realism can be defined as *performativity*: instead of reifying societal representations of gender, they presented themselves and their perspectives through their works in ways that challenged normative behavior. They created what Judith Butler calls "gender trouble" by "subverting and displacing" naturalized expressions of gender.[28] Moreover, some of these writers redefined class identity, and African American women writers challenged the images of race as well as gender identity. It was this presentation of themselves, a reconstitution of gender identity and sometimes of race and class, that enabled them to produce literary realism. They found much in the standards of the dominant culture that did not correspond to their own experience, and, rather than reifying their society's notions of gender, race, and class, they established their own.

Through their performativity—their assertion of new identities—these antebellum women writers were able to write realistically by ignoring the cultural essentializing that precluded such writing. According to accepted definitions, these writers were realists: they used conversational language and created recognizable characters and plausible plots; their writing reflected the exterior and interior lives of real people, portraying details of quotidian events involving money, social class, and the individual in social relationships. If these writers wrote realistically, meeting the criteria for literary realism, why have they not been considered realists? Here we need to differentiate between the genre and the literary practice. In practice, the women writers were realists. But they have not been classified as realists because the genre of American realism is a construction that has excluded women writers.

Twentieth-century critics and literary historians reaffirmed the opinion of the nineteenth-century male realists concerning women writers. In 1930, for example, V. L. Parrington wrote antebellum women out of the realist canon in his influential *Beginnings of Critical Realism in America, 1860–1920*, and in 1940 Van Wyck Brooks decried the "feminization of literature."[29] Until recently, antebellum women writers have been invisible to twentieth-century literary critics, who have based their theories of American literature only on the works of male writers, and those theories in turn have been used to exclude female texts. In *The American Novel and Its Tradition* (1957), for example, Richard Chase developed his thesis that Americans (as opposed to Europeans) did not write social fiction but instead wrote romance: tales of an isolated hero in a symbolic world.[30] To reach this conclusion, Chase had to omit any consideration of mid-nineteenth-century women writers who, unlike most of their male contemporaries, wrote primarily social fiction. Ultimately, because women writers did not fit into Chase's thesis, his thesis helped to preclude them from the canon.

Although most twentieth-century writers on realism have not discussed mid-nineteenth-century women writers, the few critics who do mention them have concluded that although women writers might have been "precursors of realism," they were not "realists."[31] An examination of the reasons proffered by the critics writing on realism provides us with an understanding of how the gendered construction of realism in America continued to exclude mid-nineteenth-century women writers throughout most of the twentieth century. The arguments against antebellum women as realists are, first, that their works are "too feminine" (they focus on "women's subjects" and elevate women) and, second, that they are not "objective" because the writer implicitly or explicitly adopts a moral or religious position.

The first objection assumes that "men's subjects" are the norm and questions the "reality" of a picture that is painted from a woman's point of view. Alfred Habegger, one of the few writers on realism who considers antebellum women writers, concludes in *Gender, Fantasy, and Realism in American Literature* (1982) that although their works might contain realistic elements, the women writers were not "classic" realists. They wrote "fantasies," he says, portraying "ideal femininity" leading to marriage.[32] From the woman's point of view in nineteenth-century America, however, it might not have been unrealistic to believe that "ideal femininity" led to marriage. Habegger also maintains that women writers who portrayed failed marriages were not realists because they portrayed women who were oppressed by their husbands, and he criticizes the implication that, as he says, man's effect on woman was to "stifle" her (45–54). Might not this have been a "realistic" view of a failed marriage from the woman's point of view, however? As most divorce lawyers will testify, the portrayal of a failed marriage will certainly differ depending on who is telling the story.[33]

The other reason critics cite to withhold the realist label from women writers is the stipulation that the author must be "objective," writing without comment, implicit or explicit. Most antebellum women writers assumed a belief in God and included in their work either implicit or explicit moral or religious comment. "Objectivity," of course, is part of the nineteenth-century credo of realism.[34] As postmodern criticism has made clear, however, no writing is wholly objective.[35] Even writing that claims to be objective is expressing someone's point of view. The mere selection of materials constitutes a judgment. If antebellum women realists made moral or religious judgments, the work of postbellum male realists contains other judgments. Despite the realists' attempt to portray characters "scientifically," the author often revealed his attitude toward his characters, thus indicating his subjective opinion. Howells clearly does not like the Dryfooses' materialism in *A Hazard of New Fortunes*. In *Maggie, A Girl of the Streets*, Stephen Crane condescendingly portrays Pete's and Maggie's lower-class tastes as vulgar.[36] In *An American Tragedy* Theodore Dreiser condemns the selfishness of American individualism. As Dreiser himself noted, what an author writes is necessarily filtered through his own perceptions.[37]

Ironically, the mid-nineteenth-century women writers whose feminine point of view has been derided were, in fact, more realistic in their writings than many of the late-nineteenth- and early-twentieth-century male writers who have been designated realists (e.g., Jack London, Ernest Hemingway). The male realists' portrayal of a male-centered universe in which the aggressive male confronts and tames or is vanquished by other males or by the natural environment reflects an idealization of maleness that is influenced by our culture and was given credence by Social Darwinist theory; it is a romantic vision of American individualism and portrays "male fantasies" as fully as the courtship novels that Habegger cites might be said to fulfill "female fantasies." But the mundane realism of the mid-nineteenth-century women writers is more "realistic," that is, it more nearly approximates the life of the average man and woman — life that is more pedestrian than panoramic.

The gendered construction of realism artificially set the date for the beginning of realism in the United States as the late nineteenth century, neatly excluding mid-nineteenth-century women writers. If we examine the works of antebellum women writers, however, it becomes clear that American literary realism began much earlier. The women writers who formed part of this early school of realism include Caroline Kirkland, Alice Cary, Susan Warner, Harriet Beecher Stowe, Fanny Fern, Harriet Wilson, Harriet Jacobs, Rose Terry Cooke, and Rebecca Harding Davis. In this essay I will focus on the work of three of these writers, analyzing their performativity and the ways in which their discursive challenge enabled their realism.

Caroline Kirkland (1801–64) has been called a "pioneer" in American literary realism and the "first American realist."[38] Yet no major studies of American realism mention her work. *A New Home, Who'll Follow?* (1839)[39] introduces into American fiction a kind of writing that had not been seen before.[40] In *A New Home* Kirkland states that she intends to write "a veracious history of actual occurrences, an unvarnished transcript of real characters, and an impartial record of every-day forms of speech" (3). She apologizes for the lack of dramatic adventure, such as readers had seen previously in romantic tales of the West: "I have never seen a cougar—nor been bitten by a rattlesnake." Her writings, she says, will be about "common-place occurrences" and "every-day people" (3). In her second work, *Forest Life* (1842),[41] Kirkland reiterates this credo. Her work, she says, will "delineate some of the very ordinary scenes, manners and customs of Western Life. . . . Common-place all." There will be "no wild adventures,—no blood-curdling hazards,—no romantic incidents" (1:10). Her picture may contain unpleasantnesses, she says, because only a poor painter would "leave out a wart" (1:14). In insisting that an artist must portray what he or she sees, warts and all, Kirkland articulates Stendhal's criterion for realism—that art is like a mirror on the roadway: it reflects what is there, and if there is mud on the road, it reflects the mud.

Kirkland's frankness, her ability to write about the "warts," derives from her performativity. Her experience with frontier life—living away from eastern prescriptions of the proper behavior for middle-class women and forced to deal with situations in which such behavior would have been silly or even suicidal—enabled her to recognize that her society's definitions of gender were neither natural nor essential. Early in *A New Home*, the narrator, Mary Clavers, realizes that the expectations of behavior for women are different in the West. She very deliberately modifies her performance, which contrasts with the normative behavior of eastern middle-class women: "However we may justify certain exclusive habits in populous places, they are strikingly and confessedly ridiculous in the wilderness" (65). In writing about the reality that she has experienced (which is at variance with the definition of respectable middle-class femininity), Kirkland warns the fashionable reader that she intends to be "decidedly low" (4).

Throughout her two books, Kirkland contrasts her story of "actual occurrences" with poetic views of pastoral life and with romantic adventure stories of the West. The first part of *A New Home* portrays the gradual disillusionment of the narrator, Mary Clavers, whose experiences do not match her expectations. When she first comes to Michigan, she thinks of the nature poetry of the British romantic poets and expects to find the beauty of the woods "delicious to one 'long in populous cities pent'" (5). Not only is she influenced by poetic pictures of nature, her impressions of the West derive from the colorful images she has seen in American adventure stories of the West: "But I confess, these pictures, touched by the glowing pencil of fancy, gave me but incorrect notions of a real journey through Michigan" (6).

In *Forest Life*, Kirkland uses the metaphor of "glorification glasses" to describe the unrealistic image of the West that comes from looking at things through the filter of romance and eastern notions of propriety. The narrator puts on a pair of glasses, and everything that she sees through the glasses is beautiful. But when a child breaks the glasses, Clavers finds that the world looks very different: the child, which she had previously described as an "infant cherub," is "a dirty little urchin" standing in front of a "tumble-down log-house" (1:15–23). Clavers concludes that she is better off "seeing with [her] own eyes." She says she will tell the truth about what she sees even if some people don't want to hear it (1:24).

The incidents that Mary Clavers recounts early in chapter 1 of *A New Home* en route to her "new home" provide a graphic introduction to the reality that she will have to deal with. First, her family encounters a mud-hole—which becomes a metaphor for the reality of Michigan life as compared with the idealized images of romance and adventure (6–7). Second, whereas the adventure stories contain sensational events, her family spends the night in a "wretched inn" deep in the woods, where the "terrors" are more sordid than sensational, "owing to the horrible drunkenness of the master of the house, whose wife and children were in constant fear of their lives, from his insane fury. I can never forget the countenance of that desolate woman, sitting trembling and with white compressed lips in the midst of her children [with] the father raving all night" (7).

Chapter 2 introduces the vernacular. Unlike other authors who used dialect only to create humorous or low characters, Kirkland uses dialect to characterize significant characters. Mrs. Danforth, the hostess at the log-cabin "hotel," who will become an important character in the novel, is the first of many who speaks in dialect: "Why do tell if you've been upsot in the mash? why, I want to know!—and didn't ye hurt ye none? Come, gals! fly round, and let's git some supper" (8). Kirkland's writing is without adornment—except when she is satirizing romantic discourse. As she says in the preface to *Forest Life*, she claims the right to "plainness of speech" (1:4).

Clavers is soon cured of her romantic notions, and the rest of the novel portrays daily events, as she says, without "colouring." Here are no refinements: women comb their hair over the food (14), Mrs. Jennings drinks from the spout of the teapot (51), and the school ma'am smokes a pipe and spits into the hearth (56). Elegant sketches of western life or romantic idealizations of forest life such as one finds in Chateaubriand, says Clavers, do not say anything about the "realities" of life.

Many of the "important omissions" in such books are particularly noticeable from a woman's point of view. Clavers cites the "inexorable dinner hour" and the constant baking of bread which require an inextinguishable baking fire. This fire makes the heat in the log cabin so intense that no one can stay inside (43, 49). She notes that such "vulgar inconveniences" are not mentioned in male-authored romances. Clavers discusses other aspects of women's "reality": the devastation when the wife and mother is ill (60–62) and the difficulty of dealing with tired and hungry crying children when the mother is overworked and tired herself (38).

Writing from the perspective of her new identity, Kirkland's female persona also subverts the image of what is appropriate for ladies to write about by describing aspects of women's experience that would have been regarded as unsuitable for public writing: she describes the death of a young woman from a botched abortion and says that she knows of other instances "of a similar kind, though with results less evidently fatal" (111); she discusses the need for a breast pump when a child is temporarily unable to suckle (72); and she portrays the tragedy of a woman with a dissipated husband (104) and the sad but not uncommon phenomenon of a woman attempting to hide her husband's drunkenness (37).

Kirkland's regendered identity not only enables her to discuss material of particular interest to women; it also gives her the perspective needed to question the glorious tales of male adventure and achievement which acquiescent femininity would not dare to question. She describes how elections and town meetings, particularly those that take place at some distance, are used by men as an excuse to get out of work, even when their family is suffering from hardship and desperately needs money (48). And she undercuts — by telling the truth about — a male adventure in the wilderness: the men quarreled among themselves, lost their way, slept badly, and ultimately found that the land they had set out to buy had already been sold (25–27).

Of particular significance is Kirkland's critique of speculative capitalism. In *A New Home* she comments on the difference between men's and women's attitudes toward new settlers: women "have a feeling of hostess-ship toward the new comer. . . . Men look upon each one, newly arrived, merely as . . . somebody more with whom to try the race of enterprize, i.e. money-making" (64). Mr. Mazard cheats her husband out of money and then absconds, and the bank owners issue worthless money, becoming rich at the expense of the farmers. When the bank collapses, the owners flee with their profits, but the people who had trusted them are left destitute (126). Kirkland critiques the speculators in land and money, calling the fraudulent banks a "fungous growth" and the speculators "cunning and stealthy blood-suckers" (121).[42]

In 1852 Fanny Fern (1811–72) titled one of her weekly newspaper columns "A Whisper to Romantic Young Ladies." Responding to an idealized view of marriage that she had seen printed in the popular press, she wrote: "Girls! that's a humbug! . . . This humdrum life, girls, is another affair, with its washing and ironing and cleaning days. . . . All the 'romance' there is in it, you can put under a three-cent piece!"[43]

Fern was the most outspoken of the early women realists. The circumstances under which she began to write in 1851 provided her with a good lesson in realism and drove her to redefine her femininity. Her husband died, leaving her destitute with two children. Her father pressured her to remarry so that he would not have to support her. Her abusive second husband forced himself on her sexually and withheld money from her so that he could impose his will on her. When she left him, he retaliated by spreading scandalous stories about her. Her father-in-law rewrote his will disinheriting her children unless she agreed to give them up. Her brother refused to help her. Clearly none of the men—husband, father, father-in-law, or brother—was the protective guardian that womanhood had been trained to rely on. "Woman should find in man her guardian," Ralph Waldo Emerson told women at a women's rights convention in 1855.[44] That same year Fern published her autobiographical novel *Ruth Hall* in which she satirized the men who had failed her. The heroine of the novel finds that it is best to rely on herself—financially as well as emotionally—and instead of relying on man as her guardian, she herself realizes the American Dream. In Fern's view, a woman need not be the passive, dependent creature that peopled romantic novels by men. Fern came to this realization when she discovered that men in general—even family members—could not be relied on for "protection" in the way that middle-class femininity had been trained to expect. Protection could be withdrawn, that is, the money that came with it could be used as leverage to force compliance. Male "protection" of women could be used as a form of control.

In addition to the realization that came from this hard lesson in the realpolitik of gender relations, another reason for Fern's ability to reconstitute gender identity for herself and her protagonist was her enforced redefinition of her class identity. When she was thrust into poverty, she was able to see that the conventional definition of "woman" was not universal. Attempting to earn her living as a seamstress and then as a newspaper writer, she found that she was vulnerable to insult as she had not been as the protected daughter and wife of a middle-class household. In the novel *Ruth Hall* Fern tells of how the men in the newspaper offices treat Ruth disrespectfully. The editors are "incapable of comprehending" that their manner lacks "that respectful courtesy due to a dignified woman" (122).

Not only was Ruth not treated with the same respect she had enjoyed as a dependent middle-class woman, she was also subjected to sexual harassment. Because she is poor and working for a living, men assume that she is fair game. The men she sews for make lewd comments and sexual propositions. In chapter 36 Fern portrays the attitude of the boardinghouse loungers who see the widowed and impoverished Ruth as easy prey. After discussing her physical appearance and desperate situation, they conclude "that any of the sex may be bought with a yard of ribbon, or a breastpin" (73–74).

Fern learned that the old rules did not apply in her new situation. Although she had always been spirited (which was a factor in her metamorphosis), after her shift from middle- to working-class status, she reshaped her performance. One of the characteristics of her new persona was the ability—need—to work for a living. She explicitly stated her culture's denial of this identity to a middle-class white woman: "There are few people who speak approbatively" of a woman who earns money of her own (318). The reality, Fern asserted, was that women did work—not only working-class women but middle-class women who were unmarried or widowed or whose male providers were unable or unwilling to support their families.

Fern's experience showed that the idealized view of middle-class white women as dependent and passive did not apply to her new situation—or to the situations of many other women. Like Caroline Kirkland in the West, she had to present herself in a new and radical way to accommodate herself to the new situation. She created a new identity: assertive, self-sufficient, financially independent, outspoken—even vulgar by the standards of proper femininity. She renamed this new persona "Fanny Fern." Like Kirkland, she found that the old qualities of femininity were useless in her new position and to attempt to retain them would have been suicidal. Although Fern's rejection of conventional gender identity caused her to be severely criticized,[45] it was this performativity—her presentation of herself in a new way—that led to her ability to write about her experience. Had she retained the gender and class identity of her middle-class background, she would not have been able to write so frankly and satirically about her society's conventions, revealing the hypocrisy behind the facade of such sacred ideals as marriage, motherhood, male sovereignty, and "true womanhood." A "lady" would not have written openly about such things. Moreover, it was only in her new persona that she could write in the straightforward, down-to-earth language that conservative critics criticized as "vulgar" and "unladylike."

Fern's novel *Ruth Hall* reflects the realism of her perspective. In the preface she describes her technique, differentiating her novel from the typical romantic novel of the period: "I am aware that it is entirely at variance with all set rules for novel-writing. There . . . are no hair-breadth escapes. . . . I have avoided long introductions and descriptions, and have entered unceremoniously and unannounced, into people's houses" (3). As Fern wrote in 1861 in the *New York Ledger*, the fiction writer should portray the "commonplace."

In *Ruth Hall* Fern recounts the daily events in the life of the protagonist: what she eats; how much her food costs; the lack of fifty cents for the train ride to visit her daughter at the Halls; the games she plays with her children; what happens when her child is sick; her relationship with her in-laws; how she takes her child with her when she peddles her manuscripts.

Ruth Hall is realistic rather than romantic in other, more general respects as well: it begins instead of ends with the heroine's marriage; the bride questions the possibility of happiness in marriage; instead of their "living happily ever after," the heroine's husband dies; the tone throughout the novel is satirical and cynical; the novel ends not with a marriage but with the heroine's acquisition of ten thousand dollars in bank stock. Ruth realizes that she cannot rely on her male relatives and resolves to be independent; like her author, she reconstitutes her gender and class identity.

If through their performativity Caroline Kirkland and Fanny Fern reconstitute gender and class identity, Harriet Wilson (1827–?) reconstitutes not only gender and class but also racial identity. *Our Nig, or, Sketches from the Life of a Free Black* (1859)[46] is the autobiographical story of a racially mixed New Hampshire woman. Wilson's performativity, her assertion of an identity that is contrary to that prescribed for her by her culture, derived from her realization that the reality of her life differed from the prescription. Just as Kirkland and Fern recognized that the reality for women on the frontier or in poverty was different from the idealized image of "true womanhood," Wilson recognized that the reality for her was different from the cultural definitions of blacks: free African Americans in the antebellum North were idealized by the abolitionists (to contrast with slavery in the South) and blacks were objectified by the culture generally. Having lived with racism in New Hampshire, Wilson knew that racism existed in the North. Her story principally reveals the racism of Mrs. Bellmont, but the evidence indicates that Mrs. Bellmont was not alone in her racist attitudes. In 1835, for example (a year when the protagonist of *Our Nig*—and the author—would have been in school in New Hampshire), a group of New Hampshire farmers were so angry that black children were enrolled in the local school that they hitched their oxen to the school and dragged it into a swamp.[47] Wilson hints at some of this racism in the children's taunts: "Black, white and yeller," the children call out (21); "See that nigger. . . . I won't play with her" (31).

Apparently Wilson felt that she could not look to abolitionists for support. Milford, New Hampshire, where she grew up, was considered a hotbed of abolitionism, and the family she lived with had abolitionist connections.[48] Yet as Wilson says in her preface, her "mistress was wholly imbued with southern *principles*." Moreover, as the text shows and as a letter in the appendix points out, Wilson was "a slave, in every sense of the word" (139). Surrounded by abolitionists, Wilson and her protagonist lived under conditions that rival the story of any escaped slave. *Our Nig* was not promoted by the abolitionist press, nor was it reviewed or advertised for sale in any of the contemporary periodicals.[49] One of the principal reasons why Wilson's book was ignored probably derived from the abolitionists' desire to focus on slavery in the South: they would not have wanted to have their cause complicated by reports of racism in the North which would give fuel to the contentions of southern apologists for slavery such as George Fitzhugh, who claimed that slaves were better off in the South than white wage earners were in the North.[50]

Wilson's text suggests that she is bitter about the abolitionists' failure to help her. She writes in her preface that she has left out many incidents from her book that would reflect badly on the abolitionists: "I have purposely omitted what would most provoke shame in our good anti-slavery friends at home." Yet simply by mentioning that she has had to omit such incidents, she inculpates the antislavery North. Her anger at the abolitionists does not derive simply from her experience growing up in Milford, however. During her travels in Massachusetts, she apparently found herself maltreated by people who called themselves abolitionists. Later in the book she denounces the hypocrisy of "professed abolitionists, who didn't want slaves at the South, nor niggers in their own houses, North. Faugh! to lodge one; to eat with one; to admit one through the front door; to sit next one; awful!" (129). Wilson's bitterness toward the abolitionists was probably intensified by their eagerness to accept the fraudulent claims of her husband while rejecting her own legitimate claims. Her husband, Samuel, who was hired by the abolitionists to give talks about his experience as a slave, turned out to be a fake. Just before he deserted Wilson and their unborn child, he told her that "he had never seen the South and that his illiterate harangues were humbugs for hungry abolitionists" (128). How angry she must have been to realize that the abolitionists not only did not help her in New Hampshire as a child but were "hungry" to hear her husband's story (though rambling, illiterate, and false), whereas they did not want to hear her story about racism in the North, although it was well-crafted, literate, and true.[51]

Given this recognition of the failure of reality to meet the ideal, Wilson could not look to traditional culture for concepts of gender, racial, or class identity. Instead of adopting the traditional roles ascribed generally to womanhood or specifically to black womanhood, she invented her own identity.[52] First, the African American woman of her day, particularly the working-class woman, would not have been expected to be educated. Wilson apologizes for being literate, writing in her preface the hope that her "colored brethren . . . will not condemn this attempt of their sister to be erudite." African American male writers of the mid–nineteenth century did not apologize for their erudition; rather, they displayed it proudly as a badge of honor and achievement.[53] White women writers did apologize for coming before the public, which was regarded as unfeminine, but although they were modest about their accomplishments, they did not expect to be condemned for their literacy. Wilson needed to overcome the stereotype not only of race and gender but of the combination of both race and gender as well as class. To write a novel was for an African American woman an assertion of identity. Wilson's 1859 novel is the first by an African American woman in the United States;[54] the next novel by a black woman was Frances Harper's *Iola Leroy*, published in 1892.

In addition to constituting herself as a literate black woman, Wilson also challenged her culture's image of the black woman as object. The title of Wilson's work defiantly proclaims the identity of the author/protagonist as "our nig," parodically subverting the culture's objectification of blacks: although the title suggests that "nig" is the property of the speaker (*our* nig), in fact, "nig" is the protagonist of the novel, and at times she *is* the speaker. (The first three chapter titles are in the first person.) Moreover, by using the words "Our Nig" for her pseudonym, Wilson ironically appropriates a term of denigration, authorizing herself. The novel is Alfrado's story; instead of being the "other" in somebody else's narrative, the black woman is the protagonist. The black woman of the title is subject, not object.[55]

Not only does Wilson assert her subjectivity in the title and in the fact of writing, she portrays her protagonist as the reverse of the traditional image of mid-nineteenth-century black womanhood. White womanhood was guided by the image of the "true woman": pure, pious, submissive, dependent, domestic, and selfless. The free black woman was expected to conform to a similar standard.[56] Moreover, as a member of the servant class, Alfrado would have been expected to be subservient to her mistress. Thus the combination of gender, race, and class identities would define Alfrado as submissive. Wilson's protagonist, however, is strong-willed and assertive. As a child, she is said to have "an exuberance of spirit almost beyond restraint" (17); she has "a wilful determined nature" (28). She retains her spirit despite the harsh treatment she receives from Mrs. Bellmont. This is particularly apparent when she becomes a favorite among the children at school (38). Ultimately, with encouragement from Mr. Bellmont, Frado defies Mrs. Bellmont. In this new performative act she realizes her power:

> "Stop!" shouted Frado, "strike me, and I'll never work a mite more for you;" and throwing down what she had gathered, stood like one who feels the stirring of free and independent thoughts.
> By this unexpected demonstration, her mistress, in amazement, dropped her weapon. . . . Frado walked towards the house, her mistress following with the wood. . . . She did not know, before, that she had a power to ward off assaults. Her triumph . . . repaid her for much of her former suffering. (105)

Wilson's performativity enabled her to write in the realistic tradition. Throughout the novel, Wilson undermines racial stereotypes, both white and black, negative and positive. The book begins by subverting the stereotype of white motherhood. A white mother abandons her child to the care of a woman whom she knows to be a "she-devil" (17); certainly this undercuts the image of maternal affection believed to be inherent in the definition of white motherhood. Conventional definitions of white womanhood are further challenged by the portrait of Mrs. Bellmont. Cruel not only to Frado but even to her own children, Mrs. Bellmont represents everything that "true womanhood" was not: she is not passive, acquiescent, gentle, kind, maternal, nurturing, or religious. Wilson describes her as "self-willed, haughty, undisciplined, arbitrary and severe" (25).

If white womanhood is reversed in Mrs. Bellmont, white manhood is similarly subverted in Mr. Bellmont, who does not fit the image of aggressive maleness contained in nineteenth-century individualism. A "kind, humane man" (24), he is afraid to oppose his wife, and although he is upset by her cruelty to Frado and occasionally protests, he does not stop the abuse. When Aunt Abby asks her brother why he cannot rule his own house, he says, "Women rule the earth, and all in it" (44).

In addition to its subversion of white womanhood and manhood, Wilson's novel critiques many myths in nineteenth-century American culture.[57] First, the story of Frado counters the myth of female dependency. Frado's goal is to be economically independent, "to take care of herself" (124). The novel also counters the success myth. Frado works hard and perseveres, but she is *not* successful; the American Dream does not work. Hard facts get in the way: her health is bad, she is lame from a fall, her husband deserts her, she has a child. In spite of all her efforts, the novel does not end with the "rags-to-riches" formula of triumphant success. Another myth that the novel subverts is that of marriage. Frado does not "live happily ever after." Her husband turns out to be a fraud, and he deserts his pregnant wife. As a letter in the appendix notes, Frado/Wilson would have been better off if she had never met her husband: the day that she met him "was a sad occurrence" for her (134). Frado learns that she cannot rely on a man for protection. All of the men in her life fail her for different reasons: Mr. Bellmont is weak; James dies; and her husband deserts her.[58] Wilson's text reveals the myth behind society's convention of male protection of the "weaker vessel."

Our Nig also does not conform to the pattern of conventional slave narratives, which follow a progression from slavery to triumphant freedom.[59] Wilson's protagonist is free from the beginning, yet her freedom gives her little joy. And instead of progressing to a happy conclusion, her narrative chronicles one setback after another until the final one occurs offstage: Wilson's stated purpose in writing her novel was to earn money to support her son, but a letter in the appendix tells us that Wilson's son died soon after the novel was published.

As a realistic novel, *Our Nig* not only undercuts traditional myths and stereotypes; it also provides realistic detail and characterization. The language is spare and concise, and the characters speak in dialect. Wilson describes Frado's hard life with a minimum of comment and with no hyperbole. Moreover, as Kirkland would say, she does not neglect to portray the "warts."

These three antebellum women realists are representative of the writing American women writers were doing before the so-called "birth" of American realism. Their names and those of other antebellum women writers have not been included in the roster of American literary realists because of the gendered construction of the concept of American realism. Reconstituting their own identity, early women realists challenged hegemonic definitions of gender, class, and racial identities, creating a body of work, the acknowledgment of which repositions the beginning of American literary realism.

NOTES

1. Warner Berthoff, in *The Ferment of Realism: American Literature, 1884–1919* (New York: Free Press, 1965), was, as Michael Davitt Bell notes, "simply expressing established

critical consensus when he began . . . [his book] by writing that 'the great collective event in American letters during the 1880s and 1890s was the securing of "realism" as the dominant standard of value.'" See Bell, *The Problem of American Realism: Studies in the Cultural History of a Literary Idea* (Chicago: University of Chicago Press, 1993), 1. That American realism began in the late nineteenth century is asserted by, among others, George Becker, *Realism in Modern Literature* (New York: Frederick Ungar, 1980), 5–6, and the Introduction to *Documents of Modern Literary Realism* (Princeton: Princeton University Press, 1963), 6; Daniel Borus, *Writing Realism: Howells, James, and Norris in the Mass Market* (Chapel Hill: University of North Carolina Press, 1989), 1; Eric Sundquist, "Realism and Regionalism," in *Columbia Literary History of the United States*, ed. Emory Elliott et al. (New York: Columbia University Press, 1987), 501.

2. See, e.g., Nina Baym, *Woman's Fiction: A Guide to Novels by and About Women* (Ithaca: Cornell University Press), 34; Judith Fetterley, *Provisions: A Reader from 19th-Century American Women* (Bloomington: Indiana University Press, 1985), 8, 118–19, 123; Lucy M. Freibert and Barbara A. White, *Hidden Hands: An Anthology of American Women Writers, 1790–1870* (New Brunswick: Rutgers University Press, 1985), 183; Joanne Dobson, "The American Renaissance Reenvisioned," in *The (Other) American Traditions: Nineteenth-Century American Women Writers*, ed. Joyce W. Warren (New Brunswick: Rutgers University Press, 1993), 164–202; and Robyn R. Warhol, "Poetics and Persuasion: *Uncle Tom's Cabin* as a Realist Novel," *Essays in Literature* 13 (Fall 1986)): 283–97. Annette Kolodny, in "The Integrity of Memory: Creating a New Literary History of the United States," *American Literature* 57 (May 1985), decries the crippling "habits of chronology and labelling" which cause us to "periodize 'realism' in fiction to the postbellum decades," thus preventing us from recognizing it in the works of antebellum women writers (296–97).

3. Discussions of late nineteenth-century realism sometimes include Edith Wharton and such regionalist writers (who are denominated "minor" realists) as Sarah Orne Jewett and Mary E. Wilkins Freeman but exclude antebellum women writers.

4. See J. P. Stern, *On Realism* (London: Routledge & Kegan Paul, 1973), 38–39. See also René Wellek, "The Concept of Realism in Literary Scholarship" *Neophilologus* 45 (1961), 1–20; and George J. Becker, *Realism in Modern Literature*, 37–39.

5. This point is also made by George Watson, "The Coronation of Realism," *Georgia Review* 41 (Spring 1987): 7–8.

6. Apparently, the first time the word was applied to literature in England was in an article on Balzac in the *Westminister Review* in 1853. The *Mercure de France* article in 1826 referred to "this literary doctrine which gains ground every day and should lead to faithful imitation not of the masterworks of art but of the originals offered by nature could very well be called *realism*." See Becker, *Realism in Modern Literature*, 38; and Stern, *On Realism*, 38–39.

7. See, e.g., Charles C. Walcutt, *American Literary Naturalism: A Divided Stream* (Minneapolis: University of Minnesota Press, 1956), and Harold Kolb, *The Illusion of Life: American Realism as Literary Form* (Charlottesville: University Press of Virginia, 1969). An additional discussion of realism during this period was Lionel Trilling's criti-

cism of Vernon Parrington, whose ideas in *Main Currents in American Thought* (1927–30), Trilling said, reflected a belief that literature should mechanically reflect "material reality," whereas Trilling thought it should also reflect the reality of the mind. See Trilling, *The Liberal Imagination* (New York: Viking, 1950), 1–19, 206–7, 221–22.

8. See, e.g., Georg Lukacs, *Studies in European Realism*, trans. Edith Bone (London: Hillway, 1950), and "Marx and the Problem of Ideological Decay," in *Essays on Realism*, ed. Rodney Livingstone, trans. David Fernbach (Cambridge, Mass.: MIT Press, 1981). See also the writings of American Marxist critics such as Granville Hicks and Bernard Smith in the 1930s. For a contemporary analysis of the varying responses to realism from a Marxist perspective, see Terry Lovell, *Pictures of Reality: Aesthetics, Politics, Pleasure* (New York: BFI Publishing, 1980).

9. For a discussion of feminist responses to realism, see, e.g., Toril Moi, *Sexual/Textual Politics: Feminist Literary Theory* (London: Methuen, 1985), 4–8, 45–49, 150–73; and Penny Boumelha, "Realism and the Ends of Feminism," in *Grafts*, ed. Susan Sheridan (London: Verso, 1988): 77–91.

10. See, e.g., Moira Monteith's Introduction to *Women's Writing: A Challenge to Theory* (Brighton: Harvester Press, 1986), 2–3. Toril Moi, in *Sexual/Textual Politics*, suggests that modernism is the true realism (47).

11. For the deconstructionist position on realism, see Jacques Derrida, e.g., *Of Grammatology*, trans. Gayatri Spivak (Baltimore: Johns Hopkins University Press, 1976). The signifier, writes Derrida, "has no 'natural attachment' to the signified within reality" (46).

12. Penny Boumelha, in "Realism and the Ends of Feminism," criticizes "the collapse into and on to one another of realism as an epistemology and realism as a mode of writing" (15). Terry Lovell, in *Pictures of Reality*, agrees that the two should not be connected but argues for epistemological realism from a Marxist perspective (91).

13. Lovell, *Pictures of Reality*, 6.

14. For an excellent discussion of the construction of American literary realism, see Amy Kaplan, *The Social Construction of American Realism* (Chicago: University of Chicago Press, 1988).

15. Judith Butler, "Contingent Foundations: Feminism and the Question of 'Postmodernism,'" in *Feminists Theorize the Political*, ed. Judith Butler and Joan W. Scott (New York: Routledge, 1992), 4. See also Louis Althusser, *For Marx*, trans. Ben Brewster (New York: Pantheon Books, 1969), who, as Patricia Waugh pointed out in *Feminine Fictions: Revisiting the Postmodern* (London: Routledge, 1989), refused to separate "a domain of the 'real' from a domain of the 'represented'" (2–3).

16. The *Mercure de France* wrote in 1826 that realism was "the literature of the true," and in the United States, William Dean Howells maintained that literature should portray the "Truth" (*Documents*, 38–39, 136).

17. As Michel Foucault points out, what the dominant discourse establishes as "true" is assumed to be natural or a given, and individuals are not able to see that it is socially constructed. See, e.g., Foucault, "The Discourse on Language," in *The Archaeology of Knowledge*, trans. A. M. Sheridan Smith (New York: Pantheon Books, 1972), 218.

18. As Everett Carter puts it, "an attack on the sentimental was, then, the initial force in the development of American realism." See *Howells and the Age of Realism* (Philadelphia: J. B. Lippincott, 1954). Elise Miller, in "The Feminization of American Realist Theory," *American Literary Realism* 23 (Fall 1990), however, notes that although late nineteenth-century male realists were "bent on organizing themselves against feminine enemies and threats" and attempted to purge literature of women's writing as though it were a disease, they appropriated much from their female predecessors (21).

19. Charles Dudley Warner, *As We Go* (1894), cited in Van Wyck Brooks, *New England: Indian Summer* (New York: E. P. Dutton, 1940), 100.

20. See, e.g., William Dean Howells, *Criticism and Fiction* (New York: New York University Press, 1959), 361.

21. See, e.g., Henry James, "An Animated Conversation," in *Essays in London and Elsewhere* (London: J. R. Osgood, McIlvaine and Co., 1893). This essay concludes with the resolution by the two men in the conversation that male readers and writers must unite against women.

22. Frank Norris, "A Plea for Romantic Fiction" (1901), in *The Literary Criticism of Frank Norris*, ed. Donald Pizer (Austin: University of Texas Press, 1964).

23. For a discussion of the disparaging remarks made by Edith Wharton and Willa Cather regarding women writers, see Elaine Sargent Apthorp, "Sentiment, Naturalism, and the Female Regionalist," *Legacy* 7 (Spring 1990), 18–19. For Wharton's attitude toward local-color writers, see Donna M. Campbell, "Edith Wharton and the 'Authoresses': The Critique of Local Color in Wharton's Early Fiction," *Studies in American Fiction* 22 (Autumn 1994): 169–83.

24. For a good discussion of the realists' devaluation of their female contemporaries as "minor," see Michael Davitt Bell's analysis of local-color writer Sarah Orne Jewett, *The Problem of American Realism*.

25. For analyses of the male effort to write women writers out of the canon, see, e.g., Paul Lauter, "Race and Gender in the Shaping of the American Literary Canon: A Case Study from the Twenties," *Feminist Studies* 9 (Fall 1983): 435–63; Nina Baym, "Early Histories of American Literature: A Chapter in the Institution of New England," *American Literary History* 1 (Fall 1989): 459–88; Joyce W. Warren, "Canons and Canon Fodder," Introduction to *The (Other) American Traditions*, ed. Warren, 1–25; and Elizabeth Ammons, "Men of Color, Women, and Uppity Art at the Turn of the Century," *American Literary Realism* 23 (Spring 1991): 14–24. Ammons calls this effort the "twentieth-century project of suppression" (21).

26. Henry James, "Nana," in *Documents*, ed. Becker, 236–243; Frank Norris, *The Responsibilities of the Novelist* (New York: Greenwood Press, 1902), 234.

27. Rose Terry Cooke described this editorial policy in "A Letter to Mary Ann," *Sunday Afternoon* 3 (August 1879): 752–55; for a discussion of the literary double standard with respect to Cooke, see Elizabeth Ammons, Introduction to *How Celia Changed Her Mind and Other Stories*, by Rose Terry Cooke (New Brunswick: Rutgers University Press, 1986). For a discussion of the changes that the publisher requested in Rebecca Harding

Davis's *Margret Howth* see Jean Fagan Yellin, Afterword to *Margret Howth* (New York: Feminist Press, 1990), 287–90. The criticisms of Fanny Fern's writing are discussed in Joyce Warren, *Fanny Fern: An Independent Woman* (New Brunswick: Rutgers University Press, 1992), e.g., 124–28, 139–42, 208–10. Nina Baym discusses the restrictions on nineteenth-century women writers in *Novels, Readers and Reviewers: Responses to Fiction in Antebellum America* (Ithaca: Cornell University Press, 1984), 257.

28. Judith Butler, *Gender Trouble: Feminism and the Subversion of Identity* (New York: Routledge, 1990), 33–34.

29. See V. L. Parrington, *Main Currents in American Thought*, vol 3, *The Beginnings of Critical Realism in America, 1860–1920* (New York: Harcourt, Brace, 1927–30), and Van Wyck Brooks, *New England: Indian Summer* (New York: E. P. Dutton, 1940), 99–101. Identifying "a new spirit of realism" after the Civil War (4), Parrington established the date for the realist period in the United States which was adopted by later scholars. Elise Miller notes in "The Feminization of American Realist Theory" that twentieth-century critics perceived mid-nineteenth-century women's writing as an "aberration" and rejoiced that it was finally overcome at the end of the century (38). More recent criticism has not been as overtly hostile, but the emphasis remains on the male writers. Elizabeth Ammons, in her review of Kenneth Warren's *Black and White Strangers: Race and American Literary Realism* (Chicago: University of Chicago Press, 1993), notes that the book suffers from an "underrepresentation" of women writers; it is "primarily a conversation among men" (*Studies in American Fiction* 22 (Autumn 1994): 250–52).

30. Richard Chase, *The American Novel and Its Tradition* (New York: Doubleday, 1957). For a good discussion of the impact of Chase's thesis on American literary criticism, see Amy Kaplan, *The Social Construction of American Literary Realism* (1988), 2–4. Other theorists whose discussions of American literature omit women include F. O. Matthiessen, *The American Renaissance* (1941), R. W. B. Lewis, *The American Adam* (1955), and Lionel Trilling, *The Liberal Imagination* (1950).

31. For example, George Becker in *Documents of Modern Literary Realism* (1963) cites Rebecca Harding Davis among writers who show early realist tendencies (17).

32. Alfred Habegger, *Gender, Fantasy, and Realism in American Literature* (New York: Columbia University Press, 1982), 10–11. All page references in the text are to this edition.

33. Particularly problematic is Habegger's conclusion that Elizabeth Stuart Phelps's *The Story of Avis* is not realistic. He asserts, for example, that Avis's assumption of a "maternal" role with her husband is not as realistic as Isabel Archer's behavior in Henry James's *Portrait of a Lady* (54). What Habegger fails to consider is that whereas Osmond is a villain, Avis's husband is well-meaning but weak. Avis's assumption of a maternal role is not unrealistically "noble" (as Habegger says) but simply a realistic way of coping with a not-uncommon situation.

34. See, e.g., Flaubert: "A novelist *does not have the right to express his opinion* on anything whatsoever. . . . Great Art is scientific and impersonal" (Becker, *Documents*, 90–96).

35. See e.g., Joan Scott, "Experience," in *Feminists Theorize the Political*. Scott ques-

tions the "authority of experience," pointing out that the evidence of experience discursively reproduces given ideological systems (26–36).

36. As Elaine Sargent Apthorp notes in "Sentiment, Naturalism, and the Female Regionalist," Crane creates pity in the reader for his characters because they "can never have access to our enlightened perspective" (9).

37. Dreiser wrote in the *New York World* in 1930 that he saw himself as an "individual compelled to see life through the various veils or fogs of my own lacks, predilections and what you will, yet seeking honestly always to set down that which I imagine I see" (Becker, *Documents*, 156).

38. See Langley C. Keyes, "Caroline M. Kirkland: A Pioneer in Realism," Ph.D. dissertation, Harvard University, 1936. Critics who have agreed with Keyes include John Nerber, Introduction to *A New Home, or Life in the Clearings* (New York: Putnam's Sons, 1953); William S. Osborne, *Caroline M. Kirkland* (New York: Twayne, 1972); Alfred Habegger, *Gender, Fantasy, and Realism in American Literature* (1982); Annette Kolodny, *The Land Before Her* (Chapel Hill: University of North Carolina Press, 1984); Judith Fetterley, *Provisions* (1985); Sandra Zagarell, Introduction to *A New Home, Who'll Follow?* (New Brunswick: Rutgers University Press, 1990); and Joanne Dobson, "The American Renaissance Reenvisioned."

39. Caroline Kirkland, *A New Home, Who'll Follow? or, Glimpses of Western Life*, ed. Sandra A. Zagarell (New Brunswick: Rutgers University Press, 1990). All page references in the text are to this edition.

40. As Judith Fetterley notes in *Provisions*, "Kirkland recognizes that she is doing something new in American literature" (120).

41. Caroline Kirkland, *Forest Life*, 2 vols. (New York: C. S. Francis, 1844). All page references in the text are to this edition.

42. Kirkland's realism precedes and parallels the evolution of mid-nineteenth-century European theories of realism. Internal evidence, however, suggests that she looked to the eighteenth century to frame her narrative. *A New Home* ends with "a conclusion wherein nothing is concluded" (189)—which Kirkland puts in quotation marks. The phrase is taken from the title of the last chapter of Samuel Johnson's *Rasselas*, "The Conclusion, in which nothing is concluded." Kirkland's novels are similar to *Rasselas* in other respects. Johnson's episodic work (which may or may not be a novel) chronicles the impossible attempt to find happiness; in Kirkland's episodic works (which may or may not be called novels) she describes the settlers' constant movement (buying and reselling farms and moving on every year or two), which in *Forest Life* she calls "this blundering search after happiness" (1:27).

43. Fanny Fern, "A Whisper to Romantic Young Ladies," *True Flag* (June 12, 1852), in *Ruth Hall and Other Writings*, ed. Joyce W. Warren (New Brunswick: Rutgers University Press, 1986), 229–30. All page references to Fern's work are to this edition.

44. Ralph Waldo Emerson, *Complete Works*, ed. Edward W. Emerson, 12 vols. (Boston: Houghton Mifflin, 1903–4), 11:403–26.

45. Examples of the criticism Fern was subjected to include (on the public side) re-

views that castigated her for her "unfeminine" writing and (in her personal life) the hostility of her third husband's relatives. See Warren, *Fanny Fern*.

46. Harriet Wilson, *Our Nig, or Sketches from the Life of a Free Black*, ed. Henry Louis Gates Jr. (New York: Vintage, 1983). All page references are to this edition.

47. See Thomas A. Bailey and David M. Kennedy, *The American Pageant* (Lexington, Mass.: D. C. Heath, 1994), 364.

48. See Barbara White, "'Our Nig' and the She-Devil: New Information About Harriet Wilson and the 'Bellmont' Family," *American Literature* 65 (March 1993): 34–38.

49. Henry Louis Gates reports in his Introduction to *Our Nig* that he and his assistants checked contemporary newspapers and found no reviews or notices of the book (xxx).

50. See George Fitzhugh, *Cannibals All! or Slaves Without Masters* (1857).

51. Barbara White makes this observation in "'Our Nig' and the She-Devil" (40).

52. For an interesting comparison of how two antebellum black women redefined themselves, see Beth Maclay Doriani, "Black Womanhood in Nineteenth-Century America: Subversion and Self-Construction in Two Women's Autobiographies," *American Quarterly* 43 (June 1991): 199–222.

53. Frederick Douglass, for example, although he apologized for his "ignorance," was proud of his learning, which he says he recognized early as his "pathway" out of slavery. See, e.g., Douglass, *Autobiographies*, ed. Henry Louis Gates Jr. (New York: Library of America, 1994), 4, 216–18.

54. Henry Louis Gates in his Introduction to *Our Nig* establishes that Wilson's work is the first novel in the United States by a black woman (xiii). Barbara White, "'Our Nig' and the She-Devil," concludes that although it is apparently based on the facts of Wilson's life, the work should be considered a novel rather than an autobiography since Wilson has shaped her narrative (41–44).

55. As Henry Louis Gates writes in the Introduction to *Our Nig*, the "heroine of *Our Nig* transforms "herself into a *subject*" (li). John Ernest, in "Economies of Identity: Harriet E. Wilson's *Our Nig*," *PMLA* 109 (May 1994), points out that not only is Wilson regarded as object because of her race, she is also "woman-as-object" and "worker-as-object" (429).

56. See Frances Foster, "Adding Color and Contour to Early American Self-Portraitures: Autobiographical Writings of Afro-American Women," in *Conjuring: Black Women, Fiction, and Literary Tradition*, ed. Marjorie Pryse and Hortense J. Spillers (Bloomington: Indiana University Press, 1985), 205. The role of the free black woman after Reconstruction was constructed to meet the standards of whites, notes Henry Louis Gates Jr., "The Trope of a New Negro and the Reconstruction of the Image of the Black," *Representations* 24 (Fall 1988): 129–55.

57. Barbara Christian points out that Wilson "questioned the progressive platform of her time" (331). See "'Somebody Forgot to Tell Somebody Something': African-American Women's Historical Novels," in *Wild Women in the Whirlwind: Afra-American Culture and the Contemporary Literary Renaissance*, ed. Joanne M. Braxton and Andrée Nocola McLaughlin (New Brunswick: Rutgers University Press, 1990).

58. As P. Gabrielle Foreman notes, Frado's abandonment comes about through the death or silence of the male characters. See "The Spoken and the Silenced in *Incidents in the Life of a Slave Girl* and *Our Nig*," *Callaloo* 13 (Spring 1990): 320–21.

59. Hazel Carby describes *Our Nig* as an "allegory of a slave narrative, a 'slave' narrative set in the 'free' north." See *Reconstructing Womanhood: The Emergence of the Afro-American Novelist* (Cambridge: Oxford University Press, 1984), 43.

WOMEN'S MASTERPIECES

Josephine Donovan

> Did women have a Renaissance?
>
> —Joan Kelly

The distinguished historian Joan Kelly opened her classic essay by charging that "one of the tasks of women's history is to call into question accepted schemes of periodization." For women, she concluded, "There was no renaissance . . . —at least, not during the Renaissance."[1] Kelly's point was that women's and men's cultural histories are different. What may have been a period of growth and efflorescence for one may not have been so for the other. Similarly, ethnic and racial groups and classes have had differing histories.

Although women may not have fully participated in the Renaissance in fourteenth- and fifteenth-century Italy, they have had renaissances of their own. One such was the tradition of local-color realism that flowered from about 1830 to 1900 in the United States. Its main authors were Harriet Beecher Stowe (1811–96), Rose Terry Cooke (1827–92), Sarah Orne Jewett (1849–1909), and Mary E. Wilkins Freeman (1852–1930). Their school produced a series of masterpiece works, which unfortunately continue to be marginalized by the gatekeepers of the American literary canon. Like many other works of women's literature, they have become pawns in the so-called canon wars, because of which women's literary traditions continue to be misrepresented in leading cultural media.

As recently as 1994, for example, William A. Henry 3d pronounced, "The unvarnished truth is this: you could eliminate every woman writer, painter and composer from the cave man era to the present moment and not significantly deform the course of Western culture."[2] This benighted opinion, typical of contemporary conservative revanchism, betrays, among other things, an appalling ignorance of women's literature and art. Equally disturbing is the smug acquiescence of the *New York Times*'s reviewer of Henry's book, Roger Kimball another conservative (author of *Tenured Radicals*), who observed, "It is painful to admit it, I know, but Henry is right. The only real question is what to do about it."[3] Kimball concluded his review by evoking the barbarians-at-the-gates shibboleth, expressing the hope that true standards of excellence and intelligence will soon replace the corrupt "politically correct" impositions that have allegedly reigned in recent years, forcing us to read shoddy and inferior works by women (as well as by men who are deviant by reason of race, class, or sexuality). One is tempted to look the other way at such embarrassing, if pompous, assertions of ignorance, but these opinions were expressed in the ostensibly liberal *New York Times* and thus given a cachet of respectability.

In this essay I will not extensively discuss the theoretical questions raised by Henry's comment about the historical process of canon formation, that is, the determination of what in fact *is* Western culture (and who determines it), but instead will respond to the challenge on its own terms. I will argue, in short, that by *traditional* standards of literary excellence women writers *have* produced masterpieces, which continue to be ignored, even though their existence has been heralded over and over by feminist critics. The "unvarnished truth" is that works by women are still *not* being read, still *not* being seriously studied, and that is why self-appointed custodians of culture like Henry can *still* in 1994 proclaim that they do not exist.

In fact, the women's nineteenth-century local-color movement constituted an important period in American literature, an American Renaissance, that has yet to be fully valued. Remarking the "imaginative gain" the local colorists wrought from a culturally "impoverished" milieu, Lawrence Buell comments in his *Environmental Imagination* (1995): "We are only now beginning to appreciate how historically important this largely female-sponsored project was."[4]

Before proceeding, however, let me point out that historically, the determination of what constitute the canonical works of a culture has been done by a small politically powerful group—yes, an elite—in that culture. Never in history has a canon been chosen according to strictly "objective" criteria of aesthetic and intellectual excellence, if such criteria could indeed be determined. Rather, the terms by which canons have been selected have been, like all human decisions, historically and politically contingent.[5] Often canons are selected according to thematic criteria; often these themes are chauvinistic, vaunting the virtues of a particular nation or group.

A paradigmatic instance of canon formation remains the Council of Jamnia where in 90 C.E. a group of rabbis decided which of the ancient Hebraic writings were to be considered canonical—that is, official expressions of Hebrew culture—thus determining the constitution of the Old Testament. The historical context for the Council of Jamnia was that Jerusalem had fallen (to the Romans) in 70 C.E. The temple had been destroyed, and Israel as a state was not to exist again until the twentieth century.

Thus the council met during a crisis of national identity, and the determination of the canonicity of the Bible was governed by a desire to retain a sense of national identity among the Israelites. Hence one of the guiding criteria according to which canonicity was determined was whether a work dealt (thematically) with God's alleged covenant with the Hebrews. Thus the Book of Job, for example, which had been written several centuries earlier, was accepted as canonical at this time, whereas several other writings, now called the Apocrypha, were excluded. My point is that the contents of the book conservatives hold as almost definitional to Western culture were selected according to standards of political correctness many centuries ago.

It goes without saying, therefore, that since the elites that have determined the makeup of the course of Western culture have been white men, works that have not fit into their thematic (political) concerns have been designated apocryphal. As Henry's comment conveniently illustrates, that includes most work by women. Nina Baym's now classic article "Melodramas of Beset Manhood" shows how those thematic concerns have governed canonical selection of much American literature.[6]

I am, however, going to lay aside what we know of the politics of canon formation and consider that conceivably persons of goodwill might be able to establish criteria of aesthetic, intellectual, and moral excellence that were genuinely unbiased, that genuinely reflect "the best that has been thought and said" in Western culture (to reinvoke the Arnoldian notion of the "touchstone") — recognizing, of course, the problematics involved in determining the meaning of "best."

But I am going to propose that even by traditional standards of excellence (which I specify below) numerous works by nineteenth-century American women writers qualify as "masterpieces." I do not say *touchstone* because that implies the work is meritorious only insofar as it reflects certain parochial concerns of a given culture. Rather, I use *masterpiece* to suggest that the work has a transcending appeal, that it deals with issues of vital interest to all human beings.

That indeed is the first criterion traditionally implied by the term "masterpiece."[7] In reflecting on the great works of the Western tradition — works like *Hamlet, Oedipus at Colonus, To the Lighthouse* — readers have generally agreed that they deal with the "big issues," of human mortality, suffering, evil, and redemption: how to wrest meaning from the human passage.

Second, the usual definition of a masterpiece includes the understanding that it does not provide evasive or simplistic answers; it does not deny the complexity and enigma of human existence but develops its themes with honesty, intelligence, sophistication, and depth. Moreover, it presumably teaches one something about the human condition; great literature expands the moral imagination.

Third, masterpiece literature often provides a rich variety and depth of characterization. It affords the reader personal encounters with characters whom one comes to know intimately, as if they were real people. Such literature often presents as well a dense, detailed, and convincing sense of reality—whether it be psychological reality; a sense of locale, environment, or social setting; or the complexities of moral life. It introduces one to that reality. Finally, a great work hangs together; it has an inherent design, a unifying thought, or what Aristotle called *dianoia*.

According to the traditional definition of masterpiece, then, the women writers of the nineteenth-century New England local-color school produced at least twenty masterpieces, which belong in the canon of the great works of American literature. They include three novels by Harriet Beecher Stowe *Uncle Tom's Cabin* (1852), *The Minister's Wooing* (1859), and *Oldtown Folks* (1869); several stories by Rose Terry Cooke, including "Alcedama Sparks; Or, Old and New" (1859), "Miss Lucinda" (1861), "Freedom Wheeler's Controversy with Providence" (1877), "Mrs. Flint's Married Experience" (1880), "Clary's Trial" (1880), "Some Account of Thomas Tucker" (1882), and "How Celia Changed Her Mind" (1891); Sarah Orne Jewett's *Country of the Pointed Firs* (1896)—which Willa Cather considered one of three American works destined for immortality (the other two being *Huckleberry Finn* and *The Scarlet Letter*), as well as several Jewett stories, including "A White Heron" (1886), "The Courting of Sister Wisby" (1887), "Miss Tempy's Watchers" (1888), "The Flight of Betsey Lane" (1893), "The Only Rose" (1894), "Martha's Lady" (1897), and "The Foreigner" (1900); and, finally, several stories by Mary E. Wilkins Freeman, including "A Wayfaring Couple" (1885), "A New England Nun" (1887), "Sister Liddy" (1891), "Christmas Jenny" (1891), "A Poetess" (1891), and "Old Woman Magoun" (1905).

Here in the interests of space I will confine myself in making my case to one work by each of these writers: *Uncle Tom's Cabin*, "Freedom Wheeler's Controversy with Providence," "Miss Tempy's Watchers," and "Sister Liddy."[8]

Uncle Tom's Cabin has become a lightning rod in the canon wars. Until recently dismissed as a minor, if popular, work of propaganda, it has, under the influence of feminist and New Americanist criticism, finally begun to receive the serious critical attention it deserves. Some critics have at last recognized that far from being a stereotypically superficial work of "pop" culture, it is a theologically and aesthetically complex work of art; that it is, yes, a masterpiece. The guardians of the traditional canon, however, seem to have singled out Stowe's great work for especial attack. When Jane Smiley dared to suggest in a

1996 *Harper's* article that *Uncle Tom's Cabin* is a greater work than *Huckleberry Finn*, she was roundly excoriated. "Ernest Hemingway," she commented in the article, "thinking of himself, as always, once said that all American literature grew out of *Huck Finn*. It undoubtedly would have been better for American literature, and American culture, if our literature had grown out of one of the best-selling novels of all time, another American work of the nineteenth century, *Uncle Tom's Cabin*."[9]

For this judgment Smiley is reported to have received a mountain of "hate mail."[10] In a panel discussion of her article broadcast on C-SPAN, the historian Shelby Foote, in damning Smiley's position, offered this enlightened assessment of Stowe's novel: "I judge a book by its writing. *Huckleberry Finn* is a great novel. *Uncle Tom's Cabin* is a bad novel. I can't back it up. I just feel it. I never finished *Uncle Tom's Cabin*."[11]

Applying the traditional criteria for a masterpiece outlined above, I believe we can make a case based on more than feeling that *Uncle Tom's Cabin* merits the epithet "great." First, we can readily agree that it engages in weighty, universal themes. The central issue in the novel is, of course, slavery — that is, a particular nineteenth-century American institution; however, Stowe clearly sees slavery as a manifestation of a universal issue, the problem of evil. Thus, while the institution of slavery may be a local and historically delimited phenomenon, the problem of evil persists and Stowe's analysis of the issue, through the varied responses of her characters to it, remains relevant today. Indeed, one could argue that it is because of Stowe's unflinching examination of this issue that the novel bears a haunting contemporaneity for the modern reader. It still works to enlarge our moral understanding.

The "problem" of evil, simply stated, is the question of why human suffering exists, why humans inflict it upon one another, why God allows this to continue, and what can be done about it. Stowe's characters give various answers. George Harris, for example, a slave who escapes north, takes an essentially atheistic approach, saying that a benevolent God would not permit such atrocities as slavery to exist; Tom, the protagonist, takes a Christian approach, that suffering is redemptive and that evil will be atoned for; the slave woman Cassy takes a stand of political activism. She believes that violence is the only way by which evil can be vanquished. Mrs. Shelby, the white plantation mistress in Kentucky, and a number of Quakers who operate on the underground railway, advocate instead nonviolent resistance and personal acts to alleviate suffering on an individual level. St. Clare, the relatively benign plantation owner from the Deep South, counsels apathy — tending one's garden — saying there is nothing one can do to end suffering and oppression. In short, Stowe encompasses a range of responses to the problem of human suffering, and her development of these responses is consistent throughout, providing the great moral threads that bind the work thematically.

Second, even a superficial reading of the novel (which is all it has received until recently) reveals the richness and variety of Stowe's characterization. Indeed, as Smiley recognizes, this is one of her great strengths as a writer. Over a hundred characters are fully developed—from every class and from several regions, including men, women, and children, free and slave blacks, northern and southern whites. Similarly, the epic scope of the work, the range of its settings, and the prodigious detail of its realism provide the reader with an unrivaled sense of the texture of nineteenth-century American life.

Finally, Stowe's novel, which even today is still wrongly faulted for allegedly poor construction,[12] is in fact carefully constructed according to a clear and identifiable moral and aesthetic architecture. Stowe conceived *Uncle Tom's Cabin* as an argument against slavery; it is constructed according to a rhetorical pattern of moral antithesis.[13] It proceeds by means of a series of antithetical characters or sets of characters building dialectically to the climactic allegorical final scenes in which Tom, who has assumed the status of a Christ figure, contends with Simon Legree, the Antichrist. The powerful confrontation between the two, in which Tom endures physical death but gains a spiritual triumph ("the sharp thorns became rays of glory"),[14] brings Stowe's work to an effective moral and formal resolution.

The landscape against which the dialectical unfolding of the plot occurs is a moral geography. The map of America becomes a symbolic domain, ranged according to moral antipodes: to the north lies the good, to the south, evil. The two principal plots in the work—the passage of Uncle Tom south and the Harris family north—are not disconnected, as some commentators have charged but rather held in dialectical counterpoint.

The novel is in fact symmetrically organized. Approximately eleven chapters take place in relatively benign, comfortable domestic spaces in the border states or the North, approximately eleven chapters concern people in transit—in taverns, on boats, in slave auctions, and so on. Twelve chapters cover events at the St. Clare estate and nine at the Legree plantation.

Moreover, the moral geography is expressed in several subtextual symbolic codes: from north to south means from good to evil, but the novel's landscape also ranges from cool to hot, from order to disorder, from reason to the irrational, from sacred to profane, from active to passive, from agent to victim, from egalitarian to master-slave relationships, from planned economies (socialist kitchens) based on use-value production in which people are treated with dignity and the primary concern is with human welfare, to unbridled capitalism in which people are treated as commodities and the primary motive is profit; from a world of plenty to one of deprivation.

The principal characters follow these loci. Early in the novel, after he is sold, Tom leaves the benign, middle ground of Kentucky in early spring, where he has had a modicum of control over his life; it is cool; life is orderly. He moves south, where experience is increasingly hot, disordered, irrational, and evil. The nadir, the hell, of the novel is Legree's plantation, which is intensely hot, disorderly, irrational, and profoundly evil. An antithetical alternative further north is the Quaker kitchen in Ohio, which is cool, ordered, rational, and benignly egalitarian.

The fundamental ritual that underlies these dialectical transitions is the one that subtends most great literature — the vegetative passage of the year, from life to death and from death to life, expressed in a range of cultural forms from classical tragedy to the Christian resurrection myth. Thus, after the suffering and death of Tom follow the happy, resurrectory scenes of the Harrises in Canada on their way to a utopian future. In the conception of its moral geography, if not in its structure (Dante began his work with *Inferno*, but Stowe ends there), *Uncle Tom's Cabin* bears a resemblance to the *Divine Comedy*. Tom and Eva's beatific visions of the afterlife and Stowe's utopian dream of Africa suggest the *Paradiso*, whereas the middle areas of Kentucky and the St. Clare estate recall the *Purgatorio*.[15]

Thus, if traditional standards for what constitutes a masterpiece were invoked fairly, *Uncle Tom's Cabin* would certainly qualify. It was indeed saluted as such by numerous nineteenth-century authors who had themselves produced masterpieces, including George Sand, George Eliot, Heinrich Heine, Charles Dickens, Ivan Turgenev, and Victor Hugo. Leo Tolstoy called it "an example of the highest art."[16] In this country the *Atlantic Monthly* in 1879 called it the great American novel, an opinion echoed by William Dean Howells in 1898.[17] In the first half of the twentieth century, however, like most women's literature, its critical fortunes fell for a variety of reasons, suggesting the vagaries of literary evaluation.

Similarly, nineteenth-century critical opinion of Rose Terry Cooke's work was high. Mark Twain in an 1877 letter to Howells called "Freedom Wheeler's Controversy with Providence," which I discuss below, "a ten-strike. I wish," he added, "she would write 12 old-time New England tales a year."[18]

"Freedom Wheeler" is perhaps best understood in the context of the shifting winds of nineteenth-century theology, registering in its thematics the conflict between a rigidly authoritarian Calvinism and a more compassionate, "feminized" doctrine.[19] Like other great works, however, it transcends its time and can easily be appropriated to classical tragedy in its focus on the hybris of the title character, Freedom Wheeler.

The plot is that Freedom, a willful, determined young farmer, decides that he must have a son named Freedom. Providence, however, continually intervenes to thwart his desire, which he nevertheless pursues relentlessly, causing (indirectly) the death of his wife and (directly) the death of an infant son. After bearing him three daughters whom Freedom refuses to name because "gals ain't worth namin'," [20] his exhausted wife, Lowly, dies in childbirth. The infant, the second boy named Freedom, also dies (as had the first).

Freedom, pursuing his quest, soon marries another woman, Melinda Bassett, who is more assertive than the first, refusing to name their first child, a boy, Freedom, insisting that he be named after her grandfather. Freedom then comes down with typhus fever, but after he recovers, he resumes his determination to wrest from Providence a son named Freedom, which he is finally granted only to lose in infancy in an accidental fall. In the wake of this loss, and chastised by his wife's rebuke, Freedom finally relents, and, transfixed by the dying compassionate gaze of a favorite aunt, he weeps and achieves a kind of tragic wisdom. Appreciating Freedom's newfound humility, his wife willingly names their next son Freedom.

The author sees his transformation as the triumph of grace, which Freedom's willfulness had previously "like the thorns in the parable . . . choked the struggling blades of grain" (88). Cooke thus engages in the grace versus works theological debate — a critical issue in American literary culture. Cooke also addresses the problem of evil.

> Why do we pant and thirst and find the draught poisonous? or, after long exile, come home, only to find home gone? Alas! these are the conditions of humanity, the questions we all ask, the thwarting and despair we all endure, and also the mystery and incompleteness which tell us in hourly admonition that this life is a fragment and a beginning, and that its ends are not peace and rapture, but discipline and education. (86)

Thus Cooke's story deals with weighty themes, thereby satisfying the first criterion above. It also, like much local-color literature, presents a range of diverse characters. Freedom's aunts Huldah and Hannah are well-developed, amusing figures.

> The two old women had stuff petticoats and homespun short-gowns, clean mob-caps over their decent gray hair, and big blue-check aprons: hair-dye,

wigs, flowering chintz, and other fineries had not reached the lonely farms of Dorset in those says. "Spinsters" was not a mere name. The big wool wheel stood in one corner of the kitchen, and a little flax-wheel by the window. In summer both would be moved to the great garret, where it was cool and out of the way (59).

The sisters operate as choral figures, again as in Greek tragedy but using homespun humor, commenting on the events of the story. They provide the story's unifying theological thematics, presented humorously in their opening exchange. Noting Freedom's bad humor, one suggests he needs some "wormwood-tea"; the other protests that she is reducing original sin to "a bad stomick" (60). Another important minor character who adds to the work's richness is the half-Indian herbalist Moll Thunder, who tends Freedom when he is ill with "squawvine, pep'mint, cohosh, fever-wort" and is paid "with a piece of pork, a bag of meal, and a jug of cider-brandy" (79).

The story is unified by its themes, by the sisters' chorus, and by the plot, which, again, follows the death-resurrection pattern. As Freedom's selfish and willful ego dies, the grace of compassion and connection is born.

Sarah Orne Jewett's "Miss Tempy's Watchers" (1888) similarly deals with death and resurrection but more subtly. This brilliant story concerns two old schoolmates who are called upon to wake their friend Temperance Dent. The action takes place one evening in Temperance's home with her body present (it is upstairs and the two watchers are downstairs chatting, sewing, and knitting). Tempy had chosen the two women — Mrs. Crowe and Miss Binson — in a final act of charity, hoping "that they might become closer friends in this period of intimate partnership, and that the richer woman [Mrs. Crowe] might better understand the burdens of the poorer [Miss Binson]."[21]

Mrs. Crowe is "a stingy woman," and "socially she stood much higher than Sarah Ann Binson" (234), but she is unusually afraid of death, which Miss Binson comes to realize in the course of the evening. As the women reminisce about Tempy and talk of their own lives, they become more sympathetic to each other's situations. Tempy, known for her generosity and charity, begins to operate as an example. Mrs. Crowe acknowledges, "It ain't so easy for me to give as it is for some. . . . I ain't such a generous woman as poor Tempy . . . and I made up my mind this morning that Tempy's example should be my pattern henceforth" (235).

The story is not simplistically moralistic, however. Tempy is present in the story as a kind of spiritual power, not simply as a didactic example. The women recall "what excellent [quince] preserves" she made (241), noting how every spring she would tend her old quince tree, almost forcing it to bloom by the power of her energy: "She'd . . . look at it so pleasant, and kind of expect the old thorny thing into bloomin'" (241). Miss Binson adds, "She was just the same with folks. . . . She always sensed things, and got just the p'int you meant" (241).

Thus the story evokes the power of Tempy's spiritual presence, which continues to work even in death, "expecting" the watchers into moral and spiritual "bloomin'," just as she had the old quince tree. The story takes place in April, which highlights the resurrection theme.

In a few deft, masterful strokes Jewett produces a profound and complex comment on human relationship by presenting us with three memorable characters, unified in the universal pattern of death and rebirth. In my opinion, it stands as one of the great short stories of all time.

"Sister Liddy" (1891) by Mary E. Wilkins Freeman is another great but neglected story. Like many of Freeman's stories, it is informed by a modernist, even absurdist, sensibility, set in a New England almshouse (where the poor, the aged, and the insane were often relegated indiscriminately in the nineteenth century), which becomes in Freeman's handling a microcosm of the human situation.

In the evening the inmates of this asylum gather after dinner and tell stories about their more prosperous pasts. One woman, Polly Moss, an aged deformed woman whom one resident describes as "a dretful-lookin' cretur,"[22] never speaks during these sessions. "She alone had never had anything in which to take pride. She had been always deformed and poor and friendless. She had worked for scanty pay as long as she was able, and had then drifted and struck on the almshouse, where she had grown old" (173). She did not even know where she was from: "She went humbly where she was told" (174).

As they recount their own past glories, the other residents lord it over Polly, knowing that she will have nothing to compare: "Their conversation acquired a gusto from this listener who could not join in. When a new item of past property was given, there was always a side-glance in Polly's direction" (174).

One evening, however, Polly suddenly speaks up: "You'd orter have seen my sister Liddy," she announces (174).

> "My sister Liddy was jest as handsome as a pictur'," Polly returned.
> The pretty old woman flushed jealously. "Was she fair-complected?" she inquired.
> "She was jest as fair as a lily." (175)

Polly continues to elaborate on her sister; she lived in a beautiful house in Boston, had beautiful clothes, a wealthy, attentive husband, and servants. The others are skeptical and ask how they could have left her in an almshouse if they were so wealthy. She replies that they are all dead.

> Every day Polly Moss was questioned and cross-examined concerning her sister Liddy. She rose to the occasion; she did not often contradict herself, and the glories of her sister were increased daily. Old Polly Moss, her little withered face gleaming with reckless enthusiasm, sang the praises of her sister Liddy as wildly and faithfully as any minnesinger his angel mistress, and the old women listened with ever-increasing bewilderment and awe. (177)

On her deathbed Polly confesses that Liddy was a fabrication.

The pathos and irony in this story are poignant; Polly's fantasy evokes the universal theme of the vanity of human pride, recalling Lear's anguished cry on the heath, "O, reason not the need!" Polly's imaginative construction is in fact a form of art; she is in a sense a creative artist. Her story is an attempt to wrest transcending meaning from the paltry circumstances of her life. Freeman's story, thus, though deceptively simple on the surface, becomes a parable for the human need to tell stories, to justify our existence, to redeem our lives through the transfigurations of narrative, however vain such efforts may be. Moreover, Freeman's characterization of Polly as "gleaming with reckless enthusiasm" is great literature by any standard. Shelby Foote wants to judge a work by its writing; this is great writing.

A culture's identity is determined in part by its stories, its literary canon. Were the "course" of Western culture "deformed" (to reprise Henry's sophomoric phrase) by the admittance of works like these, produced by the New England local-color school in the American Women's Renaissance — a *women's period* in American literature — we might have the grounds for a new and more positive concept of that culture's identity. But because traditional criteria of excellence, such as those outlined above, have not been applied fairly, we have instead a cultural identity and a canon that have been narrowly defined according to the chauvinistic thematics of male culture. It is one that privileges (in the case of American literature) hybristic juvenile fantasies of escape and redemption through violence, notions that still pervade popular culture. Reconceiving American literature, and indeed Western culture, to include women's masterpieces might help to establish new bases for that culture's identity, away from one characterized by dominance, escapist violence, competition, and exploitation toward one governed by a sense of humility, humanity, and compassion, born of the realization that, as seen in the works discussed above, the deaths and resurrections of everyday life, the wresting of story from infirmity, are the stuff of great literature.

NOTES

1. Joan Kelly, "Did Women Have a Renaissance?" in Kelly, *Women, History, and Theory* (Chicago: University of Chicago Press, 1984), 19.
2. As cited in the *New York Times Book Review*, 16 October 1994, 30.
3. Ibid.
4. Lawrence Buell, *The Environmental Imagination: Thoreau, Nature Writing and the Formation of American Culture* (Cambridge, Mass.: Belknap Press of Harvard University Press, 1995), 177. Buell focuses mainly on the nonfiction nature writers who are associated with "regional realism" (Celia Thaxter and Susan Fenimore Cooper, for example). I hope to make the case for the women's local-color school constituting another American Renaissance more fully in a future article or book.
5. See Barbara Hernstein Smith, "Contingencies of Value" (1983), in *The Critical Tradition*, ed. David H. Richter (New York: St. Martins, 1989), 1321–44.
6. Nina Baym, "Melodramas of Beset Manhood: How Theories of American Fiction Exclude Women Writers," *American Quarterly* 33 (1981):123–39. See also Paul Lauter, *Canons and Contexts* (New York: Oxford University Press, 1991), 22–47, and Gerald Graff, *Professing Literature: An Institutional History* (Chicago: University of Chicago Press, 1992), 209–25.
7. An earlier version of this discussion appears in my *Uncle Tom's Cabin: Evil, Affliction, and Redemptive Love* (Boston: Twayne, 1991), 11–14.
8. For a more detailed discussion of these and other works by these writers, see my *New England Local Color Literature: A Women's Tradition* (1983; New York: Continuum, 1988), *Sarah Orne Jewett* (New York: Ungar, 1980), and "Breaking the Sentence: Local-Color Literature and Subjugated Knowledges" in *The (Other) American Traditions*, ed. Joyce Warren (New Brunswick: Rutgers University Press, 1993), 226–43.
  Uncle Tom's Cabin is not, strictly speaking, a work of local color, but it is a central work in the women's realist movement I am labeling the American Women's Renaissance.
9. Jane Smiley, "Say It Ain't So, Huck: Second Thoughts on Mark Twain's 'Masterpiece,'" *Harper's Magazine*, January 1996, 64.
10. Brent Staples, moderator, "About Books," panel discussion on the Smiley article, C-SPAN, 10 June 1996 (rebroadcast).
11. Shelby Foote, panelist, "About Books," panel discussion on the Smiley article, C-SPAN, 10 June 1996 (rebroadcast).
12. For a recent misperception, see Alfred Kazin, "Her Holiness," *New York Review of Books*, 1 December 1994, 39, who calls it "diffuse in its organization."
13. Stowe was highly trained in rhetoric and indeed taught it for several years.
14. Harriet Beecher Stowe, *Uncle Tom's Cabin: Or Life Among the Lowly* (New York: Penguin, 1981), 554.
15. For a fuller development of these ideas see my *Uncle Tom's Cabin*, 13, 31–33, where an earlier version of the above analysis appears.
16. Leo Tolstoy, *What Is Art?*, trans. Almyer Maude (Indianapolis: Bobbs-Merrill, 1960), 152.

17. Thomas F. Gossett, *"Uncle Tom's Cabin" and American Culture* (Dallas: Southern Methodist University Press, 1985), 340–41.

18. *Mark Twain-Howells Letters: The Correspondence of Samuel L. Clemens and William D. Howells, 1872–1910*, ed. Henry Nash Smith and William M. Gibson, 2 vols. (Cambridge, Mass.: Belknap Press of Harvard University Press, 1960), 1:187.

19. On this issue, see Barbara Welter, "The Feminization of American Religion, 1800–1860," in *Clio's Consciousness Raised*, ed. Mary Hartman and Lois W. Banner (New York: Harper, 1974), 137–54.

20. Rose Terry Cooke, "Freedom Wheeler's Controversy with Providence," in Cooke, *"How Celia Changed Her Mind" and Selected Stories*, ed. Elizabeth Ammons (New Brunswick: Rutgers University Press, 1986), 68. Further references follow in the text.

21. Sarah Orne Jewett, "Miss Tempy's Watchers," in *The Country of the Pointed Firs and Other Stories* (Garden City, N.Y.: Anchor, 1956), 234. Further references follow in the text.

22. Mary E. Wilkins [Freeman], "Sister Liddy," in *Selected Stories of Mary E. Wilkins Freeman*, ed. Marjorie Pryse (New York: Norton, 1983), 165. Further references follow in the text.

FRANCES HARPER, CHARLOTTE FORTEN, AND AFRICAN AMERICAN LITERARY RECONSTRUCTION

Carla L. Peterson

As literary critics, we have found the task of reconstructing Reconstruction daunting. We are still hard-pressed to account for the literary moment that lies between the American Renaissance on the one hand and American realism on the other. In his 1993 book *Cultures of Letters: Scenes of Reading and Writing in Nineteenth-Century America*, Richard Brodhead has suggested one approach to analyzing the literature of this postwar period. According to Brodhead, postbellum culture reorganized the literary field by encouraging "new sorts of internal differentiation within the American literary system"; these distinctions reworked existing configurations of "high" and "low" cultures located on either side of the prewar "domestic or middlebrow world of letters." For many antebellum authors writing was often conceived as a "tutelary activity" that centered on the domestic household and promoted a middle-class ethos of "disciplinary intimacy" through which those in authority relied on love and moral influence rather than corporal punishment to regulate the American home. In contrast, the postbellum world of letters came to promote high-cultural literary values embodied primarily in the new "quality" monthlies—the *Atlantic Monthly, Harper's New Monthly Magazine, Scribner's Monthly Magazine,* and *Century Illustrated Monthly Magazine*—that flourished from the 1850s on. These magazines encouraged the development and institutionalization of new aesthetic interests: a "cosmopolitan and classical production" derived from Europe and a home-grown "vacation art," both of which were addressed to a newly emergent leisured elite.

In elaborating his cultural history, Brodhead examines the postbellum fiction of white women writers such as Louisa May Alcott and Sarah Orne Jewett. African American writing enters this history only belatedly in the form of Charles Chesnutt's magazine stories of the late 1880s. According to Brodhead's chronology of black authorship, Chesnutt was the "first" African American writer whose aim was "to have a literary career" and who "conceived of writing as a largely autonomous zone of verbal creation."[1] Such an interpretation profoundly misreads African American postbellum cultures of letters whose writers refused to disassociate literary career from political participation; they insisted instead that verbal creation could never be an autonomous cultural zone and that one of its current functions was to intervene in and comment on the politics of national Reconstruction.

Countering Brodhead's version of American literary history, I propose to analyze the literary careers of two African American women writers, Frances Harper and Charlotte Forten, from 1864 to 1878. Their Reconstruction writings point to interests that are intensely political; they indicate the degree to which both women were vitally concerned with questions of nationhood and turned to writing—in particular periodical publication—to ponder how African American men and women could work together to achieve full citizenship in the newly reconstructed nation.

Indeed, the politics of Reconstruction were a vital concern to African Americans of this period. As Eric Foner has noted, Reconstruction represented a national effort to fulfill the ideals of democracy by granting citizenship to black Americans and protecting their right to reap its benefits. These efforts were implemented even before the war's end with the Emancipation Proclamation, passage of the Thirteenth Amendment, and establishment of the Freedmen's Bureau. They were continued under Radical Reconstruction (1866–72) with the enlargement of the Freedmen's Bureau, passage of the Fourteenth and Fifteenth Amendments, and deployment of federal troops in the South to protect blacks.

But Foner also emphasizes the degree to which Reconstruction was a complex process involving both the active participation of African Americans and the hostile opposition of southerners. Radical Reconstruction enabled the achievement of significant black political power as well as grassroots activism. These efforts toward racial equality were strongly resisted under Presidential Reconstruction (1865), however, as Andrew Johnson ceded authority back to the southern states, instituted Black Codes, opposed the work of the Freedmen's Bureau, and refused to protect black civil rights. After 1873, resistance became even more pronounced as a result of several converging factors: the continued mourning of the lost cause by southerners; a rising tide of conservative opinion among northerners willing to accede to southern sensibilities; and dominance of a national economic agenda culminating in an alliance between northern and southern capital. The demise of Reconstruction was inevitable by 1874 with the ascendancy of a Democratic Party determined to dismantle black civil rights, the rise of white mob violence in the South, and finally the withdrawal of federal troops from the region in 1877.[2]

Both Harper and Forten engaged these issues directly in their Reconstruction periodical publications; yet their writing suffered strikingly different fates. As early as 1893, African American essayist Lawson Scruggs praised Harper as "a great and profound writer in both prose and poetry, a lecturer of no ordinary tact and ability, a master-hand at whatever she applies herself. . . . Her pen is ever at work; her writings are many and varied." In contrast his evaluation of Forten (Grimké) is more muted: "Her life in the District has not been an eventful one, much of her time being spent in church work, and therefore she has not done as much literary work as she had hoped to do. She sometimes tries to find some consolation in the thought that possibly this is why her long-cherished dreams of becoming an authoress have never been fully realized."[3]

To account for such differences we need to look beyond personal circumstances, which provide only partial clues. A well-established social activist widowed in 1864 after a brief marriage, Harper was free to continue her prewar lecturing and writing. In contrast, as a single young African American woman until her marriage to Francis Grimké in 1878, Forten undoubtedly needed a more remunerative career; thereafter, as Scruggs notes, marital and social obligations as well as ill health prevented her from doing much writing. Fully to understand the differences between Harper's and Forten's Reconstruction literary careers, however, we need to look for clues of a broader nature in the different strategies of patronage, production, and cultivation of readership pursued by each woman in the years following the Civil War. In so doing, Harper and Forten serve as vehicles through which to consider the politics of African American writing and publication during Reconstruction and its relationship to the newly emerging American nation. Such considerations will result, I believe, in the construction of an American literary history different from the one commonly told.

Harper's and Forten's Reconstruction publication choices nicely illustrate the critical role of the newspaper or periodical as a vehicle through which members of a nation, or a subordinated group within it, come, in the words of Benedict Anderson, to "imagine community": the newspaper unites readers who otherwise might have no contact with one another by encouraging conversation among them over the various meanings of nationhood.[4] Each woman, however, pursued different paths to achieve her goals. Harper chose to write within and for the black community, taking advantage of its publishing instruments, in particular the African Methodist Episcopal (AME) Church's *Christian Recorder*. Her work configures the middlebrow model of domestic-tutelary writing, which informed an important body of nineteenth-century African American fiction from William Wells Brown to Chesnutt, and rethinks the distinction between high and low cultures. As she addressed a black readership, Harper articulated a vision that insisted on the familiarity of the African American household in American society and made it foundational to the process of national reconstruction. In striking contrast, encouraged by the patronage of white men of letters, Forten sought recognition by the new monthlies that functioned as the gatekeepers of the nation's high-cultural domain. Working to situate herself within the nation's community of primarily white writers and readers, Forten aspired to become an active participant in the reconstruction of America's national culture. In the process, however, she was to discover the degree to which such participation depended on the representation of blacks as foreign.

Historians of journalism have noted the rapid proliferation of African American newspapers after the Civil War. The *Christian Recorder*, however, had its roots in the antebellum period; begun as the *Christian Herald* in Philadelphia in 1848 under the auspices of the General Conference of the AME Church, it changed its name in 1852. It appears to have fared well in its first months but suffered a reversal of fortune in the years 1854–56.[5] Indeed, the paper's history from 1854 on points to its lengthy struggle in helping African Americans imagine community, inviting them both to craft a group identity based on a shared past and to work toward the achievement of full national citizenship. In 1854, an AME Church bishop voiced his concern: "We live too much estranged from one another, and will ever be so until we will support a weekly paper that can connect every portion of the Church by weekly intelligence"; and in 1856 another complained that "the chief cause [of the paper's failure] lay in the people.... Twelve months after the issue of the first number of the *Christian Recorder* there were not more than one hundred subscribers in the city of Philadelphia." The Church's goals were achieved only when Benjamin Tanner, one of its most illustrious bishops, became the paper's editor in 1868. Journalism historian I. Garland Penn's comment in 1891 about "the wide reputation of [Tanner's] journal, outside of his own denomination" suggests that the *Recorder* finally was able to serve as a vehicle through which African Americans nationwide could imagine community.[6]

Harper's writings appeared regularly in the pages of the *Christian Recorder* throughout the postbellum period. Born a free black in Baltimore in 1825, by the 1850s Harper was already a well-established antislavery lecturer, activist in the causes of racial uplift, temperance, and women's rights, and author of at least two volumes of poems in which she gave literary expression to her social concerns. Several of her public lectures and poems were published in the *Liberator, Frederick Douglass' Paper,* and the *Christian Recorder;* after the war Harper's contributions to the *Recorder* became even more extensive: many poems, a series of short sketches, and three serialized novels, *Minnie's Sacrifice, Sowing and Reaping,* and, in the post-Reconstruction era, *Trial and Triumph.*

Harper's fictional narratives conform in many respects to antebellum middlebrow notions of writing as a tutelary activity concerned with the welfare of the domestic household. But Harper adapted this model to an African American perspective. Although she remained committed to the values of discipline, her model was no longer that in which authority figures (often female) exercise discipline—whether through coercion or through love—over their charges. Instead, these latter must learn to discipline themselves. Moreover, the practice of self-government applies not only to individuals but to communities and the nation as well: "feminine" domestic values now extend into the wider political domain. This disciplinary ideology reinforced African American antebellum concepts of self-control as a strategy of resistance and survival for both slave and free black populations. Given her ethical beliefs, Harper could only view the postbellum expansion of a high-cultural aesthetic as suspect, responsible for encouraging self-indulgence and moral laxity both in the home and in society at large.

In her writing practice, however, Harper challenged the distinctions of high, middle, and low cultures by appropriating the "high-cultural" form of poetry for democratic purposes. Her efforts are fully evident in her sketches, at least seven of which were published in the *Recorder* between October 1871 and January 1874. Most of the sketches are simply titled "Fancy Etchings," and they focus on the same set of characters—Aunt Jane, her nieces Jenny and Anna, and her brother Uncle Glumby. Reflecting the interests of her creator, Jenny voices her aspirations to become a great writer: "I think poetry is one of the great agents of culture, civilization and refinement. . . . I would teach men and women to love noble deeds by setting them to the music, of fitly spoken words." Such a definition might well appear an endorsement of an elitist aesthetic; this is certainly the view of the "sober and prosaic" Uncle Glumby, for whom poetry is "all moonshine."[7] But for Harper the true function of this "high-cultural form" was to promote the disciplinary ethos outlined above to a broad audience for the purpose of community building.

Indeed, the point of departure of Harper's fictional narratives is the domestic household; by insisting on its very familiarity, Harper sought to construct a vision of home that would transcend race and class distinctions to situate itself within the larger national culture. To convey her vision, Harper relied on the narrative strategy of conversation, which, according to Jenny, "ought to be made one of the finest and most excellent of all arts." Conversation is in fact a particularly important communicative tool for the sketches' women characters. It enables Jenny, Aunt Jane, and others to debate, and propose solutions to, the major problems facing African American communities; it further enables them to build links across generations and bring forgotten historical knowledge to light. This potential of dialogue is replicated in the *Recorder*'s own efforts to foster the imagining of community among its readers. Its success may be measured in the comments of one reader: "The *Recorder* [is] truly the colored people's organ in the United States, and the best family paper (colored) now published. . . . Fathers and mothers that cannot read, when the day's work is done, press the school children or some friend into service and the *Recorder* is read in the family circle. The sayings of the different writers are commented on, the news is discussed, and pleasant, instructive evenings are spent. It is thus giving food for thought during the day. The question is quite common now when a friend meets another to ask, 'What does the *Recorder* say this week?'"[8]

Even before writing her sketches, Harper had turned to serial fiction as a way of promoting conversation within the black community; the *Christian Recorder* published *Minnie's Sacrifice*, a novel of slavery and Reconstruction, in its March 20 through September 25, 1869, issues; and it would later print a temperance story, *Sowing and Reaping*, which ran from August 10, 1876, to February 8, 1877. It is not clear whether Harper actually composed these novels as serial fiction or whether it was the *Recorder* that determined the installment procedure. In either case, serialization functioned as a future-oriented process that affirmed both the author's and the editor's commitment to the gradual development over time not only of the story but of the newspaper and the social group that supported it.

Nineteenth-century serial composition actively affected both writers and readers. Authors were often influenced by ongoing events, leading them to reshape their narratives and incorporate recent factual occurrences into their fiction. In turn, serial publication encouraged reader participation. As the reader of the *Recorder* quoted above suggested, newspapers could be passed from neighbor to neighbor for perusal or even read aloud in groups. As they read "in parts," readers had time to reread the story at their leisure, to interpret and reinterpret it; installment endings left them thinking as they waited for the next issue. Furthermore, readers never read the serial fiction in isolation from other "texts"—items in the same newspaper issue, other novels, or even the readers' own lives and the world they lived in—but in close conjunction with them. Such an interplay meant that readers often immediately brought extraneous material to their reading of serial fiction, or conversely, took the fiction into their own lives; at the extreme, fact and fiction merged in their imaginations.[9]

As members of the African American community perused the pages of the *Recorder*, then, they found not only articles on current issues but also installments of Harper's serial novels in which she fictionalized many public events. In reading each episode, readers could relate its contents to the more factual articles printed nearby as well as to their own lived experiences and then discuss their reactions with others in the community. Moving well beyond traditional female preoccupations, Harper's fictions concern themselves directly with the state of the nation.

Minnie's Sacrifice dominates the issues of the *Recorder* in which it appeared. A fictionalization of the history of African Americans from antebellum slavery through 1867, the novel reflected the chief concerns of the paper and nicely complemented the many contributions that focused on the social and political work of Reconstruction that had been, or was yet to be, accomplished. One regular column titled "Information Wanted" sought the whereabouts of relatives dispersed under slavery. Other articles addressed the importance of "home building" and the quest for education within the African American community. Turning to national issues, still other contributions excitedly but anxiously debated the passage of the Fifteenth Amendment.

In contrast to *Minnie's Sacrifice*, *Sowing and Reaping* appears to be a purely domestic story in which neither time, place, nor race is specified. But this apparent narrowness belies a broader agenda: temperance is a national problem because the nation as a whole has become intemperate. In the words of Harper's fictional spokeswoman, Mrs. Gladstone: "I hold . . . that a nation as well as an individual should have a conscience."[10] And if the novel's characters are not racialized it is because temperance transcends racial categorization. Hence the characters are to be imagined not as either white or black but as both/and.

The rapid expansion of the temperance movement during Reconstruction was a response to the increase in the number of liquor dealers and of alcohol consumption after the Civil War. Contemporary commentators variously ascribed this social phenomenon to the bad habits of war veterans, the pressures of urbanization and industrialization, the economic panic of 1873, the influx of European immigrants whose cultures tolerated greater production and consumption of alcohol, and changing attitudes that had turned drinking into a violation of a moral code. Whatever the causes, the consequences were clear: intemperance was undermining the strength of the nation and encouraging social disorder; in fact, according to Mother Stewart, a women's temperance Crusade leader, it was a "curse, more fearful than southern slavery." At the historical juncture that was witness to both the celebration of the nation's centennial and the demise of Reconstruction, reformers were convinced that the United States could be saved only by its rebirth as a temperate nation. This vision was shared in particular by women, both black and white. With some confined to the home, many others financially dependent and physically vulnerable, and all politically disenfranchised, women remained the primary victims of intemperate fathers and husbands. Hence, from the 1870s on they were at the forefront of the temperance movement, marching in Crusades, organizing, and disseminating information through the press. This activity culminated in the formation of the Women's Christian Temperance Union (WCTU) in 1873.[11]

Harper's commitment to the temperance movement dates to the antebellum period and continued unabated during Reconstruction, evidenced by her affiliation with the WCTU. The editors of the *Recorder* evinced a similar interest in temperance, particularly during the early 1870s, when the women's Crusade was especially active. Surprisingly, however, little temperance writing appears in the later issues in which *Sowing and Reaping* was published; rather, these are filled with articles that chronicle the end of Reconstruction and most especially the violence that accompanied it. Particular attention is devoted to those acts of violence against blacks in which public officials either actively collaborated or passively refused to intervene: the murder of Professor Gilliard in Texas, the Hamburg Massacre in South Carolina, and the "Bargain of 1877" that resulted in the newly elected president Rutherford B. Hayes's surrender of federal authority to southern state interests.[12] Yet these articles are thematically linked to Harper's temperance concerns because they suggest a nation become intemperate, a nation whose intemperance has brought about the social evils that beset it. Temperance, then, is the tool that will reform the nation.

For Harper, novel writing became *the* tutelary activity through which to press for national reformation. In *Minnie's Sacrifice* and *Sowing and Reaping*, she offered readers a program that promoted the self-disciplining of both individuals and a society rendered intemperate not only by drink but also by the elite's accumulation of wealth and consumption of a cosmopolitan high culture that was finding its way into the new monthlies. This program emphasizes not only women's roles in the work of Reconstruction but the collaborative efforts that must be undertaken by both black men and women.

The early chapters of *Minnie's Sacrifice* take place in the antebellum period and are organized around a sectional contrast of South and North that has significant moral implications. The protagonists, Louis and Minnie, are born into southern families as the products of the rape of slave women by their masters;

although the readers know the secret of their birth, they do not. In Harper's literary imagination, southern slaveholding culture has its origins in the foreign Creole culture of prerevolutionary Haiti and is characterized by ostentatious displays of wealth and moral self-indulgence. It thus stands in negative contrast both to the many accounts of the independent black Republic of Haiti published in the *Recorder* and to Harper's vision of the North as a site of industrious free labor. Given Louis's dual racial heritage, these early chapters hint at the possibility of future sectional and racial reconciliation under his leadership. He is in fact presented to us as a Moses figure in a typological narrative that underscores the theme of heroic male leadership.

Harper's vision of the "free" North centers on her portrayal of the Quaker abolitionists who adopt Minnie; in contrast to southern slaves and slaveholders, they embody free, self-disciplined labor. And yet several ironies are at work here. Unlike in the South, black voices are not heard; rather, it is the white antislavery community that speaks for African Americans, arguing for their freedom and equality but also denying them the possibility of tracing their "origin back to any of the older civilizations." Nor can Minnie or Louis speak for blacks because they remain ignorant of their ancestry and believe themselves to be members of the white elite. This silencing of black voices in the novel contrasts sharply with the lively debates on "skilled labor" and "home influences" that were being carried out on the same pages of the *Recorder*.[13]

The national crisis of the Civil War brings about a personal crisis for both Minnie and Louis as each is informed of the secret of his and her birth. But whereas the nation is torn apart by sectional conflict, the self-divided protagonists are quickly reconciled to their racial heritage; they meet again and unite in marriage. The last five chapters address the possibility of postwar national union. African American voices now proliferate as male *and* female, elite *and* folk characters come together to discuss and participate in the work of Reconstruction. Foremost is the issue of racial identity and passing: if Minnie lists scorn for concealment, loss of self-respect, and love of mother as reasons for her refusal to pass, even more important is the need to disprove that racial characteristics are innate and to affirm the potential for black achievement. For Minnie and Louis, now the Moses of his people but not of the nation, this process involves providing education, encouraging land ownership and the building of homes, and gaining the vote. But leadership is not the exclusive right of the elite characters, for in return the folk teach Minnie and Louis the important lessons of faith and endurance. Their collaborative efforts continue until Minnie's death at the hands of a white mob. The novel's ending thus emphasizes the shared cultural values — including those of self and community discipline —

around which both elite and folk characters unite to carry out the work of reconstruction.

Discipline is at the center of *Sowing and Reaping*, which perceives intemperance as a breakdown of discipline that pervades the nation. The narrative deconstructs two important dichotomies set up in the opening chapters to illuminate how intemperance has contaminated all spheres of life. Intemperance exists in the elite's drawing room as well as the lower-class saloon; through this observation Harper continued her critique of a self-indulgent high culture no longer confined to southern aristocracy but infecting a national population driven by the acquisition and display of wealth. Even more significantly for women, intemperance exists in the domestic as well as the public sphere as the intemperate husband or father brings excessive drinking into the home in the form of physical abuse, emotional distress, and financial hardship; as a consequence, women are forced out into the public sphere to fight for their survival. The tutelary functions of the novel are given to the protagonists, Paul Clifford and Belle Gordon, who work collaboratively to reform a series of characters, the saloon keeper John Anderson, the young and wealthy Charles Romaine, the working-class Joe Gough. Through their stories, Harper suggests that even if intemperance may be viewed as an act of victimization on the part of the liquor industry, it is foremost an issue of individual moral responsibility.

The novel's most significant episodes center around Charles Romaine and his fiancée (and later wife), Jeanette Roland, as well as Mary and Joe Gough, who are introduced late in the story. The names of these last two characters suggest Harper's awareness of the national dimensions of the temperance movement as they recall Joe and Mary Morgan, the central characters of T. S. Arthur's famous *Ten Nights in a Bar-Room*, as well as John Gough, a well-known temperance lecturer whose 1869 *Autobiography and Personal Recollections* detailed his own intemperate youth, conversion, and marriage to his wife, Mary. In Harper's novel, the lesson that Joe Gough provides the reader lies in acceptance of moral responsibility for his intemperance following a conversion episode reminiscent of religious evangelical experience. Convinced by his wife and Belle to attend a meeting at the Reform Club, he listens to the temperance speaker, is persuaded, and signs the pledge. Joe has learned to discipline himself.

The fate of Charles Romaine stands in sharp contrast to that of Joe Gough. A victim of his elite culture's self-indulgence, Charles lacks the will to resist the temptations of social drinking offered him by Jeanette and his father. Portrayed as the victim of both an increased availability of liquor and a poor genetic makeup, Charles is nonethelesss censured for his moral weakness; his inability to discipline himself brings about his death. The physical and moral dangers of intemperance are reinforced finally by the misfortunes that befall John Anderson and his family. At the beginning of the novel the saloon keeper had voiced his support of separate-sphere ideology, maintaining that he could keep his profitable liquor business separate from the moral welfare of his home. Yet by the novel's end Anderson's family is in total disarray: his wealth has infected the household, contributing to the self-indulgent and undisciplined behavior of his wife and children. All these characters stand in stark contrast to the now married Belle and Paul, whose home represents the ideal of the familiar American household, characterized not by luxury but by its "moral and spiritual nature," not by lack of discipline but by firmness in "household government."[14]

The conclusions of both novels are all the more effective for the ways in which Harper introduced references to current events further to remind her readers that her fictions were indeed based on historical fact. At the end of *Minnie's Sacrifice*, for example, Louis moves beyond community issues to consideration of the Reconstruction Act of 1867 and his fear of President Johnson's betrayal. This act represented a triumph of black politics in the South in providing for both land acquisition and the franchise, but it was immediately followed by northern Republicans' abandonment of African Americans at the polls and the growth of white mob violence in the South. We do not know whether Harper wrote the concluding chapters while these events were occurring or at a time closer to publication, suggesting in the latter instance a parallel between the periods right before the impeachment of Johnson and the passage of the Fifteenth Amendment. But such parallels are readily established by the context of the *Recorder* itself: Louis's anxiety about Republican betrayal in 1867 may be read in relation to the paper's articles on the anticipated battle over the Fifteenth Amendment. Similarly, his recognition that under the Johnson administration blacks cannot count solely on federal government support is echoed in an article warning that the ballot alone cannot solve African Americans' social and economic problems.

The historical realities on which *Minnie's Sacrifice* is based affirm that blacks cannot wholly depend on the efforts of the nation but must rely on community discipline. In contrast, the ending of *Sowing and Reaping* embraces a national women's project recently adopted by the Women's Christian Temperance Union. Although Harper had long been a proponent of women's right to vote, the WCTU had remained silent on this issue until Frances Willard's endorsement of female suffrage as a weapon of "home protection" at its Philadelphia Convention in October 1876, most probably attended by Harper, as well as the Newark Convention held later that fall.[15] In the last installments of the novel published in early 1877, Harper doubled her argument on individual moral responsibility with advocacy of women's suffrage as a necessary disciplinary tool to combat intemperance; expanding on comments made by Minnie in the earlier novel, Mrs. Gladstone insists on women's need to possess not only "persuasive influence" but also the "enlightened and aggressive power" of the ballot.[16] For Harper, then, the self-indulgent values of the elite's high culture must be replaced by disciplinary ideologies at work within the American household, community, and nation at large.

Harper's literary career stands in striking contrast to that of Charlotte Forten. In a diary entry written in May 1856, when she was nineteen years old, Forten confided her ambition to become a great writer: "Oh! that I could become suddenly inspired and write as only great poets can write, or that I might write a beautiful poem of two hundred lines in my sleep as Coleridge did."[17] Born into Philadelphia's black elite, a graduate of the Salem public school system, and a member of an interracial circle of prominent abolitionists, Forten certainly possessed the necessary literary skills to accomplish her goals. Yet she did not; I have analyzed elsewhere the social and psychological factors that might have prevented her sustained publication.[18] Forten's antebellum writings consist then of a private journal, kept from 1854 to 1864, and a few published pieces—poems and travel sketches—that appeared primarily in the white abolitionist *Liberator* and *National Anti-Slavery Standard*; only one poem was printed in the *Christian Recorder*.

During and after the Civil War, Forten continued to seek a broad national readership beyond that of the black community. To do so, she turned to the patronage of two prominent men of letters: John Greenleaf Whittier, the abolitionist poet whom she had known since childhood and who had encouraged her to go to the South Carolina Sea Islands in 1862 to teach the newly emancipated slaves, and Thomas Wentworth Higginson, antislavery clergyman, soldier, and essayist, who had befriended her during her Sea Islands stay and become her literary mentor. It was through the intermediation of Whittier that the *Atlantic Monthly* published Forten's essay "Life on the Sea Islands" in its May and June 1864 issues. For his part, in 1869 Higginson arranged for Forten to translate Erckmann-Chatrian's *Madame Thérèse* for Scribner's. And it was undoubtedly one of these two men who was responsible for *Scribner's Monthly*'s publication of her essay "A Visit to the Birthplace of Whittier" in its September 1872 issue and her translation of an Erckmann-Chatrian short story a month later.

In contrast to Harper, then, Forten's literary practice represents a bold new departure for African American writers. Indeed, Forten appears to have been convinced of her membership in, and authority to address, the nation's postbellum elite: former white and black abolitionists, New England and Yankee humanists, but also the new cosmopolitan and leisured social class that was emerging in the postwar years. As she wrote, the community that Forten imagined was not only that of African Americans working for social and political reconstruction on both local and national levels but also a community transcending racial borders and devoted to the creation of a new American high culture.

Forten was undoubtedly heartened by the *Atlantic Monthly*'s acceptance of her "Sea Islands" article. Yet her successes thereafter were few and far between. When Whittier wrote *Atlantic Monthly* editor James Fields in 1865, asking whether he could offer Forten "employment in translating French stories," his request appears to have gone unanswered. And in 1885, Higginson proved unable to persuade the *North American Review* to publish her essay "One Phase of the Race Question."[19] From 1872 on, she appears to have published primarily, and sporadically, in two of Boston's abolitionist-inspired newspapers, the *Christian Register* and the *Commonwealth*. Forten had long been accustomed to interracial situations and relationships: she had participated in the activities of integrated antislavery societies in the antebellum period, mingled with white abolitionists and black freed people on the Sea Islands during the war, maintained friendships with Whittier, Higginson, and other white Bostonians in the 1860s and 1870s, and, most significantly, become engaged to a young white man during this same period.[20] Yet Forten was to find that the emerging postbellum literary system was rapidly reinstituting racial barriers that she ultimately could not transcend. How did this process occur? Beyond the intercession of Whittier and Higginson, what made Forten's early writings acceptable to the new monthlies? And why did they stop publishing her despite Whittier's and Higginson's continuing patronage?

In its early days, the ethos of the *Atlantic Monthly* under its first editor, James Russell Lowell, had been one of Yankee humanism that preached rationality, tolerance, and open intellectual inquiry; as the war approached, it became unreservedly antislavery and anti-South. This tradition of progressive politics was continued under its second editor, James Fields, who espoused Radical Republicanism and published essays by Frederick Douglass. But Fields also brought to the magazine a concern for the market that had not previously existed; still further changes could be detected when William Dean Howells became Fields's assistant in 1866 and was charged with implementing "new developments" which were consolidated when he assumed the editorship in 1871.[21]

During this period, a shift was occurring in Boston from "the expansive, socially engaged, liberal idealism" of the 1850s that reflected the vision of thinkers like Harper to a high literary culture that appealed to the tastes of the new leisured elite while purporting to represent the nation's most essential values. As a result of this shift, Howells was obliged to publish works that would cater to this elite's highbrow pretensions. As Brodhead has noted, one of the social markers that distinguished this upper class from the lower orders was leisure, which manifested itself most particularly in the enjoyment of travel and the emergence of an "imagination of acquisition." One form of travel was the grand tour of Europe that enhanced the tourist's connoisseurship of European art; it produced a refined cosmopolitan literature best exemplified by the writings of Henry James. Another was the rustic-domestic vacation in which travelers could indulge in observing how rural folk lived. Their descriptions found literary expression in the genre of "vacation arts."[22] What characterizes these two genres is the degree to which they depend on an appreciation of the foreign in contrast to the domestic-tutelary model rooted in the familiarity of home to which Harper had turned.

Forten worked in both modes as she sought to adapt her writing to the conventions of this new high culture. Her "Sea Islands" essay falls in the tradition of vacation arts, a genre cultivated as well by postbellum white women writers such as Harriet Beecher Stowe, Rose Terry Cooke, and Sarah Orne Jewett. Most often written from the distanced perspective of the dominant culture and functioning as a form of literary tourism, these travel sketches transported readers to unfamiliar locations and entertained them with tales of quaint folk characters. Critics have pointed out the degree to which many of these pieces appear to emphasize the purely local; portraying the visited place in terms of geographical and temporal containment, they offered readers a nostalgic vision of a homogeneous prelapsarian people untouched by historical change. More recent scholarship has argued that this local-color writing was in fact vitally concerned with reimagining the nation and "solidifying national centrality"; and it did so in one of two ways. Either the local place is inhabited by the primitive exotic other; if so, it is depicted as isolated; social difference is contained and national purity assured. Or the local place is envisioned as the repository of a shared past and inheritance; it represents, then, the common origins of the nation itself. Yet critics have also noted that contrary tendencies are embedded within the genre which work against national centralization. Characters or people are often geographically mobile, and the local place is traversed by translocal connections. Hence its population is marked by heterogeneity, racial and ethnic difference, social hierarchy, and economic friction; the nation is not pure but inhabited by the foreign.[23]

Viewed in the context of this emerging local-color writing, Forten's "Sea Islands" article underscores her problematic position as a black writer imagining herself as part of America's postbellum high-cultural community. She could not apprehend the "foreign" in quite the same way that writers of the dominant culture could. Born into a well-to-do family but witness to its declining fortunes, upper-class but African American, protected by the interracial abolitionist community but the object of white racial hostility, Forten was constituted by elements sufficiently "foreign" to one another that she could not construe any social entity as either totally familiar or totally foreign. Forten's composition of the "Sea Islands" essay, based on entries taken from her diary, points to her consequent difficulties in self-representation. In the earlier Salem and Philadelphia entries these difficulties led to self-censorship; indeed, many passages read like a public document of abolitionist activity characterized by emotional self-repression rather than open expressions of racial hurt and anger. In contrast, the later Sea Islands entries betray a much greater degree of self-revelation which, however, is then again suppressed in the published *Atlantic* essay.[24]

At the close of the Civil War, the Sea Islands had become a geographical crossroads into which people from different social groups and provenances poured to cohabit with the newly emancipated slave population. In Forten's diary, this mingling of heterogeneous peoples is best exemplified by the store kept by Mr. Hunn, a northern Quaker, to which the former slaves came to buy provisions and newcomers, like Forten herself, came to make their acquaintance: "I foresee that his store, to which people from all the neighboring plantations come, — will be a source of considerable interest and amusement" (395). Forten positions herself here as a tourist, yet her stance as insider/outsider to the observed culture is much more complex. Her initial perspective on the former slaves is indeed that of an outsider who perceives their customs as foreign. Forten tried at times to alleviate this sense of strangeness by emphasizing the degree to which the freed people exhibited traits familiar to, and valued by, the dominant culture: duty, honesty, industriousness. Yet she was also deeply appreciative of the African-based folkways that had given them the strength to survive slavery. And as her stay lengthened, the foreign became increasingly familiar as Forten found herself drawn to the former slaves' ceremonies. For example, recording her observation of a shout one night she acknowledged her shy participation in it: "L.[izzie] and I, in a dark corner of the Praise House, amused ourselves with practicing a little" (482).

Many of Forten's diary entries reflect on the complex forms of cultural exchange that can occur when heterogeneous peoples mingle with one another. She herself maintained an ambivalent stance toward the freed people's culture in which affective involvement alternated with amused distance. Yet she worried about their ultimate assimilation into the dominant culture, noting, for example, "We c'ld . . . hear them singing hymns;—not their own beautiful hymns, I am sorry to say. I do so fear these will be superseded by ours, which are poor in comparison" (477). Interestingly enough, in this observation Forten's use of pronouns indicates that the third person refers to the black freed people and the first to northern white Christians; she aligns herself here with the dominant culture. Yet if Forten was not a freed slave, neither was she a white abolitionist. In fact, for the entire period that she spent on St. Helena, she remained a self-divided figure ambiguously poised between these two social groups. Her sense of her own profound cultural difference is poignantly suggested in a November 1862 diary entry: "The effect of the [former slaves'] singing has been to make me feel a little sad and lonely to-night. A yearning for congenial companionship *will* sometimes come over me. . . . Kindness, most invariable,—for which I am most grateful—I meet with constantly, but congeniality I find not at all in this house [of whites]" (403).

Significantly, such discussions of cultural in-betweeness and self-division are entirely absent from Forten's published writings: two letters to William Lloyd Garrison, printed in the December 12 and 19, 1862, issues of the *Liberator*, and the later *Atlantic* article. In a letter to Fields, Whittier had promised to "omit a portion of it [the 'Sea Islands' essay] and reduce it to Magazine proportions."[25] We have no way of knowing to what extent he might have reshaped it nor whether the changes were designed to accommodate the sensibilities of the *Atlantic*'s readership. Yet the fact remains that the published version works within the most conservative parameters of local-color writing: it presents itself as a piece of literary tourism in which the visitor perceives the visited place as geographically confined and its inhabitants as a picturesque primitive people; racial boundaries are firmly reestablished and social differences contained.

Forten's 1862 *Liberator* letters still evince an ambivalence evident, for example, in her efforts to mediate between the strangeness of the freed people's folkways and the familiarity of their values. Her "Sea Islands" essay, however, is marked by a repression of intimate personal experience and her retreat into the stance of an outsider who, unlike Harper, observes the former slaves' culture from a distanced perspective. Forten began her article by narrating the scene of arrival in which she gazes freely upon her subjects: "A motley assemblage had collected on the wharf,—officers, soldiers, and 'contrabands' of every size and hue: black was, however, the prevailing color."[26] Most of the rest of Part I is organized according to a temporal chronology based on the activities of the observer rather than the people observed. This chronological structure then gives way to description, which is continued throughout Part II. Most of these descriptions are based on accounts of public events that Forten culled from her diary: the reading of the Emancipation Proclamation on Thanksgiving Day, attended by General Saxton; Emancipation Day itself; encounters with the rebels; the death of Colonel Shaw. The little new material that is included consists of portraits of the former slave population in which Forten attempts to individuate specific people; yet even here, these individuals remain picturesque stock figures representing black folk naïveté, religiosity, and wit.

Suppressed in this article, then, is the narration of Forten's intimate experiences with slave culture whereby the *I* comes familiarly to inhabit the foreign, insider/outsider distinctions are questioned, and racial boundaries troubled. In its stead the reader is presented with an indeterminate and pluralized "we"—agents of civilization from the North—who observe "the people" now deemed to be in need of assimilation into the dominant culture. To the extent that the *I* is employed, it is most often not an experiencing *I* but a narrating *I*, the writing subject engaged in observing and analyzing what she has seen. On the few occasions when Forten represents herself in the text, she does so as a detached ahistorical *I*. She portrays herself, for example, as constructing a history for the freed people from a safe pedagogical distance: "I told them about Toussaint, thinking it well they should know what one of their own color had done for his race" (591). Or she inserts herself through generalized commentary as when she adopts an ethnocentric Christian perspective to interpret the shout as the "barbarous expression of religion, handed down to them from their African ancestors, and destined to pass away under the influence of Christian teachings" (594). Forten admits identification with the freed people only in the concluding paragraph by speaking through the voice of another, that of the biblical woman of Shunem in 2 Kings: "While writing these pages I am once more nearing Port Royal. . . . I shall dwell again among 'mine own people'" (676). In this published account, the freed people remain culturally contained and, in striking contrast to Harper, Forten leaves unaddressed the question of their agency in the reconstruction of the nation.

As Reconstruction progressed and Forten matured, I believe she could no longer tolerate the constraints demanded by local-color writing and hence found it difficult to publish in the new monthlies. A personal conflict between Howells and Higginson resulted in the latter's abandonment of the *Atlantic* in favor of *Scribner's* and other New York magazines. But even the appearance in 1870 of *Scribner's*, which quickly became the *Atlantic's* chief competitor, did little to facilitate Forten's further publication. *Scribner's* proved in fact to be less than welcoming to black writers in its linkage of the newly emerging postbellum national culture with the South. Indeed, the 1870s were characterized by the reimagining of national community based on sectional reconciliation—a "romance of reunion," to use Nina Silber's phrase, in which the new monthlies played a vital role and from which not even Whittier and Higginson were immune.[27]

Virginia-born Thomas Nelson Page succinctly summed up the monthlies' participation in this romance of reunion when he noted that "the great monthly magazines were not only open as never before to Southern contributors, but welcomed them as a new and valuable acquisition."[28] In *Scribner's*, this trend was inaugurated in 1873 with a series of articles, "The Great South," by Edward King, which were then followed by the local-color, plantation, and dialect stories of George Washington Cable, Joel Chandler Harris, and Page. Promoting tourism in the South to the new leisured elite, King emphasized the charm and hospitality of its white inhabitants while celebrating the beauty of the physical landscape in which blacks were featured as primitive figures performing quaint folk rituals. If King portrayed the southern black population as picturesque, other writers such as George Cary Eggleston, a contributor to the *Atlantic* from South Carolina and a self-proclaimed rebel, insisted on their savagery and incapacity for civilization.

In the words of an editor, one of *Scribner's* chief missions was "to enlighten our country concerning itself, and to spread before the nation the wonderful natural resources, the social condition, and the political complications of a region which needs but just, wise, and generous legislation, with responding goodwill and industry, to make it a garden of happiness and prosperity."[29] In this comment, knowledge of nation is linked to knowledge of a particular region, the South, envisioned as *the* local place that will solidify national centrality. By now, however, Forten was well aware that she could not participate in this romance of reunion. So it is not surprising that she should have turned away from the vacation arts that promoted it. Eight years after her "Sea Islands" essay, Forten could no longer position herself as a detached writing subject reporting on a "primitive" people whose lack of subjectivity the nation assumed; nor was she willing to place herself within her text as a performer of this "foreign" culture.

As noted earlier, Forten published a short essay, "A Visit to the Birthplace of Whittier," in *Scribner's* in 1872. To my mind, this piece represents Forten's most successful negotiation of a middle ground betweeen her own artistic sensibilities and the new aesthetic tastes of the monthlies' readers; it fully expresses her ideal of American culture. Written in the tradition of the "country life" writings of British authors William Howitt and Mary Russell Mitford, the sketch differs sharply from the vacation arts. No longer positioned as an outsider witness to strange customs, Forten explores cultivated country life within a paradigm of liberal humanism familiar both to her and to her readers. In her sketch she travels to the places of Whittier's childhood — the town of Haverhill, the Seminary, Kenoza Lake, the old schoolhouse and homestead. The pleasures afforded by the visit depend entirely on her familiarity with Whittier's poetry and her ability to associate places seen with poems read; likewise, the impact of Forten's piece on her readers rests on her assumption of shared literary associations, indeed of a shared national culture.

Scribner's increasing sectional favoritism was undoubtedly enough to bar Forten from further publication, but her exclusion might also have been compounded by a letter she wrote that appeared in the June 27, 1874, issue of the *Christian Register*. Written in response to an article, "The Co-education of the White and Colored Races," published the month before in *Scribner's*, it represents a critical turning point in Forten's expression of racial consciousness. The article is a brief against interracial education in the South in which the writer insisted that, given the moral degradation of blacks, prejudice against them is natural, and decried the attempts of the Civil Rights Bill to legislate social change. In her response Forten countered that if moral degradation had occurred under slavery it had affected both white and black populations. Prejudice exists, she maintained, against "condition" rather than "color"; hence "co-education is the surest means by which prejudice can be rooted out."[30]

It is difficult to imagine that *Scribner's* would have printed any of Forten's future writings, and indeed from late 1872 on she seems to have published chiefly in two Boston-based papers, the *Christian Register* and the *Commonwealth*. The *Christian Register* was the main organ of Boston Unitarians; it was nondenominational, socially liberal, and reform minded, and it had been unequivocally antislavery before the war. Actively supported by Garrison and Wendell Phillips, the *Commonwealth* was even more radical in its racial politics.[31] It was also at this time that Forten started experimenting with new forms of writing designed to appeal to the elite readership's emerging taste for the high-cultural aesthetic that Harper's novels so forcefully condemned. Forten published several such pieces in the *Christian Register*, in particular a three-part account of the 1876 Centennial Exposition in Philadelphia that appeared in the July 22, 29, and August 5, 1876, issues. They reflect her persistent hope that, in sharing the highbrow values of the elite, she too could participate in the work of national reconstruction.

The Centennial Exposition was designed to celebrate the newly reconstructed American nation, in particular its material and industrial progress, to the international community. It also promoted the new cosmopolitan aesthetic with which the postbellum elite had become fascinated by providing a grand world tour that exposed visitors to the arts of Europe and Asia. Forten's articles record in great detail the vast display of luxury items from foreign lands that her readers had come to see as central to the formation of high culture. Thus on the one hand Forten appears here to participate in the highbrow culture of the elite; on the other hand she was well aware that she could never gain full acceptance into this dominant class, as her deteriorating relationship with the *Atlantic* and *Scribner's* made evident.

Indeed, despite her association with the new elite's high-cultural values, the mature Forten was now more than willing to express racial anger and demand racial justice. Thus in a letter to the editor recounting a return trip to Port Royal, published in the September 21, 1872, issue of the *Commonwealth*, Forten condemned the economic alliance of northern and southern elites and the impatience of "Northern settlers . . . who, coming down solely to make money, seem to expect perfection from a people so recently delivered from slavery and are disgusted with the whole race because they do not find it." Still another letter, "Mr. Savage's Sermon, 'The Problem of the Hour,'" published in the December 23, 1876, issue of the *Commonwealth*, elucidates even more forcefully Forten's wrath over continuing racial injustice. In the first part of the letter she angrily denounced Savage's justification of slavery, then proceeded to a critique of the present failure of Reconstruction: white southerners "had not, and have not, any desire to grant their rights to the colored people, but, on the contrary, a determination to reduce them to a condition as nearly like that of slavery as possible." Forten's Reconstruction writings are characterized, then, by a bifurcation of sensibility and subject matter that resulted, I believe, in her increasingly problematic relationship to literary publication.[32]

Postbellum American literary history is considerably more complex than Brodhead has suggested. For one, African Americans did engage in literary composition during the Reconstruction era. The careers of Charlotte Forten and Frances Harper attest to the complex issues of publication, patronage, and audience faced by black writers as they suddenly found themselves part of a new citizenry that determinedly sought a hearing from various sectors of the reading public. Writing primarily—and successfully—for the African American community, Harper reconfigured the antebellum middlebrow model of domestic-tutelary writing; in the process, she constructed an image of blacks that emphasized the familiarity of their domestic households as the basis for inclusion in

American society. In contrast, Forten aspired to participate in the high culture of the new emerging elite and write for the new national monthlies; but she found her efforts hampered by the requirement that she acquiesce to the dominant culture's representation of blacks as foreign.

In the post-Reconstruction era, African American writers—Forten Grimké and Harper included—still found it necessary to negotiate these same issues. Hence it is not enough to note, as does Brodhead, that this is the period when African Americans visibly enter the American literary scene, when Chesnutt publishes for Houghton Mifflin and W. E. B. Du Bois is accepted by the *Atlantic Monthly*. Indeed, Harper published several book volumes of poetry as well as an 1892 novel, *Iola Leroy*, that was reviewed by both the African American and mainstream presses but also continued to work for the *Christian Recorder*. And although Forten Grimké's work still appeared occasionally in such monthlies as the abolitionist-inspired *New England Magazine*, she came to follow Harper's lead and seek an African American readership, publishing in the *A.M.E. Church Review* and participating in the literary activities of the Bethel Historical and Literary Society. In order fully to comprehend postbellum American cultures of letters, then, we need to gain a better understanding of the publishing careers of Harper and Forten Grimké as well as of those of other African American writers whose works still lie buried in the archives waiting to be discovered.

NOTES

An earlier version of this essay was given as the American Antiquarian Society's Fifteenth Annual James Russell Wiggins Lecture in the History of the Book in American Culture. This essay is revised from the essay printed in the *Proceedings of the American Antiquarian Society* 107 (1998): 301–34.

I wish to thank the members of my Washington, D.C., writers' group, Thorell Tsomondo, Carolyn Karcher, Jeannie Pfaelzer, and Andrea Kerr, for their insightful comments and suggestions for the revision of this essay.

1. Richard Brodhead, *Cultures of Letters: Scenes of Reading and Writing in Nineteenth-Century America* (Chicago: University of Chicago Press, 1993), 77, 79, 17–21, 125; see also Lawrence Levine, *Highbrow/Lowbrow: The Emergence of Cultural Hierarchy in America* (Cambridge, Mass.: Harvard University Press, 1988), for a discussion of the configuration of high and low cultures from the antebellum period to the end of the nineteenth century.

2. Eric Foner, *Reconstruction: America's Unfinished Revolution, 1863–1877* (New York: Harper & Row, 1988).

3. Lawson A. Scruggs, *Women of Distinction: Remarkable in Works and Invincible in Character* (Raleigh: L. A. Scruggs, 1893), 13, 196.

4. Benedict Anderson, *Imagined Communities: Reflections on the Origin and Spread of Nationalism* (London: Verso, 1991), 30–36.

5. Daniel A. Payne, *History of the African Methodist Episcopal Church* (Nashville: A.M.E. Sunday School Union, 1891), 279–305.

6. Ibid., 306, 335; I. Garland Penn, *The Afro-American Press and Its Editors* (Springfield, Mass.: Wiley, 1891), 80.

7. "Fancy Etchings," *Christian Recorder*, April 24 and May 1, 1873.

8. "Fancy Etchings," *Christian Recorder*, February 20, 1873; letter, January 18, 1877.

9. For recent discussions of serial fiction, see Linda K. Hughes and Michael Lund, *The Victorian Serial* (Charlottesville: University Press of Virginia, 1991); Michael Lund, *America's Continuing Story: An Introduction to Serial Fiction, 1850–1900* (Detroit: Wayne State University Press, 1992); Carol A. Martin, *George Eliot's Serial Fiction* (Columbus: Ohio State University Press, 1994).

10. *Sowing and Reaping, Christian Recorder*, January 4, 1877.

11. Mother Stewart, *Memories of the Crusade* (Columbus: Wm. Hubbard, 1888), 27; Ruth Bordin, *Woman and Temperance: The Quest for Power and Liberty, 1873–1900* (Philadelphia: Temple University Press, 1981), 6–14; Annie Wittenmyer, *History of the Woman's Temperance Crusade* (Philadelphia: Office of the Christian Woman, 1878), 25–27; Jack S. Blocker, *"Give to the Wind Thy Fears": The Women's Temperance Crusade, 1873–1874* (Westport, Conn.: Greenwood Press, 1985).

12. *Christian Recorder*, August 10, October 12, 1876, January 25, 1877.

13. *Minnie's Sacrifice, Christian Recorder*, June 26, 1869; *Christian Recorder*, May 1, 1869.

14. *Sowing and Reaping, Christian Recorder*, February 8, 1877.

15. Frances E. Willard, *Glimpses of Fifty Years: The Autobiography of an American Woman* (Chicago: H. J. Smith, 1889), 351–53; Bordin, *Woman and Temperance*, 57–59.

16. *Sowing and Reaping, Christian Recorder*, January 4, 1877.

17. Charlotte Forten Grimké, *The Journals of Charlotte Forten Grimké*, ed. Brenda Stevenson (New York: Oxford University Press, 1988), 156. All further references to the diary are to this edition and page numbers are placed parenthetically in the text.

18. Carla L. Peterson, *"Doers of the Word": African-American Women Speakers and Writers in the North (1830–1880)* (New Brunswick: Rutgers University Press, 1995), 177–79.

19. Whittier to Fields, August 28, 1865, *The Letters of John Greenleaf Whittier*, ed. John B. Pickard, 3 vols. (Cambridge, Mass.: Belknap Press of Harvard University Press, 1975), 3:99; Grimké, *Journals*, 519, 607n.

20. Judith A. Roman, *Annie Adams Fields: The Spirit of Charles Street* (Bloomington: Indiana University Press, 1990), 69.

21. Ellery Sedgwick, *The Atlantic Monthly, 1857–1909* (Amherst: University of Massachusetts Press, 1994), 80.

22. Ibid., 123; Brodhead, *Cultures of Letters*, 123–138.

23. June Howard, "Unraveling Regions, Unsettling Periods: Sarah Orne Jewett and

American Literary History," *American Literature* 68 (June 1996): 366, 372–80; Amy Kaplan, "Nation, Region, and Empire," in *The Columbia History of the American Novel*, ed. Emory Elliott (New York: Columbia University Press, 1991), 250–53.

24. For a fuller discussion of Forten's Sea Islands diary entries and published writings, see Peterson, *"Doers of the Word,"* 189–95.

25. Whittier to Fields, December 25, 1863, *Letters of John Greenleaf Whittier*, 3:55.

26. "Life on the Sea Islands," *Atlantic Monthly* 13 (May and June 1864): 587. All further page references to the essay are placed parenthetically in the text.

27. Sedgwick, *Atlantic Monthly*, 134–35; Nina Silber, *The Romance of Reunion* (Chapel Hill: University of North Carolina Press, 1993).

28. Quoted in Silber, *Romance of Reunion*, 113.

29. Quoted in Frank Luther Mott, *A History of American Magazines*, 5 vols. (Cambridge, Mass.: Harvard University Press, 1938–69), 3:464.

30. See also Peterson, *"Doers of the Word,"* 218. The reader may also wish to refer to Forten's incisive critique of Rebecca Harding Davis's novel *Waiting for the Verdict* for an earlier expression of racial anger, *National Anti-Slavery Standard*, February 22, 1868.

31. George Willis Cooke, *Unitarianism in America: A History of Its Origins and Development* (Boston: American Unitarian Association, 1902), 114–16, 356; Moncure Daniel Conway, *Autobiography: Memories and Experiences of Moncure Daniel Conway*, 2 vols. (1904; rpt. New York: Negro Universities Press, 1969), 1:369.

32. See also Peterson, *"Doers of the Word,"* 218–22.

"A QUEER LOT" AND THE LESBIANS OF 1914:
Amy Lowell, H.D., and Gertrude Stein

Susan McCabe

> I say someone in another time will remember us.
>
> —Sappho

> When this you see remember me.
>
> —Stein

Amy Lowell's poem "The Sisters" searches for a matrilineage, invoking the phantom-like yet sustaining Sappho:

> I know a single slender thing about her:
> That, loving, she was like a burning birch-tree
> All tall and glittering fire, and that she wrote
> Like the same fire caught up to Heaven and held there,
> A frozen blaze before it broke and fell.[1]

Lowell further calls attention to the female poet's eccentric position within a "man-wise" world and aligns herself with the Sapphic "fragment":

> Taking us by and large, we're a queer lot
> We women who write poetry. And when you think
> How few of us there've been, its queerer still.
> I wonder what makes us do it,
> Singles us out to scribble down, man-wise,
> The fragments of ourselves.

Lowell references her lesbian orientation by regarding herself as part of a "queer" and endangered "lot";[2] the poet must be "man-wise," writing *like* a man, or alternatively, writing with the knowledge of how gender, as it is culturally formulated, constricts literary success. Significantly, what survives of writing and the self are "fragments," a word that signals both preservation and destruction. Sappho is invoked but can never be fully restored. H.D. similarly enacts Sapphic returns throughout her writing, and considers the Greek poet the emblem of the creative union of body, soul, and mind in her *Notes on Thought and Vision* (1919). But Sappho cannot fully mediate between H.D. and the heterosexist tradition she finds herself pitted against. Likewise, Stein writes in a work partly composed in 1914 while she and Alice Toklas were living in Mallorca: "Lifting belly is a language. It says island. Island a strata. Lifting belly is a repetition."[3] Stein, like Lowell and H.D., cannot reside in a Lesbos that is not tinged by present violence: "Sometimes we look at the boats. When we read about a boat we know it has been sunk" (*LB* 1–2). In counterpoint to World War I, Stein returns, again and again, to the very female "belly." Lowell, H.D., and Stein each struggle to remember and to assemble a lesbian poetics.[4]

This essay considers how a lesbian poetics challenges our assumptions about modernism; certainly, modernism looks very different if we think of a "renaissance" period of lesbian poets, including Lowell, H.D., and Stein.[5] Such reconsidering allows, at the least, for a new reading of modernism, or of "the lesbians of 1914." Modernism signifies both a period and a style, and as such, it rests on implicit and explicit assumptions about gender and sexual differences. If the modernist canon constitutes itself as a specific configuration of literary styles, the lesbian poets of the modern period become the silenced specter on which such a configuration depends. A lesbian version of modernism has always existed; constructions of masculinist modernism include it through their very act of exclusion. Literary history has fixated on Ezra Pound and T. S. Eliot as the prime movers of Anglo-American poetic modernism, occluding in the process women as active, desiring, speaking subjects, and even more so, making women the beloved addressee of poetic discourse. In particular, I will adumbrate how the inclusion of Lowell, H.D., and Stein as significant lesbian voices reshapes modernist poetic claims that have been sexed and canonized as masculine. Instead of an impersonal anti-Romantic aesthetic, these poets foreground desire and embodiment. Their work, infused with homoerotic energies, enacts a collaborative relation with the "beloved" as muse that breaks down divisions between subject and object. Operating not as some essential or wholly coherent identity but as "the lesbian-as-sign,"[6] these poets disrupt heterosexist paradigms of desire. Lesbian sexuality inflects their work through the simultaneous silencing and affirmation of lesbian desire, and becomes integral to experimentations in voice, language and lyric style.[7]

By confining myself to the years 1912–1919, a period in which interest in poetry was renewed, I locate these three poets as pivotal agents in the shaping of modernism.⁸ They clearly possess many differentiated aims, with Stein seemingly at the far end of the spectrum of what is considered "experimental" and Lowell at the other end.⁹ Stein revolutionizes language, exulting in the fragments that many of her heterosexual peers wish to shore up and recohere; if, as a lesbian signifier, she reconsolidates her relationship to poetic language, it is through her radically divining the lesbian as muse. The Sapphic fragment represents both the mythic survival and erasure of lesbian identity, and as such replicates the lesbian modernist's presence and suppression within literary history. Lowell, H.D., and Stein each actively rejects the heterosexual imperative that underwrites the dominant model of masculinist modernism. Connecting Lowell, H.D., and Stein as contributing to a "lesbian period" reveals their recuperation of homoerotic desire.

In the first part of this essay I will elaborate on how modernism has been fashioned through literary history and periodization to exclude and repress the lesbian signifier. This repressed signifier, in particular, works in defiance of a period and style that privileges disembodiment in favor of viscerally expressed desire. I then examine some specific instances of lesbian signs of desire through the remaking of imagism, an influential doctrine that implicitly silences the lesbian voice. My final section develops the idea of a lesbian divining of the muse, of a subversion of the literary convention that insists on a rigidly gendered hierarchy of poet and muse, lover and beloved.

THE LESBIANS OF 1914

Under current theoretical interrogation, all of the interrelated terms of this essay — period, lesbian, modernism, tradition, canon — are so volatile that it is impossible to assert any unproblematic definition of any of them.¹⁰

Although there have been attempts to establish a "lesbian tradition,"¹¹ sexual orientation remains a subterranean subject in discussions of modernism. *Lesbian Texts and Contexts: Radical Revisions*, allows for a remapping of diverse modernisms (yet none of its essays discuss Lowell's or Stein's relationship to tradition). Bonnie Zimmerman notes that throughout the collection, "lesbian" denotes "a disrupter of heterosexuality, a presence standing outside the conventions of patriarchy, a hole in the fabric of gender dualism." Even as she acknowledges that "in the anti-essentialist nineties . . . tradition-building is a much more troublesome task" than it was in the seventies, she advises that we "approach lesbian history and literary tradition as a shifting matrix of behaviors, choices, subjectivities, textualities and self-representations that is always situated in a specific historical context."¹² Zimmerman recommends, then, a necessary resistance to essentialist, transhistorical representations of women and lesbians: we can examine their traditions only as local, fragmentary and shifting. By reconsidering Lowell, H.D., and Stein, in their very specific poetic endeavors, as actively contributing to a silenced aspect of the early modernist period, we burn a hole in the fabric of a literary history that has posited Pound and Eliot as central figures around whom Lowell, H.D., and Stein are only refractively constellated.

Although modernism is often viewed in antithetical relationship to "tradition,"[13] it is in the context of discontinuity and loss of historical grounding that modernists such as Pound and Eliot enjoined the necessity of literary tradition, the recovery of lost textual history as well as the modernist dictum, in Pound's phrasing, "to make it new." Eliot's plea for the "historical sense" which "compels a man to write not merely with his own generation in his bones, but with a feeling that the whole of literature of Europe from Homer and within it the whole of the literature of his own country" renders the poet a disembodied and universal figure: "The progress of an artist is a continual self-sacrifice, a continual extinction of personality."[14] The gender bias and partiality (think of Eliot's conception of "the whole of literature"; think even of the more "personal" poetics of Wallace Stevens, which imagines "the figure of the youth as virile poet") of such modernist theories of writing have been adroitly revealed: "Modernism is not the aesthetic, directed, monological sort of phenomenon sought in their own ways by authors of now-famous manifestos," that in fact modernism "was unconsciously gendered masculine" in spite of its purported neutrality.[15] From this perspective, tradition itself becomes a phallocentric construct, explicitly exclusive of female, and especially lesbian, voices.[16]

Some "antimodernist" aspects of "fluid explorations of sexuality and gender" in H.D. apply to both Lowell and Stein. The modernist, and specifically imagist, rejection of Romanticism, entailed the rejection of women's writing:

> One recognizes the familiar dismissals of women's writing in the charges leveled by the male modernists against Romanticism: sentimentalism, effeminacy, escapism, lack of discipline, emotionalism, self-indulgence, confessionalism, and so forth. . . . T. E. Hulme's "Romanticism and Classicism," . . . divided literary history into strict gender categories: the "Romanticism" of Swinburne, Byron, and Shelley was defined as "feminine," "damp," and "vague"; Classicism, which formed the model for Imagism, "dry," "hard," "virile," and "exact." Explicit or implicit rejections of "women's writing" for the "masculine" virtues of intellect, "unity," objectivity, and concreteness lay behind Pound's professed "contempt" for the "softness of the 'nineties,'" Eliot's arguments against Romantic "dissocia-

tion" of intellect and emotion, and Yeats's scorn for the "womanish introspection" of the "tragic generation."[17]

Such a catalog could be extended to include, for example, the privileging of intellect in Eliot's "objective correlative" and in Pound's phallic characterization of the mind as "an up-spurt of sperm" and "the phallus or spermatozoid charging, head-on, the female chaos."[18] These intransigent makings of a virile modernism inevitably obfuscate, if not foreclose, any "queer" construction of the romantic impulses or desires in poets like Lowell, H.D., and Stein. In "Composition as Explanation," Stein contrastingly regards "romanticism" (using a demoted "r") as a necessary vital difference, not as inappropriate emotionalism: "This then was the period that brings me to the period of the beginning of 1914. Everything being alike everything naturally would be simply different and war came and everything being alike and everything being simply different brings everything being simply different brings it to romanticism."[19] Stein marks this period as not "simply different." The lesbian signifier is a complex, necessary difference, if unspoken, for the formulation of modernism as both a period and a style.

Peter Nicholls points toward a clarification of the complex reasons behind the exclusion of female (particularly lesbian) writers within the founding definitions of the period when he considers the ideas promulgated by Pound, Eliot and Wyndham Lewis: "What is of interest about this otherwise conventional misogyny is its function as a criterion of literary style." While acknowledging that "beginnings of modernism, like its endings, are largely indeterminate," he locates one of its "traces" in Baudelaire's portrait of a beggar girl; the poet is attracted to the girl's beauty, but it is her inadequacy as agent, her "feminine 'naturalness,'" which allows him an "ironic distance": he can objectify her, see her as "self-presence incarnate" and, in the process, attain "a contrasting disembodiment." This "trace" reappears significantly in the particular modernism of "the men of 1914" in their insistence on the impersonal and objective, an insistence, he observes, that is "concerned with developing models of psychic order which reinstate the divide between art and life, frequently in terms of a parallel re-fixing of sexual difference." The "triumph of form over bodily content" for these poets often signals a rejection of the feminine or the maternal. Such a rejection, however, allows us to perceive the lesbian poet's refusal to make the female body into an impersonal object; her resistance has acted as the silenced underside of a modernism constructed as hegemonically masculinist and exclusive.[20]

If the modernist disavowal of desire and the body serves a vision of self as sharply divorced from objects and others, a lesbian version of early modernism might take "an intellectual and emotional complex in an instant of time" (Pound's definition of the image) and show its relations to the desiring body and to the beloved. In fact, the poetry of Lowell, H.D., and Stein is embodied in the body of their beloved, their work often obscuring the divide between artist and muse. This embodiment stands in contrast to the compression of Pound's prototypic imagist poem, "In a Station of the Metro," which reduces thirty-six lines to two, the "containment of an erotic response" with "the platonic maternal cave transmogrified into a hell of the degraded modern."[21] Compression in Lowell, H.D. and Stein, in contrast, uses not containment but a paradoxical overflowing, a scission of expectations regarding female sexuality and poetics.

For each poet, such an aesthetics emerges from a specific matrix of lesbian embodiment and erotics. Lowell knows she must write an alternate poetry after she has seen Eleanora Duse perform *La Giaconda*; she writes of this moment in bodily language: "I just knew that I had to express the sensations that Duse's acting gave me, somehow, I knew nothing whatever about the technique of poetry, I had never heard of vers libre, I had never analyzed blank verse . . . I sat down, and with infinite agitation wrote this poem . . . it loosed a bolt in my brain and I found out where my true function lay."[22] It would be ten years before the publication of her first volume of poetry in 1912, and it was through her relationship to Ada that her modernist poetic priorities crystallize. From *Sword Blades and Poppy Seed* (1914) forward, Ada becomes so collaborative in her creations that Lowell wants to inscribe over their doorway at Sevenels "'Lowell & Russell, Makers of Fine Poems.'"[23] H.D.'s *Sea Garden* (published in 1916 but which included poems written between 1912 and 1915), acclaimed as a product of imagist work under the seal of Pound's approval, establishes a homoerotic poetics, sensual and interpersonal, which ultimately refuses to conform to the overbearing modernist models erected by poets such as Pound and Eliot. Although she did not meet Bryher until 1919, her amorous relationship with Frances Gregg in 1911 (memorialized in her novella *Paint It Today*) signaled a pervasive attraction to what Susan Friedman calls "Artemesian discourse." Stein's *Tender Buttons* (begun the year after she met Alice in 1911), published in 1914, is energized by the overthrow of the Leo and Gertrude "family romance" and its replacement with a lesbian menage. And as Catherine Stimpson has argued, Toklas is more collaborative in Stein's writing than we have been able to conceive.[24] From such tracking, a lesbian modernism surfaces; yet when modernist studies consider the works of Lowell, Stein, and

H.D., their alternate version of modernism usually becomes subsumed by and misinterpreted according to the implicitly heterosexed doctrines of "the men of 1914."

IMAGISM AND THE RECOVERY OF DESIRE

If Pound's influential "imagism" both obscures Lowell's following his dictum "to make it new" in her identification of herself as an imagist and creates H.D. in its own image, both poets remake the ultimately sketchy, nebulous movement into their own. Hilda Doolittle assumed her debut signature as H.D., *Imagiste*, in *Poetry* magazine of January 1913 through her well-known encounter with Pound in the tearoom across from the British Museum; Lowell's shock of recognition, that she too is an imagist, occurs through her reading of H.D's featured poems. If imagism, as fashioned by Pound, consists of "direct treatment of the thing," economy and precision of language, and the breaking away from metrical in favor of musical composition, Lowell, H.D., and Stein are only partially successful practitioners of this new mode, creating very different aesthetic results than those of their male colleagues. Lesbian modernists share with Pound an enthusiasm for the concrete image, but they are not, it would seem, interested in fixing or mastering it, but rather in showing its tactile and sensuous relation to a more unbounded self. At the same time, their poems are filled with images of sharpness, tearing, and harshness—qualities suggestive of a fragmentation within tradition.

It is not surprising that Lowell would admire H.D's work—it, like her own, exuberantly expresses a homoerotic sexuality; if H.D.'s poems are "hard" and chiseled, they also partake of the fluid, as most poems of her first volume, *Sea Garden*, reveal. H.D. wrote to Lowell in December 1916 after receiving a copy of *Sword Blades and Poppy Seed* that she "like[s] the Aquarius—the swish or swirl of colour" and that "the best is colour and warmth—as I say very warm, exotic even, against this northern grey." After Pound's abandonment of the imagist movement (the poets associated with it were, in his words, "a bunch of goups"), Lowell continued to champion several anthologies of imagist poetry (1915, 1916, 1917) in spite of Pound's threats to interfere with publication.[25] But to expect Lowell or H.D. to live up to imagism as defined by Pound blurs the provocative aspects of their work, lines measured without subordinating the primacy of desire. Louis Untermeyer refers to the odd critical assumption that Lowell "had everything a poet should have except passion, that she had perception but lacked feeling, that (in the words of one of her critics) she substituted motion for emotion";[26] Lowell's affectional preferences certainly could engender such blind spots. Other critics point to H.D.'s coldness, even frigidity; Lowell herself remarks in her *Tendencies* that "there are people who find this poetry cold," but then, with erotic undertones, she proceeds to "liken 'H.D.'s' poetry to the cool flesh of a woman bathing in a fountain—cool to the sight, cool to the touch, but within is a warm, beating heart" (276).

Lowell's polyphonic sequence *Spring Day* opens with "Bath" (MWG 145),[27] a poem interested in embodiment and its interstitial connections to image. In the "anti-poetic" setting of a bathtub, the poem begins with simple observation: "The day is fresh-washed and fair, and there is a smell of tulips and narcissus in the air." As the sun "cleaves the water into flaws like a jewel, cracks it to bright light," the poet is ready to find herself in it: "Little spots of sunshine lie on the surface of the water and dance, dance, and their reflections wobble deliciously over the ceiling; a stir of my finger sets them whirring, reeling. I move a foot, and the planes of light in the water jar. I lie back and laugh, and let the green-white water, the sun-flawed beryl water, flow over me." Such a passage of sensuous enjoyment and immersion has no place within the constructs defined by master narratives of modernism. "Bath" returns us at the end to images it begins with, but with a difference (a method reminiscent of Stein's use of repetition with continuous alteration): "The sky is blue and high. A crow flaps by the window, and there is a whiff of tulips and narcissus in the air." Seeing in "planes of light" does not effectively separate the poet from what she perceives and experiences.

Another poem, "The Basket" (*SBPS* 58), reveals a figure very like Baudelaire's beggar girl, yet Lowell counteracts ironic objectification by deflating the poet's impulse to rigidly contain meaning:

> See! She is coming, the young woman with the bright hair. She swings a basket as she walks, which she places on the sill, between the geranium stalks. He laughs, and crumples his paper as he leans forward to look. 'The Basket Filled with Moonlight,' what a title for a book! The bellying clouds swing over the housetops.

As she returns throughout the poem to images of moon and cloud, they transmute through "the shock of one colour on another," unmastered by the poetic eye and "bellying," a distinctively female-gendered word (which Stein employs in *Lifting Belly* as noun, verb and adjective). By section III, the basket of nuts has vividly changed—presumably under the influence of moonlight—into a basket of eyes:

> Blue, black, gray, and hazel, and the irises are cased in the whites, and they glitter and spark under the moon. The basket is heaped with human eyes. She cracks off the whites and throws them away. They ricochet upon the roof, and get into the gutters, and bounce over the edge and disappear. But she is here, quietly sitting on the window-sill, eating human eyes. The silver-blue moonlight makes the geraniums purple, and the roof shines like ice.

Is this a castration fantasy, with the slang reference of "basket" as the male genitals? Even if it is not, the passage represents an attack on masculinist scopophilia (as present in Baudelaire's rendition of the beggar girl). This ingestion allows the quiet observer to "take in" the fluid shifting of light and color, to displace the dry and hard image within a poetics of dispersal and metamorphosis. Such a context provides Lowell an alternative locus, not strictly imagist, from which to figure forth lesbian desire.

"Anticipation" (*SBPS* 42), like the poem above, defies the "impersonal"; in the context of Eliot's notion of poetry as "an escape from emotion," Lowell's writing appears to escape *in* emotion, even as its heady and blunt lines control the releasing of it. The poem opens: "I have been temperate always, / But I am like to be very drunk / With your coming." Variation in line length modulates an experience of breathlessness, the last foreshortened line suggestive of orgasmic arrival. We are not in the world of safety and acceptance as the speaker depicts a kind of terror:

> There have been times
> I feared to walk down the street
> Lest I should reel with the wine of you,
> And jerk against my neighbors
> As they go by.

Even with the archaic "Lest" (in Pound the word would be a "medievalism), the poem potently expresses desire under duress. Such desire is not inevitably encoded as lesbian, but if we consider the possibility of a woman speaking to another woman, the poem appears to fit less into a model of feminine love poetry and becomes more radical, more flexible in its romantic revelations.

If I teach any of Lowell's "imagist" poems to introductory classes without indicating to them the author, students invariably assume a male writer, and once they find out the author's gender, they readily construct a male persona, persistent in perceiving a heterosexual dynamic. When Lowell's sexual orientation is introduced into the discussion, the notion of a definitely sexed persona becomes more questionable. Is imagining a lesbian speaker, a female voice so resonant with desire for another woman, unthinkable? Elizabeth Grosz writes that "it seems impossible to think lesbian desire," given the terms provided by psychoanalytic and patriarchal discourse; in an effort to escape "the ontology of lack," she looks to Deleuze and Guattari as a starting point where "desire is presence, not lack."[28] Lowell's poems become illumined through such a model of "presence," even as they simultaneously encode "lack." The above lines register a brazen "difference," no metrical smoothness denying that the lover here will "jerk against [her] neighbors." In spite of the poet's forthright expression of desire, a potential silencing of the tongue continues even as an internal phantasmic orgy prepares for fulfillment, a spilling over of abundance:

> I am parched now, and my tongue is horrible in my mouth,
> But my brain is noisy
> With the clash and gurgle of filling wine-cups. (42)

"Vintage" (*SBPS* 42), another so-called imagist poem, begins with this assertion:

> I will mix me a drink of stars,—
> Large stars with polychrome needles,
> Small stars jetting maroon and crimson,
> Cool, quiet, green stars.
> I will tear them out of the sky,
> And squeeze them over an old silver cup,
> And I will pour the cold scorn of my Beloved into it,
> So that my drink shall be bubbled with ice.

Lowell manipulates the gender position of the speaker with the personification of the drink as a serpent and the use of the masculine pronoun: "His snortings will rise to my head, / And I shall be hot, and laugh, / Forgetting that I have ever known a woman." Throughout her work, Lowell doubly upsets heterosexist claims to language, here both parodically rejecting the conventional trope of the "beloved" and reclaiming it; the violence in the poem denotes an anger, directed towards the paradigm of feminine love poetry, grounded in the female-as-object of the gaze and the female-as-vessel, she must revision.

Grosz's version of a lesbian desire that is interested in diffuse surfaces inscribing presence rather than in a narrowly genital sexuality is useful in reconceiving Lowell (as with H.D. and Stein) as displacing a scopic body, one designated by its lack, with tactile and oral bodies. "Decade" (*PFW* 217), with imagistic compression, contracts Lowell's time with her lover into six lines, both sensuous and unsentimental:

> When you came, you were like red wine and honey,
> And the taste of you burnt my mouth with its sweetness.
> Now you are like morning bread.
> Smooth and pleasant.
> I hardly taste you at all for I know your savor,
> But I am completely nourished.

Transubstantiation becomes secular, the wine and the bread turning into familiar yet erotic comfort. Without limiting lesbian desire to the genital or to the rhetoric of lack, the unnamable image of oral sex between women becomes a possible scenario in a world of everyday enactments.

To reread Lowell as a lesbian (with other lesbians) allows us to see her writing in defiance of, not in sentimentalizing cooperation with, a heterosexual love tradition. Nor is she writing the modernist poem as advocated by her peers. She can retain the personal and the passionate; at the same time, she can assume several of the classical traits applauded by T. E. Hulme (her stars can be "polychrome needles," and as with H.D. in *Sea Garden*, her sharpness becomes a reappraisal of feminine stereotypes), but she does not have to forsake the fluidity of emotion. Written under the influence of Ada, *Sword Blades and Poppy Seed* permits her a break from her previous collection, *A Dome of Many-Coloured Glass* (1912), and its almost complete abidance to meter and rhyme. Her new style of 1914, variously cadenced and unrhymed, searches for more precise depiction of a subjective experience, without the emphasis upon the "object," as suggested by Pound's brand of imagism.

H.D.'s "imagist" poems, like Lowell's, similarly defy the imagist criteria they apparently fulfill, and foreground a desiring subject. When *Sea Garden* is read as a whole, it appears expansive, passionate, even hyperbolic, rather than contained by a return to classicist restraint. Sparseness works in tension with excessiveness, rather than part of an exclusionary aesthetic program. In referring to H.D.'s "imagism," critics often cite one or two poems as exemplary, usually "Oread" and "Sea Rose." Friedman, in her attempt to distinguish H.D.'s prose as "personal narrative discourse in opposition to the impersonal discourse of her early lyrics" (14), offers "Mid-day" as perfectly fulfilling modernist dictates: "Intense, concentrated and passionate, the poem is nonetheless completely impersonal in Eliot's sense of the term."[29] Although it is impossible to make absolute correspondences between biography and the poetry, the poem does not appear as thoroughly impersonal and contained as Friedman would have it.

The images do not have definitive causal relation to the emotions that follow, nor do the images contain the emotions. Here are the first two stanzas:

> The light beats upon me.
> I am startled —
> a split leaf crackles on the paved floor —
> I am anguished — defeated.
>
> A slight wind shakes the seed-pods —
> my thoughts are spent
> as the black seeds.
> My thoughts tear me,
> I dread their fever.
> I am scattered like
> the hot shriveled seeds.[30]

"Startled," "anguished," "defeated," "scattered," "spent," "shriveled": in this spare poem, there is much emoting and rupturing (as indicated by her dashes). The poem closes with an image of a poplar "great / among the hill-stones," not perishing as she is on the ground; H.D. is perhaps in the process of resigning her post as Pound's "dryad."

As in Lowell's "Bath," an embodied, sensual exploration dissolves the notion of a singular ego in H.D.'s early lyrics. "Oread," in its imagist brevity and intensity, previews her gynocentric poetics; she speaks in the plural personae of Greek mountain nymphs, but her invocation is not contained by these voices:

> Whirl up, sea —
> whirl your pointed pines,
> splash your great pines
> on our rocks,
> hurl over green over us,
> cover us with your pools of fir. (CP 55)

The boundaries between sea and mountains dynamically blur: the sea has "pointed pines," "great pines," and reflection here prevents distinction between self and other. The last line is particularly tactile and erotic with the desire to be "cover[ed]" with "pools of fir."

H.D.'s "Sheltered Garden" forthrightly rejects patriarchal boundaries and rigid standards of sexual identity. H.D. declares immediately: "I have had enough. / I gasp for breath."[31] As she discards stereotypes for feminine propriety, H.D. invokes the sublime extreme of a romantic topos:

> I have had enough —
> border-pinks, clove-pinks, wax-lilies,
> herbs, sweet-cress.
>
> O for some sharp swish of a branch —

There is an excessiveness in H.D. that one may overlook if examining one or two poems as they appear to fit Pound's notion of imagism; without objective correlative, she apostrophizes and emotes, her consciousness keenly attuned to sensory experience that beauty can be too much, beyond language. "Orchard" begins with simple perception and turns into the insistent demand to "spare us from loveliness":

> I saw the first pear
> as it fell —
> the honey-seeking, golden-banded,
> the yellow swarm
> was not more fleet than I,
> (spare us from loveliness)
> and I fell prostrate
> crying:
> you have flayed us
> with your blossoms,
> spare us the beauty
> of fruit-trees.

Like the pear she identifies with, she falls and becomes "prostrate." The visual becomes lacerating in its merging with psychic experience.

With similar obfuscating of boundaries, of one thing becoming another with implosive immediacy, "Garden," with the hard petals of a rose "cut in rock" compared to "spilt dye," gives the poet the energy to "break a tree" and to "break you," an unidentified second person. Pound becomes a likely candidate, for he had addressed her as his treelike muse in his collection of poems, *Hilda's Book*: this is certainly a moment she seizes to construct her position as outside of modernism's masculinist imperatives.

Much of the impetus and energy of H.D.'s lyrics, like Lowell's, resides in their recovery of desire. "In the Cliff Temple," she asks: "Shall I hurl myself from here?" (*CP* 27); in "Orion Dead," with Artemis speaking, she declares: "I will tear the full flowers" (*CP* 56); and in "The Gift": "I endure from moment to moment —/ days pass all alike, / tortured, intense" (*CP* 17): these brief examples should indicate lack of ironic distance and inviolable impersonalism.

The desire to break free of confining, rigid notions of sexuality and poetics often emerges in extremely violent, adversarial language. H.D. invokes, for instance, in "Sea Lily": "Reed, slashed and torn / but doubly rich—" (CP 14). The reed signals the lyric mode, here surviving the slashing and tearing of a antagonistic environ:

>   Yet though the whole wind
>   slash at your bark,
>   you are lifted up,
>   aye—though it hiss
> to cover you with froth.

Often embodying herself as a flower, she revises the image by showing herself as both "fragile" and "fronting the wind" ("Sea Violet," CP 25); an Artemesian beauty with strength ("Sheltered Garden," CP 19), her "Sea Rose" is a "harsh rose" that "caught in the drift" is "marred and with stint of petals," "meagre," and "sparse of leaf" (CP 5). Such tropes potentially adumbrate lesbian presence, even as it is queerly "deformed." "At least I have the flowers of myself," her Eurydice can articulate by the end of H.D.'s poem about embracing a gynopoetic project of repossessing Orphic power; in Irigarayan inversion, she gains presence within the cave of lack and passive receptivity, asserting that "against this stark grey / I have more light" ("Eurydice" 55).[32] Through this long poem, H.D. certainly alters what it means to be imagist, and her refashioning of the Victorian garden becomes a potential site for lesbian desire.

Stein, perhaps even more than Lowell and H.D., masks homoerotic desire yet her encodings insist on their encodedness to such an extent that they radically enact lesbian desire. *The Autobiography* notes a shift in Stein's writing from "the insides of people" to wanting "to express the rhythm of the visible world,"[33] and yet this shift is synchronous in establishing a whole new household with Alice, a process memorialized by *Tender Buttons*; language must be deconstituted and reconstituted, and these two activities foreground the lesbian as desiring subject. Examine "A Piece of Coffee" for example:

> A PIECE OF COFFEE
> More of double.
> A place in no new table.
> A single image is not splendor. Dirty is yellow. A sign of more in not mentioned. A piece of coffee is not a detainer. The resemblance to yellow is dirtier and distincter. The clean mixture is whiter and not coal color, never more coal color than altogether.[34]

Stein subverts Kantian categories of perception and knowing: our definitions, however clear and precise, must become a "mixture." She swiftly manages to undermine imagism: "A single image is not splendor"; resemblances become distinctions, differences lose their edges.[35] *Tender Buttons*, at least in one reading, revitalizes how lesbian desire can be located or spread around the body, the erotogenic zones becoming less fixed. The often quoted opening testifies to such sexual difference:

> A CARAFE THAT IS A BLIND GLASS
> A kind in glass and a cousin, a spectacle and nothing strange, a single hurt color and an arrangement in a system to pointing. All this and not ordinary, not unordered in not resembling. The difference is spreading. (*TB* 9)

The rearrangements Stein makes with language reflect her household's rearrangement: the felt betrayal of Leo, the "hurt color," and a defense of the "not ordinary" as "nothing strange." Objects lose their solidity and become kindred; they spread rather than retain singularity. Nevertheless, Stein must separate and cut away from the conventional, in poetic and sexual terms. A *CHAIR* reflects such repositioning and necessary veiling; here is a portion of it:

> A widow in a wise veil and more garments shows that shadows are even. It addresses no more, it shadows the stage and learning. A regular arrangement, the severest and the most preserved is that which has the arrangement not more than always authorised.
> A suitable establishment, well housed, practical, patient and staring, a suitable bedding, very suitable and not more particularly than complaining, anything suitable is so necessary.
> . . . .
> If the chance to dirty diminishing is necessary, if it is why is there no complexion, why is there no rubbing, why is there no special protection. (*TB* 18–19)

Perspective, placement, and orientation become enmeshed terms. The "dirt" she refers to so much throughout is the taint she sees ascribed to her illegitimate relation, her anti-Oedipal menage. Without an "authorised" arrangement, there is "no rubbing" and "no special protection." Nevertheless, she claims "a suitable bedding, very suitable." Erotic suggestiveness circulates throughout; she reclaims abstract thinking and imbues it with the sensuous: lesbian sexuality cannot be pinned down or fixed in images rescued from flux and complexity. A *PETTICOAT*, compressed as if in imagist homage, is indirect and proliferative in its four panels of rhythmic flaps: "A light white, a disguise, an ink spot, a rosy charm" (*TB* 22). Such incantatory language charms: the "disguise" and the "rose" both belong to a series of changing surfaces. ORANGE enacts another recovery of desire, while resisting imagist containment: "A type oh oh new new not no not kneader kneader of old slow beef-steak, neither neither" (*TB* 57). We can find no ordinary "orange" here. But her line is charged with an emotional current, the "oh oh" echoing the "o" in orange — the absence of most punctuation allows this; there is urgency in the rejection of kneading (not needing the "old slow beef-steak"). "Neither" echoes "kneader" and rejection also slips into "need her." Such slipperiness is an aesthetic as well as an erotic move. That a reader can be lost in the language and its possibilities points toward the disruptive presence of lesbian desire.

Although Lowell's and H.D.'s experiments with language are certainly not as radical as Stein's, each nevertheless was committed to a poetics that questioned both previous models of poetry and the performances of the day. Peter Nicholls helpfully describes Stein's alternate modernism (which he perceives as "at odds in about every respect with Pound, Eliot and Lewis") as one that, like H.D.'s, operates with a "fantasy of sameness," with identity "no longer predicated on lack." He cites Stein's anti-referential concern with words, with the "self-sufficiency of language," her "refusal of irony," her conception of writing as "a passionate activity," her "felt connection with the world," and her poetics as a refusal to name.[36] In these particulars, Stein operates antithetically to the tenets of imagism. And perhaps it is Lowell's articulated alliance with this "movement" that clouds her resistance to its mimetic implications; she says, in fact, in *Tendencies* that "imagism is presentation, not representation" (245). Like Stein and H.D., Lowell foregrounds process and method, and her interest in bodily experience and sensation make her language an investment in flexible boundaries; if she does not always "catch" the image, it is because she does not want to. Even though Lowell's work is not nearly as invested as Stein's is in language itself as the subject of poetry, she shares with Stein an exploratory sensibility, her caressing the edges of the thing or emotion under scrutiny, her repetition a process of transformation.[37] In contrast to the coldness imputed to both H.D. and Lowell and the cerebral incomprehensibility often attributed to Stein, I discover in them the denigrated traits of emotionalism and passion. Although I am by no means suggesting that emotional or sexual expressiveness is exclusively lesbian, their particular positions as lesbians (or as women who chose another woman as their primary, significant relationship) encouraged a poetics that often became overflowing, even excessive in its blurring of one thing with another: lover and beloved, self and perception. When Stein writes in *Pink Melon Joy*—"I cannot express emotion. / Any house is a home"—she seems, flatly and clearly, to dissemble;[38] as with H.D. and Lowell, emotion and desire permeate her texts, disrupting the artificial containments of imagist and antiromantic modernism.

DIVINING THE LESBIAN MUSE

That one was then one always completely listening. Ada was then one and all her living then one completely telling stories that were charming, completely listening to stories having a beginning and a middle and an ending. Trembling was all living, living was all loving, some one was then the other one. Certainly this one was loving this Ada then.[39]

Stein's portrait of Alice as "Ada," written in 1910, describes a collaborative union in which "some one was then the other one," an oscillation between listening and telling stories the very fabric of the relationship. Similarly, Lowell's divining of the muse commits her not primarily to overthrowing patriarchal infringement but more directly to including *her* Ada.

The ending of Lowell's "The Garden by Moonlight" reflects a paratactic grace and blurring, perhaps threatening to a virile poetics:

Then you come,
And you are quiet like the garden,
And white like the alyssum flowers,
And beautiful as the silent sparks of the fireflies.
Ah, Beloved, do you see those orange lilies?
(*PFW* 212)

Objects become indeterminate, matter for investigative meditation. Lowell, like H.D., frequently invokes the figure of a "beloved" as the lesbian muse. "The Captured Goddess" (*SBPS* 31) is inflected with Sapphic urgency to recover a lost female beauty. As the poet pledges her devotion, the "shiver of amethyst" turns into a spectrumed and resounding vision:

I followed her for long,
With gazing eyes and stumbling feet.
I cared not where she led me,
My eyes were full of colors:
Saffrons, rubies, the yellows of beryls,
And the indigo-blue of quartz;

> Flights of rose, layers of chrysoprase,
> Points of orange, spirals of vermilion

This is not a descent into the underworld, but a recognition of the limits of the upperworld. When the poet "found her," she is "bound and trembling," a commodity of exchange.

In this same manner of searching for the muse but more successfully, "Madonna of the Evening Flowers" (*PFW* 210) concretely links the goddess figure with the real Ada and so makes the transposition between the real and the visionary vivid and tender. The poem begins quite simply: "All day long I have been working, / Now I am tired. / I call: 'Where are you?'" This call provokes a search, but the poet remains rooted in the earthly world of her desire. She discovers her beloved in a spare vision that builds until synesthesia crosses over the boundaries of sight and hearing:

> Then I see you,
> Standing under a spire of pale blue larkspur,
> With a basket of roses on your arm.
> You are cool, like silver,
> And you smile.
> I think the Canterbury bells are playing little tunes.

The speaker addresses her beloved with emotion that threatens to "overrun all bounds" but does not:

> You tell me that the peonies need spraying,
> That the columbines have overrun all bounds,
> That the pyrus japonica should be cut back and rounded.
> You tell me these things.
> But I look at you, heart of silver,
> White heart-flame of polished silver,
> Burning beneath the blue steeples of the larkspur,
> And I long to kneel instantly at your feet,
> While all about us peal the loud, sweet *Te Deums* of the Canterbury bells.

The poem resounds with worship. "A Sprig of Rosemary" (*PFW* 216), another poem written in celebration of the beloved, renders Ada's hands metonymic with her being; Lowell uses repetition to foreground their significance, suspending them on their own line:

> I cannot see your face.
> When I think of you,

> It is your hands which I see.
> Your hands
> Sewing,
> Holding a book,
> Resting for a moment on the sill of a window.

The poem begins once more with absence; and then through imaginative vision, finishes with the ecstatic recreated presence of the loved one, framed in memory. A later poem, "In Excelsis" (WO 444) also refers to Ada's hands, here as "moving, a chime of bells across a windless air," in synesthesic displacement. If lesbian desire, as Grosz recommends, is refigured as production, as making rather than as lack, hands become significant in figuring forth an alternate sexual economy. The rosemary, a perennial flower linked with remembrance, suggests that this momentary, fragmentary vision can be perpetually reenacted.

The invocational nature of so much of H.D.'s *Sea Garden* suggests its posture of devotion, simultaneously enacted with the experience of splitness; this is a landscape where "each leaf is rent like split wood" (CP 36); at the same time, she enacts Sapphic ritualized worship: in part II of "Sea Gods," the garlanding central to Sappho's homoeroticism appears as an offering of violets:

> But we bring violets,
> great masses — single, sweet,
> wood violets, stream-violets,
> violets from a wet marsh.

Sappho writes:

> for with many a crown of roses
> mixed with crocus and violets
> you were garlanded while you were at my side
>
> and with many a flower necklace
> you encircled your tender throat,
> plaiting blossoms together to make a wreath [40]

Like Lowell's "The Captured Goddess," H.D. registers the allure involved in the following of a Sapphic trail. Although "Pursuit" (CP 11–12) does not clearly delineate pursuer and pursued, it references her other poem, "The Huntress" with its Artemesian declaration of "our bare heels / in the heel-prints" (CP 23–24) and its call for followers. It begins passionately:

> What do I care
> that the stream is trampled,

the sand on the stream-bank
still holds the print of our foot:
the heel is cut deep.

In the second section of "The Shrine," the poet invokes:

O but stay tender, enchanted
where wave-lengths cut you
apart from all the rest—
for we have found you,
we watch the splendour of you,
we thread throat on throat of freesia
for your shelf.

To garland "the salt stretch" of this beach becomes an act with homoerotic charge. The center stanza of "Pear Tree" is worshipful with sexual overtones:

no flower ever opened
so staunch a white leaf,
no flower ever parted silver
from such rare silver;

O white pear (CP 39)

One of H.D.'s signature methods is her use of repetition and anaphora; by returning again and again to a phrase she pushes us back to a present: it is a return that represents a desiring and a loving. H.D.'s novel *Hermione*, a text layered with repetitions, articulates this: "Writing. Love is writing."[41]

Repetition is an important feature to each of the poets under discussion here, especially in relation to their recuperation of desire. Stein's conception of the sexual / texual aspect of repetition resonates in this divining of the lesbian muse: "You can love a name and if you love a name then saying that name any number of times only makes you love it more, more violently more persistently more tormentedly."[42] *Lifting Belly*, with the title phrase repeated in multiple permutations makes this pertinent for her lesbian poetics. Four lines—declarations of sexual difference—must do for the present:

She is my sweetheart.
Why doesn't she resemble an other.
This I cannot say here.
Full of love and echoes. Lifting belly is full of love. (LB 34)

For H.D. (along with Stein and Lowell), beauty and love have a violent aspect to them, an aspect much more "romantic" than "classical." Certainly, *Sea Gar-*

den is romantic in tenor (belied by its "hard" or chiseled lineation), spilling over in its ecstatic search for "a new beauty / in some terrible / wind-tortured place" ("Sheltered Garden"), foreshadowing an overthrow of the heterosexual economy. Her "Huntress" (CP 23–24) is an invitation to join Artemis:

> Can you come,
> can you come,
> can you follow the hound trail,
> can you trample the hot froth?

One wonders if these lines didn't resonate loudly for Bryher, who had memorized all of H.D.'s *Sea Garden* before meeting the poet.

As with H.D. and Lowell, Stein's resistance to literary tradition and its oppressive monumentalism includes identifying herself with a new language of lesbian desire:

> Lifting belly what is earnest. Expecting an arena to be monumental.
> Lifting belly is recognized to be the only spectacle present. Do you mean that. Lifting belly is a language. It says island. Island a strata. Lifting belly is a repetition.
> Lifting belly means me.
> I do love roses and carnations. (*LB* 17)

Even with this "spectacle" of intensive loving, the work does not attempt to portray a relationship without conflict, without disagreement: one voice often modifies the other, disagrees as it realigns reciprocity; no voice inhabits a fixed register, or point on the hierarchy, and thus the assertions, bold and confident, can be made without quotation, but in a process of mutual reconceptualizing. Such a method breaks down the pattern of egocentric writing, of a single creative ego working in isolation to create monumental art, the muse carefully poised in otherness. Here is confluence, expression unchecked, overflowing and multiple: "lifting belly" is never singly defined. Language remains an arena for apostrophe, lavishing, and praise, with verbs enjambed:

> Lifting belly is so strong. I love cherish idolise adore and worship you.
> You are so sweet so tender and so perfect. (*LB* 19)

While Stein possesses a kind of romantic readiness and exuberance distinctive in both H.D. and Lowell, she more radically separates herself from inherited poetic traditions. Her cadences operate in a process of constantly alternating positions; her desiring subject is not sublated within a monumentalist form: her divining of the muse appears with bodily directness. Consider this passage from "Emp Lace" (1914):

> Come out.
> Come come out.
> Out.
> Mercifully mercifully mercy fully mercifully.
> Which is a lit.
> Lighter.
> Wedding chest.
> Wedding chest pansies.
> Hat is across.
> Across far.
>
> Next to next to near soled tip, next to next to near to next to near to next to next to. Next to next to next to near to next to near to.
>
> Cow come out come out cow come out come out cow cow come out come out cow cow come out cow come out cow come out come out cow cow come out come out cow cow come out cow come out cow come out cow come out cow cow come out cow come out.
>
> Honey is wet.[43]

One notices echoes from and in other Stein works; echoes and repetitions are part of a model of writing as loving. Repeating is a making and emp(lacing) of presence, to reuse Grosz's terms. In spite of its disjunctiveness, each articulation is a simple act, each declaration a playing upon the aural connections between words, finding the "fully" in "mercifully." As she immerses herself in language, what could become a cerebral exercise of seeking out puns becomes instead a site of revelatory desire and sensuality, with the urgent rhythm of "Come come out" expanding into the extended incantation to female pleasuring with the four lines beginning with "Cow come out"; the urgency of lesbian desire becomes metonymic with the plainly erotic assertion: "Honey is wet." The bodily involvement required by the unexpected proximities within language precludes the distancing from the female body enacted by so much of masculinist modernism. "Next to" and "near to" are adjacencies, and she permits no ironic distancing between subject and object, à la Baudelaire. There is no firm separation between language and experience, between assertion and becoming.

OUTLAWED MODERNISM

Reconfiguring modernism in terms of the silenced lesbian requires a spatial rearrangement, a foregrounding of previously marginal identifications. Instead of thinking of tradition in Eliot's terms of layered accretion and continuity, of simultaneous historicity laden and enfolded with the truly great poets, we might prefer to think of Stein's sense of time, of her "continuous present" that insists on necessary forgetfulness: "There was a groping for using everything and there was a groping for a continuous present and there was an inevitable beginning of beginning again and again and again."[44] As a lesbian poet, Stein positions herself in a state of perpetual nascence, lacking contemporary validation; her work belonging to "the history of the refused," she wisely observes: "Those who are creating the modern composition authentically are naturally only of importance when they are dead because by that time the modern composition having become past is classified and the description of it is classical. That is the reason why the creator of the new composition in the arts is an outlaw until he is a classic."[45] "Outlaw" is suggestive of sexual outsiderhood as well as modern composition. In spite of the extensive networking between modernist women as outlined by Bonnie Kime Scott and others, there exists no real collective, no developed cultural support for lesbian existence. The lesbian period remains outlaw. Even as Lowell's work (like that of H.D. and Stein) defies the notion of an autonomous self, continuity and connection are only tentatively achieved. "When this you see remember me," Stein writes, aware that the process of such remembering is fragmented, tentative and provisional.

Sexual orientation and the repression of it, I would argue, promote a textual ambiguity that lesbian modernist poets possess; gender and sexuality defy poetic privileging of impersonality as advocated by Eliot and Pound. Lowell, perhaps a slack "amygist," provides another perspective on innovation, in terms of alternative sexual economies. H.D.'s so-called imagism allowed her a place in the modernist canon long before even Stein gained admittance; but H.D's place is significantly circumscribed by "the period" she has been made to fit within so neatly. The period alters when we see her outside of the shadow of Pound's poetic priorities. If we examine Stein's extensive opus, most of which remained unpublished during her life, we might daringly reconsider calling modernism "The Stein Era." Such a reconsideration, however, would not position Stein as uncritically fixed as the hierarchical substitute for any male modernist; I propose it only as it serves an always shifting configuration, as disruptive refocusing of modernism that allows the possibility of perceiving the lesbians of 1914.

NOTES

1. "The Sisters" appears in the 1925 posthumously published and Pulitzer Prize–winning *What's O'Clock* in *Complete Poetical Works of Amy Lowell* (Boston: Houghton Mifflin, 1955), 459–61. Future references to this volume will be cited in the text as WO. Future references to other volumes, all taken from *The Complete Poetical Works*, will be

abbreviated as follows: *Sword Blades and Poppy Seed* (1914) as *SBPS*; *Men, Women and Ghosts* (1916) as *MWG*; and *Pictures of the Floating World* (1919) as *PFW*.

2. "Queer" as a word designating homosexuality was already in circulation when she wrote the poem.

3. Gertrude Stein, *Lifting Belly* (Tallahassee: Naiad Press, 1989). Subsequent references will be cited in the text as *LB*.

4. Although they were starkly divergent in their self-identification as lesbians, with H.D. usually assigned bisexual status, female-to-female relationships were primary in their lives, specifically Ada Dwyer Russell in Lowell's, Alice Toklas in Stein's, and Bryher in H.D.'s.

5. Significantly, Lowell conceived herself a part of a renaissance in poetry. See her *Tendencies in Modern American Poetry* (New York: Macmillan, 1917), 237. Subsequent references to this work will be cited parenthetically in the text. I borrow from Eve Kosofsky Sedgwick's contribution to the canon discussion that raises the issue of uncharted renaissances. She advises in *Epistemology of the Closet* (Berkeley: University of California Press, 1990) that we rethink all of "the Renaissances" in which "gay desires, people, discourses, prohibitions, and energies were manifest" (59).

6. I am borrowing this phrase from Bonnie Zimmerman's "Lesbians Like This and Like That" in *New Lesbian Criticism: Literary and Cultural Readings*, ed. Sally Munt (Hertfordshire: Harvester Wheatsheaf, 1992). Another important discussion of the lesbian signifier appears in Teresa de Lauretis's *The Practice of Love: Lesbian Sexuality and Perverse Desire* (Bloomington: Indiana University Press, 1994), where she considers the lesbian as a liberatory sign for gay and straight feminists: "*What I am referring to is not the reality, the psychic and/or social reality, of lesbianism but its fantasmatic place and figuration in feminist theory*: a place from where female homosexuality figures, for women, the *possibility* of subject and desire" (156).

7. See Margaret Dickie's "Recovering the Repression in Stein's Erotic Poetry" in *Gendered Modernisms: American Women Poets and Their Readers*, ed. Margaret Dickie and Thomas Travisano (Philadelphia: University of Pennsylvania Press, 1996), where she advises: "Set back into her own time and examined in the context of her own development, Stein will appear less interested in freeing language from patriarchal strictures and more concerned with manipulating language to cover up meaning that might become too explicit for the taboo subject of lesbian eroticism, which was her central concern" (3–4). Such "covering up" is complicit with the expression of "her central concern"; this dynamic, I think, is active in Lowell as well as Stein.

8. For the purposes of this essay, I will refer to them as poets, as indication of my sense of their heightened use of language. It is clear, however, that they each (especially Stein) called into question the conventional divisions between poetry and prose.

9. To link these particular poets, I am aware, is an act of perhaps perverse reconstitution. Rita Felski's notion in *The Gender of Modernity* (Cambridge, Mass.: Harvard University Press, 1995) that the privileging of women's avant-garde texts (such as Stein's) in favor of other "modern" enterprises obscures the relationship of women to modernity is

useful here. While Felski does not mention her, Lowell's more "conventional" poetry often makes her easy to overlook in studies of modernism. Of modernist lesbian poets, Lowell (1874–1925) seems possibly in greatest need of the three in recuperation in terms of her place in any tradition, modernist or lesbian. Only recently has her poetry appeared in the Norton Anthology, yet of her eight volumes of poetry, none are in print, not even the 1957 Twayne selected edition. Even Bonnie Kime Scott's insightful *The Gender of Modernism: A Critical Anthology* (Bloomington: Indiana University Press, 1990) sees fit to give her no chapter. What accounts for this rejection? Although it cannot be pinned entirely on Pound, much of her disrepute stems from his construction of her as mispracticing imagism, or as he fashioned her brand of it, "Amygism": such constructions seem clearly motivated by divergent aesthetic sensibilities. Hugh Kenner writes of Lowell's relationship to imagism in his *The Pound Era* (Berkeley: University of California Press, 1971) with scathing irony; he refers to her "crossing like a big blue wave or like Daisy Miller in 1913 to join the movement and in 1914 to appropriate it since she had not been properly accepted" (292). In a rare attempt to place Lowell in a tradition (other than allowing her only provisional status as interloper in the imagist movement), Jeanne Larsen in *Columbia History of American Poetry*, ed. Jay Parini and Brett C. Miller (New York: Columbia University Press, 1993) groups her with Teasdale, Wylie, Millay, and Bogan, and she describes Lowell's subversion of "the previous century by writing . . . both far more explicitly and in the Imagist mode" and points to her as continuing "the feminine tradition of ardent love poems" (210); while I agree that Lowell is resisted, in part, because of her defiance of androcentric models of love poetry, the notion of Lowell's place in modernism needs to be refined in terms of her connection to other lesbian poets in their recovery of "romantic" forms of desire.

10. The notion of establishing a lesbian version of modernism remains problematic within contemporary frameworks. In his *Is Literary History Possible?* (Baltimore: Johns Hopkins University Press, 1992), David Perkins declares the incapacity of legitimating any literary remapping; from a postmodern perspective, all projects of canonization become strained. He reminds us that "history cannot represent the past but must distort it" (19), and periodization becomes a matter of "necessary fictions" (65). He conjectures: "Theorists have proposed new taxonomic categories—horizon of expectations, discourse, communicative system, episteme—that will, it is hoped, escape the objections to the traditional ones. But emphasis on particularity, difference, and discontinuity undermines confidence in all classifications" (67). Thus those "movements of liberation of women, blacks, gays" which "turn to the past in search of identity, tradition, and self-understanding" (10), from this perspective, cannot help but be deceptive, ever-mutable categories of inquiry. Such a discounting, or loss of confidence, belies a nostalgia for history that both demands the breakdown of canonical literary history and insists on the impossibility of refiguring the canon in meaningful, if tentative, alternative ways.

11. There has been substantial work in excavating a lesbian tradition. Most significant are Blanche Wiesen Cook's "Women Alone Stir My Imagination: Lesbianism and the

Cultural Tradition," *Signs* 4 (1979); Bonnie Zimmerman's "What Has Never Been: An Overview of Lesbian Feminist Criticism" (1981) in *Feminisms: An Anthology of Literary Theory and Criticism,* ed. Robin R. Warhol and Diane Price Herndl (New Brunswick: Rutgers University Press, 1991); Mary J. Carruthers's "The Re-Vision of the Muse: Adrienne Rich, Audre Lorde, Judy Grahn, Olga Broumas," *Hudson Review* 36 (1984); and Liz Yorke's *Impertinent Voices: Subversive Strategies in Contemporary Women's Poetry* (London: Routledge, 1991). Also notable here is Susan Gubar's "Sapphistries," *Signs* 10 (1984), which discusses the significance of Sappho to modernists as "an attempt to solve the problem of poetic isolation and imputed inferiority" (45). Shari Benstock's impressive *Women of the Left Bank: Paris, 1900–1940* (Austin: University of Texas Press, 1986) registers the importance of lesbian sexuality to the period; her essay "Expatriate Sapphic Modernism: Entering Literary History" in *Lesbian Texts and Contexts,* ed. Karla Jay and Joanne Glasgow (New York: New York University Press, 1990) specifically addresses orientation. Also excellent for providing contextualization for the numerous relations between women, Andrea Weiss's recent *Paris Was a Woman: Portraits from the Left Bank* (New York: HarperCollins, 1996) is a photo-documentary that vividly establishes the centrality of homoeroticism and lesbian affiliations for modernism. Since both Benstock and Weiss are interested primarily in European and expatriate writers, Lowell is once again left out.

12. Zimmerman, "Lesbians Like This and That," 4, 8, 9. The problems, nevertheless, of definition and categories remain and are not confined to notions of the canon. Zimmerman responded a decade later to her own essay "What Has Never Been" (1981). Now taking into account the "influence of poststructuralist theories" on lesbian criticism, she distinguishes "the 1970's notion of lesbianism as a variation—perhaps a privileged variation—of female experience or identity" (2) from the current emphasis on social construction in gay and lesbian studies; she cogently summarizes: "The primary strategies of the recent past, therefore, have involved the deconstruction of the lesbian as a unified, essentialist, ontological being and the reconstruction of the lesbian as metaphor and/or subject position" (3).

13. In the scope of this essay, I cannot hope to cover these diverse constructions; we must, however, think of modernisms. See Astradur Eysteinsson, *The Concept of Modernism* (Ithaca: Cornell University Press, 1990), who writes: "There is rapidly spreading agreement that 'modernism' is a legitimate concept broadly signifying a 'paradigmatic shift,' a major revolt, beginning in the mid- and late nineteenth century, against the prevalent literary and aesthetic traditions of the Western world. But this is as far as we can assume a critical and theoretical consensus to go." He points to the "making of various, often conflicting, modernist paradigms" (3). In their introduction to an anthology titled *The Modern Tradition: Backgrounds of Modern Literature* (New York: Oxford University Press, 1965), Richard Ellmann and Charles Feidelson Jr. are tentative in asserting their purpose: "Assuming that there is a 'modern tradition' and that the phrase conveys something of the ambiguous essence of modernity, this book sets out to describe

the modern movement with as much of its real complexity, and with as much depth in time and intellectual breadth, as are possible within a single volume" (vii). Published in 1965, the statement already reveals a grappling with the term "modern," a grappling that has become characteristic of constructions of modernity. In spite of their professed dedication to "complexity," these editors establish and reinforce a familiar version of canonical tradition, including only minimal entries from the work of three women: Virginia Woolf, George Sand, and George Eliot. If not Lowell or H.D., where is Stein, we might urgently demand. First published in 1976 and then reprinted in 1991, *Modernism: A Guide to European Literature, 1890–1930*, ed. M. Bradbury and James McFarlane (London: Penguin, 1991) presents itself as a "textbook on international modernism"; even with its purported "plurality," very few women modernists are mentioned (11). One very telling instance appears in the entry by Alan Bullock, "The Doubled Image," where he invokes the usual pantheon of writers—Yeats, Pound, Joyce, Eliot—and includes "those two middlemen—Wyndham Lewis and Gertrude Stein" (65). The gendering of modernism as masculine seems inescapable.

14. T. S. Eliot, "Tradition and Individual Talent" (1920) in *The Sacred Wood: Essays on Poetry and Criticism* (London: Methuen, 1983), 49.

15. Scott, *Gender of Modernism*, 4, 2.

16. Harold Bloom's *The Western Canon: The Books and School of the Ages* (New York: Harcourt Brace, 1994) contends that the attempts of feminist and minority groups to open up the canon "are destroying all intellectual and esthetic standards . . . in the name of social justice" (35). "Strength alone can open [the canon] up" (a "strength," as he depicts it, inextricable from a model of masculine privilege) and it "cannot be forced open by our current cheerleaders" (35). Bloom, not surprisingly, does not see fit to include many women writers, and lesbians get an especially poor showing; he refers disparagingly to Rich as "vehement," for instance (33).

17. Cassandra Laity, "H.D. and A. C. Swinburne: Decadence and Sapphic Modernism," in *Lesbian Texts and Contexts*, 218, 220–21.

18. Quoted in Sandra Gilbert and Susan Gubar's *No Man's Land: The Place of the Woman Writer in the Twentieth Century*, vol. 2 (New Haven: Yale University Press, 1989), 169.

19. Gertrude Stein, "Composition as Explanation" in *A Stein Reader*, ed. Ulla E. Dydo (Evanston: Northwestern University Press, 1993), 501.

20. Peter Nicholls, *Modernisms: A Literary Guide* (Berkeley: University of California Press, 1995), 194, 3, 167, 189.

21. Marianne DeKoven, *Rich and Strange: Gender, History, Modernism* (Princeton: Princeton University Press, 1991), 188–89.

22. Jean Gould, *Amy: The World of Amy Lowell and the Imagist Movement* (New York: Dodd, 1975), 65–66.

23. In Gould, *Amy*, 152. As others have suggested that Stein and Toklas reenacted heterosexual roles, it could be argued that Lowell's vision of Ada as indispensable nurse indicates a similar dynamic. But as with the former pair, I think their relationship dis-

mantles conventional gender roles and functions at the core of each poet's modernism. Romantic love expands in flexible interchange, becomes a means of accessing a Sapphic tradition as registered by critics such as Benstock and Gubar.

24. Catherine R. Stimpson, "Gertrice/Altrude: Stein, Toklas, and the Paradox of the Happy Marriage," in *Mothering the Mind: Twelve Studies of Writers and Their Silent Partners*, ed. Ruth Perry and Martine Watson Brownley (New York: Holmes and Meier, 1984).

25. H.D.'s letters are quoted in Scott, *Gender of Modernism*, 136, 134. H.D.'s letter to Lowell, December 17, 1924, tells of "Ezra's plan to prevent publication" and advises renaming the anthology *The Six*.

26. Louis Untermeyer, Introduction to *The Complete Poetical Works of Amy Lowell*, xxviii.

27. "Polyphonic verse" was a term Lowell introduced to describe the linking together of apparent prose pieces written in cadenced rhythm, and as Jeanne Larsen describes it, "the intense interweaving of vowels, consonants, and accentual patterns that [she] liked to compare to the many voices of an orchestra (*Columbia History of American Poetry*, 208) — this aspect of Lowell's work has yet to be explored. Lowell also asserts (of the prose aspect of her polyphonic poems) in her preface to *Some Imagist Poets* (Boston: Houghton Mifflin, 1915) that "the fact is, that there is no hard and fast dividing line between prose and poetry" (xii).

28. Elizabeth Grosz, "Refiguring Lesbian Desire," in *The Lesbian Postmodern*, ed. Laura Doan (New York: Columbia University Press, 1994), 74, 70, 75.

29. Susan Stanford Friedman, *Penelope's Web: Gender, Modernity, H.D.'s Fiction* (Cambridge, Eng., Cambridge University Press, 1990), 14, 48.

30. "Mid-day" first appears in *Sea Garden* (1916). My quotations are taken from H.D. *Collected Poems, 1912–1944*, ed. Louis Martz (New York: New Directions, 1983), 10. All other poetry citations to this volume will be noted as *CP*.

31. A useful comparison can be made with Lowell's "Patterns," a poem that also invokes the garden as trope for restrictive patterns of poetry and sexuality.

32. This poem was not only published in *The Egoist* (name changed from the *Freewoman*) but also in Lowell's *Some Imagist Poets* (1917).

33. Gertrude Stein, *The Autobiography of Alice B. Toklas* (New York: Random House, 1933), 119.

34. Gertrude Stein, *Tender Buttons* (rpt. Los Angeles: Sun and Moon Press, 1914), 12. Subsequent references will be cited in the text as *TB*.

35. Lowell's polyphonic pieces, in their discontinuous narrative structures, their unusual juxtapositions, and recurrences especially reveal her evasions of the image in itself. Her rendering of wartime ennui, for instance, in "The Dinner-Party" is divided into six unparallel sections, only spectrally organized: "Fish," "Game," "Drawing-Room," "Coffee," "Talk," "Eleven O'Clock" (MWG 147); in the poem's refusal to treat objects directly, it microcosmically resembles the more expansive *Tender Buttons*, Stein's revolutionary composition that defamiliarizes conventional categories of apprehending ex-

perience. Though not as engaged in linguistic play as incessantly as Stein, she nevertheless dislocates ready perceptions and leaves volatile blanks in signification. "Coffee," for instance, abandons any "object" in order to express her experience of rejection:

> They sat in a circle with their coffee-cups.
> One dropped in a lump of sugar,
> One stirred with a spoon.
> I saw them as a circle of ghosts,
> Sipping blackness out of beautiful china,
> And mildly protesting against my coarseness
> In being alive.

Lowell registers herself as "coarse" because she is an embodied, desiring subject, and in particular, because she is also a lesbian one. While her poems to Ada are sensuously rich, her work is laced with the self-deprecation associated with the outlaw: in her "Miscast," for instance she becomes "shut up, with broken crockery, / In a dark closet!" (SBPS 42).

36. Nicholls, *Modernisms*, 202–3, 207–8.

37. Gould points to numerous almost uncanny parallels in the lives of Lowell and Stein, even though they never met and disapproved of each other's work; she conjectures that "these two opposing regal personages of the hour were too much alike ever to accept each other" (191–95); she also suggests that what Stein did for poets across the continent by providing them a salon and support system, Lowell did for artists "at home," including D. H. Lawrence and Robert Frost (195).

38. Gertrude Stein, *A Stein Reader*, 303.

39. Stein, "Ada," ibid., 102–3.

40. *The Poems and Fragments of Sappho*, ed. Jim Powell (New York: Farrar, Straus and Giroux, 1993), 25.

41. Susan Stanford Friedman in *Penelope's Web* invokes the trope of Penelope to describe H.D.'s "unweaving" and "(re)weaving" in novels such as *Hermione*: "Gendering modernism—reading gender in modernism—needs to weave together these different strands of how it was (en)gendered. The tendency in male modernism to fix women in the silent space of the feminine meant that many female modernists had to release themselves from this linguistic trap as the (pre)condition of their speech" (3). Repetition belongs to this "reweaving" or reconstruction of modernism simultaneous with the necessary breaking away from the "silent space of the feminine."

42. Gertrude Stein, *Selected Writings*, ed. Carl Van Vechten (New York: Vintage Books, 1962), 232.

43. *The Yale Gertrude Stein*, ed. Richard Kostelanetz (New Haven: Yale University Press, 1980), 238–39.

44. Gertrude Stein, "Composition as Explanation," in *A Stein Reader*, 499.

45. Ibid., 496.

BLACK WOMEN WRITERS OF THE HARLEM RENAISSANCE

Crystal J. Lucky

My commitment to the study of African American women writers of the Harlem Renaissance began more than ten years ago when I was formally introduced to the period in a graduate seminar. The course readings were taken, in part, from what has become the seminal text of the period, Alain Locke's *The New Negro*. In 1925, Locke included the contributions of eight women fiction writers and essayists to support his New Negro polemic; the collection, however, contained a total of thirty-six contributors.[1] I was troubled that Locke chose to include so few women, which led me to question whether there were other New Negro women publishing in other venues, and if so, why so few of these black women's works are currently taught in university literature courses or offered to the general reading public.[2]

Since then, much of the significant work published on the Harlem Renaissance has refocused critical attention on the black women artists whose works have previously been excluded from the study of the period. From Daphne Duval Harrison's study of black women blues singers to Maureen Honey's anthology of black women poets to Cheryl Wall's study of Harlem Renaissance women writers, contemporary scholars have begun to consider how differently the period looks if the artistic contributions of black women are shifted from the margins to the center of a revisionist examination.[3] The reclaiming of these women's works provides interested scholars and educators a virtually untapped arsenal of poetry and short fiction; yet more work remains to be done. The exclusion of women from mainstream vehicles relegated their works to even more marginalized journals and poorly distributed publications. Accordingly, their works have not been consistently included in later considerations of the period or courses in African American and Euro-American literature. Thus most students of literature remain unexposed to the full range of black women's writings, perpetuating the further truncation of an African American literary ancestry.

The focus of this essay is two-tiered. Primarily, I wish to consider the pedagogical changes such a reclamation affords African American literary study, thereby joining my voice with those who through their recovery work have called for a reevaluation of the Harlem Renaissance with respect to gender in terms of who was involved in it, when, and where the movement occurred.[4] Excellent scholarship now exists noting how periodization and geography shift when black women writers are considered.[5] And whereas the beginning and ending dates for the period have heretofore been confined to the 1920s, scholars have lately become liberal enough in their conceptualization to include the 1930s, often continuing into the 1940s.[6] Yet the work of incorporating the newly discovered women's texts into the structure of the American classroom remains to be tackled adequately given the abbreviated list of black women regularly included on Harlem Renaissance course syllabi. To that end, as the second focus of this essay, I wish to present one model for teaching the lives and works of these lesser-known women writers by offering representative unrecognized writers alongside familiar black women writers of the period.

The juxtaposition of traditional Harlem Renaissance artists and texts with those less recognized sheds new light on the period. Likewise, it resists privileging a canon of black male and female artists whose works are repeatedly admitted to the exclusion of many others. It also provides a context within which to ask and to begin to answer the question, Where have all the women gone? At first glance, one might assume that only a small number of women were publishing their work in Harlem and other major metropolises; however, constant resurfacing of black women's writing of that period indicates otherwise. Initially, one might point to the obvious problem of plain sexism. It is interesting, for example, to observe how someone like Charles S. Johnson, editor of *Opportunity* magazine, noted his contributors. During the early 1920s, Johnson provided brief, individual personal and professional sketches for each of his male contributors toward the end of each issue, but he tended to group all the women writers together with a "thanks." Or taken a step further, the answer might emanate from the cultural context out of which the Renaissance materialized. The close group of male and female writers, in particular, associated with the major intellectual figures of the time created an intimate artistic inner circle. Women (and men) writing and attempting to publish outside of that clique would certainly have had a difficult time getting their work recognized. As materials resurface, it is owing to the tireless efforts of scholars willing to scour the pages of *Challenge, Crisis, Fire!!, Harlem,* and *Opportunity* magazines to recelebrate prize-winning stories, buried essays, and forgotten writers and to reintegrate the work into our literary imagination.

A call for the revamping of reading lists and course curricula necessitates a discussion concerning the formation of African American literary canons. Critic Paul Lauter argues the problem eloquently: "Obviously, no conclave of cultural cardinals establishes a literary canon, but for all that it exercises substantial influence. For it encodes a set of social norms and values; and these, by virtue of its cultural standing, it helps endow with force and continuity. Thus, although we cannot ascribe to a literary canon the decline in attention to the concerns of [white] women [and blacks] in the 1920s, the progressive exclusion of literary works by [white] women [and blacks] from the canon suggested that such concerns were of lesser value than those inscribed in canonical books and authors. The literary canon is, in short, a means by which culture validates social power."[7] Scholars of American literature are increasingly emphasizing the reevaluation of an exclusory and racialist American literary canon. The canon's ability to reinscribe particular social values and assumptions necessarily demands that those concerned with canon revision consider the foundations of its construction. My revisional and inclusive efforts focus primarily on the specific problems of literary pedagogy and textual realignment, particularly with respect to the teaching of African American women's literature in the twenty-first century. In fact, many of the concerns faced twenty years ago by literary scholars attempting to collect and recover the work of black women writers remain at the forefront of this work. In the early 1970s, when both the late Toni Cade Bambara and Mary Helen Washington were editing the first contemporary anthologies of black women's writings, they did so to confront the rampant development of stereotypes about black women in this country as depicted in print and television media, film, and various forms of advertising.[8] Washington, in particular, was concerned that women such as Toni Morrison, Nella Larsen, Zora Neale Hurston, Gwendolyn Brooks, Dorothy West, Ann Petry, Paule Marshall, and Alice Walker were not being taught in college-level American literature courses. Fortunately, many of these women's works are now regular components of course syllabi, but the process remains unfinished.

What is particularly helpful for me about Washington's project is that she articulated in 1975 the attraction to literary recovery I would feel more than twenty years later. Why is literary recovery necessary? "Because so many countless generations of men and women have been deprived of the insight and sensitivity of these writers."[9] A widening of the proverbial literary canon allows for a greater diversity of literature to be taught, deliberated, and written about. Such admittance of diversity is extremely important because so often discussion of literary texts is intimately interwoven with political and economic agendas and human values. Students' partially developed moral values and political orientations are more fully developed and set in the high school and college classrooms. They must be encouraged to confront the lifestyles, social practices, culture, and history of traditionally marginalized groups in the United States since, for the most part, the extremely closed and exclusory nature of the classic American literary canon treats marginal groups as if they simply do not exist.

The problem for many educators is not their unwillingness to teach a broader range of materials; desire fails to translate into practice because of the inaccessibility of heretofore uncollected texts. Three current collections are excellent repositories of Harlem Renaissance black women's writing, making the task of teaching marginalized material less difficult. Marcy Knopf has collected twenty-seven short stories in *The Sleeper Wakes*, titled after Jessie Redmon Fauset's story of the same title. In addition to the stories of well-known writers like Fauset, Dorothy West, and Georgia Douglas Johnson, Knopf has included the work of Maude Irwin Owens, Leila Amos Pendleton, Anita Scott Coleman, Ottie Beatrice Graham, and Eloise Bibb Thompson. *Shadowed Dreams: Women's Poetry of the Harlem Renaissance* (1989), edited by Maureen Honey, has arranged the verse of over thirty women writers of the 1920s and 1930s under four themes: Protest, Heritage, Love and Passion, and Nature. And *Harlem's Glory: Black Women Writing, 1900–1950* (1996), edited by Lorraine Elena Roses and Ruth Elizabeth Randolph, includes the writings—in all genres—of more than fifty women writers of the Renaissance and beyond. Each of the book's ten parts, for example, "Native Daughter," "Harlem's Glory: A Woman's View," and "The Offering," begins with an explanation of the rubric under which the pieces are set. For me, what is important is the existence of these collections, for they—in the words of two of the editors—"signal the diversity and complexity of the black women writers who preceded today's more celebrated figures. Taken together, the pieces—some quite sophisticated, others rough-hewn—allow us to repossess a sensibility we were not even aware of before.... The writings hold meaning for us today insofar as they articulate, in another voice, a gendered voice, many issues that recur now in other guises and continue to elude resolution."[10] Moreover, it is still the case, as Washington has argued in another context, that "we should be about the business of reading, absorbing, and giving critical attention to those writers whose understanding of the black woman can take us further."[11] To that end, I would like to turn to a few of the exemplary artists to whom this essay is dedicated by introducing their lives and works.

Since the publication of Alain Locke's compilation of essays, short fiction, poetry, and drama, the anthology has remained of interest to scholars and students of the period. The collection's objective, as set forth in the title essay, heralds a new day for post-Reconstruction black Americans. Locke, as a professor of history at Howard University in Washington, D.C., was one of the chief architects of this intellectual, artistic, and political movement made up of young black American artists and thinkers. What was required, according to Locke, was that "the Negro of to-day be seen through other than the dusty spectacles of past controversy. The day of 'aunties,' 'uncles' and 'mammies' is equally gone. Uncle Tom and Sambo have passed on, and even the 'Colonel' and 'George' play barnstorm rôles from which they escape with relief when the public spotlight is off. The popular melodrama has about played itself out, and it is time to scrap the fictions, garret the bogeys and settle down to a realistic facing of facts."[12] As Locke envisioned it, the next logical step for black America to take was toward the acquisition of full American citizenship, which would be accomplished through production of art and literature. His description of this New Negro goes on to submit that "the Negro to-day is inevitably moving forward under the control largely of *his* own objectives. What are these objectives? Those of *his* outer life are happily already well and finally formulated, for they are none other than the ideals of American institutions and democracy. Those of *his* inner life are yet in process of formation, for the new psychology at present is more of a consensus of feeling than of opinion, of attitude rather than of program. Still some points seem to have crystallized."[13] As he describes him, Locke's New Negro is male, forward-moving, in control of his own objectives, integrationist yet race-conscious, and in possession of a new sense of spirituality and creativity. He is acutely aware of his divided self, one part Negro, one part American, and is determined that if the "more intelligent and representative elements of the two race groups" get in "vital touch with one another," surely those in power will concede that the historically oppressed are worthy of tasting American democracy.[14] This New Negro stands in stark contrast to the *old* Negro, a savage member of a dark, segregated ghetto, in effect, a naïve child.

This New Negro also stands in stark contrast to other viable and equally noteworthy models of blackness for both men and women during those early decades of the twentieth century; yet, throughout the century, what has survived as the paradigm for how to study the period most often is the one that stems from the talented tenth theory adhered to by more conservative intellectuals like Locke, Howard University dean Kelly Miller, novelist, editor, and linguist Jessie Redmon Fauset, and W. E. B. Du Bois.[15] This integrationist and aesthetic-based ideology has provided a backdrop against which to read primarily those fiction and nonfiction writers included in *The New Negro* and to interpret narrowly the political activities of the time. For example, the New Negro A. Philip Randolph conceived of bears little resemblance to Locke's, although it was Randolph who first coined the phrase in the years preceding and during World War I. As a staunch socialist and political activist, the "Harlem Radical" was unencumbered by the demands of a white patron—unlike many of the Harlem Renaissance notables—academic restrictions, or elitist motives. Rather than concern himself with the desires and preferences of white Americans, Randolph outlined his agenda quite narrowly in the *Messenger*, the magazine he coedited with Chandler Owen for eleven years—that blacks should focus on their acquisition of full enfranchisement, the overturning of Jim Crowism, and the problem of lynching.

Equally, little is mentioned in courses of the period about the essays of Marcus Garvey and his Universal Negro Improvement Association (UNIA) or the thoughts and contributions of his second wife, Amy Euphemia Jacques-Garvey. Usually, we are left with Elise Johnson McDougald's description of the New Negro woman in "The Task of Negro Womanhood," also included in Locke's anthology. The essay chronicles the brief professional history of black women since Reconstruction and simultaneously laments white society's failure to recognize the multiplicity of black women's arduous difficulties: the twofold quandary of being sexually and racially discriminated against; social, familial, and economic oppression; and their portrayal in society as having low morals and values. In its celebration of the achievements of black women as academic, health care, and industry professionals, McDougald's essay is quite different from the work of Amy Jacques-Garvey, which contested notions of a supposed talented tenth and acted as a clarion call to black women to join the ranks of what had been traditionally considered men's work.

The daughter of well-educated parents, Amy Jacques emigrated to the United States from Jamaica in 1917 and became affiliated a year later with Marcus Garvey's UNIA, the grassroots, Pan-Africanist organization that was characterized by resistance to white supremacy, diasporic pride, and colorful and rousing parades through Harlem's neighborhoods. Jacques-Garvey began her tenure with the UNIA by serving as Garvey's private secretary; the two married in 1922. During her years in the United States, Jacques-Garvey served as the editor of the woman's page of the UNIA's weekly newspaper and was outspoken about her belief that women should be politically active in their communities. During her husband's incarceration for alleged mail fraud, she worked tirelessly on behalf of the UNIA and her husband to secure his freedom. After Garvey's deportation to their native Jamaica in 1927, the Garveys continued the work of the UNIA until the movement dissolved. As the organization's archivist and because of her intense commitment to her husband's beliefs, Jacques-Garvey kept fastidious records, enabling her to publish a collection of his essays and speeches,

The Philosophy and Opinions of Marcus Garvey, or, Africa for the Africans in two volumes. Originally published in 1923 in New York City, the collection included many of Garvey's epigrams, essays, and two of his "best speeches." Before her death in 1973, Jacques-Garvey also published *Garvey and Garveyism*—her own treatment of her husband's work and philosophy—and *Black Power in America*.[16] She maintained her bitterness toward mainline New Negro intellectuals even thirty years after the movement's demise. In a letter to historian Jervis Anderson, Jacques-Garvey described the New Negro intellectuals of the 1920s and 1930s as a "self-opinionated, isolationist minded set who felt that 'integration'—miscegenation—was an easy way out as a solution to the 'Negro problem.'"[17]

The inclusion of alternative perspectives does not suggest that the solution to this problem of cultural astigmatism is to disregard the classic collection completely. If we recur to the eight women originally included in Locke's project, we find that at least four—Hurston, Johnson, Fauset, and Gwendolyn Bennett—have maintained their critical prominence. One method for introducing the lesser-known writers is to do so alongside these and others of their stellar sisters. One example is Beatrice M. Murphy.

> Tis not the parting
> That means so much.
> Ah! No!—
> It is the frequent
> After meetings
> That carry
> The deeper sting.
>
> When your eyes meet mine
> (Those eyes once full of love)
> In a chilling stare—
> When your lips say
> A curt "good day"
> (Those lips that once clung to mine)—
> When your arms
> (That held me once in such a tight
> embrace)
> Are raised now
> Only to tip your hat
> Or for formal handshakes—
> When we meet again

At the old trysting places
Among the old
Familiar scenes
And cannot recall
Even by a glance
The sweet memories
That flock about us
As bees about honey—

Ah! these! These
Hold the deeper sting![18]

I stumbled on Beatrice M. Murphy's poem "The Parting" in the May 1928 issue of *Crisis* magazine and later discovered that she had been the editor of two books of poetry—*An Anthology of Contemporary Verse: Negro Voices* (1938) and *Ebony Rhythm: An Anthology of Contemporary Negro Verse* (1941). Murphy serves as an excellent example of the contributions we miss by focusing exclusively on Harlem during the 1920s and 1930s. Born in Pennsylvania, Murphy spent most of her life in Washington, D.C., where she received her education. In addition to serving as the secretary to the head of the sociology department at Catholic University in Washington, D.C., Murphy was also part-owner and operator of a circulating library and public stenography shop. As a poet, journalist, librarian, and stenographer, Murphy's career led her to publish in several newspapers—including the *Baltimore Afro-American* and the *Washington Tribune*—journals, and anthologies.[19] Although little is known of Murphy's life, one cannot help but wonder whether the poet struggled for a period with the dissolution of an important personal relationship, for much of her poetry published toward the end of the 1920s and beginning of the 1930s expresses intense emotion. "The Parting" focuses on the pain that the speaker experiences at the ending of a love affair. It is not the parting of the two lovers that pains the speaker, however, but the subsequent meetings, polite and formal encounters, and remembrances of the past in a dismal present that disturb the woman most. She expends a great deal of energy reliving the pleasantries of the failed relationship with full knowledge that reconciliation is not an option.

Although no source links the two poets, it is reasonable to imagine that Murphy would have had artistic and perhaps personal interaction with poet, playwright, and novelist Georgia Douglas Johnson. Her contributions to the New Negro movement included not only her work but her Washington, D.C., home, which she opened as a literary salon to both budding and experienced writers. Reared and married in Atlanta, Georgia, Johnson moved with her husband to

Washington, D.C., in 1910. In 1916, three of her poems were published in *Crisis*, and two years later, her first book of poetry, *The Heart of a Woman*, appeared in print. The themes of Johnson's poetry vary between love and racial protest, for which she was often criticized by Renaissance leaders, but it is her exploration of women in love relationships that most solidly links Murphy to her.[20] An example is Johnson's "I Want to Die While You Love Me" from her third collection, published in 1928, *An Autumn Love Cycle*, and Murphy's poem "Hatred."[21]

> My hatred for you is a beautiful thing
> Made up on songs you would not let me sing,
> It's tended in anguish and grows in pain.
> Your taunts were its sunshine; your scorn its rain.
> When you gleefully hurled at me jibes and jeers,
> I watered this plant with my falling tears.
> Rooted in bitterness and pruned with care,
> It grew very fast; and oh, how fair!
>
> My hatred for you is a healthy thing.
> It thrives in winter as well as in spring.
> Sweet as the opening flowers in May;
> Perfect and lovely in every way;
> Strong as the love that once was your due,
> Nurtured with pride is my hatred for you!

Using a lyrical a-a-b-b-c-c rhyme scheme, the speaker in "Hatred" describes her loathing for a lost love in terms of beauty: songs, sunshine, foliage, winter, and spring. Apparently, all of the elements of life that she has been unable to experience in the stifling relationship are realized in the transformation of her hatred for the individual. Hatred, a consuming, bitter, and often destructive emotion, is turned into a channeling of positive energy that manifests itself in the singing of songs, sunshine, rain, and new growth. The object of her scorn has suppressed her voice in the past, but her hatred motivates her to sing. The speaker has experienced great pain from taunts, jibes, and jeers, but she has directed her focus toward the nurture and care of some lovely growth. And so, though hatred might have been destructive for the speaker, through great fervor and passion, she moves from the past toward the promise of a healthy future. Likewise, the lines of the first stanza of Johnson's poem, "I want to die while you love me, / While yet you hold me fair, / While laughter lies upon my lips, / And lights are in my hair," places side by side love and death, pleasure and pain, nurture and destruction. For the speaker in Johnson's poem, death is romanticized in the prospect of preserving utter and complete happiness—"I want to die while you love me, / And never, never see, / The glory of this perfect day, / Grow dim or cease to be!"

Two other writers whose works are new to a study of the Renaissance are Anita Scott Coleman and Ottie Beatrice Graham. Coleman writes that she "was born . . . in our neighboring country, Mexico, State of Sonora, City of Guaymas. Education—ordinary, though it culminated in the profession of teaching. I did teach—long enough to consider it the most interesting work I've ever done. . . . And then I married."[22] She was born in 1890 to a Cuban man who had purchased her black slave mother, and she attended school in Silver City, New Mexico. After marrying, Coleman and her husband settled in Los Angeles, California. She is another writer we miss by focusing exclusively on Harlem. Her work as a poet, short-story writer, and essayist led her to publish in several journals—including *Crisis, Opportunity, Half Century,* and the *Messenger*—anthologies, and two books of her own poetry—*Reason for Singing* (1948) and *The Singing Bells* (1961). Her short story "Three Dogs and a Rabbit" won her third prize in a *Crisis* literary contest.

The story, a reinvention of a familiar African American tale of slavery, pursuit, and miscegenation, is told by first-person narrator Timothy Phipps, whose voice gives way to that of the "loveliest woman" Phipps has ever known. The reader learns abruptly at the end of the well-crafted and detail-laden story that this woman has saved him from the pursuit of police officers and is subsequently brought to trial for aiding and abetting a criminal. Phipps begins by confessing, quite erroneously and perhaps facetiously, that the story he is about to relate "isn't much of a story" and that he "isn't much of a talker or a writer." Yet it is the nontalker and nonwriter who declares that "there is no joy in life so satisfying, so joyous, as that of having our belief strengthened—to watch iridescent bubbles—our castles in the air—settle, unbroken upon firm old earth. To hear our doubts go singing through the chimneys of oblivion. Ah, that's joy indeed. And it is what I experienced that never-to-be forgotten day in the dinkiest courtroom in the world." Contrary to Phipps's confession, we are presented with a sophisticated discussion about the beauty of women, the process of writing and storytelling, and the elements necessary for a good story. Coleman's characters speak with tenderness and sentimentality, but her task is focused, to relay to her readers the brutal and lasting effects of black chattel slavery.

In her engaging testimony concerning her harboring of the fugitive, the old woman, who, despite her Negroid features, was improbably "anything other than a white American," relates an earlier experience involving three of her master's hunting dogs in pursuit of the family's would-be dinner.

What a din they made yelping, yip, yap, yap and Master halooing and urging them to the race. The frightened rabbit ran like the wind, a living atom with the speed of a flying arrow. Straight as a shooting star, it sped: until turning suddenly it began bounding back along the way it had come. The ruse worked. The dogs sped past, hot on his trail of the dodging rabbit, many paces forward before they were able to stop short and pick up the scent once more. And the rabbit ran, oh, how he ran tumbling, darting, swirling down the hillside, terror-mad, fright-blind, on he came, the dogs on his trail once more, bounding length over length behind him. One last frantic dash, one desperate leap and the rabbit plunged into my lap. I covered the tiny trembling creature with my hands, just in time, before the great hounds sprang towards me. With great effort I kept them off and managed to conceal my captive in the large old-fashioned pocket of my wide skirt.[23]

Her hungry master, disgusted by the dogs' failure to capture the rabbit, questions her as to the creature's whereabouts. When the young slave girl replies that she does not know where the rabbit has fled, the master beats her. It is the invocation of this scene, that of the frightened, trapped "terror-mad" animal, that prompts the woman to protect Phipps on the afternoon of his flight and thereby forces her to reveal her own black identity. Coleman, like Graham to follow, writes specifically with a New Negro sensibility. On the one hand, she considers the problematics of early-twentieth-century racism through the lens of nineteenth-century slavery. On the other, she ponders the New Negro's desire to partake freely of her rights as an American citizen, in this instance by way of the phenomenon of miscegenation and subsequent passing.

Ottie Beatrice Graham, perhaps the youngest addition to the group, was born in 1900 and educated at both Howard and Columbia Universities. She contributed short stories and a play to both *Crisis* and *Opportunity* magazines and won a literary contest offered by the Delta Omega Chapter of the Alpha Kappa Alpha Sorority in 1923 for her story "To a Wild Rose." Graham demonstrates her ability to create effectively by drawing on both the European and African American literary and cultural traditions. "To a Wild Rose," the tale of an old man thinking back on his days of slavery, is written almost totally in dialect. She works with ideas of African ancestry as it is spoiled through miscegenation in "To a Wild Rose," while she struggles with the harmful effects of racism on the psyche and creativity in her later story, "Slackened Caprice."[24]

"Slackened Caprice," my favorite of the two, tells the story of a young, unnamed woman, traveling through the South with her friend Carlotta. On their way home, presumably back to some northern city, the two women stop to visit a friend of Carlotta's and her eccentric son. "Too old to be young and too young to be even middle-aged," the son is an accomplished pianist who performs an intriguing Caprice for the two women. The son attempts to perform the piece, which has several passages with "something of Grieg wonder in them," but is repeatedly interrupted by household disturbances. Once he does progress further, he is unable to advance beyond a disturbing crash in the music, "high in treble, like a quick, shrill scream." The son's performance leaves him physically altered after each effort.

After one such unfinished attempt, the woman reveals that her son, a veteran of World War I, has returned home to her "a wreck from gas. His nerves were almost gone, and sometimes his head was wrong; but he began to get back to normal after a while." With the help of his music and the composing of the Caprice, the son continues to improve until "one little incident ruined everything." The woman tells the two northern travelers how she and her son witnessed a disturbing scene involving a group of black children playing happily in a public park. As mother and son begin to move away, a "big, burly white man, a watchman or keeper or something" tells the children that they cannot stay there: "No niggers in there." The effect on the war-torn son is disastrous, manifesting itself in his inability to complete the performance of the musical composition until one day he forces himself to do so, causing his own death. The story, which in one way celebrates the access that socially disfranchised black Americans have to a European cultural tradition by way of their inalienable rights as Americans, is a fascinating study of race that examines the beautiful and idyllic South as the seat of violent racism that silences and suffocates aesthetic sensibilities and artistic achievements.

Both Coleman and Graham fit into a dyadic black women's literary tradition of the Harlem Renaissance which is epitomized by Zora Neale Hurston, on the one hand, and both Jessie Redmon Fauset and Nella Larsen, on the other. The one is firmly rooted in African American folk ways and myths, while the other more readily explores the possibilities of combining European and African forms and themes. "Slackened Caprice," in particular, lends itself to a reading of Nella Larsen's *Quicksand*, for her novel interrogates the problematics of the New Negro's return to the southern landscape after experiencing northern and European modernity. Contemporary readers are familiar with Helga Crane and her search for an elusive racial identity, which leads her south to her demise. Graham's eccentric young man of "Slackened Caprice," though positioned in the South during the story, has experienced the racial contradictions of both Europe and America but has chosen to use his southern locale as a way of attempting emotional, racial, and aesthetic reconciliation. The results for both protagonists are devastating.

One final word. Presumably, widening the canon with the inclusion of a greater diversity of texts and subsequent candid, informed discussion will further address the issues of African American literature which focus on more than racism, sexism, and classism in this country. The texts include equally important notions of celebration, self-reflection and examination, spirituality, and the development of various inter- and intraracial relationships. Mary Helen Washington speaks to such expansion of issues in the definition of her threefold objective for writing: the destruction of stereotypes about black women, the creation of a larger space in which black women can create, and the portrayal of the movement in literature from past brutalization to future healing and reconciliation.[25]

In my call for expansion of the canon, I am not calling for the formation of an African American canon that furthers an exclusive hierarchy. Let me be clear. I would concur with Cornel West that "the mere addition of Afro-American texts to the present canon without any explicit and persuasive account of how this addition leads us to see the canon anew reveals the worst of academic pluralist ideology. Serious Afro-American literary canon formation cannot take place without a wholesome reconsideration of the canon already in place."[26] I have attempted careful, critical expansion, rather than employing the same exclusionary, restrictive techniques as the original guards of the classic American literary canon. The work of women like Anita Scott Coleman, Mae V. Cowdery, Blanche Taylor Dickinson, Ottie B. Graham, Beatrice Murphy, Mary Effie Lee Newsome, Esther Popel, and Lucy Ariel Williams—to name a few—are only now beginning to gain recognition. It is my hope that these writers will be read and taught in the classroom, allowing fresh interpretations of black women's work of the Harlem Renaissance to enter the existing dialogue. There is beauty in the pieces, which speak to the voluminous needs, interests, joys, and pains of black women. New readings call for widened perspectives and reevaluations, enabling us at the end of the millennium to begin to answer some of the questions posed by black women at its beginning.

NOTES

1. The women include the following: Zora Neale Hurston, Georgia Douglas Johnson, Anne Spencer, Angelina Grimké, Jessie Redmon Fauset, Gwendolyn B. Bennett, Helene Johnson, and Elise Johnson McDougald. See Alain Locke, ed., *The New Negro* (1925; rpt. New York: Atheneum, 1986).

2. An analysis of the major anthologies published during the period reveals similar

gender ratios as those in *The New Negro*. James Weldon Johnson's *Book of American Negro Poetry* (1922) contains the work of seven women out of a total of forty contributors—Alice Dunbar-Nelson, Georgia Douglas Johnson, Jessie Redmon Fauset, Anne Spencer, Gwendolyn B. Bennett, Helene Johnson, and Lucy Ariel Williams. Three years after the publication of *The New Negro*, Countee Cullen published *Caroling Dusk: An Anthology of Verse by Negro Poets*. Cullen's collection included the poetry of thirteen women, along with lesser-known writers Blanche Taylor Dickinson, Clarissa M. Scott Delaney, Gladys May Casely Hayford, Mary Effie Lee Newsome, and Lula Weedon. And in 1929, a white man, Victor Francis Calverton, edited *Anthology of American Negro Literature* and included what he called "six major women poets," plus Nella Larsen and Georgia Douglas Johnson's award-winning folk drama, *Plumes*. In total, *Caroling Dusk* contained the most complete subcollection of black women poets during the 1920s and 1930s before the 1936 publication of Mae V. Cowdery's *We Lift Our Voices, and Other Poems* and Beatrice M. Murphy's 1938 publication, *An Anthology of Contemporary Verse: Negro Voices*. Murphy published the poetry of more than thirty women, most of whom were new, young voices.

3. See the following works on black women's writing during the Harlem Renaissance: Thadious M. Davis, *Nella Larsen, Novelist of the Harlem Renaissance: A Woman's Life Unveiled* (Baton Rouge: Louisiana State University Press, 1994); Joyce Flynn and Joyce Occomy Stricklin, eds., *Frye Street and Environs: The Collected Works of Marita Bonner* (Boston: Beacon Press, 1987); Daphne Duval Harrison, *Black Pearls: Blues Queens of the 1920's* (New Brunswick: Rutgers University Press, 1988); Maureen Honey, ed., *Shadowed Dreams: Women's Poetry of the Harlem Renaissance* (New Brunswick: Rutgers University Press, 1989); Marcy Knopf, ed., *The Sleeper Wakes: Harlem Renaissance Stories by Women* (New Brunswick: Rutgers University Press, 1993); Charles R. Larson, ed., *An Intimation of Things Distant: The Collected Fiction of Nella Larsen* (New York: Anchor Books, 1992); Lorraine Elena Roses and Ruth Elizabeth Randolph, *The Harlem Renaissance and Beyond: Literary Biographies of the 100 Black Women Writers, 1900–1945* (Boston: G. K. Hall, 1989); Roses and Randolph, *Harlem's Glory: Black Women Writing, 1900–1950* (Cambridge, Mass.: Harvard University Press, 1996); and Cheryl A. Wall, *Women of the Harlem Renaissance* (Bloomington: Indiana University Press, 1995).

4. When I first began thinking about this problem of gender and the ways it affects the rendering of literary history, I found a useful and theoretical model to be Joan Scott's *Gender and the Politics of History* (New York: Columbia University Press, 1988). Her critical paradigm later enabled me to take as a given the necessity for a reevaluation of the Harlem Renaissance in terms of gender.

5. A reading of the creative works of black women throughout the United States during that time yields evidence that Americans were experiencing more than a "Harlem" Renaissance but a black American Renaissance with a very visible concentration in Harlem. Midwestern black women, for example, include artists like Marita O. Bonner, who was publishing in Chicago. Dorothy West and Helene Johnson had their beginnings in Boston and contributed to the Boston-based *Saturday Evening Quill*. And the Washing-

ton, D.C., group of artists, which at critical points in the period's development included Georgia Douglas Johnson and Zora Neale Hurston, offered significant and essential contributions to this new aesthetic. See Cheryl Wall's *Women of the Harlem Renaissance*, and for an earlier version of this geographical argument, see Crystal J. Lucky, "The Harlem Renaissance: A Revisionist Approach," in *Focus on Robert Graves and His Contemporaries* 1 (Summer 1991):25–29.

6. This debate is taken up by three scholars, in particular, whose texts have helped to form our present notions of the Harlem Renaissance: Houston A. Baker Jr., *Modernism and the Harlem Renaissance* (Chicago: University of Chicago Press, 1987); Arna Bontemps, *The Harlem Renaissance Remembered* (New York: Dodd, Mead, 1972); and Nathan Huggins, *The Harlem Renaissance* (New York: Oxford University Press, 1971). In *Women of the Harlem Renaissance*, Cheryl Wall generously demarcates the period using the publication of two major texts: James Weldon Johnson's *Book of American Negro Poetry* (1922) and *The Negro Caravan* (1941) edited by Sterling Brown, Arthur P. Davis, and Ulysses Lee. In addition, three widely recognized contemporary anthologies of African American literature do similarly: *The Norton Anthology of African American Literature* (New York: Norton, 1997) outlines the period as 1919 to 1940; *Call and Response* (New York: Houghton Mifflin, 1998) liberally describes the period in terms of the Great Migration, 1915 to 1945; and *The Heath Anthology of American Literature* (New York: Houghton Mifflin, 1998) tracks the period into the 1940s.

7. Paul Lauter, *Canons and Contexts* (New York: Oxford University Press, 1991), 23. The additions in brackets are mine.

8. See Toni Cade Bambara's *The Black Woman: An Anthology* (New York: New American Library, 1970) and Mary Helen Washington's *Black-Eyed Susans: Classic Stories by and About Black Women* (Garden City, N.Y.: Anchor/Doubleday, 1975).

9. Washington, *Black-Eyed*, x.

10. Roses and Randolph, eds., *Harlem's Glory*, 6.

11. Mary Helen Washington, "Black Women Image Makers," *Black World* 23 (August 1974): 11.

12. Locke, *Negro*, 5.

13. Ibid., 10, emphasis added.

14. Ibid., 9.

15. I thank Professor Farah Jasmine Griffin, whose careful reading of drafts of this essay helped me to think more broadly about the New Negro movement and its varied facets.

16. See *The Philosophy and Opinions of Marcus Garvey, or, Africa for the Africans*, Vols. 1 and 2 (Dover, Mass.: Majority Press, 1986) and *Garvey and Garveyism* (New York: Collier Books, 1970). For an examination of the active roles women played in the UNIA, see Barbara Bair, "True Women, Real Men: Gender, Ideology, and Social Roles in the Garvey Movement," in *Gendered Domains: Rethinking Public and Private in Women's History*, ed. Susan Reverby and Dorothy O. Helly (Ithaca: Cornell University Press, 1992) and Darlene Clark Hine, ed., *Black Women in America: An Historical Encyclopedia* (New York: Carlson, 1993).

17. Jervis Anderson, *A. Philip Randolph: A Biographical Portrait* (New York: Harcourt Brace Jovanovich, 1973), 137.

18. Taken from *Crisis*, May 1928.

19. Little is known of these women's lives. What is known is largely the result of the painstaking efforts of librarian and scholar Ann Allen Shockley. The biographical information included on Beatrice Murphy, Anita Scott Coleman, and Ottie Beatrice Graham comes from *Afro-American Women Writers, 1746–1933: An Anthology and Critical Guide*, ed. Shockley (Boston: G. K. Hall, 1988).

20. For a complete discussion of Johnson's life and the complexities of her poetry regarding her lesbianism, see Gloria T. Hull, *Color, Sex and Poetry: Three Women Writers of the Harlem Renaissance* (Bloomington: Indiana University Press, 1987).

21. Taken from Beatrice M. Murphy, *An Anthology of Contemporary Negro Verse: Negro Voices* (New York: Poetry Publisher, 1938).

22. Ibid.

23. Taken from *Crisis*, January 1926.

24. Taken from *Opportunity*, November 1924.

25. Washington, *Black-Eyed*, xii–xiii.

26. Cornel West, "Minority Discourse and the Pitfalls of Canon Formation," in West, *Keeping Faith: Philosophy and Race in America* (New York: Routledge, 1993).

COMPLICATIONS OF FEMINIST AND ETHNIC LITERARY THEORIES IN ASIAN AMERICAN LITERATURE

Shirley Geok-lin Lim

Johnnella Butler notes that Women's Studies scholars in their "task of changing the world . . . are cast with (Black Studies, Asian American Studies, Latino Studies, and American Indian Studies) with whom in many ways we are uneasy." The tensions between Women's Studies and Ethnic Studies, according to Butler, rise from the fact that Women's Studies scholarship, theory, and pedagogy are being radically altered by the scholarship of women of color; that Women's Studies is being asked to be accountable also to race, class, and ethnicity; and that, compared to Ethnic Studies, "Women's Studies is privileged because it is peopled largely by white women who move more freely than men or women of color throughout the academy."[1] Butler's candid account of the contested site within Women's Studies to accommodate the experiences and scholarship of women of color counters the usual attempts to gloss over the unease that she has characterized in Euro-American feminist responses to ethnic scholarship.

Butler's account recognizes the absence of symmetrical, like-minded relations between the two groups, one concerned with gender issues, especially the imbalance of power and the attempt to rectify these historical imbalances between men and women, and the other concerned with analysis of race and ethnicity, specifically the imbalance of power between dominant white groups and people of color, and the attempt to change the unequal sets of relationships. The asymmetrical goals of feminist and ethnic scholars within the same institutional structures have given rise to conflict and hostility.[2] The gender/ethnic split is mirrored, moreover, in *both* communities, among white feminists who, according to some women of color, have been defining feminism in narrow terms privileged by their positions as whites, and among men of color who, "desiring to maintain power over 'their women' at all costs, have been among the most willing reinforcers of the fears and myths about the women's movement, attempting to scare us away from figuring things out for ourselves."[3]

Nevertheless, feminist and ethnic literary discourses, although demonstrating this asymmetry, are often inextricably intertwined. Both practices have led to personally charged readings whose impetus and power relate critically suspect notions such as experience, the subjective, and the local to ideologies undergirding literary evaluation. Feminist and ethnic literary criticisms resist and interrogate the claim that aesthetic criteria form a dominant, autonomous, objective, privileged position.[4] Both are said to lack a specifying theory. Although feminist literary criticism is seen as more sociopolitically driven than literary by critics such as Ellen Messer-Davidow,[5] other critics such as Hazel V. Carby have questioned the value of an essentially black theory and practice of criticism, noting of Henry Louis Gates's ethnic-based theory that "the exposition of uniquely black literary strategies is accomplished as much through the work of Geoffrey Hartman, Harold Bloom, Jacques Lacan and others as it is through the insights of a wide range of African American critics, including Houston Baker, Amiri Imamu Baraka and Sterling Brown."[6] Generally, feminist and ethnic critics oppose hegemonic disciplines. Many have presented themselves as cultural pluralists and revisionists calling attention to, among other things, neglected or omitted texts that, even by established standards, should be admitted into the canon.[7] They operate as interventionists disrupting the totalizing naturalization of white male culture.

These common purposes, however, do not imply that feminist and ethnic criticisms share inherently sympathetic identities or areas of overlap that allow them to synthesize critical orientations. Even when, bound together in a common cause of revising the canon, both feminist and ethnic critics select similar ethnic texts, one cannot assume that they share integral or identical traditions. My essay attempts to unpack textual instances in which ethnic and feminist issues have intersected to analyze how their diverging emphases necessitate an ethnic cultural nuancing of conventional Euro-American feminist positions on gender/power relations and a feminist critique of ethnic-specific identity. In the analysis of ethnic identity, politics, and feminist ideological conjunctions, I argue, first, that much of Asian American literature has been an active site of masculinist views and feminist resistance; and second, that these women's texts are symptomatic of the struggle to refigure the subject between the often oppositional demands of ethnic and gender identity. In addition, I argue that the increased presence of Filipino Americans and the entry of immigrants from recently decolonized Asian countries to the United States after the 1965 revision of the immigration laws, together with the introduction of postcolonial studies into the university, point to a further complication of periodization for Asian American women's writing. Thus postcolonial Asian American women's writing, foregrounding a globalized rather than U.S. domestic historical context, has made provisional earlier attempts at periodizing an Asian American women's literary tradition. The tension, to my mind, is not merely or wholly over the question of who should be read — male or female writers, whose canon is it, anyway? — but over how representation of the subject is negotiated between ethnic and feminist thematics and how a consideration of gender and of other categories such as nation and postcolonialism, in addition to ethnicity, problematizes issues of canon formation and periodization.

The polarities between masculinist and feminist assertions of identity were already in place in the traditional East Asian patriarchal constructions of society.[8] They were further exacerbated by a history of racism (similar histories apply to Chinese, Japanese, South Asian, and Filipino male immigration and delayed or difficult entry for women) that disempowered Asian males and separated them for long periods from women and families, and by the entry of Asian social norms into a differently restrictive American culture.[9] These polarities can be seen as still operative in the debates over Asian American women marrying out and in the debates that occasionally flare up to illuminate the problems of power relations between Asian American men and women.[10]

It was only in the 1970s that the notion of a body of Asian American literature recognizable as a separate canon became common. This literature can be said to represent that paradoxical phenomenon known as a "new tradition." Even as the texts are self-conscious expressions of "a new political consciousness and identity," their commentaries locate them in a "recovered" ethnic history. Texts like Maxine Hong Kingston's *Woman Warrior* and *China Men* are like a slow development of photographs taken years ago; even as their textuality appears for the first time before our eyes, we are reminded that the images were posed in a time already past, that history and textuality form one subject.[11] The commentator observes the coloration of the text as it appears for the first time with a postmodern consciousness of the text's belatedness, an awareness that the images are to be understood in the contexts of a lapidary of discourses on and from the past: memoir, myth, family and community history, folktales, talk-story.[12] This insistence on past narratives, whether as Old World culture and values, immigrant history, race suffering, communal traditions, or earlier other language traces, is a marked feature of much Asian American literature and criticism, just as the recovery of a woman's culture, woman's language, and neglected women's texts and traditions forms a major feature of feminist criticism.[13]

DEFINING THE FIELD

Three publication events mark the increasing acceptance of an Asian American canon: the appearance of three anthologies (*Asian American Authors*, 1972; *Asian-American Heritage: An Anthology of Prose and Poetry*, 1974; *Aiiieeeee!: An Anthology of Asian American Writers*, 1974) in the early 1970s; the first book-length study of the literature, Elaine H. Kim's *Asian American Literature: An Introduction to the Writings and Their Social Context* in 1982; and the 1988 *Asian American Literature: An Annotated Bibliography* edited by King-Kok Cheung and Stan Yogi, which conferred academic legitimacy to the field through its publication by the Modern Language Association Press.[14] These publications relate coherent historiographies of an Asian American literary tradition and of the contesting of that tradition. In doing so, they also provide a grounding for the culture and affect its identity formation for the future.

Like feminist critics, these ethnic-identified critics share the task of identifying and countering stereotypes. Their criticism in the 1970s, exemplified by the influential introduction of *Aiiieeeee!*, was restricted to a critique of stereotypes of the emasculated Asian American male. These critics modeled their thinking on the militant African American antiacademic rhetoric manifested in Ishmael Reed's work.[15] Unfortunately, they also adopted Reed's sexist stance. Ironically, the attack on male stereotypes reiterated and reinforced stereotypes of females. In the *Aiiieeeee!* introduction, the animus against stereotypes appears specially reserved for women writers of Chinese American descent who were accused of collaborating with white supremacists in propagating the stereotypes of the submissive, patriotic, model and "dual-personality" (a psychological term used by sociologists of the 1950s to explain the consequences of biculturality on Japanese Americans) Asian American.[16]

Chinese American women writers were conspicuous for their absence from these anthologies. In the issue of the *Yardbird Reader* (1974), guest-edited by Frank Chin and Shawn Wong, only four women writers are represented: two Japanese American short story writers, Hisaye Yamamoto and Wakako Yamauchi, a Filipina poet, Cyn. Zarco, and a Chinese-German American poet, Mei Berssenbrugge, against eleven men, of whom eight are Chinese Americans. In *Aiiieeeee!*, again only four women writers are included against ten men, and only one of the women was Chinese American, as opposed to five Chinese American male writers. One may be led to conclude from these selections that this ethnic literature up to the 1970s was full of talented male writers and most deficient in women writers. The 1991 *Big Aiiieeeee!*, which despite the title is a completely different anthology from the 1974 work, fails to include any Chinese

American women writers.[17] That the 1974 selection is distorted is evident from the editors' introduction, which is replete with references to Chinese American women scholars and writers whose works are critiqued and denigrated. The 1974 anthology can be said to be superseded by the 1991 work, but its editorial arguments are still significant today because they helped form a generation of opinion on Asian American cultural identity.

Aiiieeeee! set out to be more than a collection of works by writers of Asian descent. The editors asserted an authority as culture makers and namers, authorizing their version of Asian American sensibility. In their introduction, they assailed the assumption of continuity between Asian American culture and Asian culture. The positive valuation of Asian culture undergirding the American perception of the Asian American, they argued, was "a work of racist art" to keep the Asian American estranged from America. This reified representation insists on an identity as Old World Asian, preventing the perception of dynamism, hybridity, New World vitality, and other more interactive qualities that characterize a burgeoning ethnic culture in the United States. Offering black American culture as their model, the editors argued that Asian Americans should "invent" their culture, not passively accept the distortions of high Asian cultural elements that white Americans foist on them. Consequently, they certified as authentic only those writers who exhibited "Asian American," rather than an Asian or Euro-American, sensibility. This sensibility, the editors concluded, was specifically constructed through male-centered language and culture: "Language is the medium of culture and the people's sensibility, including the style of manhood. . . . On the simplest level, a man in any culture speaks for himself. Without a language of his own, he is no longer a man."[18] The assumption, therefore, is that Asian American men who assert "manhood" decide, possess, and exhibit the legitimate cultural national sensibility.

Elaine H. Kim's chapter "Chinatown Cowboys and Warrior Women" in her study *Asian American Literature: An Introduction to the Writings and Their Social Context* provides an early critique of the masculinism evident in the *Aiiieeeee!* introduction. Analyzing Frank Chin's essays and dramas, Kim concludes that his "sexism, cynicism, and sense of alienation (among other factors) have prevented him from creating protagonists who can overcome the devastating effects of racism on Chinese American men."[19] In a later essay, Kim revises her critique to render a more harmonious, less oppositional reading of Asian American writing. Agreeing in part with the *Aiiieeeee!* editors, Kim argues that U.S. race and gender hierarchies have objectified Asian Americans as permanent outsiders and sexual deviants: "Asian men have been coded as having no sexuality, while Asian women have nothing else." While such social realities have resulted in differences between nationalist and feminist concerns, the woman's voice in works such as Kingston's *Tripmaster Monkey*, she asserts, "dissolves binary oppositions of ethnicity and gender."[20]

My own reading of Asian American literature demonstrates less a solution than a continuous negotiation between often conflicting cultural constructions of ethnicity and gender. To my mind, in the years after publication of Kingston's *Woman Warrior* in 1976, Asian American literature has often been the site of conscious and explicit conflict, between women's ideas of culture and cultural nationalism as claimed by some males, preeminently presented in the *Aiiieeeee!* introduction and more curiously elaborated as neo-Confucianist ideology in Frank Chin's essay in *The Big Aiiieeeee!*[21] This gender split was explicitly caused by the intervention of feminist issues and is marked historically in the publication of two anthologies of women's writing in 1989, *The Forbidden Stitch: An Asian American Women's Anthology* and *Making Waves: An Anthology of Writings by and About Asian American Women*. These anthologies, though not directly addressing the masculinist ideology that undergirded the 1970s literary movement, exhibit a difference from the earlier anthologies in their constituting of ethnic subject and culture. Primarily, they are a stage for women who claim, not the minor representation given in the 1970s anthologies, but all of the attention. Men are present in the work, but they often appear as aggressors or ignorant of women's needs: "He beat me with the hem of a kimono"; "Father's belt"; "Men know nothing of sex."[22] Moreover, the works counter stereotypes of Asian American women in Asian and white cultures. *Making Waves* features sociological and historical essays that analyze images of Asian women in the media ("Lotus Blossoms Don't Bleed: Images of Asian Women") and express the dilemma of living biculturally in societies that insist on a hegemonic identity ("Growing up Asian in America").[23]

More significantly, in contrast to the 1970s male critique of the concept of "dual personality," the anthologies foreground the instabilities of identity and represent the oscillating and crisscrossing of national, racial, and subjective borders that characterize the experience of biculturalism: "How is one to know and define oneself? From the inside—within a context that is self defined, from a grounding in community and a connection with culture and history that are comfortably accepted? Or from the outside—in terms of messages received from the media and people who are often ignorant?"[24] Kesaya E. Noda's essay, for example, beginning in "confusions and distortions," resolves itself in its construction of "I am racially Japanese," "I am a Japanese American," "I am a Japanese American woman." This tripartite construction of Asian American identity, affirmatively propositional, counters the 1970s syllogistic construction:

"I am not Asian," "I am not white American," "I am Asian American (male)." The feminist intervention in the evolving tradition of this writing has led to a reclamation of mother/other origin, an affirmation of continuity or relation between origin and present tense, and a new foregrounding of gender identity. Paradoxically, the absence of an attempt to illuminate an Asian American sensibility has resulted in the affirmation of sensibilities marked by softened categories, elastic cultural spaces, and a more global antihegemonic construction of identity.

In contrast to the *Aiiieeeee!* anthology, neither women's anthology attempts to explicate an exclusive boundary of ethnic sensibility. In fact, the selection of works that manifest emotional and physical bonds to a non-American homeland indicates an elastic sense of identity to encompass the past of Asian national identity as well as an American writing in the present. Moreover, no attempt is made to separate the selections into ethnic groups; work by South Asian, Korean, Filipino, Japanese, Chinese, and other Asian American women appear side by side organized thematically or sequentially. Thus, together with an increased diversity of Asian national representations is a decreased emphasis on categorical national difference. The very multiplicity appears to result in a blurring of national boundaries and an assertion of organizational principles through commonalities of experience rather than differences of attributes.

The 1980s selections of Asian American women's writing share with the 1970s anthologies general themes of immigrant concerns and first-generation conflicts, acknowledgment of cultural sources and roots in Asian societies, and thematics of family bond and conflicts. *The Forbidden Stitch* foregrounds new writing that manifests "subjectivity as gendered," inclusive of a "contemporary Asian American culture [that] is not dictated from a central committee."[25] The editors of the 1980s anthologies worked in collectives, as communities of women. The ethnic culture of these anthologies is nonauthoritative, decentered, nondogmatic, unprogrammatic, uncategorizing, inclusive, qualities that some feminist theoreticians such as Carol Gilligan argue characterize female sensibilities.[26]

The editors avoided propositions that constructed universalist notions of Asian American women's experiences. In the introductory essay to *Making Waves*, for example, Sucheta Mazumdar argues that for Asian Americans whose histories of exclusion, isolation, discrimination, exploitation, and internment result in "severe trauma," "ethnic identity supersedes gender and class. For women of color, concerns arising out of racial identity are an integral aspect of their overall identity." Yet many exceptions exist to this general observation. As Mazumdar elaborates: "The impact of gender on Asian women in America varies enormously even within the same class and ethnic group. While the idea that female children are of less value than male children permeates all Asian cultures . . . the effect of this value-system on an American-born woman is quite different than on an immigrant one."

For the Asian-born woman, moving away from a relatively closed patriarchal world into a relatively democratized, egalitarian, interrogative America, immigration can be a liberalizing and freeing experience. Mazumdar cites a national survey of college-educated women from India living in the United States that showed 33.3 percent of the women working in the technical fields and 50 percent in the academic fields describing themselves as feminists.[27] Traditional Asian valuation of authoritarian husbands is frequently subverted by the working woman's growing economic independence and interaction in larger social relations that reflect different, more positive values of the female.

INVENTING NEW PLOTS

For the woman writer whose ethnic community is patriarchal, ethnic and feminist values and identities must inevitably intersect in potentially uneasy, conflicting, or violent ways. In male-centered ethnic societies, the woman usually remains on the margin, invisible, mute, or constrained to limited stereotypical roles of possession, child or mother, domestic worker, or sexual object. Most assertions of female identity or qualities falling outside the subordinate ranks and delineated kinship roles may be read as subversive of male power and, by implication, of one's ethnic community. To be a free woman, such a woman must be at some level a "no name woman," that is, outcast from her ethnic community. Thus in *The Woman Warrior*, the narrator's aunt, a "No name Woman" who carries an illegitimate child, has broken the Chinese patriarchal laws of kinship and descent, has become a non-Chinese, nonhuman, and drowns herself in the well, an act of retribution for breaking the name of the father, the final patriarchal control over all women. In the intersection of race and gender identity, the woman who represents the urgencies of her gender (her sexuality, her maternality) against a race imperative is in a position to be violently erased. But that is in the traditional master plot of ethnic patriarch as villain and ethnic woman as victim.

Rejecting this originary race and gender plot (encompassing female infanticide, clitoridectomy, child brides, dowries, bride burning, catalog brides, enforced purdah, suttee—the archetypal patterns of female oppression and male masterhood),[28] Asian American women have been busy inventing new plots that are complicated by race and class issues. One alternative narrative to the representation of woman as a victim to patriarchy is that of the disempowering of the central male figure in the Asian kinship nexus by a racist and classist white American society. Through the eyes of Asian American daughters, the father's humiliations, losses, and pathetic struggles against white social authority are both indictments against racism (and therefore an assertion of ethnic protest) and evidence of patriarchal impotence (and therefore a stripping away of ethnic core identity). Jeanne Wakatsuki Houston and James Houston's 1974 *Farewell to Manzanar* constructs this double-edged critique of Asian/American cultures in its portrayal of the gradual emasculation of the powerful Papa figure. Because Papa "didn't want to be labeled or grouped by anyone," the daughter has grown up in an all-white neighborhood. Because he had terrified her with the threat, "I'm going to sell you to the Chinaman," she grows up with "this fear of Oriental faces." "Papa had been the patriarch," she tells us explicitly. The internment process changed him to "a man without a country. . . . He was suddenly a man with no rights who looked exactly like the enemy." The Japanese values that supported his patriarchal role have become erased by the internment; he is now "without a country," "the enemy." In the face of the FBI arrest, "all he had left . . . was his tremendous dignity."²⁹

A similar intergenerational conflict between Old World patriarch and American daughter is manifested in Chinese American women's writing. For example, the strict patriarch in Jade Snow Wong's *Fifth Chinese Daughter* (although he escapes the emasculation that the Japanese father suffers in *Farewell to Manzanar*) is compelled finally to change his views on the inferior status of his fifth daughter.³⁰ Wong offers an alternative ethnic/gender plot in which the patriarch retains his position and the daughter represses her female subjectivity so that she can succeed in her ethnic identity as her father's *son*.³¹

These two Asian American daughters' narratives demonstrate that their identities form sites of conflict between the different ideological valuations of the individual, the community, and gender that distinguish Asian cultures from U.S. culture. In the process of countersocialization, from Asian and Confucianist values to Euro-American values, inevitable conflicts occur within each woman simultaneously with external difficulties in her roles as obedient daughter and independent individual and professional. The contradictions between Asian and U.S. (that is, Euro-American) socially inscribed positions for woman and the Asian woman's internal resistance to those cultural elements that seemingly would liberate her from patriarchal constraints are evident in the 1984 novel *Clay Walls*, by a second-generation Korean American woman, Kim Ronyoung.³²

The novel traces the lives of a Korean couple who flee the Japanese imperialists in Korea for a Korean immigrant community in Los Angeles. In the power relation between Chun and Haesu, potentially feminist issues of patriarchal oppression staged in the arranged marriage and of male violence represented in the scenes of marital rape are diffused and dispersed by more pressing representations of the bondage of the male, of female psychosexual punishment of the male, of male frustration, disempowerment, and erasure. *Clay Walls* reminds us that in U.S. culture, the immigrant Asian male, burdened by racial legislation, is more threatened with dysfunction than the Asian woman. The woman, supported by the presence of her children and the social network of her ethnic community, survives. The novel also demonstrates how in U.S. culture, certain values are disabling for Asian males, such as the male's primary identity with the economic function of provider and the construction of masculine pride and stoicism. Yet other Korean cultural values help Haesu survive. The traditional seclusion of women in the home offers her the psychic resources to support her children through piecework sewing, and the traditional value of children gives her an overriding motive for economic struggle.

Clay Walls does not provide a Euro-American–style feminist text. Its focus is on the transformation of individuals caught between ethnic cultures rather than between gender roles. Moving from gender to ethnicity, the perspective inevitably moves from women's "domestic" issues to ethnic social issues. In communities where men appear to be under as much or greater adaptive stress as do women, generally the case for people of color in the United States, the cultural/social perspective also foregrounds men and their struggles in a race- and class-, as well as gender-divided, society.

ASIAN AMERICAN FEMINISM

In the texts discussed, the Asian American female, to pursue her interests in a race-conscious society, has to modify her rejection of patriarchal ethnic identity. Mitsuye Yamada asserts that "being a feminist activist is more dangerous for women of color" and that feminist agendas should be accommodated within an affirmation of ethnic culture: "Asian Pacific women need to affirm our culture while working within to change it."[33] Her position assumes an overlapping of categories that will enable the conventional and stereotypical hostility between ethnic cultures, with elements organized for patriarchal ends, and emerging women's identities, expressed in socially transforming concerns for the rights of women, to be defused, synthesized, or merged into a new sensibility. The construction of gender need not be contingent on the ethnic versions of female roles and experiences, nor need the construction of ethnicity depend on patriarchal constructions of an ethnic group; feminist identity, therefore, should be recoverable inside Asian American culture and history. Yet Kim's *Clay Walls*, Wong's *Fifth Chinese Daughter*, and Jeanne Wakatsuki Houston's career provide a caution against too easily assuming the merger of ethnic and feminist identities.

While Houston's memoir, *Farewell to Manzanar*, demonstrates her resistance to ethnic-identified patriarchy, her 1985 autobiographical essays in *Beyond Manzanar: Views of Asian American Womanhood*, like the narrative of Faye's growing up in *Clay Walls*, erase that earlier resistance and return as if without a memory to the usual constructions of Japanese cultural values that mute women's voices and concerns. In *Beyond Manzanar*, Wakatsuki Houston recuperates her "Japanese roots" by recuperating a Japanese mother whose figure integrates the American mode of individualism (she marries for romantic love) and "a prized identity" of peers and community almost exclusively of Japanese descent. Wakatsuki Houston privileges the maternal component in the ethnic community, equates it with "service," and conflates the narrative of maternal service with that of approved female subordination: "My mother, already inherently prepared to subordinate herself in their relationship . . . zealously sought for ways to elevate [the husband's] position in the family." The author's internalized conflict, between aggressive, assertive attitudes, identified as "Caucasian" in ethnic culture, and submissive, passive, receptive characteristics, identified as Japanese woman, surfaces in her marital relation to her Caucasian husband. Wakatsuki Houston "solves" this "double identity" by claiming "cultural hybridness," an acceptance of cultural and psychological divergence in her personality. Her "resolution," however, can be read as itself a compliance with both racist and sexist constructions of female identity; as she admits in her essay "The Geisha, the Good Wife, and Me," there are roles that "Westerners, including me, have amalgamated into one stereotype . . . [:] the submissive, docile, self-sacrificing, artlessly perfect Japanese wife."[34] Wakatsuki Houston's later essays move the dilemma of the woman in a patriarchal ethnic community from the problem of patriarchy to the "solution" of sexist role-playing.

Farewell to Manzanar had foregrounded a plot in which the female protagonist seeks and finds a woman's identity, no matter how partial and unsatisfactory, outside the Japanese father's version — a self-representation that locates content in white America's version of the princess, exotic native, or Hollywood heroine. This ethnically transgressive yet American assimilative mode of self-representation is one common form of the intersection of ethnicity and feminism in much Asian American writing. In two randomly selected poems in the 1986 Asian American Special Edition of *Contact ll*, for example, Genny Lim and Karen Tei Yamashita situate their representations of woman in recognizably feminist yet seemingly nonethnically identified codes.[35] Treating sexuality with a remarkable candor and explicitness, associated with the emphasis on writing the body that feminist literary criticism has privileged, both poems break any stereotypical notions the reader may have concerning Asian American female modesty, submissiveness, and passivity. Indeed, stereotypes aside, they transgress common social rules of female behavior that still pervade middle-class societies of any ethnic camp. Lim's title, "If Sartre Was a Whore," immediately places the poem in a Western cultural orientation; the stanzas describe a larger-than-life female energy principle:

> They call her whore
> because she fucks with pleasure
> They sneer
> because she loves women
> Queen bee
> She sucks life's nectar
> from one-night stands.

This figure of bisexual energy and the pleasure principle contains nothing of stereotypes of Asian American women in its representation.[36] Similarly, Yamashita's "Midwifs," with its playful use of jazz rhythms and linguistic registers, borrows its diction and images from African American blues lyrics:

> Say man lady
> hootche kootche woman
> huddled on your hootche kootche womb
> baring breasts to wet
> lips and tongues of father the son, ghosts
> in dreams caress the nights
> in middle age sing crazy like a loon.[37]

Both poems appear to demonstrate that the construction of female sexual energy need not be ethnic-bound. Yet, although these poems operate outside the context of Asian ethnicity, or at least allude to it chiefly by transgression and exclusion, as representations they are no less culture-bound because they displace references to images, ideas, and behavior commonly associated with Asian ethnic societies and locate their women's content instead in European and African American contexts. The choices of that preeminent European philosopher Jean-Paul Sartre and the jazz-influenced diction and rhythms offer a counter-European and African American ground in these poems, illustrating that when Asian American writers write from non–Asian American centers, they are already situated in another ethnic domain. We should read the poems of Lim and Yamashita as constructed within a Western tradition of *l'écriture féminine*.[38] In this Western feminist poetics, women's physicality, maternality, sexuality, and eroticism are foregrounded as a defiant inscription of female experience outside the forms of phallocentric and logocentric poetics. As Susan Rubin Suleiman suggests, women's writing is claiming the right to "dirty" words and to subjects long forbidden to women by a patriarchal discourse that, in idealizing women as other than material, had deprived women of the power of the material.[39] In these two poems, their subjects, idioms, jazz syncopations, metaphors, and figures are coded Euro-African American. These poems construct women's bodies but go outside Asian-American culture-specific codes to do so.

It is generally accepted that one tradition of women's writing in the French-Anglophone tradition concerns the body as reflected in thematics and choice of diction. A tradition of ethnic immigrant writing is also grounded on a body of thematics (Old World/New World conflict; alienation/assimilation; intergenerational tensions rising out of cross-cultural differences, and so forth). In such a contrasting morphology, *Farewell to Manzanar* and *Clay Walls* may be considered more ethnic than feminist texts. But if we also consider that the theme of women's oppression by patriarchal structures and the representation of women's struggles to free themselves from these ancient bonds form another tradition of women's writing, then surely these two books, which unreel the twisted strands of the cultural pressures of descent (being born into an ethnic community) and consent (attempting to constitute a woman's identity of one's own outside the imprisonment of culture), meet at the intersection of ethnic and feminist traditions.

In contrast, by placing their poems in a European and African American rhetorical context, Lim and Yamashita demonstrate a conscious decision to forgo the complexities of intersecting Asian American and feminist cultures, choosing instead to position themselves in other cultural contexts in which female sexuality can be assertively represented without the countering repressions of culture-specific patriarchal attitudes. Reading the different representations of woman by these writers, we are reminded of how ethnic and gender identities are continuously negotiated in tension against each other, the very act of naming and representing, that is, of writing, composed of strategies of identity that challenge each other in a dialogical mode within the texts themselves.

THE INTERVENTION OF POSTCOLONIALITY

The pioneering work done by the two 1980s anthologies, *The Forbidden Stitch* and *Making Waves*, was carried forward by other women-centered anthologies in the 1990s, many of them more explicitly bounded by regional and more strictly defined identities.[40] Despite the complaint that South Asian American communities have been usually neglected in Asian American Studies, South Asian American women's anthologies now lead in numbers of publications.[41] These and other more recent publications, especially of Filipino American and Southeast Asian American works,[42] point to a further complication with the intersection of three, rather than two, emergent fields: not simply Women's Studies with its emphasis on the saliency of gender in constructing knowledge overlapping with Asian American literature, usually read within the interpretative practices of literary scholarship, most recently within a deconstructive unpacking of identity thematics, but also postcolonial writing, which foregrounds a global historical context, testifying to "the problem of oppression, of one nation or people constructing a discourse of violence to dominate others." The three overlapping contextual concerns, shared thematic resonances, and common theoretical terms are sutured in these texts — for example, Theresa Hak-Kyung Cha's *Dictee* and Jessica Hagedorn's *Dogeaters* — even as Trinh T. Minh-ha and other critics have attempted an integrated theory that will take into account feminist epistemology and postcolonial theory.[43]

Indeed, in addressing the overlaps, commonalities, and signal resonances among these tripartite fields, I note, for example, that each "field" shares an interdisciplinary approach that is enlivened by the different methodologies associated with the humanities and social sciences: history, literary criticism, sociology, anthropology, art history, film studies, and so forth. Scholars also have noted the tendency in all three fields not only to blur disciplinary boundaries or to be pluri-disciplinary but to engage in antidisciplinary work. And more and more, paradigms drawn from cultural studies have moved into feminist, postcolonial, and Asian American literary inquiry.

The attempt at integrating interpretative practices specific to these fields goes against a deeply installed criticism of "unity" as an intellectually suspect concept, a criticism that may also appear to come out of paradoxically hegemonizing, reductive, and conservative impulses that seek to reify particularism as another form of totalizing principle. Indeed, the overlapping concerns have little to do with articulating a principle of unity as they are asking how we can effect a praxis of coalitional interpretative practices among feminist, postcolonial, and Asian American critical studies.

The analytical categories of imperialism, colonialism, and globalism raised, for example, in the chapters on Filipino American and South Asian literature, in *Reading the Literatures of Asian America*, one of the first edited volumes to focus on Asian American writing, resist the institutional erasure of feminist Asian American productions as also part of a postcolonial literature.[44] In the last fifteen years at least, feminist theory has grown in complexity and reach, including, most recently, a "cultural studies' broadening of feminist scholarship [and] intellectual currents that transcend national boundaries." According to Deborah A. Gordon, "the transnationalizing of North American feminism has changed its subject matter, methodology and sense of political purpose. Feminism's object is no longer only patriarchy or male dominance but also society, consumption, interpretation, nature, and culture. . . . Its subjects are most often modern, industrial states including the shifts of a global economy, ethnic hostilities, gender struggle, right-wing populism, and the demise of socialist governments," so setting into question "the ascendancy of a bourgeois feminism that seeks to win citizens' hearts and minds through free-market ideology."[45] Chandra Mohanty et al.'s edited volume, *Third World Women and the Politics of Feminism*, is one of the few texts to address what Cheryl Johnson-Odim conceptualizes as "common themes, different contexts" that interlink postcolonial matrixes of race, class, and imperialism in the U.S. First World territory.[46] Mohanty's introduction argues ably for a "focus on dynamic oppositional agency that clarifies the intricate connections between systemic relationships and the directionality of power" to demonstrate that "systems of racial, class, and gender domination do not have identical effects on women in the third world."[47] The feminist argument that simply adding the category of woman or of race to criticism as usual is "inadequate to address their lives . . . [and] yields inadequate accounts of *everyone else's* relationships to issues"[48] can be similarly extended to the interpretation of South, Southeast, and East Asian American texts in which the category of nation is a crucial analytical and thematic feature. As I have argued elsewhere, feminist literary praxis, from Nina Baym's criticism of male-centered U.S. traditions and themes to Sandra Gilbert and Susan Gubar's *Norton Anthology of Literature by Women*,[49] can be said to reproduce uncritically a Eurocentric-biased canon that also encodes, to paraphrase Sandra Harding, racial and national messages "in the very definition of their most abstract projects."[50] Decoding their messages, we can see how white U.S. feminist literary epistemology frequently takes "American" national identity as an unproblematized, unmarked center that functions as the condition for inclusion and so excludes consciousness of differently marked relations to a hegemonic imagination of U.S. national identity. Thus, even when race is admitted as an intersecting category for inquiry, with the admission of the work of women of color into the feminist canon, the category of nation often still remains unacknowledged.[51]

TRANSNATIONALISM AND ASIAN AMERICAN WOMEN'S WRITING

From its first inception in the student protest movements of 1968, Asian American Studies was posited as part of a Third World movement drawing its intellectual base from the anti-imperial struggles of colonized people. Gary Okihiro testifies to this tradition in his introduction to the 1988 collection *Reflections on Shattered Windows* that Asian American Studies, originating in and symbolized by the "demand of Third World strikers at San Francisco State [that] education . . . must be 'decolonized' . . . arose out of struggle, out of a critique of American society and the educational system that buttresses it, and out of a profound commitment to community."[52] Other Asian American scholars such as Michael Omi, together with sociologists like Robert Blauner, took a Marxist model in their analysis of Asian American history and communities. Asian Americans, identified with other ethnic Americans, belong historically to a proletariat class, internally colonized by a ruling class that owns the means of production.[53] "Assimilation" thus becomes theorized as a coercive process by which institutionalized racism deprives these communities of civil rights, economic advancement, and cultural integrity.

This colonial reading is still powerful in effecting a resistant reading of Orientalist representations and in instating an oppositional identity politics that has invigorated the work of authors such as Frank Chin and Jeffrey Paul Chan. But it is inadequate to explain the contemporary writing coming out of new Asian American immigrant writers (e.g., Jessica Hagedorn, Shirley Geok-lin Lim, Chitra Divakaruni)[54], who, paradoxically, have come from newly independent former colonies; nor the work of a younger group (such as Cynthia Kadohata)[55] that rejects the reified essentializing cultural nationalist separatism of the 1970s. Contemporary Asian American writing such as Kingston's *Tripmaster Monkey* or David Hwang's *M. Butterfly*[56] operates in a postmodern or postcolonial space where gendered subjectivity is playfully performed or critically constructed rather than naturalized and where postmodern strategies of narrative destabilize and disavow fixed categories of race, class, and gender identity. American feminists have tended to read the works of Maxine Hong Kingston, Bharati Mukherjee, and Gish Jen[57] in the frame of Western feminism and so miss the colonial/postcolonial locations from which these writers speak. These authors, for example, repeatedly narrativize, even if they do not equally problematize, a U.S.

national identity. Although the reiterative strategies and constructions of the American nation in their works raise questions as to their purpose, their deconstructive elements, erased referents, rhetorical address, the relations between imagined nation and female subject suggested, and so forth, in the main, Euro-American feminists have read such fictive American-nation-enunciation moments as unproblematically transparent statements mimetic of social realities.

Intersections of ethnic and feminist theories that are not inflected by other complicating categories, such as nation and diaspora, are inadequate fully to illuminate the relations between and among such Asian American texts, that is, to account for the complexities of their diverse literary traditions. We see these complex traditions at work when we place Kingston's *Woman Warrior*, for example, in relation to Diana Chang's 1956 novel *The Frontiers of Love*.[58] Like Kingston's text, Chang's novel narrates the coming of age of a young Chinese American girl. But Chang's protagonist is a Eurasian, Sylvia Chen, who arrives at sexual and political consciousness at a historical moment of Japanese and European imperialism in China. The novel narrativizes the identity crises of race, sex, class, and nation that are so au courant today. But, although published almost twenty years before *The Woman Warrior* and set in World War II Shanghai, Chang's fiction hardly notes those Chinese patriarchal evils and attitudes that *The Woman Warrior*, despite its setting in a chiefly post–World War II U.S. space, continuously narrates. Clearly, instead of a chronological progression in the development of feminist-identified themes, we find discontinuities in the characterization of patriarchal Chinese and Chinese American society in these two narratives. Do we conclude that Shanghai in the early 1940s was a less patriarchal world than Stockton's Chinatown in the 1950s and 1960s? What accounts for the apparent anomalies and discontinuities between these two imagined Chinese/Chinese American communities? Can acts of contextualization help us understand the differentiating social consequences of class on women's bodies? On the one hand, when we contextualize Chang's novel in a cosmopolitan, transnational, mixed-race, elite social history, we can better understand the operations of colonial racism in undermining any emergent national self and the densely woven reiterative third-person interiorized monologues that star the fiction. Kingston's putative memoir, on the other hand, must be contextualized in the working-class, segregated history of Chinese American communities during the era of the Exclusion Acts. The widely different contexts of these two books, when both are read within a canon of Chinese American women's writing, suggest that there are other continuities than those offered by feminist theory that link them as sister texts. That is, although an Asian American literary tradition is discernible in reading these women's narratives side by side, as the most recent Asian American publications increasingly demonstrate, feminist and ethnic identity theorization cannot account fully for the astonishing diversity and divergences contained in this tradition.

When we ask, What are the important texts that have formed the attitudes and approaches of those who are now writing Asian American fiction and critical studies, and how can we periodize this canon? — we are merely asking from a contingent and provisional base, for Asian American writing is being produced at an amazing pace, perhaps even more amazing in reference to the entire previous history of Asian Americans.[59] More significantly, while the opening salvo in the 1970s on the absence of Asian American writing was derived from an exclusionary criterion constructing an authentic ethnic identity, the interrogation and dismantling of this authentic essential ethnic subject has been the project and the catalyst for much of the efflorescence of Asian American writing in the 1980s and 1990s. The project is complicitously related to the contingent presence of postcolonial subjects and theory in U.S. cultural discourses, including the migrancy of South Asians geographically and intellectually into Asian American cultural sites, and so is directly linked to the production of a new and different literary tradition for Asian American writing. Contemporary Asian American literary tradition, marked by a fluidity or open-endedness in which the "national" origin/U.S. natal identity of the author is blurred or left undetermined or at least not pivotally signified as totalizing correspondence between text and social reality, opens up a space where the aesthetics or textual production can be submitted for appropriate scrutiny as signifying form.

One clear collection of texts in which postcolonial theory bears a relevant weight is that produced by diasporic and émigré or newly immigrant authors who are claiming or have been identified with an Asian American location. Among these I include the plethora of writing by South Asian immigrant women, beginning with Bharati Mukherjee and now including authors such as Sara Suleri, Bhapsi Sidhwa, Ginu Kamani, and a throng of women writers represented in the numerous South Asian women's anthologies that have appeared in the last five years.[60] Because South Asian American writing is produced within different cultural boundaries from U.S.-born authored texts, they inscribe different reconstitutions of memory and give rise to different fabrications of tradition, deploying in some instances transgressive, appropriative, and disavowing strategies. The narratives of the Burmese-born Wendy Law-Yone and the Vietnamese refugee Le Ly Hayslip[61] suggest that any survey of Asian American writing now must wrestle with the destablizing notions of Asian American ethnic, national, and gender identities and the congruent problematizing of traditional authorial voicing, genre boundaries, and narrative stylistics that these new Asian American immigrant (and émigré/green card) literatures introduce.

The new horizon of postcolonial and feminist expectations illuminates older texts and permits a different reception of them. The recovery of diasporic identification complicates and inflects the master narrative of becoming American, suggests a postmodern, post-1960s tradition that brings into a different relief the older tradition of English-language memoirs and novels written by Asians in the United States in the period of transition between 1945 and 1969. This postcolonial reading, however, needs to take into greater account the category of gender, which is an especially vexed subset of inquiry in the postcolonial world. Incorporating a feminist epistemological dimension will allow us to revise simple reductions of social relations in these texts to Asian patriarchal structures. A critical feminist inquiry will subvert the unidirectional, univocal structuring of sexism as something that is done to women by men; instead, deessentializing gender attributes will permit us to note that sexism is also something that is done to Asian American men by U.S. society, sometimes with Asian American women as duplicitous agents. Kingston powerfully retells the story of white men turning Asian American male subjects into disempowered, that is, feminized, sex objects in the opening fable of Tang Ao in *China Men*, and David Hwang critically scrutinizes the overlapping of colonialist, imperialist, racist ideologies in the overdetermined gendering of female subjectivity in *M. Butterfly*. Similar demasculinization themes are sounded in narratives as historically apart as Jeanne Wakatsuki's *Farewell to Manzanar* and Law-Yone's *Coffin Tree*. Gender renegotiations, specifically in more feminist militant forms, have thus been interpreted not simply as social in character but as denoting a teleological shift in the de/structuring of Asian "manhood."

In Asian American women's texts, such as Chuang Hua's *Crossings* and Hua Ling Nieh's *Mulberry and Peach*,[62] of coming to the United States and staying; coming, returning, then re-returning; coming and returning repeatedly; born in the United States; traveling, traversing, in transition, unsettling rather than settling into a prescribed U.S. national identity, working out a schizophrenic epistemology rather than the paranoid rigid surveillance of the ideological nation, the impatience with the question of an authentic and authenticating Asian American identity in works points to what is emergent and different about recent Asian American literature. These works articulate a postcolonial, global consciousness—not simply cosmopolitan or binational or diasporic or immigrant—but all these strands bound together, imbricated within U.S.-based ideologies of society and the individual, within the English language, and within the genres of prose narratives.

The transition of the tradition from a cultural national to postcolonial consciousness has been elided by its contingent side-by-sideness with postmodern theorization. Asian American critical and literary consciousness seems to have moved from the national to the postmodern moment with hardly a glance at the contents of modernity in the cultural forms. Perhaps illustrating the collapse of temporal sense in the face of the spatially urgent globalization of Asian American identity formations, young Asian American critics have appropriated postmodern theories for Asian American studies, as seen in the 1995 volume *Privileging Positions: The Sites of Asian American Studies*. As the editor, Gary Okihiro, notes, four of the chapters "consider the intersections and divergencies of Asian American Studies and postmodernism and feminism."[63] The authors of these chapters look for an "affirmative postmodernism" that will "work toward alternative futures" and that will have "an integrative impact upon the disciplines across the academy," and they argue that the centrality of Asia puts Asian Americanists "in an excellent position to make powerful interventions in the dominant understanding of postmodernism and late capitalism." This intervention by young Asian American acadamics impatient with standing "at the edge of theoretical debates rather than sit[ting] in their midst"[64] resituates and redraws identity/subject formation but to my mind spectacularly elides any notion of the postcolonial, a lapse that has perhaps everything to do with the privileging of the East Asian over the South Asian in the volume, as Okihiro himself noted in his introduction. In the focus on late capitalism's penetration of the Pacific Rim sphere, class rather than nation forms the pivotal discursive category, with commodification taking the place of oppression under this paradigm of postmodernism.

To repeat, in Asian American literary studies, the entry of feminist epistemology has been particularly enlivening and productive in constructing standpoint knowledge of Asian American women's experiences and in the foregrounding of women's issues and examination of gender representations, as seen in the critical studies by Amy Ling and King-Kok Cheung, the first being a study of women writers of Chinese descent and the latter interpreting notions of silence and articulations in Asian American women's fictions.[65] But the absence of postcolonial critiques in these 1980s studies, like the absence of feminist critiques in the colonial readings of Asian American literature in the 1970s, have tended to a reification of specific binaries, for example, of assimilation versus cultural nationalism, immigrant versus diasporic models, or masculinist versus feminist ideological representations, binaries that reflect the sameness versus difference camps that dominated feminist discourse in the 1980s. Feminist, postcolonial, and postmodern theorization breaks open these binaries, leading to further transformations of a once culturally nationalist Asian American literary tradition. Antihegemonic and antiauthoritarian, Asian American women's writing cannot be periodized or uniformly classified. The challenge of pluralism, of an ideology that seeks to include divergent, even conflictual, cultural components, is acutely articulated in such texts, situated in the intersections of ethnic and feminist identities.

NOTES

This essay is a revised and expanded version of an article originally published in *Feminist Studies* 19 (Fall 1993): 571–96, by permission of the publisher, Feminist Studies, Inc.

1. Johnnella E. Butler, *NWSAction* 2 (Winter 1989): 1, 2.

2. Many women of color scholars have written of what Barbara Christian has called the "conflict of choice and possibility" caused by divergent ethnic and feminist lines of inquiry. See her article, "But Who Do You Really Belong to—Black Studies or Women's Studies?" in *Across Cultures: The Spectrum of Women's Lives*, ed. Emily K. Abel and Marjorie L. Pearson (New York: Gordon and Breach, 1989), 18. Patricia Zavella indicts "the early feminist criticisms of the nuclear family" and asserts that for some Chicanas "the white, middle-class focus of American feminism" implied a form of racism ("The Problematic Relationship of Feminism and Chicana Studies," ibid., 26).

3. Barbara Smith, Introduction to *Home Girls: A Black Feminist Anthology* (New York: Kitchen Table, Women of Color Press, 1983), xxv.

4. See Donna Perry, "Procne's Song: The Task of Feminist Literary Criticism," in *Gender/Body/Knowledge: Feminist Reconstructions of Being and Knowing*, ed. Alison M. Jaggar and Susan R. Bordo (New Brunswick: Rutgers University Press, 1989). Perry nicely summarizes feminist literary criticism's political agenda, pointing out that "it originates in the critic's recognition that women, whatever their race or color, experience the world differently from men, that their status outside the dominant white male middle-class culture allows (or even compels) them to critique it.... The feminist literary critic is committed to changing the world by challenging patriarchal assumptions, judgments, and values, particularly as they affect women" (293).

5. Messer-Davidow argues that the "subject of feminist literary criticisms appears to be not literature but the feminist study of ideas about sex and gender that people express in literary and critical media" and from that premise concludes for a position of "perspectivity" which assumes that "we as diverse knowers must insert ourselves and our perspectives into the domain of the study and become, self-reflexively, part of the investigation." See "The Philosophical Bases of Feminist Literary Criticisms," *New Literary History* 19 (Autumn 1987): 11, 88.

6. Hazel V. Carby, "Telling Fruit from Roots," *Times Literary Supplement*, December 29, 1989–January 4, 1990, 1446.

7. For a critique of the problematics of pluralism raised by feminist literary inquiry, see Annette Kolodny, "Dancing Through the Minefields: Some Observations on the Theory, Practice, and Politics of a Feminist Literary Criticism," in *The New Feminist Criticism*, ed. Elaine Showalter (New York: Pantheon Books, 1985), 144–67. While Ko-

lodny acknowledges that pluralism "seems to threaten a kind of chaos for the future of literary inquiry," she asserts that the task for feminist critics is "to initiate nothing less than a playful pluralism, responsive to the possibilities of multiple critical schools and methods" (161).

8. For discussions of women's positions in traditional Asian patriarchal social structures, see Kay Ann Johnson, *Women, the Family, and Peasant Revolution* (Chicago: University of Chicago Press, 1983); Marilyn Blatt Young, ed., *Women in China: Studies in Social Change and Feminism* (Ann Arbor: Center for Chinese Studies, University of Michigan, 1973); Judith Stacey, *Patriarchy and Socialist Revolution in China* (Berkeley: University of California Press, 1983); Sharon L. Sievers, *Flowers in Salt: The Beginnings of Feminist Consciousness in Modern Japan* (Stanford: Stanford University Press, 1983); Susan Pharr, ed., *Political Women in Japan* (Berkeley: University of California Press, 1981); Takie Sugiyama Lebra, *Japanese Women: Constraint and Fulfillment* (Honolulu: University of Hawaii Press, 1984); Alice Chai, "Korean Women in Hawaii," in *Women in New Worlds, 1903–1945*, ed. Hilah F. Thomas and Rosemary Skinner Keller (Nashville: Abingdon Press, 1981), 77–87; Sheila Rowbotham, *Women, Resistance and Revolution* (New York: Vintage, 1972), especially the chapter "When the Sand-Grouse Flies to Heaven," 170–99; Sylvia A. Chipp and Justin J. Green, eds., *Asian Women in Transition* (University Park: Pennsylvania State University Press, 1980); Judy Chu, "Southeast Asian Women in Transition," paper presented at the Immigrant Women Project, Long Beach, California, September 1984; Beverley Lindsay, ed., *Comparative Perspectives of Third World Women* (New York: Praeger, 1980); and Perdita Huston, *Third World Women Speak Out: Interviews in Six Countries on Change, Development and Basic Needs* (New York: Praeger, 1979). Recent studies of the role of international corporate capital and development in further eroding Asian women's human rights include Rachel Grossman, "Women's Place in the Integrated Circuit," *Southeast Asia Chronicle–Pacific Research* 66 (January–February 1979): 2–17; Marlyn, "The Sale of Sexual Labor in the Philippines: Marlyn's Story," introduced and translated by Brenda Stoltzfus, *Bulletin of Concerned Asian Scholars* 22 (1990): 13–19.

9. Sexual dysfunction and misogyny among Chinese immigrants, resulting from long separations from their womenfolk, a social phenomenon created by the various Asian Exclusion Acts between 1882 to 1943, are documented, for example, in Paul C. P. Siu's *The Chinese Laundryman: A Study of Social Isolation*, ed. John Kuo Wei Tchen (New York: New York University Press, 1987), esp. 250–71. Sucheta Mazumdar points out that "for immigrant women arrival in America can be liberating. Societal norms of the majority community frequently provide greater personal freedom than permitted in Asian societies" (p.15). See "General Introduction: A Woman-Centered Perspective on Asian American History," in *Making Waves*, ed. Asian Women United of California (Boston: Beacon Press, 1989), 1–22. Psychological studies have posited that "conflicts between traditional Chinese roles and feminist orientations may exist for many Chinese American females" (Stanley Sue and James K. Morishima, "Personality, Sex-Role Conflict,

and Ethnic Identity," in *The Mental Health of Asian Americans* [San Francisco: Jossey-Bass, 1982], 93–125).

10. The hostility roused in Asian American men at Asian American women who date or marry outside their ethnic community has not yet been documented, but various personal writings testify to its existence. See, for example, Tommy S. Kim's "Asian Goils Are Easy," in *Tealeaves* (University of California Berkeley, Fall 1989), 24:

> Oriental sluts with attitudes:
> I'm so, special so unique — no
> boy Chinee
> understand me — no
> satisfy need. . . .
> A race of Wong —
> wanna-be's: Suzie
> feeling sick
> 'cause she needs white dick
> to fix an itch
> in her too-tight twat.

11. See Carol Neubauer, "Developing Ties to the Past: Photography and Other Sources of Information on Maxine Hong Kingston's *China Men*," *MELUS* 10 (1983): 17–36, for a discussion of how Kingston uses photographs to help develop her strategy of memory in her memoirs.

12. For discussions of Kingston's postmodernist genre collages, see Linda Ching Sledge, "Maxine Hong Kingston's China Men: The Family Historian as Epic Poet," *MELUS* 7 (1980): 3–22, and Marilyn Yalom's "The Woman Warrior as Postmodern Autobiography," in *Approaches to Teaching Kingston's The Woman Warrior*, ed. Shirley Geok-lin Lim (New York: Modern Language Association Press, 1991).

13. For examples of historical and archival recoveries, see Marlon K. Hom, *Songs of Gold Mountain: Cantonese Rhymes from San Francisco Chinatown* (Berkeley: University of California Press, 1987); Him Mark Lai, *A History Reclaimed: An Annotated Bibliography of Chinese Language Materials on the Chinese of America*, ed. Russell Leong and Jean Pang Yip (Los Angeles: Resource Development and Publications, Asian American Studies Center, University of California, 1986); Mark Him Lai, Genny Lim, and Judy Yung, eds. and trans., *Island: Poetry and History of Chinese Immigrants on Angel Island, 1910–1940* (San Francisco: HOCDOI, 1980); and Sau-ling Wong, "Tales of Postwar Chinatown: Short Stories of the Bud, 1947–1948," *Amerasia* 14 (1988): 61–79.

14. Kai-yu Hsu and Helen Palubinskas, eds., *Asian-American Authors* (1972; rpt. Boston: Houghton Mifflin, 1976); David Hsin-Fu Wand, ed., *Asian-American Heritage: An Anthology of Prose and Poetry* (New York: Washington Square Press, 1974); Frank Chin et al., eds., *Aiiieeeee! An Anthology of Asian-American Writers* (1974; rpt. Washington, D.C.: Howard University Press, 1983); Elaine H. Kim, *Asian American Literature:*

An Introduction to the Writings and Their Social Context (Philadelphia: Temple University Press, 1982); King-Kok Cheung and Stan Yogi, *Asian American Literature: An Annotated Bibliography* (New York: MLA Press, 1988).

15. Ishmael Reed encouraged Frank Chin and Shawn Wong; Chin appeared in *Yardbird Reader* 2 (1973): 21–46; and *Yardbird Reader* 3, vi–x. Chin and Wong guest-edited a special Asian American issue of *Yardbird Reader* 3 (1974). Reed's invective against African American women writers for their feminist critiques of African American male abuse, which he claims is a form of scapegoating that plays to racist sentiments, is manifest in his polemical satire, *Reckless Eyeballing* (London: Allison & Busby, 1989).

16. See Chin et al., eds., *Aiiieeeee!*, 14–15, for a criticism of the stereotype of the demasculinized male in Asian American culture.

17. *The Big Aiiieeeee!*, ed. Jeffery Paul Chan, Frank Chin, Lawson Fusao Inada, and Shawn Wong (New York: Meridan, 1991).

18. Chin et al., eds., *Aiiieeeee!*, 35.

19. Elaine H. Kim, *Asian American Literature: An Introduction to the Writings and Their Social Context* (Philadelphia: Temple University Press, 1982), 189.

20. Elaine H. Kim, "'Such Opposite Creatures': Men and Women in Asian American Literature," *Michigan Quarterly Review* 29 (Winter 1990): 69, 71.

21. Maxine Hong Kingston, *The Woman Warrior: Memoirs of a Girlhood Among Ghosts* (New York: Knopf, 1976); Frank Chin, "Come All Ye Asian American Writers of the Real and the Fake," in *The Big Aiiieeeee!*, 1–92.

22. Shirley Geok-lin Lim and Mayumi Tsutakawa, eds., *The Forbidden Stitch: An Asian American Women's Anthology* (Corvallis, Ore.: Calyx, 1989), 85, 91. 79.

23. *Making Waves*, ed. Asian Women United of California, 308, 243.

24. Kesaya E. Noda, "Growing Up Asian in America," ibid., 244.

25. Lim and Tsutakawa, *Forbidden Stitch*, 14.

26. Carol Gilligan, *In a Different Voice: Psychological Theory and Women's Development* (Cambridge, Mass.: Harvard University Press, 1982).

27. Sucheta Mazumdar, "General Introduction: A Woman-Centered Perspective on Asian American History," in *Making Waves*, 15, 16.

28. Although such a catalog of social phenomena oversimplifies and overgeneralizes Asian women's status as victims of patriarchy, it does point to a history of unequal power relations in Asian societies.

29. Jeanne Wakatsuki Houston and James Houston, *Farewell to Manzanar* (New York: Bantam, 1974). See Mary V. Dearborn, *Pocahontas's Daughter: Gender and Ethnicity in American Culture* (New York: Oxford University Press, 1986), particularly Dearborn's discussion of the ethnic woman's "compromised authorship," 17–30. Dearborn elucidates the theme of the immigrant daughter's struggle against the Old World patriarch in texts as diverse as Mary Antin's *Promised Land* and Anzia Yezierska's *Bread Givers*: "If one's own father is renounced, indeed, erased, the bastardized immigrant is free to adopt the founding fathers as her own. Moreover, by this act, she adopts an American identity" (88). Anzia Yezierska, *Bread Givers* (1925; rpt. New York: Persea Books, 1975). See

Thomas Sowell, *Ethnic America: A History* (New York: Basic Books, 1981), 170. On the disintegration of the Issei families during the internment, see also Ann Umemoto, "Crisis in the Japanese American Family," *Asian Women* (Berkeley: University of California Press, 1971), 31–34.

30. Snow Wong, *Fifth Chinese Daughter* (1945; rpt. Seattle: University of Washington Press, 1989).

31. See an expanded discussion of Jade Snow Wong's autobiography in Shirley Geok-lin Lim, "The Tradition of Chinese-American Women's Life-Stories: Thematics of Race and Gender in Jade Snow Wong's *Fifth Chinese Daughter* and Maxine Hong Kingston's *The Woman Warrior*," in *American Women's Autobiography*, ed. Margo Culley (Madison: University of Wisconsin Press, 1992).

32. Kim Ronyoung, *Clay Walls* (1984; rpt., Seattle: University of Washington Press, 1990).

33. Mitsuye Yamada, "Asian Pacific American Women and Feminism," in *This Bridge Called My Back*, ed. Cherríe Moraga and Gloria Anzaldua (Watertown, Mass.: Persephone Press, 1981), 74, 73, 35.

34. Jeanne Wakatsuki Houston, *Beyond Manzanar: Views of Asian American Womanhood* (Santa Barbara: Capra Press, 1985).

35. Genny Lim, "If Sartre Was a Whore," *Contact II* (Winter–Spring 1986): 28; Karen Tei Yamashita, "Midwifs," *Contact II* (Winter–Spring 1986), 29.

36. For discussions of popular American stereotypes of Asian American woman as erotica, see Frank Gibney, "Those Exotic (Erotic) Japanese Women," *Cosmopolitan* 178 (May 1975): 166, 180–81; Elaine Louie, "The Myth of the Erotic Exotic," *Bridge* (April 1973): 19–20; Kay Carter, "Dragon Lady/Geisha Girl: Hollywood's Mythical Asian Female," *Neworld* 2 (Fall 1975): 37–53.

37. Yamashita, "Midwifs," 29.

38. For an example of discussions on *l'écriture féminine*, see *New French Feminisms*, ed. Elaine Marks and Isabelle de Courtivron (New York: Schocken Books, 1981), esp. 161–86, which takes up the questions, In what ways does women's writing call attention to the fact that the writers are women, and Isn't the final goal of writing to articulate the body?

39. Susan Rubin Suleiman, "Re-Writing the Body: The Politics and Poetics of Female Eroticism," in *The Female Body in Western Culture: Contemporary Perspectives*, ed. Suleiman (Cambridge, Mass.: Harvard University Press, 1986), 7–29.

40. See, for example, the sequel, *Making More Waves*, edited by Elaine H. Kim et al. (Boston: Beacon Press, 1997).

41. *Home to Stay: Asian American Women's Fiction*, ed. Carol Bruchac and Sylvia Watanabe (New York: Greenfield Press, 1990); *Our Feet Walk the Sky: Women of the South Asian Diaspora*, ed. Women of South Asian Descent Collective (San Francisco: Aunt Lute, 1993); *A Lotus of Another Color: An Unfolding of the South Asian Gay and Lesbian Experience*, ed. Rakesh Ratti (Boston: Alyson, 1993); *The Very Inside: An Anthology of Writing by Asian and Pacific Islander Lesbian and Bisexual Women* (Toronto:

Sister Vision, 1994); *Living in America: Poetry and Fiction by South Asian American Writers*, ed. Roshni Rustomji-Kerns (Boulder: Westview, 1995).

42. See the works of the Filipino American authors such as Jessica Hagedorn, especially *Dogeaters* (New York: Penguin, 1990) and M. Evelina Galang, *Her Wild American Self* (Minneapolis: Coffee House, 1996); also Malaysian American Shirley Geok-lin Lim, *Among the White Moon Faces: An Asian-American Memoir of Homelands* (New York: Feminist Press, 1996).

43. Theresa Hak-Kyung Cha, *Dictee* (1982; rpt., Berkeley: Third Woman Press, 1995); Trinh T. Minh-ha, *Woman, Native, Other: Writing Postcoloniality and Feminism* (Bloomington: Indiana University Press, 1989); and Minh-ha, *When the Moon Waxes Red: Representation, Gender, and Cultural Politics* (New York: Routledge, 1991).

44. Shirley Geok-lin Lim and Amy Ling, *Reading the Literatures of Asian America* (Philadelphia: Temple University Press, 1992).

45. Deborah A. Gordon, "Feminism and Cultural Studies," *Feminist Studies* 12 (Summer 1995): 364, 367.

46. Chandra Mohanty, et al., eds., *Third World Women and the Politics of Feminism* (Bloomington: Indiana University Press, 1990).

47. Ibid., 13.

48. Sandra Harding, " . . . and Race"? Toward the Science Question," in Sandra Harding, *Whose Science? Whose Knowledge?: Thinking from Women's Lives* (Ithaca: Cornell University Press, 1991), 194.

49. *The Norton Anthology of Literature by Women*, compiled by Sandra M. Gilbert and Susan Gubar, 2d ed. (New York: Norton, 1996).

50. Harding, " . . . and Race," 199.

51. Chicana literary critics were among the first to include a problematizing of national identity in their critical consciousness, seen especially in the popularization of their tropes of the borderland and the mestiza identity. In Gloria Anzaldua's work, for example, the borderlands and the mixed-race/cosmic-race metaphors are also literal, and textual production, genre hybridity, bilingual stylistics, multiplying linguistic registers, and lesbian/bisexual addresses are ruptures of and into political consciousness. Arguably, in the centrality of the contested category of nation and the differently nuanced articulations of a colonized/diasporic/borderlands/mixed or hybrid ethnic subject, Asian American literary tradition has as much in common with Chicana literature as it does with African American and Euro-American writing. See Gloria Anzaldua, *Borderlands/La Frontera: The New Mestiza* (San Francisco: Aunt Lute, 1987); Anzaldua, ed., *Making Face, Making Soul* (San Francisco: Aunt Lute, 1990).

52. Gary Okihiro, Introduction to *Reflections on Shattered Windows* (Pullman: Washington State University Press, 1988), xvii, xviii.

53. Robert Blauner, in *From Different Shores: Perspectives on Race and Ethnicity in America* (New York: Oxford University Press, 1987); Michael Omi and Howard Winant, *Racial Formation in the United States from the 1960s to the 1990s* (New York: Routledge, 1994).

54. Chitra Divakaruni, *Arranged Marriage: Stories* (New York: Anchor, 1995); *The Mistress of Spices* (New York: Anchor, 1997).

55. Cynthia Kadohata, *The Floating World* (New York: Ballantine, 1989); also *In the Heart of the Valley of Love* (New York: Penguin, 1992).

56. Maxine Hong Kingston, *Tripmaster Monkey* (New York: Knopf, 1989); David Henry Hwang, *M. Butterfly* (New York: New American Library, 1988).

57. Bharati Mukherjee, *Wife* (New York: Penguin, 1987); Mukherjee, *The Middleman and Other Stories* (New York: Viking Penguin, 1988); Mukherjee, *Jasmine* (New York: Viking Penguin, 1989); also Gish Jen, *Typical American* (New York: Penguin, 1993); Jen, *Mona in the Promised Land* (New York: Knopf, 1996).

58. Diana Chang, *The Frontiers of Love* (1956; rpt. Seattle: University of Washington Press, 1994).

59. See "Asian American Literature, January 1992–June 1996: An Annotated Bibliography," compiled by Shirley Geok-lin Lim and Noelle Williams, *ADE Bulletin*, no. 116 (Spring 1997): 53–58.

60. Sara Suleri, *Meatless Days* (Chicago: University of Chicago Press, 1989); Meena Alexander, *Fault Lines: A Memoir* (New York: Feminist Press, 1993); Bhapsi Sidhwa, *An American Brat* (Minneapolis: Milkweed, 1993); Ginu Kamani, *Junglee Girl* (San Francisco: Aunt Lute, 1995).

61. Wendy Law-Yone, *Irrawaddy Tango* (New York: Knopf, 1993); Le Ly Hayslip with Jay Wurts, *When Heaven and Earth Changed Places* (New York: Plume, 1989).

62. Chuang Hua, *Crossings* (1968; rpt. Boston: Northeastern University Press, 1986); Hua Ling Nieh, *Mulberry and Peach* (1981; rpt. New York: Feminist Press, 1998).

63. *Privileging Positions: The Sites of Asian American Studies*, ed. Gary Okihiro, Marilyn Alquizola, Dorothy Fujita Rony, and K. Scott Wong (Pullman: Washington State University Press, 1995), 4.

64. Ibid., 41.

65. Amy Ling, *Between Worlds: Women Writers of Chinese Ancestry* (Elmsford, N.Y.: Pergamon Press, 1990); King-Kok Cheung, *Articulate Silences: Hisaye Yamamoto, Maxine Hong Kingston, Joy Kogawa* (Ithaca: Cornell University Press, 1993).

TWO

RE(DE)FRAMINGS

"AMERICAN PURITANISM" AND MARY WHITE ROWLANDSON'S *NARRATIVE*

Teresa A. Toulouse

> In every era the attempt must be made to wrest tradition away from a conformism that is about to overpower it.
>
> —Walter Benjamin, "Theses on the Philosophy of History," in *Illuminations: Essays and Reflections*

In 1977 Joan Kelly asked, "Did women have a Renaissance?" and irrevocably altered the notion of "accepted schemes of periodization." Kelly did not discount the need for something like periodization, however. As a social historian, she viewed periods as involving "changes in the social order" which fell into a certain "causal sequence." Thus rather than dismissing broad temporal categories such as "medieval" or "Renaissance," she claimed that "what is more promising about the way periodization has begun to function in women's history is that it has become relational. It relates the history of women to that of men."[1] Kelly did not discount historical periodization as such; rather, periods would change from within rather than from without as the object of what was studied within them changed.

Nearly twenty years later, some literary historians indebted to Kelly's early insights call not only accepted schemes of periodization into question, but also the very concept of periodization itself, dealing as it does with suspect assumptions about possibly totalizing "causal sequence[s]." Under the influence of a variety of theories disputing the essential nature of "man" and "woman," Kelly's concept of the "relational character" of women's history, particularly the connections it bears to "institutional reasons" for gendered inequalities, has likewise been transformed.

For Americanists, the interlinked distrust of periodization and of older constructions of a unified (fe)male "subject" has taken a variety of practical shapes in recent literary histories and anthologies. In the *Columbia Literary History* (1988), for example, the editors explain that selections were arranged chronologically only for "organizational convenience." Readers were encouraged to see thematic spillover and overlap among sections, a process to be aided by extensive indexing. Such reading practices would allow readers to "do" American literary history rather than simply to "read" it. Their multiple readings would force this history to emerge as kaleidoscopic rather than unidirectional,[2] something made, or something making them "American," rather than something simply given. More recently, a specialized anthology in my own area of interest, early American studies, has similarly stressed the variety of ways in which this literature can be used other than the strictly chronological. While it, too, employs a chronological framework, *The English Literatures of America* also points out, "Some chapters focus on regions; others on genre; others on contexts of discourse, or topic."[3] For this anthology, such categorical variations are intended to show up the wider imperial and inter/national contexts in which the concept of an exceptional "American" subject—male and female—comes to be constructed in English texts.

Such practical efforts at dislodging traditional assumptions about historical periodization have been accompanied by explicit theoretical claims by other Americanists. Annette Kolodny, for instance, took up the call resonating throughout literary studies that the dissolution of the idea of a (largely white male) canon called for an equal dissolution of the notions of periodization on which it was presumably based. Texts by formerly disenfranchised groups could not simply be included in an "expanding" canon based on traditional notions of periodization: they would instead call for a total reworking of any concept of literary history itself.[4] Such reworking would not only affect more traditional readings of periods, it would also affect newer terms invoked to critique such periodization such as "margin" and "center." Elaine Hedges suggested that the questioning of these terms would further increase the need for different ways of conceptualizing relationships among texts—perhaps "repositioning a text" in a variety of different contexts.[5]

Central to both traditional and contemporary concerns about periods, however, seems to be the question, touched on by Hedges and indirectly acknowledged by editors and anthologists, of what organization newer and older texts "should" take once traditional periodizing has been drawn into question by theories of gendered, ethnic, "racial," sexual, and now, national, difference. Hedges's concept of repositioning suggests an implicit egalitarian impulse at work in such efforts that could, but not necessarily would, be related to a concept of historical categorization.

If such an unspoken moral, as opposed to, say, explicitly historical, basis of some of these arguments would seem to call for historical analysis, so does such critics' own historical positioning. Paradoxically, the notion of repositioning as well as many current antiperiodization claims could be produced out of what is, in fact, implicitly assumed to be a period. Surely, as one scholar has recently done, we should ask to what extent the current concept of history as chaotic, fragmented, and nonperiodizable (for whatever reasons) is often grounded in critics' own unspoken sense that they themselves speak from the vantage point or view of a uniquely postmodern or postperiod "period."[6] Debunking periods, they still assume themselves to speak from some unique temporal ground.

Suggesting that even an antiperiod position is levied from the position of a period underscores the need to be extremely self-conscious about our own historical embeddedness when we theorize about how to reorganize past texts. It also suggests the need to be careful about too easily taking a position that is a priori for or against any notion of historical periodization simply because of our own period's interest in the construction of "difference." If "difference" can, under certain circumstances, lead to particular repositionings of texts, does difference always and necessarily mean an abandonment of all, even traditional periodization?

In several essays, including most pertinently "Periodizing the Sixties," Marxist theorist Fredric Jameson has explored both the usefulness and the necessity of retaining a notion of periods. Specifically, he has argued that concepts of "difference" can be understood only in their relation to historically particular concepts of a "dominant." For Jameson, "exceptions" cannot exist (or be understood) outside the structural framework of what is considered a "norm." The problem with those who debunk periodization, he argues, is that they have too often misread it as simply referring to some "omnipresent and uniform shared style or way of thinking or acting" rather than "as the sharing of an objective situation, to which a whole range of varied responses and creative innovations is then possible, but always within that situation's structural limitations."[7]

Feminist historians like Joan Scott have nuanced, expanded, and criticized Marxist critics like Jameson, either for their tendency to explain issues of difference largely in economic terms or for their discounting of the importance of social differences other than class.[8] At the same time, Scott herself is troubled by the wealth of abstract and descriptive models currently available and the corresponding lack of complicated causal models. The challenge for feminist historians, as she viewed it in the late 1980s, was to come up with methods still analyzing change that involved not "single origins," but "processes so interconnected that they cannot be disentangled."[9]

In spite of the criticism feminists have levied at some Marxists (and Marxist feminists), Scott's notion of entangled "processes" that nonetheless can be said to emerge and to change is—on a very broad level—not all that different from Jameson's notion of periods as both heterogeneous and bounded. It is simply that the two scholars differently construe what is to be seen as historically entangled and/or interconnected. Similarly, even though her well-known essay on gender as a category of historical analysis does not directly address issues of re/periodization as such, Scott supports the notion that a cultural dominant and its "alternatives" can be read only in relation, not separation. Neither Scott nor Jameson opposes periodization, but both call for its refining and its justification on different grounds. While Scott is now criticized for not considering the "gender" system in enough relation to other discursive systems—particularly "race"—her analysis and Jameson's still provide useful frames for thinking about ways at once to reconfigure and to retain a notion of periodization.

Taking a cue from both Scott and Jameson, I focus in this essay not on a "problem" called "periodization" that a concept of "difference"—in this case, gendered difference—can "solve" only by somehow destroying. Instead, on a far more modest scale, I consider what an exploration of three contemporary analyses of a single early modern "American" woman's text can add to the process of formulating the questions we might ask as we reconsider possibilities and problems involved in the retention or transformation of certain concepts of periodization. To this end, though I will not feel limited to their analyses, I draw loosely on Scott's and Jameson's shared sense that periods are both heterogeneous and bounded and that periods, though circumscribed, can be said to change precisely because of the nature of the relationships they express and shape between dominants and their differences. Performing densely embedded analyses, centered on specific historical cases and their broader implications, seems to me one of the basic steps we need to take to address responsibly the question of how we should or should not change our ways of organizing and thereby interpreting literary texts in time.

Before turning to my three examples, I will offer a brief historical sketch that will set my discussion of their analyses of Mary Rowlandson's narrative in the fairly recent context of early American literary studies. What constituted a "colonial period" in American literary history used to be easily defined—by negation. First, it had nothing to do with Native American "literature"—of which there clearly was none, according to then definitions of the literary. Second, it did not deal with colonial literary traditions other than those of the English. It was not that American literary historians of the 1950s and early 1960s were unaware of other histories of colonization—French and Spanish to name only two—but their Cold War interest in tracing and celebrating the "origins" and "fruition" of the "American republic" led them to focus on the New England and southern colonies. In the *Literary History of the United States* (1948), Robert Spiller and his fellow editors viewed New England writers, in particular, as providing the "seeds" of the country's cultural future. This mode of perceiving literary history is mirrored in the contents page, which divides pre–Civil War literature into the following periods: The Colonies, The Republic, The Democracy, Literary Fulfillment.[10] A colonial New English woman's text such as Mary Rowlandson's *The sovreignty and goodness of God, together with the faithfulness of his promises displayed; being a narrative of the captivity and restoration of Mrs. Mary Rowlandson* (1682), which was not viewed as helping to create the metaphors of "fruition" and "evolution" valued in such a historical reading, received no mention in such attempts at periodizing.[11]

Though ignored by the Spiller group, selections from the Rowlandson text were included in a well-known anthology, *The Puritans* (1938), compiled, edited, and introduced by two New England intellectual and literary historians, Perry Miller and Thomas Johnson. Johnson had also served as one of Spiller's editors. In this collection, however, Miller and Johnson were less interested in describing "organic" continuities in "American" culture than in locating a beginning and end of a "Puritan" period in American intellectual history, dating from approximately 1620 (with the landing at Plymouth) and ending in approximately 1725 (with the rise of Jonathan Edwards). Selections were largely guided by the assumptions of a specific kind of intellectual history: the editors chose texts because they shaped a narrative about certain white male colonists' early-seventeenth-century development of, and later seventeenth-century declension from, an exceptional "New English" construction of colonial mission. Miller and Johnson included Mary Rowlandson's narrative because it drew on what they considered especially "American" Puritan frames of understanding—providential history and the jeremiad, to name two.[12]

For Miller, Johnson, and those who followed them, American history did not organically "flower." History "moved," in their terms, not by evolution but through conflicts between an intellectual system and material reality, as a fragmenting "New England mind" confronted the "fact" of the "American" frontier. Mary Rowlandson's text, dealing as it does with Indian raids and wilderness events as well as an orthodox understanding of their meaning, could have provided a clear site for examining a variety of parameters of this conflict between "mind" and "frontier." It also, obviously, could have opened up a range of interpretive questions about literary responses to contact with Native Americans. Curiously, it was not so used. The place of her text in expressing or its use in interpreting a major historical shift, at least as Miller and Johnson construed it, was thus minor—Rowlandson was simply representative of certain assumptions in third-generation Puritan religious thought rather than in any sense transformative.

Contemporary criticism of Rowlandson, much of which has focused on the central importance of gender as a concept necessary for understanding her text's relation to its context, has challenged the model of a unified colonial "New England mind" that fragments under external pressures from a number of directions. "Early modern" theorists such as Margreta de Grazia would view both Spiller's loosely evolutionary and Miller's more dialectical model as based on a psychologization of history that simply assumed the unified subject(ivity) of the growing/declining/contesting New England/American "mind" they analyzed.[13] Believing in a unified subject, in the coherence of signifier/signified relationships, and in the "truth" value of particular historical narratives, these earlier Americanists simply did not conceive of the possible role played by gender and other socially constructed differences in helping to shape either a distinctively "American Puritan" period or its transformations.

In the following exploration of three recent approaches to Rowlandson, I ask to what extent the newer critical assumptions they employ help us to reconceptualize our theories about a woman's text in relation to an "American Puritan" period. In doing so, I will briefly consider each approach in the light of past Americanists' assumptions about "Puritanism" as well as in the broader light of Jameson's and Scott's comments about periodization. The works I have chosen are, first, that of literary historian and theorist Mitchell Breitwieser, second, a study by intellectual and social historian Tara Fitzpatrick, and last an essay jointly written by literary theorists and historians Nancy Armstrong and Leonard Tennenhouse.

My discussion here does not presume some absolute truth value of their claims any more than this can be presumed about older analyses. I seek instead to locate and to set in conversation certain possibilities and problems that each approach poses for rethinking aspects of the relationship of a variously conceived historical periodization—American Puritanism—to the category of gender. This discussion is thus a preliminary inquiry rather than an attempt to provide some final adjudication of varying claims. Given the profound ramifications of retaining, dismissing, or reconceiving historical periodization in all areas of literary study, including "American," it seems far more important at this stage to raise larger questions out of smaller instances rather than too easily to assume their answers.

In *American Puritanism and the Defense of Mourning* (1990), Mitchell Breitwieser assumes the historical givenness of an "ideological formation" called

"American Puritanism." Reading what he calls this "highly functional cultural machine" in largely synchronic terms, Breitwieser analyzes what he considers its violent response to any alternative readings to its own interpretation of history.

The primary means through which "Puritanism" defended and maintained its interpretive hegemony over events and persons was "typology." "The progressive refinement of the holy community," as it was conceived by Puritan ideologues, was dependent on movement "through a series of increasingly perfected avatars" — or "types."[14] In the terms of typology, Old Testament figures such as David, Jonah, and Job did not simply provide ahistorical models for the Puritan community, they were "types" — models moving through historical time whose full meanings (or antitypes) had not yet been revealed. From this perspective, the place for the types' continuing revelation was no longer in the Bible but in the lived world of current human experience. This theory provided Puritanism with "an historical scheme that searched for abstractions realized or actualized in present conditions such as Rowlandson's captivity."[15] Aware of alternative ways of reading particular experiences, the Puritan "cultural machine" set out, through its use of typology, to assimilate or erase any difference from its own modeling of meaning.

Because Mary Rowlandson's narrative presumably fulfilled the needs of Puritan male elites for a typological reading of the meaning of the devastating events of "King Philip's" (Metacomet's) War (1676–77), it was allowed publication, despite its female author. According to Breitwieser, however, the narrative draws typology into question as much as it uses it. In fact, the Rowlandson text's ultimate inability to offer a closed typological reading of her wilderness experience reveals both a new way of viewing other cultures and an alternative way of reading colonial history that challenge "Puritan" typology and, by extension, the Puritan "cultural machine."

What does such a reading contribute to a rereading of a "Puritan" period? Clearly, the notion of an evolution found in earlier literary histories is missing here. "Puritanism" becomes a more or less spatialized "ideological formation" rather than a period, its interpretive hegemony over temporal movement supported by a particular method of reading biblical figures into history. If, however, Breitwieser's "formation" rewrites what older scholars had viewed chronologically, he nonetheless retains the notion that Puritanism is bounded and characterized by certain modes of interpretation. Given that this is the case, his model might seem in some ways little different from that of Miller and Johnson: it simply devalorizes a Puritanism that they valorized.

But is this strictly true? In earlier scholars' readings, American Puritanism followed a chronological trajectory emerging out of internal and external conflicts arising over time: if it ever were a "formation," it was almost immediately questioned. In Breitwieser's reading, however, the "ideological machine" of the 1670s seems no different from that of the 1620s—Puritanism as cultural formation can be threatened only by what seem to be equally synchronic alternatives.

The alternative to Puritanism that Breitwieser locates lies in the phenomenological experience of Rowlandson's mourning. Mary Rowlandson's experience of the loss of her daughter, Sara, precipitates a process of personal mourning for a particular person that the abstracting demands of typology for exemplification simply cannot foreclose. Such mourning, condemned as effeminate and irreligious in male Puritan writing, opens Rowlandson to a process of hesitant counterexemplification. If Sara's death and her own experience cannot be made available for abstract social uses, neither can her Indian captors any longer be viewed in the demonizing terms demanded by typology. For Breitwieser, Rowlandson's experience as mourning mother in the wilderness pushes her—if not to complete awareness or outright denial of her own system—at least to an intimation of the constructed quality of cultures and of differential power relations within them. In so (unconsciously) threatening Puritanism, Rowlandson's text, Breitwieser argues, provides the contours of a "Puritan social unconscious" which not only her period but also our own, has sought to assimilate or to repress.[16]

On one level, Breitwieser's sense that Puritanism was threatened by contact with the Indians again resembles Miller's: his "unconscious" comes into contact with "alternatives" just as Miller's "mind" confronts the "frontier." On another level, however, Breitwieser's focus on the Indians as cultural and not simply material threats to Puritanism differentiates him from Miller in ways that add a new dimension—Native American history—to our thinking about the relationship of periodization and "difference." Clearly, too, Breitwieser's focus on a Puritan "social unconscious" disrupts the presumed coherence/declension model of the "New England mind." In Scott and Jameson's terms, Breitwieser has located new strands in variable relation to a so-called dominant that should now be considered when we use a chronological and interpretive frame called "American Puritanism" as a way of explaining early texts.

At the same time, one might also question Breitwieser's spatialized reading of Puritanism from the point of view of Jameson and Scott as lacking a concern precisely for the historical dimensions both of the ideological formation it discusses and of the alternatives it proposes—particularly a Puritan social unconscious. Instead of simply positing a "mind" versus an "unconscious," could we not examine in more historical and textual detail how multiple religious and social tensions within late-seventeenth-century Puritanism, ranging from debates over the Halfway Covenant to intergenerational conflicts, to fear of new royalist English and/or French imperial intentions all could have contributed in helping to shape the "unconscious" critique offered in a text like Rowlandson's? Along the way could we not locate other forms of perhaps conscious resistance to Puritan norms which, if examined closely, could be said to be equally Puritan? Here, I think particularly of Rowlandson's own complicated Biblicism: her text does not simply represent her as a reflex of the "types" she mentions; rather, it demonstrates how she uses them as much as she is used by them. Furthermore, her sense of her own interpretive rights within the Puritan ideological formation demands attention not simply for what it reveals about a Puritan unconscious but more specifically for what it suggests about women church members' growing conscious sense of their own power in late-seventeenth-century congregations. Such responses do not discount Breitwieser's insight that we might need to posit something like a Puritan social unconscious; they do, however, suggest how we must move beyond merely claiming such an unconscious to a genuine attempt at explaining its historical rise and transformations in relation to more conscious choices, especially by Puritan women, as well.

If such historical questions can be directed to a concept of the unconscious, they can be similarly directed to gender. As the comments above suggest, Puritan concepts of gender roles were in flux by the end of the seventeenth century for a variety of political as well as religious reasons. Presenting Rowlandson's personal mourning as gendered does not answer the broader question of how and why a woman's text becomes "exemplary" of a general Puritan social unconscious, male and female alike. Breitwieser's more phenomenological claims about a specific woman's gendered mourning, fascinating as they are, also demand broader historical consideration within a Puritan period that is conceived of as coming into being for certain determinate reasons (including its views on gender)—and that for equally entangled reasons (again including gender) can be said to change. If Spiller's "evolutionary" and Miller's New England mind/declension models seem at once too simplistic and limited to us now, given our interest in the social and political uses of difference and our disbelief in "progress," should we merely dismiss Puritanism as period and replace it with a fixed "ideological formation," or should we instead rigorously reexamine the roles played by historically constructed and changing differences in the creation and breakdown of such a period in the first place?

Such a use of Scott's "entangled processes" does not mean that Rowlandson's text could not be repositioned in other ways—whether in Native American history or in comparison with Spanish, French, and Native American experiences of captivity. But does acknowledging that these possibilities exist mean that Puritanism as period should therefore disappear altogether? Within the tentative model of Puritanism as both chronologically bounded and changing suggested above, historically specific and often conflicting constructions of Native Americans could be set in relation to varying views of gender, sometimes revealing similar representations, sometimes not. Jameson's and Scott's notion of how, say, a Puritan dominant is constructed only in relation to its exceptions and alternatives, traces of which still lurk within it even at its most powerful moment, could here receive a fuller treatment than ever before. The expansions and reworkings of Puritanism that Breitwieser thus offers clearly do not destroy both the historical need and the heuristic value of at once retaining and reconsidering a more complicated version of an American Puritan period.

A second way of examining the relation of a woman's text to possible methods of construing and organizing a notion of historical periodization is offered in Tara Fitzpatrick's 1991 essay "The Figure of Captivity: The 'Cultural Work' of the Puritan Captivity Narrative." Although Fitzpatrick deals with several captivities, Rowlandson's provides the chief example for a case she wishes to make about the relationship of the female captivity narrative to broader changes in New England colonial self-understanding.

Fitzpatrick shares some of Breitwieser's perceptions, especially about exemplification, but she phrases them in slightly different terms and places them in a context which, in the end, offers a quite different way of interpreting the relation of gender and historical periodization. Like Breitwieser, for example, Fitzpatrick views the captivity narratives as expressing a conflicted dialogue between the usually female captives and the wishes of their minister-editors. However much ministers might have wished to use captivity narratives to control interpretation of the relationship between the covenanted community and the frontier, the captivities themselves clearly did not abide by such directives. Like Breitwieser, Fitzpatrick argues that Rowlandson's "experience of survival, accommodation, and enlightenment in the forest resist[s] ready translation into the Puritan spiritual rhetoric of submission and self-effacement within a congregational community."[17]

But for Fitzpatrick, in contrast to Breitwieser, such female resistance does not necessarily signal an emotional and/or unconscious abandonment of Puritan modes of understanding. Rather, Fitzpatrick reads the conflicting historical impulses present in these extremely popular late-seventeenth-century narratives as reshaping and transforming Puritanism from within. The captivities perform the "cultural work" of expressing and transforming the dominant in two ways. First, they describe and affirm an individual experience of conversion under duress that cannot be directly appropriated for the older purposes of communal exemplification. The sense of personal justification and the resulting piety experienced by the individual woman in the wilderness was simply not commensurate with the standard church-proscribed methods of ministerial and congregational oversight. It was therefore difficult to construct her experience as traditionally (or typologically) exemplary. In addition, in spite of Puritan strictures against venturing beyond the "hedge" of the community, such deeply felt religious regeneration occurred only in the wilderness, indeed seemed almost dependent on it.

In Fitzpatrick's reading, the orthodox Puritan ministers who wished to make use of these women's stories were caught in a paradox. They wished to employ the stories both to uphold a vision of individual piety as linked to community piety and as a means to dissuade land-hungry colonists from moving out of their communities and onto the frontier. One could, of course, read a text like Rowlandson's as supporting such ends. At the same time, however, how and where such piety was achieved by Rowlandson and other female captives threatened the purposes the texts were presumed to express. By the end of the seventeenth century, New England ministers such as Cotton Mather, whose churches were largely filled by female congregants, came to assimilate the inevitable. In contrast to early-seventeenth-century preaching, early-eighteenth-century preaching increasingly addressed both the glories of individual piety achieved in solitude and the religious character of the once diabolical wilderness into which so many colonists were moving. The mid–eighteenth century marks a further change in the captivity narratives as they become less focused on internal religious concerns and more on colonial and imperial political rivalries with the French. For Fitzpatrick, the communal unity which the women's texts had threatened returned by mid-century in the form of the incipient nationalism in the newer texts of male captives.

Fitzpatrick's analysis of female captivities directly challenges common historical assumptions about the "rise of individualism" in America:

> Instead of the traditional interpretation's concomitant rise of secularism and individualism or the more recently emphasized continuity of communal ideals, what we see emerging in the captivity narratives is an increasingly atomistic understanding of the process of salvation developing within the narrative structure of orthodox Puritanism, particularly in instances where the experience of exclusion and transcendence was told by a woman.[18]

Here, rather than viewing the possible contradictions within these texts synchronically, or reading textual contortions as unconsciously suggesting cultural alternatives that can come only from the outside, Fitzpatrick offers new historical reasons for how and why alternatives to one version of "orthodoxy" could have emerged to change Puritanism from within.

While Fitzpatrick, like Breitwieser, also draws on Miller's "mind" versus "frontier" model, she, too, alters it. Rather than reading late-seventeenth-century Puritanism in the terms either of a progressive or a declension model, she reads it as responsive and adaptive to the possibilities as well as the threats that the wilderness presented. It is captive women's orthodoxy, their unwillingness to cede their religious experience to models that did not fit it, that transforms but does not erase Puritanism as historical dominant by the beginning of the eighteenth century. Thus retaining a notion of Puritan periodization, Fitzpatrick's reading of gendered captivities changes our sense of both its range and its applications. If, like Breitwieser, she argues that gendered experience confronts Puritanism, she does not view such experience as Puritanism's alternative but as itself, complexly reconstructing Puritanism. Such an analysis depends on a notion of periodization that is not monolithic but heterogeneous; like Jameson, it assumes that similar historical conditions give rise to many different cultural responses; like Scott, it argues that attitudes toward gender are at once part of these conditions and part of what transforms them.

Still, if Fitzpatrick's analysis, like Breitwieser's, offers new possibilities for rethinking periodization in relation to gender, it also generates new questions. For example, even if differences like gender transform a Puritan dominant at some levels, at other levels, such socially constructed differences also help to maintain structural inequalities within that dominant. Women like Rowlandson, for example, who participated in the making of newer "individualist" self-representations, were not those whom the culture then allowed to act as individuals. Who other than men had the power, after all, to act on the new individual-in-the-wilderness myth that these women's representations helped to construct? If Puritanism-as-period gave rise to certain gendered possibilities, it also allowed for the continuation of certain gendered problems. Models of period transformation could usefully consider how such transformation might also support or even be dependent on continuities.

If this is true at the level of gender, could it not also be true at the level of "race"? Fitzpatrick's argument for the transformations within Puritanism that resulted from women's responses to captivity does not account for the continuity of their typological representation of Native Americans. Breitwieser attempts to address this problem by asserting that personal experience opened up the possibility of seeing alternative cultures; nowhere in Fitzpatrick's argument do the Indians appear other than typologically. Once again, we should ask if and how gender as a category, viewed by Fitzpatrick as changing certain strands within

Puritanism, serves all the more strongly to maintain others. Is this true in all or in most of the captivities? When, how, and under what circumstances might we argue that the interrelations of "gender," "race," and "Puritanism" begin to change?

Answering such questions might move us out of a traditional frame of Puritanism-as-period, forcing us, as John Demos does, to reconstruct varying historical perspectives on one event, rather than viewing all of them within one structural frame, however adaptable. In *The Unredeemed Captive*, Demos, a colonial historian, explores the 1704 captivity of the Williams family and considers French, Native American, and English points of view toward it. The Puritan perspective here becomes only one of several possible interpretations.[19]

We might argue, however, that Demos's approach need not discount Puritanism as period altogether; rather, he simply layers three or more possible periodizations on top of one another. Surely, to posit such a layering still demands that its strands be understood as individually and chronologically separate as well as in relationship. That is, though Demos's analysis can in some ways address the question of alternative cultures more fully than Fitzpatrick's, it, too, still implicitly depends on a notion, if a complicated one, of periodization. Clearly, as Fitzpatrick's essay suggests, the answer to the question of how or why particular readings of gender support or deconstruct particular representations of other groups is not necessarily answered by moving outside a concept of periodization altogether. The issue that Fitzpatrick directly and Demos indirectly address is whether it is, in fact, ever even possible to make such a move. "Change" for both historians happens from within or as a result of an overlapping series of "withins." Although calling such an overlapping a "Northeastern colonial period" might usefully describe certain facets of change, would it in all cases necessarily explain the emergence and transformation of such overlapping any better than a concept of intersecting periods?

Fitzpatrick's use of gender not only raises new questions about the relationship of gender to other differences, it also, finally, raises the need for more analysis of gender's contribution to the "rise of individualism." For all the light she sheds on women's roles in transforming, yet retaining a notion of Puritanism as dominant, Fitzpatrick's claims about the relationship of disempowered women's texts to such individualism is more fully addressed by the last essay considered here.

For Nancy Armstrong and Leonard Tennenhouse, in "The American Origins of the English Novel" (1992), analyzing the paradox of women's role in the shift to a concept of modern individualism moves us altogether out of an organizing concept such as American Puritanism; their analysis turns us instead to an exploration of how the rise of the novel and the nation as "imagined community" are linked to the popularity and influence of colonial women's captivity narratives. Placing Rowlandson's text in the massive context of the late-seventeenth- and early-eighteenth-century meanings of literacy in the English-speaking world, Armstrong and Tennenhouse immensely enlarge the scope of critical claims about how a woman's text resists or transforms Puritanism. In offering new insights into how and why generic and nationalist frames are historically produced through a conflation of a gendered voice with print technology, these scholars offer the most radical possibilities for displacement of traditional periodization we have yet considered.[20]

For Armstrong and Tennenhouse, Rowlandson's text is crucial for understanding the "rise" of the novel, particularly the structure and the popularity of fictions like Richardson's *Pamela*.[21] As in the case of Breitwieser and Fitzpatrick, Rowlandson's text becomes exemplary but not because of its use of typology. For Armstrong and Tennenhouse, Rowlandson's popular narrative shows how the gendered body of a nonaristocratic woman came to represent a class of people rather than simple individuals. The structure of captivity places this "English" woman in a wilderness, surrounded by captors. The captive woman not only expresses a desire to return to her "English" home, but by moving out of her context and returning to it, she also names and defines signs of "true Englishness"—"English" paths, "English" houses, "English" cattle, and so forth. This "full" (meaningful) landscape is set in contrast to the cultural "emptiness" she assumes to surround her. It is not her captured body as much as her reading of such English signs that indicates the essential Englishness of her "heart."[22]

In contrast to Spiller, Miller and Johnson, and even Breitwieser, for Armstrong and Tennenhouse, the confrontation of "frontier" and "mind" here produces not "American" identity, but, most broadly, a narrative of "English" identity. Out of wilderness isolation a solitary woman's voice is able to construct "a single [English] community . . . unified on the basis of literacy."[23] In its expression of "a unique sensibility which is the source of the language composing the narrative" the Rowlandson text astonishingly "converts a form of literacy based on the print vernacular into a new basis for human identity."[24] New notions of individual "sensibility" and "English" community come together in a bodiless female voice producible and communicable only through print.

If at this point in their argument, Armstrong and Tennenhouse move beyond the concept of "American exceptionalism" based on the frontier experience, they have also moved beyond the "experience" of the captivities per se. The growing popularity and availability of the print medium expresses, shapes, and puts the nonaristocratic female captive "English" voice into circulation. Print, of course, demands content, but in the process of printing and circulating print, such content takes on new meanings. The captive's distinct "voice"—a voice that expressed her Englishness—is embodied and displayed only through print. It is through a printed female voice that an "English" readership becomes aware of itself as "English." At its broadest reaches, this printed voice aids in the reconstruction of notions of the "English" family—it is now composed precisely of such "individual" yet representative voices—and of the "English" nation/family as similarly composed of discrete yet related "individuals."[25] Through the agency of print, a colonial woman's representation of a threatened identity that returns safely "home" thus comes at once to transform the "mother" country's sense of itself as "nation" and to influence the origin and course of the "English" novel.

Armstrong and Tennenhouse's interest lies obviously in the historical interrelationship of the birth of the author and the birth of the nation. Their claims not only draw into question the "exceptionalist" frames of the other essays we have considered; they also undermine the assumed categorical split between early modern "American" and English culture produced in the institutional arrangements, criticism, and literary histories of the nineteenth through the mid-twentieth centuries. Armstrong and Tennenhouse deconstruct this split by newly and differently historicizing categories that converge in the production of nationalism: it emerges out of a print-based sense of "English" exceptionalism developing among a new middle class. The traditional question of colonial differences from the mother country here yields to a newer question about the historical process whereby an international "English" sensibility is produced in gendered texts. For such an analysis regional historical specificities no longer matter.

This approach to Rowlandson's text at once complicates Fitzpatrick's sense of how gender came to be used in the production of modern individualism and, in a manner Scott would approve, immensely widens the field of application of gender as a category of analysis. The voice of English nationalism is here shown to be centrally female. In contrast to Fitzpatrick, Armstrong and Tennenhouse argue that the texts of male captives did not produce a new sense of community after those of female captives had threatened an older one; it is precisely the individual sensibility of the helpless yet unyielding female captive that provided a new sense of "English" community. The "rise" of individualism, of nationalism, and of the novel are interlinked, not separate phenomena, and only through a historical and textual examination of a printed female voice can such links be traced and analyzed. The category of gender difference in this analysis even influences the construction and operation of modernity—"once one is willing to entertain the very real historical possibility that the modern subject was not only first and foremost a writing subject, but also a woman who could claim no political power save literacy alone."[26]

If Armstrong and Tennenhouse's argument forces us to rethink the role of the printed female voice in the production of nationalism, it also makes us rethink the relation of this voice to the history of the novel as a genre that changes from period to period. If the captivity narrative originally "influenced" *Pamela*, they ask, "how might our interpretation of Rowlandson redefine that novel and the whole tradition of sentimental and Gothic fiction that it inaugurated?"[27] Posing such a question not only breaks down assumptions about the impact of the English novel on nineteenth-century American fiction, it also problematizes the tired novel/romance dichotomy in criticism of nineteenth-century American texts, suggesting that an international form of English middle-class "mentalité" was being produced under specific nationalist and imperialist conditions in the late seventeenth century. Viewing the novel's "rise" in these terms forces a departure from older "period" theories of genre as interpretable solely in terms of form or affect, suggesting in a manner Jameson would applaud that generic boundaries and separations are historically related to other boundaries, including those of the "period" and those of the nation.

Armstrong and Tennenhouse's approach obviously offers exciting prospects for rethinking the constructed qualities of texts, gender identities, and nations. It also raises questions about the extent to which older models of periodization may have helped to naturalize such constructions. Still, as was the case with Breitwieser and Fitzpatrick, this interpretation, too, prompts other questions to consider when reconceptualizing the ways we describe and organize literary texts and/in history.

First, there seems a risk of historical overstatement in ascribing largely to the agency of print the transformations in identity and community Armstrong and Tennenhouse locate by the middle of the eighteenth century. To what extent does using a newer Foucaultian model of impersonal rather than personal "agency" here retain certain problems that Scott points out with "single origins"? Would not the intersection of print with other historical phenomena—economic, political, religious, and cultural—also need to be considered in accounting for changes in the perception of the individual and the nation by the 1740s? How could these other sources, printed and unprinted, have aided or qualified the power of printed narratives to effect such changes in concepts of self and community? Changes so major as those Armstrong and Tennenhouse describe cannot be explained solely by the increasing dominance of a single historical and technological change, however important. Should a historical reading of the "rise of print" simply replace notions of "period"? Might such a reading occlude questions that only a notion of "periodization" could make visible?

Second, even if we do accept the importance of the growing availability and popularity of printed texts by the 1740s, could not *printed* sources other than captivities, unequally distributed in England and America, have had an equal impact on the novel, on the production of the modern individual, and on the modern conception of nation? One need only think of the seventeenth-century English and "New" English Puritan obsession with sermons and conversion narratives, for example, on which the Rowlandson narrative itself draws, or of the more general English fascination with the transformative capacities of the New World as evidenced in a variety of different genres appearing throughout the "early modern" period. In newly explaining the rise of the novel, in other words, why should we necessarily begin with printed captivities rather than considering their debt to other generic sources or the existence of other unrelated printed sources that could have equally influenced this rise? This last question seems especially pertinent given Kathryn Zabelle Derounian's data, which suggest that Rowlandson's captivity narrative in fact experienced little popularity among English (not English colonial) readers.[28]

Addressing such questions would not discount current interest in the relation of print culture to constructions of individual and group identities, but it would historically complicate analysis of the ways in which different kinds of printed texts came to inform and to inhabit such constructions. It might also suggest how and why we might retain, but on different grounds, a notion of "American Puritanism" that overlaps with but is also divergent from "English Puritanism." Even if we replaced such notions with a history of the relation of nationalist and imperialist culture to technological change, surely this history, too, would need to include a history of the struggles among different kinds of texts (and nontexts) out of which assumptions about what was "dominant" emerged, and from which struggles, as Scott and Jameson argue, no concept of dominant is entirely free. This history, if it did not call for traditional periodization, would surely require its own demarcations and justifications for specific historical breaks and transformations.

Drawing attention to the notion of a heterogeneity that both contributes to and contests the production of a dominant kind of print raises a parallel question about Armstrong and Tennenhouse's use of gender to stabilize national identity. Certainly, when late-seventeenth-century women's captivity narratives are viewed structurally—a woman surrounded by others is threatened and saved—a concept of gender does seem to be stabilized. At the same time, the obsessive use of such a structure by male editors and publishers as well as by women writers could push us to ask, Why is the captive continually threatened in this particular way? To what extent could this threatening of the woman in the wilderness have engaged fe/male desires — (for escape? for contact? for assimilation with other groups?) — other than that of shaping "English" ethnic loyalty and stability? What older fears and assumptions about the exchangeability of female bodies enter into the meanings represented by and ascribed to the captive woman? In focusing on the "heart" not the "body" of the captive female narrator, does not Armstrong and Tennenhouse's analysis both scant Rowlandson's (and other captives') own obsessive detailing of their bodily sensations and neglect the cultural anxieties that the female body traditionally represented to those who wished to contain and fix its meanings?[29] If a concept of female gender-as-English(ed) could be used to measure the distance from other ethnicities and other classes, the variable historical meanings ascribed to gender could also have expressed ambivalence about and even the desire for dissociation from Englishness.[30]

An argument for different anxieties informing as well as being exacerbated by the representation of a female captive resurrects the issue of American exceptionalism that Armstrong and Tennenhouse's approach totally discounts. Reconsidering exceptionalism returns us to Fitzpatrick's claims about the cultural "work" of "New" English women's captivities and points us in directions I am currently pursuing in work on these narratives. Given New English colonial anxieties from 1660 to the late 1690s about the restored Crown's impact on colonial charters, I explore how the captive woman's position could be construed as not simply representing English ethnicity versus all others but also as representing English colonial ethnicity versus all others, including noncolonial and non-Puritan English. Even to pose the question this way could make us rethink the extent to which representations of conflicts with different Native American groups and with the French might also have figured certain "New" English colonial conflicts about English intervention in colonial affairs. Armstrong and Tennenhouse suggest that in the narrative as in the novel, Englishness is freed from the body and from territoriality, making it a state of mind or heart. If this is the case, however, why do conflicts over the nature of Englishness erupt in the eighteenth century precisely over colonial-English property rights in the New World? Clearly, a concept of "Englishness" always already includes a notion of differences within what is being "English-ed." Early colonial captivity narratives by women express this possibility: if they can be understood at different moments to construct a new model of national Englishness, they at the same time indicate the inability of such a concept ever to achieve self-consistency. If this is the case, a concept of the exceptionalism of an "American Puritan" period should certainly not be entirely discounted: as I have suggested throughout this essay, it should rather be rethought on new grounds.

Such questions do not of course deny the suggestiveness of Armstrong and Tennenhouse's Foucaultian claims about the intersections of subjectivity, community, and a new technology. They do, however, qualify them. The existence of defining contexts and knowledges other than those of print-culture technology, the availability of multiple forms of print, and the instabilities of the forms of (gendered/ethnic) identity expressed/produced in different forms of print under varying local conditions are dimensions that also demand intersecting theoretical and historical treatment. The existence of such relatively unexplored areas surely implies the need for caution before we simply exchange current limited models of periodization for an overarching model of "early modern" (European) culture whose transformation to the "modern" is grounded primarily in theories about the growing hegemony of print. Both early modern culture and the variety of exceptionalisms that resist, take shape within, and transform it are more complicated than one explanatory model, however powerful, can encompass. While such a claim does not mean that we relinquish a concept of "early modernity" and, especially, the place played by concepts of gender in defining it, it does suggest the continuing need for a variety of chronologically demarcated spaces within it. Such bounded spaces, possessing their own characteristic products and conflicts—including those deriving from or circumscribed by concepts of gender—provide the complicated yet absolutely necessary means whereby we can analyze both continuities and changes—which is the function that any periodization has always served.

What is clearly emerging in this discussion is the sense that no single way of recasting our notion of Puritan, early American, or early modern periodization has come out of our inquiries. Far from simply lauding this fact as the mark of a "pluralist" heterogeneity that simply replaces traditional concepts of a Puritan period, however, we should ask whether we really can or need to effect such a replacement. Such questions, addressed here at the level of specific approaches, have broader implications. They force us to ask to what extent some current categorical shifting really adds little to older concepts of periodization. They also force us to ask whether our understanding of American literary studies should be transformed, not merely by important acts such as addition or inclusion, but crucially by totally different conceptions of history. In what specific ways do or could concepts of "difference" serve as bridges between older and newer models of conceiving a Puritan period in early American studies? In what specific ways do or could they serve as absolute marks of the gap(s) between approaches? Does "difference" help to wrest a concept of "tradition" from "conformism" for new social ends, as the epigraph to this chapter from Benjamin suggests, or must "difference" invariably deconstruct any validity to a concept of "tradition"?

In a 1991 article, Mark Parker describes mid-twentieth-century debates about "romanticism:" is it simply a useful label or does it name a "dynamic concept" that indicates something somehow "true" about historical flux?[31] Each of the essays discussed above, drawing on different readings of the intersection of a gendered narrative with a period denoted as "American Puritan," has engaged the in/adequacy of the notion of periodization it suggests. Breitwieser's analysis argues for a model of gendered experience in New England Puritanism that unconsciously expresses alternatives to it; Fitzpatrick's model of gendered "cultural work" argues for implosions and variations within a changing Puritan dominant, and Armstrong and Tennenhouse's model of the print-based "national" subjectivity expressed in women's texts underscores the need for a reconceived historical view of late Puritanism's relations to material conditions like print which helped both to produce it and to undermine its explanatory power. In all three approaches—each of which draws on different uses of gender for historical analysis—the notion of a period emerges neither as a simple label nor as an easily discernible historical "dynamism." Each essay offers a distinct, if often intersecting, method of conceiving the story of the relation of a seventeenth-century woman's text to a differently conceived historical moment. Despite their variations, each study disallows the notion of the period as either marking historical progress or, in related fashion, as revealing some unified "New" English or English mind. Yet, at the same time, each approach does not, indeed perhaps cannot, repress its own expression of some organizational frame akin to historical periodization.

Mark Parker supports the claims that even if we dismiss the period-as-label/period-as-dynamism question posed above, we cannot rid ourselves of the notion of something like periodization. What we can and should do, he suggests, is to play within both traditional and contemporary forms of describing and organizing historical change in such a way that both their necessity and their stability (i.e., their "identity") are always drawn into question and denied self-consistency. At the same time, we should continue to interrogate our own desires as historians and critics, attempting insofar as we can to acknowledge what our own analyses leave out even as we struggle to include.[32] The different roles played by concepts of gender in re/constructing notions of periodization accordingly become only a preliminary step, leading us to question, as Breitwieser's, Fitzpatrick's, and Armstrong and Tennenhouse's work has done, the ways in which other social differences historically intersect with gender in constructing and deconstructing our assumptions about individual and national, local and imperial, textual and nontextual identity and stability.

Just as each approach to Mary Rowlandson's narrative I have considered admirably transforms our sense of past literary scholars' assumptions about and organizations of a dominant "Puritan," or "early American" period, so does each, in turn, generate new questions for us to consider as we consciously and unconsciously "play" with and within the unavoidable frames, older and emergent, through which our historical knowledges are at once produced, debated, and transformed.

NOTES

My thanks to Barbara Ewell, Cynthia Lowenthal, Mary Beth Rose, and Michael Zimmerman for comments on different versions of this essay. Since it was first written in 1995, a good deal of new and important work on Rowlandson and gender has been published.

1. Joan Kelly, "The Social Relations of the Sexes: Methodological Implications of Women's History," in Kelly, *Women, History and Theory: The Essays of Joan Kelly* (Chicago: University of Chicago Press, 1984), 4. The essay to which I refer is, of course, titled "Did Women Have a Renaissance?," reprinted in the collection, 19–50.

2. Elliott Emory et al., eds., *Columbia Literary History* (New York: Columbia University Press, 1988), xii.

3. Myra Jehlen and Michael Warner, *The English Literatures of America, 1500–1800* (New York: Routledge, 1997), xxii.

4. Annette Kolodny, "The Integrity of Memory: Creating a New Literary History of the United States," *American Literature* 57 (1985): 291–307.

5. Elaine Hedges, Introduction to "Repositionings: Multiculturalism, American Literary History, and the Curriculum," *American Literature* 66 (1994): 770.

6. Margreta de Grazia, "Fin-de-Siècle Renaissance England," in *Fins-de-Siècle: English Poetry in 1590, 1690, 1790, 1890, 1990*, ed. Elaine Scarry (Baltimore: Johns Hopkins Press, 1995), 37–63.

7. Fredric Jameson, "Periodizing the Sixties," in *The Ideologies of Theory: Essays, 1971–1996* (Minneapolis: University of Minnesota Press, 1988), 179.

8. See, in particular, Joan Wallach Scott, "Women's History" and "Gender: A Useful Category of Historical Analysis," in Scott, *Gender and the Politics of History* (New York: Columbia University Press, 1988), 15–27 and 28–50.

9. Ibid., 42.

10. Robert Spiller et al., eds., *A Literary History of the United States* (New York: Macmillan, 1948), xiv–xv.

11. In all fairness, it must be noted that for Spiller at least, this reading becomes quali-

fied by a language of "cycles" and repetitions rather than that of simple organic "progress."

12. Perry Miller and Thomas Johnson, *The Puritans* (Cincinnati: American Book Company, 1938).

13. De Grazia, "Fin-de-Siècle," 48–49.

14. Mitchell Breitwieser, *American Puritanism and the Defense of Mourning* (Madison: University of Wisconsin Press, 1990), 23.

15. Ibid.

16. Ibid., 9.

17. Tara Fitzpatrick, "The Figure of Captivity: The 'Cultural Work' of the Puritan Captivity Narrative," *American Literary History* 3 (1991): 12.

18. Ibid., 9.

19. John Demos, *The Unredeemed Captive: A Family Story from Early America* (New York: Knopf, 1994).

20. Nancy Armstrong and Leonard Tennenhouse, "The American Origins of the English Novel," *American Literary History* 4 (1992): 386–410.

21. Whereas Armstrong and Tennenhouse focus a good deal of their analysis on *Pamela*, the focus here is their comments on Rowlandson.

22. Armstrong and Tennenhouse, "American Origins," 394–95.

23. Ibid., 396.

24. Ibid.

25. Ibid., 400.

26. Ibid., 407.

27. Ibid., 398.

28. Kathryn Zabelle Derounian, "The Publication, Promotion, and Distribution of Mary Rowlandson's Indian Captivity Narrative in the Seventeenth Century," *Early American Literature* 23 (1988): 248.

29. Armstrong and Tennenhouse mention the possibility of such a counternarrative, but they neglect to analyze the part such anxieties played in what they consider ideologically "closed" texts such as Rowlandson's. See Armstrong and Tennenhouse, "American Origins," 392–93.

30. The ideal "position" of the female captive, figured as "English," would seem to set up a comfortable "us" versus "them." The social/cultural position of women, however, situated between white male Europeans and Indians, uncannily replicates a betweenness uncomfortably experienced by male colonists—they are neither "English" nor "Indian."

31. Mark Parker, "Measure and Countermeasure: The Lovejoy-Wellek Debate and Romantic Periodization," in *Theoretical Issues in Literary History*, ed. David Perkins (Cambridge, Mass.: Harvard University Press, 1991), 229.

32. Parker, whom de Grazia also cites, is here drawing on Michel Foucault, "Nietzsche, Genealogy, History," in *Language, Countermemory, Practices*, ed. and trans. Donald Bouchard (Ithaca: Cornell University Press, 1977), 139–64.

ESSENTIAL, PORTABLE, MYTHICAL MARGARET FULLER

Mary Loeffelholz

Margaret Fuller's career and reception illuminate as strikingly, perhaps, as those of any other nineteenth-century American woman writer the gendered assumptions and strategies behind periodization in the writing of literary history. As feminist critics of the past twenty-odd years have argued, Fuller's place in the construction of American Transcendentalism, or the "American Renaissance," has always been strongly conditioned by her gender; she has been variously omitted, referred to in passing as a token woman or derivative mediator of the ideas of Ralph Waldo Emerson, or (in a once popular, now dated metaphor) elevated to the position of "priestess of Transcendentalism"—a metaphor that curiously sacralized but still preserved her presumed role as a vessel of the period's presiding, generative male spirit. "A handmaiden to major talents, a sole female figure in the frieze of minor Transcendentalists," in Bell Gale Chevigny's 1976 critical summation of this reception history,[1] this Fuller still appears now and then in accounts of the period; witness the Fuller of Michael Colacurcio's massive 1991 review essay on American Renaissance literary scholarship, who "always hovered at the edges of the Concord group, of course."[2] Of course.

Through these same twenty-odd years, however, Fuller has proven difficult to assimilate into new feminist periodizing constructions of nineteenth-century American "women's culture." Ann Douglas's uncomfortable idealizing 1977 gesture toward Fuller as a lone female exception to the "feminization of American culture,"[3] however vigorously Douglas's evaluation of that "feminization" has been challenged by subsequent feminist readers, has tended to predict Fuller's still anomalous standing, frequently as prophet rather than priestess, in feminist literary histories of nineteenth-century U.S. women's literature and culture. Chevigny's 1976 demand that "we reverse the usual practice of seeing Margaret Fuller as a fascinating exception to the condition of American women of her time" has gone largely unanswered and would still be so even if we further qualified Chevigny's "American women" as middle-class white women, New England women, and women of letters.[4]

It is not clear that the explosion of recent scholarship on Fuller has entirely changed the situation; there may still be more individual biographies of Fuller than, say, chapter-length or other extended treatments of her in broader feminist literary-historical studies. It may even be more common these days to encounter Fuller in critical studies otherwise entirely devoted to male writers than in feminist work on nineteenth-century women's writing.[5] For all the brilliant feminist work that has been done both in nineteenth-century women's culture and on Fuller herself, an anxiety of exceptionalism still lingers around the figure of Margaret Fuller in feminist literary scholarship, coupled with a deep anxiety over critical anachronism and identification. The problem with Margaret Fuller in the writing of feminist literary history is both that we fear she is too unlike other (middle-class, white, New England) literary women of her period and that she is too like "us," if us means late-twentieth-century feminist literary intellectuals, mostly similar to Fuller in respect to race and class, who probably can't help sharing Fuller's will to believe that intellectual labor coincides with personal self-realization. The titles of three recent (or recently reissued) anthologies in which Fuller's work is conveniently available—*The Portable Margaret Fuller, The Essential Margaret Fuller, The Woman and the Myth*—suggest (in their own professionally conventional ways) both the hopes and the fears prompted by "our" identifications with Fuller.[6]

The troubled courses of Fuller's reputation in general accounts of antebellum American literature and her visibility in feminist literary scholarship have certainly intersected from time to time in various of our disciplinary practices, and such intersections have become more frequent of late. Outright omission of Fuller's life and work in general literary histories of mid-nineteenth-century American literature, or in specialized studies with some generalizing ambitions, is rarer now than twenty years ago. Meanwhile, however, some of the literary-historical berths into which Fuller might most readily be eased have come under fire. The Concord center around which Fuller is generously supposed to have "hovered" has lost much of its power to stand by synecdoche for the whole of antebellum American literature. Not only the "American Renaissance" but "American" literature as such is noisily in crisis as a category. As some of my own metaphors here would imply, this crisis has more often been represented in spatial than in temporal terms, as an affair of borders, centers, margins, and the outward expandability of the canon. Of course, the spatial terms in which the crisis of American literature is usually posed inevitably implicate matters of periodization: to set one or another group of writers at the center of a period is usually to establish period beginnings and endings oriented to that group's literary production or to the historical events seen as most salient for those writers. Attending to multiple "centers" of literary production during a period entails searching for common, or perhaps compromise, *termini a quo* and *ad quem*. But my own survey of anthology practices of periodization—about which I will say more shortly—suggests that while editors almost always explicitly foreground questions of which writers to include, their consequent decisions about periods in which to group those writers are usually undertaken silently and left to speak for themselves. Colacurcio's doggedly impertinent foundational question for American Renaissance studies—"What exactly *is* our interest in writing about (or merely in teaching) writers in aggregates rather than as unique instances?"[7]—more often than not goes unanswered, even by editors who plainly have given much thought to the implications of naming, or more often lately not naming, a period as the "American Renaissance."

My aim here is to track Margaret Fuller's fortunes through this semi-silent professional crisis in periodization, drawing on some standard American literature anthologies for raw material, then to assess Fuller's roles in this crisis with reference to recent feminist work on her that replies directly to some of the issues at stake, drawing from this body of work possible revisionary approaches to standard practices of periodization. My reasons for doing so are threefold. First, it seems to me that there is still room for reflection in American literary studies (and, differently, in feminist criticism) about how fundamentally gender and sexuality structure our representations of literary periods. Second, I suspect that Fuller's place in both general histories of American literature and feminist histories of women's culture will remain insecure or equivocal—she will "hover"—until the writers of those histories find more creative and consistent ways of heeding Joan Kelly-Gadol's well-known feminist insight of 1976 that feminist scholarship had to lead to the rewriting of the history of women and men in "relational" or diacritical terms.[8] Then again, perhaps this could be put differently: if Kelly-Gadol is right about how to do periodization in feminist terms, it could become a positive strength for feminist literary history if Fuller were to continue hovering, under a different understanding of what that verb conveys about the loci and meaning of her activities: not batting her wings at the glowing windows of Concord but ranging, mobile and attentive, over different realms of intellectual territory.

Finally, I think that investigating what we want by placing Fuller "in her own time"—whatever that turns out to be called—can teach us much about what we, feminists and other disciplinary Americanists at least, currently want in doing literary history. As Peter Carafiol, among other critics of American Renaissance literary scholarship, has argued, the American Renaissance by any of its possible names is still invoked to furnish Americanist literary studies with an ahistorical "American Ideal" that governs the writing of a nationalist literary history.[9] And as Julie Ellison, among other feminist critics of Fuller, has persuasively argued, Fuller's ways of inventing a feminism for her time are deeply implicated in the way we still do both literary history and feminism: feminist criticism on Fuller, Ellison suggests, is the place in which the romantic logic of Fuller's work "continues to operate," even as — even because — "feminist critics and theorists are now scrutinizing the historical connections between feminism and romanticism more closely."[10] If, as Carafiol argues, the lingering idealism of American literary histories has yet to be fully accounted for or exorcised, Ellison's work on Fuller suggests that any such accounting will have to come to terms with Fuller and with the complex genderings of our ideal literary-historical periods.

By our anthologies shall you know our periods: any scholar-teacher in American literature understands as much and has anguished over the implications of accepting one or another anthology's selections or reproducing the anthology's period labels and divisions on her syllabus. Unlike Emily Dickinson, who notoriously straddles most anthologies' two-volume structure and the border it almost invariably establishes at the Civil War,[11] Margaret Fuller has the advantage at least of being the chronological insider, her life and career falling well within the temporal bounds established by all the anthologies of antebellum American literature. And she has certainly benefited from what not one of these anthologies fails to acknowledge as the "most significant advance" of recent American literary studies, canon expansion: of the six American literature anthologies in general distribution I surveyed, Fuller appeared in five. What concerns me here, however, is not only whether Fuller appears in anthologies, not only which of Fuller's works are printed, but how the period contexts in which Fuller is placed predict the way she is represented and ultimately read. I am not arguing that the great and greatly familiar welter of anthology apparatus — prefaces, general statements of editorial principles, period divisions and titles, and introductory essays on literary-historical contexts of particular periods — entirely determines what any given anthology can make of Fuller as an individual writer, still less what any given teacher or student may read in her. Indeed, sometimes the inconsistencies between one and another arm of this apparatus tell things otherwise unsaid. But consistent and otherwise, the periodizing apparatus of our anthologies calls for more than occasional feminist critical scrutiny.

As I have observed, anthologies are more openly self-conscious (not to say self-congratulatory) about who is in them than about the period boxes in which writers are placed. Their near unanimity in beginning their statements of principles by hailing the "multiplicity and variety" achieved in each anthology's advertised "balance . . . between the traditional and the new"[12] contrasts with their relative silence on the topic of periodization. It is as if the editors sensed that different schemes of periodization conferred little comparative advantage in selling anthologies, as compared to the more vital or accessible issues of inclusion and exclusion. Several anthologies imply philosophies of periodization in calling attention to their distinctive ways of attacking the traditional foreground/background, literature/history, work/context difficulties of literary history. Prentice-Hall's *American Literature,* for instance, especially emphasizes feminist historian Linda Kerber's role as editor and claims to focus "strongly on the connections between American literature and its various contexts: historical, political, economic, religious, intellectual, and international" (xxiii). Interestingly, the Prentice-Hall focus on "connections" winds up dispersing the traditional hefty period essay-introduction. Reporting "that students are often daunted by extremely long period introductions that attempt to cover too much history and literature at once," the editors opt for "shorter introductory background segments . . . placed . . . closer to the appropriate texts," coupled with more specific introductory essays on the literary genres represented in a given period (xxiii). Along with *The Harper American Literature,* Prentice-Hall's *American Literature* also offers context by the bit or the byte, setting off snippets of quotation and sometimes illustrations in boxes next to the main text—a hypertext effect that implies a vision of literature passing into history through a latent network of linkages that may be activated at any time.[13]

The Harper American Literature both courts and defends against the networks of dispersal implied by the hypertext effect. In the only one of the anthologies to reflect in any extended way on periodization as a theoretical issue, its editors usefully worry what they call the "perennial problem of any collection of American literature": "a structure that appears to isolate careers and periods without adequate attention to the interactions of these lives, works, and times" (xxxii). Their hope is instead to "weave" a "unified approach." Yet the Harper editors don't worry—how far could any anthology committed to being a "collection of American literature" worry?—over structures that might well yoke writers together without adequately attending to their conflicts, especially if the aim is to weave a unified approach. The *Harper* editors' metaphor for their philosophy of periodization, the anthology as textile, implicitly draws on both nineteenth-century women's material cultures and twentieth-century cultural feminisms that have enshrined weaving and webs as ideal images of antihierarchical, non-conflictual, antipatriarchal social orders. Like the *Harper* editors' collective title for the anthology's context-bytes ("Cultural landscapes and interiors"), the metaphor domesticates and contains what might otherwise strike readers as the dispersive or disseminating potential of history as hypertext network. As the governing image for the *Harper's* practices of periodization, the "weaving" metaphor both reads and repeats some of the unifying ideological work done by nineteenth-century bourgeois women's culture.

What this turns out to mean is that women's culture saves the American Renaissance for *The Harper American Literature,* which is the only anthology of the six to retain Matthiesson's famous title in undisturbed glory ("The Literature of the American Renaissance, 1836–1865"). Is the Renaissance less intellectually and ideologically troublesome — kinder, gentler — if its unities are underwritten by women's culture metaphors? If *The Harper American Literature,* thanks to its self-conscious wrestling with periodization as a critical issue, almost irresistibly provokes this question, it might still be asked of the other anthologies as well.

In the remaining five anthologies, presumably intense but covert struggles over periodization and its ambitions to "unify" take place not in discussion of principles but in the naming of what might have been called the American Renaissance. Prentice-Hall's *American Literature* puts up "Progress and Crisis: The Early to Middle 19th Century" — allowing readers to pick up the period by either handle, while the rhetoric of choice and balance formally conveys a reassuring message about the (liberal, plural, free, stable) outcome of crisis in the United States. This much choice seems to unnerve James E. Miller, whose American Renaissance by any other name is redundantly titled, in *Heritage of American Literature,* "Fruition: The Coming of Age." The *Heritage* groups writers into thematic clusters within periods, and "Fruition" begins with "The Transcendentalist Spirit" (Emerson and Thoreau), answered by "The Blackness of Darkness" (Poe, Hawthorne, and Melville), followed by the "Poets of the Tradition" (Longfellow and other genteel menfolk), then by "Emerging Feminist Perspectives" — where Fuller appears. When successive sections are titled "American Humorists" and "Literature of Native Americans," it is impossible not to feel that value and representation are being assigned by a quasi-geographical criterion of increasing distance from the Renaissance centers of civilization, with women as that civilization's interior frontier and Fuller, specifically, as Concord's interior frontier. Of the six anthologies, only the *Heath* and the *Norton Anthology of American Literature* confine their master period categories for the "renaissance" to the bare bones of chronology or chronology and nation, respectively as "Early Nineteenth Century, 1800–1865" and "American Literature, 1820–1865."[14] It is only the *Heath,* true to its iconoclastic reputation, that thoroughly disperses the classic "renaissance" writers across different thematic and generic categories—"The Flowering of Narrative," where Hawthorne abuts Caroline Kirkland, "Explorations of an 'American' Self," where Fuller keeps company not only with Emerson but with Frederick Douglass, Harriet Jacobs, and George Copway/Ojibwa—and by doing so undermines Concord's role as the originary center of national cultural unity, source of moral dissent as well as visionary consensus.[15]

However discreetly and expansively, consensus continues to be managed in the anthology period once known as the American Renaissance, and Margaret Fuller continues to be placed in provocatively marginal or pivotal relationships to existing and emergent centers of consensus; to repeat Colacurcio, she hovers. Where Fuller is concerned, the most awkward tasks of managing consensus hinge on the anthologies' treatment of nineteenth-century feminism and of American culture's ongoing dependence on, or at least relationship to, Europe. Fuller's placement on these two difficult frontiers, the one apparently domestic, the other apparently external, is vividly illustrated by two of the anthologies that include her work—the Norton Anthology and the Prentice-Hall *American Literature*—and also, I think, by the only anthology that does not include her, the Macmillan *Anthology of American Literature*. Reading more closely into these anthologies' introductory entanglements with feminism and literary internationalism reveals much about their engagements with Fuller and her ghosts and about the ways gender threads itself through literary periodization.

One version of anthology consensus feminism works by collapsing the two frontiers, domestic and external, of feminism and literary internationalism in the mode of the history of ideas and then reinstalling their abstracted ideas at the heart of the culture. Thus the Prentice-Hall *American Literature*'s "Headnote" to its section on early-nineteenth-century nonfiction prose ventures:

> If . . . there is one central emphasis in nonfiction prose of the first half of the nineteenth century, it is the unfolding of the self. The romanticism that developed in Europe at the beginning of the nineteenth century was fundamentally an assertion of the self. . . . And the romantics had a pronounced effect on America's writers. The Ralph Waldo Emerson who returned to the United States in 1833 . . . was fired with a romantic belief in the power of human intuition. . . .
>
> Margaret Fuller, for two years editor of *The Dial*, the transcendentalist magazine, spent a career urging women to assert themselves. This expansion of the idea of self led naturally and logically to a conflict between the individual and society. We see it in Fuller's feminism. (1325–26)

Under the genial light of the history of ideas, feminism becomes the late fruit of the *translatio studii*, "the transfer of art and learning from the Old World to the New."[16]

Like all strategies of periodization, this one posts both gains and losses. It usefully takes aim at more extreme versions of American exceptionalism by attending to shared intellectual history between Europe and the United States. It brings feminism and Fuller herself ("long considered a rather bizarre figure on the periphery of American transcendentalism," the editors observe in their headnote to Fuller's writings, p. 1681) in from the cold fringes of the world to the center of events in Concord. Under this understanding of nineteenth-century feminism, Margaret Fuller can't help assuming her "position of significance" (1681), and her work is well represented as both feminist and international, with excerpts from *At Home and Abroad* appearing alongside the usual anthology favorites, "The Great Lawsuit" and the essay "American Literature." She assumes significance, however, at a cost. As the mediator of European romantic ideas, Fuller apparently espouses a feminism whose sources lie elsewhere than in the experiences of, and debates among, actual women. Alone, she preaches ideas of self at a seemingly passive and nonindividuated body of women readers. The editors will emend this impression later in the essay by listing Fanny Fern and Elizabeth Cady Stanton along with Fuller as writers who "called attention to the inequality of women in a supposedly democratic society" (1328), but the impression is made: Fuller is exceptional and alone in bringing the romantic ideas of "self" from their source-springs in Europe to American women.

It is not, I would stress again, that there are no persuasive and pedagogically strategic elements in this representation of Fuller's feminism, or that it is not authorized in many ways by Fuller's own romantic-ideal self-representations. What is most troubling from a present-day feminist perspective, however, is the way the Prentice-Hall's version of the *translatio studii* insistently naturalizes feminist thinking in the person of Fuller. "Logically and naturally," she entered into the conflict between "the individual and society": this description effaces not only Fuller's personal struggles but those of other women, as well as struggles *between* women for who would get to define "individual" and "society."

If there is a natural, inevitable logic of feminism, differences among feminists have no logic that could be discussed: contrast the Prentice-Hall *American Literature*'s cursory list of Fuller, Fern, and Stanton with the *Heath*'s extensive discussion of different positions in "The Debate Over Women's Sphere" (1243–47). Nor, once feminism is thus naturalized in terms of the history of ideas and the *translatio studii*, can its vicissitudes in the United States be fully accounted for. In observing that "Margaret Fuller's reputation has undergone a critical change" (in the headnote to her work, 1683), the editors cannot say exactly *who* changed it, or why it needed changing, given what they credit as the cultural inevitability of feminism's individualist logic.[17] Their final conclusion, that Fuller "transcends her own time as a model of activism and intellectualism," implies her ongoing usefulness in some present work of culture. Yet that work of present-day feminism is what the Prentice-Hall *American Literature*, along with most of the other anthologies, can perhaps least afford to acknowledge in accounting for Fuller's reemergence.[18]

The naturalizing logic of the *translatio studii* can be used to exclude Fuller on what might have been thought her distinctive cultural turf: the 1989 Macmillan *Anthology of American Literature* is alone among the six anthologies I looked at in labeling antebellum American literature "The Age of Romanticism" and alone among them in entirely leaving out Fuller's work. How could this be? The Macmillan editors' obligatory introductory bow to diversity relies more heavily than most on the rhetoric of consensus inevitability: "In 1974 [when the first edition appeared], the contributions of women and minorities to the American literary tradition lacked the secure recognition with which we regard them now, and the confirmation of that recognition has altered the face of the American literary canon."[19] Who did the recognizing, who the confirming of the original recognizing, and who declared the results secure we are left to infer for ourselves, if we can find any remaining traces in the present of a cultural work so firmly relegated to the distant (1974?) past.

Turning to "The Age of Romanticism," looking for where Fuller isn't, we can find those traces in abundance; indeed, can find rehearsed virtually the whole cultural battle repressed in the Macmillan's preface. Here as so often antebellum American literature, whether it goes under the name of the American Renaissance or not, remains the anxiously privileged mirror of current critical practice. Looking toward Europe, the Macmillan editors see more or less what the Prentice-Hall editors saw: a history-of-ideas romanticism inexorably advancing toward the United States on the wings of the *translatio studii*. But what the Prentice-Hall editors hail, the Macmillan editors view with skeptical alarm:

> The attitudes of America's writers were shaped by their New World environment and an array of ideas inherited from the romantic traditions of Europe. A new romanticism had appeared in England in the last years of the eighteenth century. It spread to continental Europe and then came to America early in the nineteenth century. It was pluralistic; its manifestations were as varied, as individualistic, and as conflicting as the cultures and the

intellects from which it sprang. Romantics frequently shared certain general characteristics: moral enthusiasm, faith in the value of individualism and intuitive perception, and a presumption that the natural world is a source of goodness and man's societies a source of corruption. (595)

Whereas the Prentice-Hall *American Literature* cheerfully associates romanticism as assimilated by Transcendentalists like Emerson and Fuller with a natural logic of progress, the Macmillan team charges romanticism with the "rejection of rationalism" and, ultimately, with all the political ills to which the antebellum United States was heir. "Political egalitarianism had brought a politics that was frequently ignorant, impulsive, and irrational.... Intense individualism and soaring optimism had deteriorated into their natural consequences: selfishness, a crippling pessimism, and a frivolous addiction to the pleasures of despair and woe" (597).

Charged with the time's woes, romanticism rises to be credited, ambivalently, with the best and worst of its legacies to the future:

> Yet romanticism remained one of the glories of the age. It accelerated the spread of democracy to the downtrodden and the poor. It revitalized art and established new ways of perceiving humanity and the universe. And it remains evident today, in the resurgence of democratic radicalism, in the fascination with the simple life, in the exaltation of love, ... and in the social and sexual upheavals that have become a characteristic of American life. (597)

"Social and sexual upheavals" is as close as the Macmillan editors come to acknowledging some connection between their very brief earlier summary of "the feminist movement" (594, which mentions Stanton, Lucy Stone, Dorothea Dix, and Amelia Bloomer but not Fuller) and anything that may have happened between 1974 and 1989 to produce the "secure recognition" of women's writing hailed in the anthology's preface. Heir to a romanticism damned by the editors as irrationalist, present-day feminism—if you will, "sexual upheavals"—cannot be understood as an intellectual, critical, or reasoned set of positions but at best as an anarchic vitalist energy badly in need of the calming discipline exercised by the all-male Macmillan editorial collective. From this perspective, a romantic feminist intellectual is an impossible contradiction in terms: there is not now, for the Macmillan, and there can never have been a Margaret Fuller.

The evidence of the Prentice-Hall *American Literature* and the Macmillan *Anthology of American Literature* suggests that literary-historical idealism in periodization—deep investments in *translatio studii* and history of ideas—can work either to elide Fuller (in the case of Macmillan) or to represent her in terms that generously foreground some aspects of her significance while silencing others. The fourth edition of the *Norton Anthology of American Literature* offers an instructive contrast to both the Prentice-Hall and the Macmillan anthologies in what seem to be its conscious efforts to avoid literary-historical idealism in its work of literary periodization. Refusing more idea-driven or interpretive labels, the Norton editors title the antebellum period "American Literature, 1820–1865" and scrupulously stick to this locution despite its awkwardness, referring always to "the period 1820–1865" rather than lapsing into the "American Renaissance," "American Romanticism," or even "antebellum American literature" (xxviii). And yet, even to the Norton editors, "the period 1820–1865" is not a period like any other. In commenting on changes made in the fourth edition, the editors speak of 1820–1865 as "this great period" (xxviii), a summary judgment their preface ventures of no other period in the anthology and which it does not explain further.

Like all the anthologies in one way or another, the Norton's introductory period essay to "1820–1865" goes some way toward explaining the period's "greatness" by framing it in cultural nationalist terms as the era of "The Quest for an American Literary Destiny"—and, if that were not enough, following through with "The New Americanness of American Literature" and "The Aesthetics of a National Literature" (883–86). More than some of the other anthologies, however, the *Norton* also displaces a history-of-ideas model of periodization with a cultural materialist frame: thus sections titled "The Small World of American Writers" and "The Economics of American Letters" precede (and thus economics presumably both prompts and enables) "The Quest for an American Literary Destiny." Cultural nationalism and cultural materialism combine in the *Norton* to push European romanticism out of its central place in the Prentice-Hall and Macmillan versions of the period. The *Norton* acknowledges that "Americans were not long behind the British in responding to the Romantics Wordsworth and Coleridge" (884) and that "in *Moby-Dick* Melville's metaphysics are recognizably of the generation of Goethe, Byron, and Carlyle" (884), but unlike the Prentice-Hall *American Literature*, the *Norton* will not concede that American individualism as an idea, or system of ideas, owed anything to European romanticism.[20]

Margaret Fuller fares poorly in the *Norton*'s muscular retelling of "The Quest for an American Literary Destiny."[21] Sounding their nationalist theme in the opening of the introductory essay by describing the imagined company of American men of letters brought together in Christian Schussele's painting *Washington Irving and His Literary Friends at Sunnyside*, the editors note that the company excludes (among others) Margaret Fuller, but they do not venture to explain why it would have seemed appropriate to the painter "to depict representative literary men (not literary women)" (879). What the painting displays as the gendered status of the "representative" American literary intellectual is either above or beneath explication by the Norton editors, who might have but did not summon up a picture of Fuller's famous, and moreover historically real, conversations by way of commentary on Schussele's "pious hoax."[22] Fuller's name does not appear anywhere in the three pivotal sections of the essay trumpeting the new Americanness of American literature or in the essay's final section celebrating "The Heroism of American Writers" for challenging "a society that often lost sight of principles, whether aesthetic, social, or political" (892).[23] The great drama of the individual against society, which, according to the romantically minded editors of the Prentice-Hall *American Literature,* "naturally and logically" encompassed Fuller's feminism, does not encompass Fuller in the *Norton's* more aggressively nationalist redaction.

If Fuller does not, for the *Norton's* purposes, adequately have a nationalism, she does have a sex. The single most astonishing thing about the *Norton's* introductory essay to "American Literature, 1820–1865" is how it collapses what feminist scholarship has come to call gender on what we commonly understand as sexuality. Paging through the introduction for what it has to say about nineteenth-century feminism or the Woman Question, readers will find only a section titled "Sex and Sexual Roles." And if a reader guesses that "sexual roles" probably passes for what a more academic vocabulary would call "gender roles," the opening of this section will confuse her quickly:

> At a time when sex was banished from the magazines and from almost all books except medical treatises, Whitman alone called for a healthy sense of the relation between body and soul and created a forum for discussing sexual joy and anguish. The other male writers made no challenge to conventional sexual roles; when Emerson, for instance, said that society "is in conspiracy against the manhood of every one of its members," he meant "*man*hood," not "manhood and womanhood." Only Whitman ... rejected the opinion that woman's proper "sphere" was a limited, subservient, supportive one. While the attitudes of most male — and female — writers of the time reflected and embodied the prevailing sexism, Whitman rejected the "empty dish, gallantry." (887)

By the time we arrive at the "other male writers" on "sexual roles," we seem indeed to be talking in the wider sense about gender roles, the division of labor and of social power on the basis of gender conventions. The first sentence, however, makes no sense unless "sex" means only "sexuality," narrowly speaking: no student of the period could imagine that discussion of *gender*, of woman's proper sphere and man's, was "banished from the magazines and from almost all books."[24]

A classic instance of what Michel Foucault describes as the "repressive hypothesis" at work,[25] this passage's casting of Walt Whitman as the lone pioneer against the sexual repression of his time massively represses whole realms of nineteenth-century public discourse, debate, and activism—including, of course, women's activism—around matters of what we today call gender roles. (And in so doing, it also represses the wealth of twentieth-century scholarship devoted to reconstructing those realms.) Leaving aside the passage's understandable oversimplification of Whitman's sexual politics, this repression radically constrains what we can know of how women writers themselves understood the "prevailing sexism"—whatever that was, since no historical specifics are offered that would help readers flesh out a picture of a sexism somewhat different in its outlines from what we know. Nor are readers helped to understand the intricate dialectical relations between nineteenth-century sentimental cultures of gender and nineteenth-century feminisms. Instead of reacting to and participating in wider social discussions, women who think about "sexual roles" can only be, in this picture, lesser versions of Whitman, the heroic lone antirepressive dissenter:

> Of the other writers only Margaret Fuller thought so deeply [as Whitman] about sexual roles. Ironically, as the mother of a tardily acknowledged child (and perhaps not the wife of its Italian father), Fuller was an incalculable threat to the little Boston literary society in the months before her death by shipwreck prevented her arrival home. Of the women writers of the time, Dickinson, who never married, was the most bitterly ironic observer of the sacrifices marriage often required of a woman. (887)

The *Norton* represents Whitman's dissent through his writings but Fuller's only through her biography. In her biography, the relations that establish her as a sexual "threat" to "Boston literary society" are those with her child and its father, not her intense intellectual friendships with, or writerly addresses to, other women. And if Dickinson is characterized as one "of the women writers of the time," to what category of "other writers" does Fuller belong?

Given their antipathy toward the *translatio studii* and their bent toward muscular cultural nationalism, with its heroic claims for American originality, it is not surprising that the *Norton* editors spend little time with Fuller's translations in drawing up her brief intellectual biography or that they eschew her writings from Europe and most of her literary criticism in compiling their selections from her work. Although Fuller's *Summer on the Lakes* might seem more promising from a literary nationalist perspective, not to mention a literary nationalist perspective that connects "Americanness" with generic experimentation in prose, it too is passed over. Represented (at least in excerpts) by three of the five anthologies that include Fuller, her essay "American Literature" does not appear in the *Norton*, further underscoring the anthology's representation of literary nationalism as a cultural work that belongs to men.[26] The fourth edition *Norton*'s Fuller is confined to excerpts from "The Great Lawsuit," confined, that is, to what both the nineteenth century and the *Norton* editors both understand as The Sex. What the *Norton*'s Fuller does not help us to see, what its construction of "American Literature 1820–1865" even actively obscures, are the wider relations among sex and gender, gender and genre, gender and literary nationalism that are crucial to the work of literary periodization.

In general, the anthologies' versions of antebellum American literature as a period and of Margaret Fuller's place in that period tend to confirm Lawrence Buell's observation that "for all its critical sophistication, the New Historicist critique of the ideological duplicity of classic American Renaissance texts (their ostensible radicalism versus their actual centrism) has not seriously challenged the assumption that these texts can be adequately understood as an internally coherent and nationally distinctive series." The American Renaissance is the period around which what Buell calls the "cisatlantic hermeticism" of American literary studies, with its "lineal succession stories like from Edwards to Emerson, Emerson to Whitman, Whitman to Stevens, and so on," historically coalesced, and around which that hermeticism still flourishes in practice today. Neither the "small but growing number" of critical works that have "taken Anglo-American or Euro-American literary relations as their main subject" nor "the Euro-American community of nineteenth-century women writers implicit in feminist criticism," Buell concludes, have "yet seriously affected the way Americanists conduct business as usual."[27]

Some of the anthology treatments of Fuller, as we have seen, do indeed mount creative challenges to one or another aspect of "business as usual" but seldom to the package as a whole. Prentice-Hall's *American Literature*, for example, by naming both Emerson's individualism and Fuller's feminism as the "natural" legatees of European romanticism, inserts Fuller into an otherwise patri-"lineal succession story" that is not exclusively nationalist in its intellectual origins. In doing so, however, the editors assume in other ways the internal coherence and consensual logic of American individualism.

And Vera Kutzinski, in her reply to Buell, raises further important questions about Buell's diagnosis and about the corrective he tentatively ventures for these entrenched professional practices, which is to read American literature, and especially the American Renaissance, as a "postcolonial" literature. Charging that Buell's "main goal" in reimagining a "postcolonial" American literary studies "is to rescue a now-neglected series of canonical American writers and texts by appropriating for them the label postcolonial without any regard for the specificity of significantly different historical situations," Kutzinski takes aim at the

> tendency on the part of some American literary historians generously to rescind external, national, and even linguistic, borders while implicitly holding fast to those internal boundaries that demarcate race, class, and gender differences. Put differently, it is still easier to open the American canon to sanitized dialogues with select masterpieces from other literatures than to reimagine American literary history as a palimpsest inscribed with traces of all kinds of promiscuous contacts and relations between different races, classes and genders (not even to mention what is euphemistically described as sexual preference).[28]

The "internally coherent and nationally distinctive series" that concerns Buell, in other words, will not fall until Emerson's individualism is seen not only as the product of an intimate argument with Europe but also as the remainder of its division from the woman, the black, the Indian—from Fuller herself, among other interlocutors.[29] By the same token, Kutzinski's argument requires us to understand Fuller's subject of feminism as produced by division from, and alliances with, not only Emerson and Europe but also African Americans, Native Americans, and other women.

Kutzinski's picture of a literary history organized around modes "of promiscuous contacts and relations" effectively enlarges for the 1990s the possibilities, as well as the obligations, of Joan Kelly-Gadol's early feminist observation that "periodization . . . in women's history . . . has become *relational.*"[30] Since 1976, feminist scholarship has added to Kelly-Gadol's stress on relations between women and men the realization that "women" and "men" are categories constituted by internal differences and contradictions, as well as by their binary relationship to one another, and by their cross-cutting with other categories of nationality, class, race, and sexuality. Margaret Fuller, as my survey of American literature anthologies suggests, is presently a figure at the crossroads between feminist criticism's demand for relational understandings of periodization and ongoing efforts to reframe the normalizing, nationalist periodizations of American literary history. Recent feminist work on Fuller by Christina Zwarg, Julie

Ellison, and Mary Wood replies directly and provocatively to the difficulties of periodization exposed by Fuller's placement in the standard American literature anthologies and helps suggest other directions for periodization to take.

Fuller's career played both sides of what both she and her American contemporaries saw as a period-defining struggle between the belated self-consciousness of criticism and the nationalist possibilities of original creation as she exploited the contradictions of the gendered division of intellectual labor that assigned critique, philosophy, and abstraction to the masculine but that also fretted about the derivative, secondary, enfeebling—read, feminine—cast of this same side of the division of intellectual labor.[31] Christina Zwarg and Julie Ellison, among feminist critics now writing on Fuller, have done the most to explicate the complex genderings of Fuller's work as a critical intellectual. If Fuller's favored "derivative" genres or writing practices—translation, editing, critique, anthology— explore her realization that, as Zwarg puts it, "gender itself depend[s] upon a collision of 'languages,'" these same writing practices also allowed her, in Ellison's words, to dramatize "the pattern of resistance to the pressure of conventional gender roles . . . through the juxtaposition of generic idioms."[32] Zwarg's and Ellison's accounts of Fuller's intellectual work strikingly echo the logic of Buell's and Kutzinski's arguments about American literary history, which urge us to see that literary periodization and literary nationalism also "depend upon a collision of languages," a collision that happens both at the national borders and within them.

In this light, a text like Fuller's *Summer on the Lakes, in 1843*, with its self-dramatizing surfeit of heterogeneous quotation (chapter 5, for instance, goes from a direct description of "Milwaukie" to an ekphrastic flight on Titian's Venus and Adonis distanced by quotation marks, to an imagined dialogue among three persons that is offered as a reaction to, in a sense a "translation" of, matters taken up in an obscure German book but that also rehearses Fuller's dialogues with Emerson—and so on)[33] offers a stronger contrast with Emerson's effort in *Nature* to simplify or purify the borders, rendering them down to the ME and the NOT ME.

As Annette Kolodny argued some years ago, *Summer on the Lakes* shows that men and women settlers had very different experiences of the frontiers; just as Joan Kelly-Gadol's historical work challenged the idea that men and women had the same "renaissance," Fuller's book challenges the idea that Euro-American women and men migrating westward (let alone Native American women and men) experienced what the anthologies call the age of "Progress and Crisis" or "Fruition" in the same ways.[34] The coincidence of Buell's and Kutzinski's critique of American literary studies with Zwarg's and Ellison's more recent feminist work on Fuller shows a way of taking Kolodny's implicitly periodizing argument one step further: Fuller's insistent "collision of 'languages'" in *Summer on the Lakes* might make paradigmatic sense for understanding the period of emergent American literary nationalism, at least as much sense as the works of the male writers credited by the *Norton Anthology* with doing the work of nationalism. Taking *Summer on the Lakes* seriously as a defining text of the period, we might be encouraged to extend the category most anthologies now feature in one form or another at the very beginnings of American literature—"The Literature of Exploration" or "Cultures in Contact"—further into the conventional anthology periods of American literary history and to remember more consistently the category's genderings; we might also consider translation more self-consciously as an issue that threads itself in different and, again, gendered ways through different periods of American history.[35]

As Julie Ellison powerfully argues, however, the Fuller who took issue with Emerson in *Summer on the Lakes* and elsewhere did so from "within romanticism," from some assumptions shared with (although, as Ellison insists, not necessarily derived from) Emerson and other American and European romantics. To contrast Emerson's *Nature* with *Summer on the Lakes* should not require us to subscribe to the version of Fuller's career that Ellison aptly calls "an allegory of literary history, in which Fuller's development spans the neoclassicism of her father's eighteenth-century curriculum and the spectrum of romanticism from Goethe to Emerson, to end in the realism of a radical and almost modern engagement with history."[36] Ellison's and Zwarg's work instead provokes us to reconsider the periodizing significance of the figure rendered invisible or impossible by the Macmillan *Anthology of American Literature* and flattened into American consensus individualism by the Prentice-Hall *American Literature*: the romantic woman intellectual. What might be the period boundaries, significant events, and significant texts for a European-American anthology of the works of romantic women intellectuals and of Anglo-American romantic women writers in all genres? What course might use such a text? One question for such an imaginary anthology, as Ellison suggests, would be to assess the as yet too little explored boundary between the "romantic" and the "sentimental," a boundary around which questions of literary nationalism (England romantic, the U.S. sentimental), literary value (too obvious to gloss), gender (men romantic, women sentimental), and chronology (British romantics up through about 1830, Victorians sentimental thereafter, but all bets off in the United States) have circulated murkily for decades.[37]

To ask about connections between "romantic" and "sentimental" cultures brings us to Fuller's implication in still another set of contested relations between general or anthology literary-historical periods and those most salient in feminist critical work on the nineteenth century United States. One of the more powerful periodizing constructions of mid-1970s feminist historiography was delivered in Carroll Smith-Rosenberg's groundbreaking article "The Female World of Love and Ritual: Relations Between Women in Nineteenth-Century America." Born of the "emotional proximity" of the nineteenth-century "world of female support, intimacy, and ritual," in Smith-Rosenberg's account, women's relations with one another in this world were "cut short" by emergent twentieth-century "cultural taboos" that sexualized interpretations of women's friendships and strictly split off "normal" from "deviant" sexualities. This interpretation of nineteenth-century women's experience took direct aim at the understanding of sexuality still to be found in the *Norton Anthology*'s representation of antebellum "sex and sexual roles": rather than being a particularly repressive time for women, Smith-Rosenberg speculated, "the supposedly repressive and destructive Victorian sexual ethos may have been more flexible and responsive to the needs of particular individuals than those of the mid-twentieth century."[38] We could look to Fuller's relations with women, rather than only to the picture of Fuller in her heterosexual tableau of the illicit drowned family, for the significance of her life and work in light of emergent feminist periodizations of the history of sexuality.

As many historians of nineteenth-century women's culture have since pointed out, of course, Smith-Rosenberg's thesis generalized freely from middle-class white women's experiences to those of all nineteenth-century American women. And even within those boundaries of race and class, Fuller makes some trouble for Smith-Rosenberg's account of this period of women's culture.

Ellison, alert to the power relations of subjectivity and interpretation at work in Fuller's conversations with women no less than in her relations with male intellectuals, raises the question of whether "assimilat[ing] the Conversations into 'the female world of love and ritual'" does not end up "transpos[ing] a scenario of inequality into the language of intimacy and exchange," in a "sentimental" reading that echoes rather than analyzes what Fuller herself wanted from other women in sentimentalizing herself with and for them.[39]

From another angle, Mary Wood's work on Fuller and lesbianism suggests that "we need to keep examining our assumptions about historical shifts," including Smith-Rosenberg's influential periodization: reading Fuller's writings "in the light of the discourse on sexuality" in the antebellum United States, she finds evidence that "notions of lesbian 'identity' were already being constructed and deconstructed well before sexologists named lesbianism as medically deviant in the 1880s." As not only a middle-class woman but more specifically an ambitious romantic woman intellectual, Fuller was "bound to reveal the contradictions" of idealized romantic women's friendships: "Fuller's sexuality was necessarily called into question precisely because she sought to place herself within a tradition of writers and philosophers. Within that tradition, to write about romantic love for a woman was necessarily to place oneself in the position of male artist or philosopher."[40] Fuller's work, like that of Dickinson and Whitman a little later in the century, suggests the ways in which gender and sexuality are both mutually dependent on and mutually fractured by each other, in still another "collision of languages" like that described by Zwarg; it complicates both traditionally received and emergent feminist understandings of her period.

If the literary periodization of standard American literature anthologies were to be reexamined in light of Smith-Rosenberg's thesis and its critique in Wood's essay, some of Fuller's texts would clearly be candidates for anthologizing. Fuller's letters to women friends (of which the *Heath* anthology prints a few) and her essay "Bettine Brentano and Her Friend Gunderode" are obvious choices.[41] Another would be "A Dialogue," included in Fuller's *Papers on Literature and Art*, in which two male figures discuss the end of their romantic pedagogical friendship by quoting and glossing poems with each other. "Dialogue" puts another twist on Wood's exploration of what it meant for Fuller to pose her sexuality "within a tradition of writers and philosophers"; the dialogue's tactics of quotation and cross-quotation produce its eros, and the fate of quotation is the fate of love.[42] "Dialogue" also uncannily anticipates later nineteenth- and twentieth-century tactics of queer reading: when Aglauron combs through Wordsworth's and Coleridge's poetry for evidence of his own lost love, composing Wordsworth's "A Complaint" and Coleridge's "A Soliloquy" into a coherent narrative sequence of lament and reply, one can be reminded of Oscar Wilde's dialogue in "The Portrait of Mr W. H.," which constructs its narrative around Shakespeare's sonnets, and other gay and lesbian attempts at composing or anthologizing buried traditions.[43] One might also be reminded of how other women intellectuals in the United States, writing in later times and from other positions of race, class, and ethnicity, have composed proscribed sexual identities out of other collisions of language, other practices of translation, quotation, genre-mixing and bending. Eve Kosofsky Sedgwick's 1987 "A Poem Is Being Written," which combines critical prose, autobiography (including the story of learning French from a gay teacher), and Sedgwick's own poetry in reflecting on how she herself came to be deeply identified with the cultural position of modern gay men, comes to mind. So does Cherríe Moraga's 1983 *Loving in the War Years*, a more radically bilingual, Spanish-English exploration of living as a Chicana and a lesbian-feminist in poetry, narrative, and critical prose.[44] The anthology that might connect Fuller's essay on Bettine Brentano (along with her translation of Brentano's *Die Gunderode*) to her "Dialogue," and then Fuller's writing to more recent generically, sexually, and linguistically transgressive works like Sedgwick's and Moraga's, however, has yet to be imagined—let alone the periods such an anthology might fall into or how its periods could reshape those of the standard American literature anthology.

But the further afield these speculations go, the more they underline the risks as well as the excitement of feminist efforts to reperiodize American literature, or any other body of literary cultures, by drawing new period paradigms from the work of any one woman writer. As Vera Kutzinski's critique of Lawrence Buell's comparativist, "postcolonial" American Renaissance cautions, the borders of nations are internal as well as external; thus too the borders of periods and of genders and sexualities. And the borders are not places innocent of inequality or power. The point of comparing Cherríe Moraga's *Loving in the War Years* to some of Fuller's generic experiments, as Kutzinski warns, ought not to be to canonize Moraga by virtue of her similarities to Fuller, whatever good intentions might lie behind such an effort. Moreover, as Ellison's work implies, such *re*periodizing efforts run the risk of obscuring the extent to which Fuller's romantic idealism, however complex and conflicted her iterations of it, *already* structures the way "we"—meaning the feminist literary intellectuals, mostly kin to Fuller in race and class, with whom I began this essay—understand both her literary period and "our" contemporary feminism. One persistent rhetorical strategy or closing gesture, common to both feminist critical work on Fuller and the standard American literature anthologies, poses the timing of Fuller's significance in what a grammarian might analyze as the future anterior tense: as the *Harper American Literature* puts it, "the real extent of her influence may well surface in the next generation of writers who read her work" (1610).[45] In some future time, Fuller will have been able to be what she already must have been in order to have influenced that future. When past and future cross rhetorically like this, it is possible to see how feminist reperiodization both anticipates the future revisions of our current revisions and grounds our current hopes in the "real" of a future past.

NOTES

1. Bell Gale Chevigny, *The Woman and the Myth: Margaret Fuller's Life and Writings* (Old Westbury, N.Y.: Feminist Press, 1976), 1.

2. Michael J. Colacurcio, "The American Renaissance-Renaissance" (Essay Review), *New England Quarterly* 64 (September 1991): 445–93, 453.

3. Ann Douglas, *The Feminization of American Culture* (New York: Knopf, 1977), 259–88.

4. Chevigny, *The Woman and the Myth*, 3. Chevigny's preface to the revised edition of *The Woman and the Myth* (Boston: Northeastern University Press, 1994) returns to this problem, observing that "with ongoing analyses of the literature of domesticity and the culture of sentiment and with emerging close studies of female activists, we can now position her various achievements in finer detail" (xx). We should be able to, but perhaps we haven't yet: the studies of domesticity Chevigny cites in evidence here, Mary Kelley's *Private Woman, Public Stage: Literary Domesticity in America* (New York: Oxford University Press, 1984), Lora Romero's article "Domesticity and Fiction" in *The Columbia History of the American Novel*, Emory Elliott, gen. ed. (New York: Columbia University Press, 1991), and *The Culture of Sentiment: Race, Gender, and Sentimentality in Nineteenth-Century America*, ed. Shirley Samuels (New York: Oxford University Press, 1992), give very little time to Fuller. One of the reasons for this lack of connection, as the inclusion of Romero's article on Chevigny's list suggests, is that scholarly studies of domesticity and sentimentalism have focused on fiction to the exclusion of other genres. The question of Fuller and sentimentalism will return later in this essay.

5. Such studies would include Larzer Ziff's *Literary Democracy: The Declaration of Cultural Independence in America* (New York: Viking, 1981), Larry J. Reynolds's *European Revolutions and the American Literary Renaissance* (New Haven: Yale University Press, 1988), Jeffrey Steele's *The Representation of the Self in the American Renaissance* (Chapel Hill: University of North Carolina Press, 1987), and Joyce Warren's *The American Narcissus: Individualism and Women in Nineteenth-Century American Fiction* (New Brunswick: Rutgers University Press, 1984), all of which include important sections on Fuller.

6. *The Portable Margaret Fuller*, ed. Mary Kelley (New York: Viking/Penguin, 1994); *The Essential Margaret Fuller*, ed. Jeffrey Steele (New Brunswick: Rutgers University Press, 1992). Bell Gale Chevigny, in her Foreword to the 1994 *The Woman and the Myth*, confides her fear that "in my passion to rescue Fuller from past distortions and despite my commitment to letting her speak for herself, I might have done her new damage by bringing her back to satisfy needs of my own, as some of her friends had so disturbingly done" (xxi). Christina Zwarg, some of whose other work on Fuller will be discussed later in this essay, directly addresses the question of feminist readers' identification with Fuller and of her motives for drawing Fuller's writing into a conversation with twentieth-century feminist theory, in her essay "Womanizing Margaret Fuller: Theorizing a Lover's Discourse," *Cultural Critique* 16 (Fall 1990): 161–91.

7. Colacurcio, "American Renaissance," 493.

8. Joan Kelly-Gadol, "The Social Relation of the Sexes: Methodological Implications of Women's History," first published in *Signs*, 1976; rpt. in *The Signs Reader*, ed. Elizabeth Abel and Emily K. Abel (Chicago: University of Chicago Press, 1983), 11–25.

9. See Peter Carafiol, *The American Ideal: Literary History as a Wordly Activity* (New York: Oxford University Press, 1991), 3–93, for an extended discussion of how Transcen-

dentalist writings have both grounded American literary scholarship's foundational investments in nationalism and idealism and troubled that grounding in practice: "Transcendentalist texts never seemed to justify [their] centrality because they failed to meet established critical standards for either intellectual or logical coherence" (7). Fuller's Transcendentalist writings have always been liable to just these charges, of course. Given the rich provocations of Fuller's career and reception for Carafiol's argument (including his critique of some present-day feminist versions of the "American Ideal"), it is the more disappointing that Carafiol does not address her—not even by reference passing enough to turn up in the book's index.

10. Julie Ellison, *Delicate Subjects: Romanticism, Gender, and the Ethics of Understanding* (Ithaca: Cornell University Press, 1990), 298, 225.

11. See Margaret Dickie's essay in this volume, "Emily Dickinson in History and Literary History."

12. James Miller, ed., *Heritage of American Literature: Beginnings to the Civil War* (New York: Harcourt Brace Jovanovich, 1991), v. The universality of this opening gesture toward pluralism should not be allowed to obscure some real differences among the anthologies as to the origin stories they tell about how the happy pluralism came to be. For example, the Prentice-Hall *American Literature*, in naming "the discovery and rediscovery of important works that had received little critical attention in the past," goes on to account for the neglect thus redressed, pointing out that these works are "for the most part . . . by women writers and members of ethnic and racial minority groups" whose interests were not represented in institutional literary criticism. See Emory Elliot, Linda K. Kerber, A. Walton Litz, and Terence Martin, eds., *American Literature: A Prentice-Hall Anthology* (Englewood Cliffs, N.J.: Prentice-Hall, 1991), xxi. Miller's *Heritage*, by contrast, a generally more conservative anthology, represents or mystifies the issues as a conflict of (or rather selection among) equal metaphors rather than unequal people: "Whatever the truth of these metaphors—melting pot, patchwork quilt, roots—there can be no gainsaying that American writers and their works are made up of a multiplicity and variety that constitute their unique character and richness" (v).

13. The *Harper's* editors call their context-bytes "Cultural landscapes and interiors," being metaphorically suggestive rather than literally accurate as to the contents of the byte-boxes, which are more often drawn from intellectual history than from material culture. See *The Harper American Literature*, 2d ed., ed. Donald McQuade et al. (New York: HarperCollins, 1994). The *Heath Anthology of American Literature*, 2d ed., ed. Paul Lauter et al. (Lexington, Mass: D. C. Heath, 1994), uses comparable byte-boxes of "context" in its long introductory period essays.

14. *The Norton Anthology of American Literature*, 4th ed., ed. Nina Baym et al. (New York: Norton, 1994). The fifth edition of the *Norton* appeared while this essay was in final preparation; for comments on its revised treatment of both Fuller and "American Literature, 1820–1865," see notes 20, 22, 23, 24, and 26, below. Unless otherwise noted, all citations in this essay are to the fourth edition.

15. Interestingly, however, the *Heath* installs Henry David Thoreau in an honorific

category of one, "A Concord Individualist," as if even the multicultural dream had to have, somewhere, its navel in Concord.

16. For some transmutations of *translatio studii* in American literature and criticism, see Lawrence Buell, "American Literary Emergence as a Postcolonial Phenomenon," ALH 4 (Fall 1992): 411–41. The definition of *translatio studii* comes from page 420.

17. The *Harper's* introductory essay to "The Literature of the American Renaissance" draws on some of the same strategies as the Prentice-Hall *American Literature* for representing nineteenth-century feminism but with less satisfying results. Feminism, or the women's movement, is not among the various social and political issues singled out for detailed treatment in the introductory essay. Two pages (1045–47), however, including a half-page illustration, are given over to phrenology as a representative instance of "self-trust, self-improvement, and perfectionism" in the nineteenth-century United States (1045).

18. See, for example, the headnote to Fuller in Miller's *Heritage:* "With all her considerable achievements, Margaret Fuller's death at the age of forty left (and still leaves) an impression of immense promise unfulfilled. So fixed was this view that for a long time the works she did leave behind her remained on the shelves, unregarded. . . . More recently, however, her literary importance has been quietly reinstated"—a reinstatement whose beginnings Miller credits to Vernon Parrington, who "some decades ago . . . made the case" for Fuller. Although Miller carefully traces the damages done by Fuller's posthumous male editors, his conclusion effaces the agency of present-day feminism in Fuller's reinstatement, which has not been "quiet" to everybody's taste. We are implicitly invited to repose in another version of the Prentice-Hall *American Literature's* faith in inevitability: if Vernon Parrington made the case so well so long ago, why should feminists agitate themselves noisily today? Again the *Heath's* headnote (by Joel Myerson) provides an instructive contrast, forthrightly acknowledging that "the emergence of a renewed women's movement in the 1960s helped revive interest in Fuller's work" (1612).

19. George McMichael et al., eds., *Anthology of American Literature*, 4th ed., Vol. 1 (New York: Macmillan, 1989), vii.

20. The fourth edition of the *Norton* acknowledges that Americans were responding to Romantics like Wordsworth, Coleridge, and Goethe but not that American individualism, the *Norton's* most prized national trait, owed anything to European romanticism; if Emerson picked over "ancient and modern philosophies" in his writing, nevertheless "what proved most enduringly 'American' about Emerson was his wide streak of Yankee individualism" (884). The fifth edition of the *Norton* has retreated considerably from this narrative of national emergence, a retreat signaled most forcibly by the new edition's deletion of three entire section titles—"The Quest for an American Literary Destiny," "The Aesthetics of a National Literature," and "The New Americanness of American Literature"—from its introductory essay "American Literature, 1820–1865." In their vacated place, roughly speaking, the fifth edition puts "The Shifting Canon of American Writers" and "The Small World of American Writers," newly stressing "the fragile status of literary reputations" (920) while extending the *Norton's* long-standing interest in rep-

resenting the economic conditions of American writing and reading. See the *Norton*, 883–86, and Nina Baym et al., eds., *The Norton Anthology of American Literature*, 5th ed., 2 vols. (New York: Norton, 1998), 1:919–20.

21. The best feminist critique of the Adamic male myth of pioneering that underlies this picture of "The Quest for an American Literary Destiny" is still Nina Baym's "Melodramas of Beset Manhood: How Theories of American Fiction Exclude Women Authors," rpt. in *The New Feminist Criticism: Essays on Women, Literature and Theory*, ed. Elaine Showalter (New York: Pantheon, 1985). Ironically, Baym is one of the editors responsible for framing the *Norton*'s "American Literature, 1820–1865" so vividly in terms of this male narrative.

22. The fifth edition of the *Norton* mentions Fuller's conversations (922) in its section "The Small World of American Writers" (920–22), in deliberate counterpoint to the imaginary small world of Schussele's idealizing canonical painting.

23. The only woman writer to appear in most of these crucial paragraphs in the *Norton* fourth edition, although not in the final section on "Heroism," is Emily Dickinson, who seems to make it on the grounds of formal radicalism. Her "wrenched syntax and rhyme" qualify her as "accomplishing things yet unattempted in the English language," along with Cooper, Melville, Thoreau, and other of the usual suspects (885). Bearing in mind Fuller's experimental ways with genre in her prose, one might suspect that the standard of heroically original formal radicalism—which is, in the *Norton*'s terms, the standard of Americanness itself—is higher here for female than for male writers. "The Heroism of American Writers" remains the final section of the introductory essay "American Literature, 1820–1865" in the *Norton* fifth edition, although in a mode somewhat chastened and subdued by acknowledgment of "National Sins" (the fifth edition's penultimate section title, replacing the fourth edition's more neutral "Politics and Wars"). See the *Norton*, 891–92, and the *Norton* 5th ed., 928–31.

24. Strikingly, the new fifth edition of the *Norton* has discarded the fourth (and previous) edition's introductory section "Sex and Sexual Roles." Material on the status of women authors and women as readers is generously included under other rubrics in the introductory essay "American Literature, 1820–1865," but nineteenth-century feminist activism and debates over gender roles drop out of the limelight as social issues to be considered on a par with "Immigration, Xenophobia, and Racism" (*Norton* 5th ed., 927).

25. See Michel Foucault, *The History of Sexuality*, trans. Robert Hurley, Vol. 1, *An Introduction* (New York: Pantheon, 1978), for an extended discussion of how the nineteenth century has been interpreted under the sway of the "repressive hypothesis."

26. The Prentice-Hall *American Literature*, the *Heath* anthology, and the *Harper American Literature* all include at least portions of Fuller's "American Literature." The fifth edition of the *Norton* reprints "The Great Lawsuit" in its entirety and Fuller's unfinished, posthumously published memoir (see the *Norton*, 5th ed., 1626–42); this considerably increased representation arguably still slights Fuller's work as a public intellectual in both the literary and political spheres.

27. Buell, "American Literary Emergence as a Postcolonial Phenomenon," 415, 413, 414.

28. Vera M. Kutzinski, "Commentary: American Literary History as Spatial Practice," *American Literary History* 4 (Fall 1992): 554–55. I am not sure why Kutzinski believes that Whitman, Emerson, and Melville are nowadays "neglected"—the MLA International Bibliography and the teaching anthologies still suggest otherwise. And Kutzinski does not directly answer Buell's demonstration that it is still surprisingly difficult to "open the American canon" *even* "to sanitized dialogues with select masterpieces from other literatures." What counts as a "sanitized" dialogue is still another question; whose Whitman could ever be "hairy" enough?

29. The *Heath* anthology points to these issues under its introductory rubrics of "Individualism and/vs. Community" (1257–60) and "Explorations of an 'American' Self" (1481). Bell Gale Chevigny makes the case for Fuller's life and work as a developing project of deconstructing "universal" Emersonian individualism's dependence on woman as other in her important essay "To the Edges of Ideology: Margaret Fuller's Centrifugal Evolution," *American Quarterly* 38 (Summer 1986): 173–202.

30. Kelly-Gadol, "The Social Relation of the Sexes," 14.

31. See in this connection David Simpson's useful work on relations among nationalism, theory, and gender in *Romanticism, Nationalism, and the Revolt Against Theory* (Chicago: University of Chicago Press, 1993).

32. Christina Zwarg, "Feminism in Translation: Margaret Fuller's *Tasso*," *Studies in Romanticism* 29 (Fall 1990): 464; Julie Ellison, *Delicate Subjects: Romanticism, Gender, and the Ethics of Understanding* (Ithaca: Cornell University Press, 1990), 225. See also Christina Zwarg's *Feminist Conversations: Fuller, Emerson, and the Play of Reading* (Ithaca: Cornell University Press, 1995).

33. Margaret Fuller, *Summer on the Lakes, in 1843*, intro. Susan Belasco Smith (Urbana: University of Illinois Press, 1991), 68–104; see Smith's introduction, xviii–xx, for a brief account of how *Summer on the Lakes*, especially chapter 5, expresses Fuller's evolving "differences with Emerson" (xix).

34. See Annette Kolodny, *The Land Before Her: Fantasy and Experience of the American Frontiers, 1630–1860* (Chapel Hill: University of North Carolina Press, 1984), 112–30, and Smith, introduction to *Summer on the Lakes*, xvii.

35. "Cultures in Contact" is the *Heath* rubric; the Prentice-Hall *American Literature* put "The Literature of Exploration" under its general term for the opening period of "American" literature, "The European Colonization of the Americas." See Eric Cheyfitz's *The Poetics of Imperialism: Translation and Colonization from The Tempest to Tarzan* (New York: Oxford University Press, 1991), for an effort to come to terms "with the theoretical/historical problem of translation as it structures the Anglo-American/Native American frontier" (xvii). Thinking about translation and "contact" as ongoing works might help reframe, for example, period discussions of American post–Civil War realism and its relationship to literatures of immigrants and immigration. The gendered poetics of translation in modernism, to take another example, have begun to be explored in relation to canonical poets such as Ezra Pound and H.D.

36. See Ellison, *Delicate Subjects*, 220, for an attack on the received picture of Fuller's dependence on Emerson for her romantic or Transcendentalist thought.

37. Ann Douglas's use of "romantic" versus "sentimental" and "Victorian" as a stand-in for "sentimental" runs these various possibilities through most of their paces; see *Feminization of American Culture*, 3–13 ("The Legacy of American Victorianism") and Part Three, "Protest: Case Studies in American Romanticism." On sentimentalism and romanticism, see Ellison, *Delicate Subjects*, 253–56. For a wide-ranging attempt to reconfigure the period of mid-century (1820–70) American literature around women's sentimental writing, see Joanne Dobson, "The American Renaissance Reenvisioned," in *The (Other) American Traditions: Nineteenth-Century Women Writers*, ed. Joyce W. Warren (New Brunswick: Rutgers University Press, 1993), 164–82.

38. Carroll Smith-Rosenberg, "The Female World of Love and Ritual: Relations Between Women in Nineteenth-Century America," in Smith-Rosenberg, *Disorderly Conduct: Visions of Gender in Victorian America* (New York: Oxford University Press, 1985), 71, 74, 76. The essay was originally published in *Signs: Journal of Women in Culture and Society* 1 (1975).

39. Ellison, *Delicate Subjects*, 253–54.

40. Mary E. Wood, "'With Ready Eye': Margaret Fuller and Lesbianism in Nineteenth-Century American Literature," *American Literature* 65 (March 1993): 4, 6.

41. The most recent anthologies of Fuller's work reflect these changes; thus the essay on Bettine Brentano and Gunderode, absent from Chevigny's 1976 *Margaret Fuller: The Woman and the Myth*, appears in the Supplement to the 1994 edition.

42. "A Dialogue," in S. Margaret Fuller, *Papers on Literature and Art* (1846; rpt. New York: AMS, 1972), 151–64. The parade of quotations between the two men closes with Aglauron's invocation of *Hamlet*, the very quotation of quotation: "Had we never read the play, we should find the whole of it from quotation and illustration familiar to us as air. That exquisite phraseology, so heavy with meaning, wrought out with such admirable minuteness, has become a part of literary diction, the stock of the literary bank; and what set criticism can tell like this fact how great was the work, and that men were worthy it should be addressed to them?" (163). Aglauron's consolation (and he knows perfectly well it is out of "stock") for the loss of romantic friendship's private "exquisite phraseology" is its transmutation into public meaning and love of mankind. The names of the dialogue's speakers, Aglauron and Laurie, suggest a doubling or narcissistic relationship between the two of them, with Laurie as the diminutive or lesser light of the other; this is worth pondering for what it may say about how Fuller understood the samenesses and differences structuring same-gender love.

43. "The Portrait of Mr W. H.," rpt. in *The Artist as Critic: Critical Writings of Oscar Wilde*, ed. Richard Ellman (New York: Random House, 1969), 152–220.

44. Eve Kosofsky Sedgwick, "A Poem Is Being Written," *Representations* 17 (Winter 1987): 110–43; Cherríe Moraga, *Loving in the War Years* (Boston: South End Press, 1983).

45. Compare the ending of the *Norton Anthology of American Literature*'s headnote on Fuller: "The evidence is at hand that may at last establish Fuller's candidacy for serious consideration as what Hawthorne said mockingly, 'the greatest, wisest, best woman of the age'" (1589; unchanged in the 5th ed., 1592).

EMILY DICKINSON IN HISTORY AND LITERARY HISTORY

Margaret Dickie

I'm ceded—I've stopped being Theirs

—Emily Dickinson

In discussing Dickinson's "I'm ceded—I've stopped being Theirs,"[1] Betsy Erkkila claims that the poet "deploys the politically charged language of secession, but the secession she imagines is not in favor of a sovereign republican self or state"; rather, she secedes into an "essentially monarchical order in which she will be 'Queen.'"[2] Thus the most recent critic committed to "historicizing" our understanding of women poets concludes that Dickinson's "revolutionary poetic practice appears to be unconnected with any real transformation of woman's historical status as 'object' and 'other' in a system of production and exchange controlled by men" (52), and, what is more, her "radical poetics was conjoined with an essentially conservative and in some sense reactionary and Know-Nothing politics" (53).

Quite apart from her conflation of the nativist politics of the decade before the Civil War with secession, Erkkila places Dickinson in history exactly where she has conventionally been—isolated from her own times. This new historicism restricts the poet to her father's politics before the Civil War and cuts her off from the post–Civil War "revolutionary struggles of blacks, women, and workers" (52). Thus the decade of the 1860s—when Dickinson was most productive and, although it is seldom remembered in this connection, the nation was at war—is written out of the poet's life.

Such "historicizing" of Dickinson distorts history and begs the question of how, if poetry and politics are intertextual, as Erkkila insists, such a revolutionary poet came from such a reactionary background. Or if the household politics must be read into the poetry, how can the poetry be called revolutionary? Entangled in the very binary oppositions she would appear to deny, Erkkila's claims not only ring false, they also defy common sense. How could the greatest

American woman poet of all times *not* have transformed woman's historical status as object? Moreover, they rely on dubious facts to illuminate the poetry, warning that "it is important that we recognize the fact that her poetic revolution was grounded in the privilege of her class position in a conservative Whig household whose elitist, antidemocratic values were still at the very center of her work" (53). Important for what, we must ask. And is it even a "fact" that we can recognize? Moreover, can revolution be centered by conservative values?

Finding Dickinson secured against the national crisis and removed entirely from the "general sorrow of the Civil War" (47) by the love of an exclusive group of female friends, Erkkila delineates a very "feminine," not to say antifeminist, role for this poet and once again relegates history and war to men. Thus she joins a long line of literary historians who have banished Dickinson from history and from the literary history that depends on it. From F. O. Matthiessen's pioneering study of the period, *American Renaissance: Art and Expression in the Age of Emerson and Whitman* (1941) through Donald Pease's more recent *Visionary Compacts* (1987) and David Reynolds's *Beneath the American Renaissance: The Subversive Imagination in the Age of Emerson and Melville* (1988), Dickinson has either not been mentioned at all or given scant consideration by comparison to the major male writers of the period.

In the new *Columbia Literary History of the United States* (1988), for example, Dickinson is accorded a separate chapter as a "major voice" in the period 1865–1910 and placed with three male prose writers, Mark Twain, Henry Adams, and Henry James, all of whom wrote at the end of the century and figure here as commentators on their civilization. In this company, Dickinson appears as "the ghost that haunts American literature,"[3] a description that acknowledges the difficulty of her place in literary history. In *The Columbia History of American Poetry* (1993), although admitting that Dickinson came from a family of sophisticated lawyers and politicians and had a firm grasp of political realities, Cynthia Griffin Wolff concludes that "the poetry was all she left; it appears to be all she *wished* to leave."[4]

Thus even when she is acknowledged as a great writer, Dickinson has never found a central place in American literary history. By contrast, such writers as John Winthrop, Benjamin Franklin, Walt Whitman, Ernest Hemingway, and Norman Mailer are easily accommodated because American literary history is always linked to American history and its narratives drawn from the writings of men interested in historical crises, chiefly war. Moreover, to be included in literary history, at least in the nineteenth century, one has had to be not only a man interested in history (as the exclusion until recently of such women writers as Margaret Fuller and Harriet Beecher Stowe would suggest) but a man with the right political interests—those that confirmed democracy, the nation, the national destiny—as the exclusion of Frederick Douglass until recently indicates. Yet today, even with Fuller, Stowe, and Douglass now allotted a place in literary history, Dickinson remains an anomaly. She has fit into a largely masculine history in exactly the terms Erkkila once again uses—as an eccentric woman isolated from the main concerns of the day.

Perhaps a literary history that would include women writers should start with Dickinson and redo the conventional story by fitting literary history around the poet, considering both how she defines the period and how literary history might be redone if she were placed at its center.[5] Starting with Dickinson means centering on her most productive years, which happened to coincide with the years of the Civil War. This war, like the poet, is usually written out of the literary history of the nineteenth century and the anthologies that derive from it, which have tended to divide the nineteenth century at 1865, focusing on the five male writers of the pre–Civil War period who were interested in the possibilities of democracy in the new republic and on the largely male regionalist and realist writers at the end of the century. Even *The Heath Anthology of American Literature* that purports to revise such notions by including a greater cultural diversity divides the century in this way and tucks Dickinson and Whitman into a section titled "Emerging American Poetic Voices." The first step in restructuring American literary history can thus reclaim the poet in the period of the war during which she wrote. Neither the male writers whom Matthiessen names as central nor the realists who came after the war can be identified so clearly with the war as Dickinson can.

Nevertheless, to place Dickinson and the Civil War at the center of the century they dominated is to confront immediately the fact that almost every critic who writes about Dickinson claims she had no interest in the war. The single exception is Shira Wolosky, who, in *Emily Dickinson: A Voice of War* (1984), has made the case for Dickinson as a war poet, arguing that she lived in an atmosphere of political commitment and controversy that was reflected in both her letters and her verse.[6] Her father was a delegate to the national Whig convention in 1852 and elected to Congress in the same year; his term spanned the period of the Kansas-Nebraska Act, the Fugitive Slave Act, and the first attempts to build a new party out of which the Republican Party eventually emerged. Cloistered in the household of such a man, Dickinson could not have avoided war talk. And as Wolosky proves, the war confirmed for Dickinson the incoherence and violence that characterized her view of ordinary life (37). War intensified her concern with death as the most incomprehensible sorrow and can account for her concentration on its mystery (41). Although critics have generally attributed the violence that marks her imagery to an inner struggle, it may, according to Wolosky, be related more directly to the civil turmoil in which she lived. Even Dickinson's religious doubts were played out in a national context as the war shook the nation's confidence in divine providence. In short, writing almost half of her poems between 1861 and 1865, Dickinson took on the issues that the war of those years presented.[7]

Wolosky's study of these issues is important; but focusing on Dickinson's metaphysical concerns over the meaning of the war and her growing conviction that the theodicean justification of loss by gain was inadequate to explain it, Wolosky tends to spiritualize the war, discounting its reality and locating Dickinson's interests in those religious and ahistorical issues familiar to conventional studies of the poet. To be sure, the war did give these issues a historical context, as Wolosky claims, but the war had a reality of its own that not only touched the poet but overwhelmed her imagination, disrupting even the emotional and spiritual turmoil of her early years. The war's devastation was not remote to Dickinson, who witnessed reports of the deaths of Amherst men and boys, nor was its impact slight on a poet obsessed with death. The speed, the suffering, and the unbearable loss of the war deaths are the subjects of many of her poems in which she puts aside religious issues and probes the psychological reality of the war experience. Mourning and guilt at surviving when so many were killed are also her subjects, as she turned her attention to the catastrophic impact this war had on every citizen. In short, quite apart from its metaphysical effect, the reality of war flooded Dickinson's imagination in her most productive years.

If she had no direct war experience herself (and, in this, she is not distinguished from Hawthorne, Melville, and Emerson, among other writers), she understood its terror so fully that, in his study of American war fiction, John Limon writes, "The Vonnegut/Heller/Pynchon generation is a late regendering of a lineage that includes Anne Bradstreet, Dickinson, Christina Rossetti, and culminates in Plath and Sexton: the tradition is female, its rhetorical device is hysteron proteron, and its theme is living death." Limon goes on, "It may be worth noting that James Jones was oddly fascinated by Dickinson. And the only poets explicitly quoted (I think) in *Gravity's Rainbow* are Dickinson and Rilke."[8]

What have these twentieth-century war novelists recognized in Dickinson that literary critics from Matthiessen to Erkkila have not? Perhaps they see not just her fascination with the theme of living death but also the understanding she shares with them that, as she wrote in 1863 to Thomas W. Higginson, who was in South Carolina commanding a black regiment, "War feels to me an oblique place."[9] She locates herself on a slant with her subject, as do those writers of war fiction from realism to postmodernism whom Limon finds engaging in a series of substitutions that lead them from war to literature. For example, Limon notes that William Dean Howells replaced the Civil War with the labor wars of the 1880s in *A Hazard of New Fortunes*, F. Scott Fitzgerald moved from the Great War to football, and Hemingway rejected the metaphoric closure of the bullfight in favor of Cohn's boxing. Nor does Limon's account omit women, as he traces the tradition from Louisa May Alcott's sequestering of the Civil War in *Little Women* to Maxine Hong Kingston's *Woman Warrior*, which, immersed in war, is still about substitutes for war. He concludes, "It is close to the truth to say that literary history progresses by inverting, rather than internalizing, the lessons . . . of contemporaneous warfare."[10]

Dickinson fits into this literary history of war writing by substituting funerals for the military, romance for warfare, psychic horror for the ineffable disaster of the Civil War. Writing in a creative frenzy that matched the war's own fury, she inverted the lessons of that war not by internalizing them, as critics have sometimes suggested, but rather by overturning the relationship of citizen to state demanded by that or any war. Validating the private over the public, the individual over the social, the psychic over the political, the sectional over the national, the fragment over the whole, she refused to succumb to the war fever, choosing instead to embody it, by speaking the unspeakable horrors it perpetrated, externalizing the inner fear and violence the war evoked, materializing its spiritual terror, in short, by making it "real." In the substitutions of her poems of the Civil War period, Dickinson, like American war novelists from Howells to the meta-fictionists of the 1960s, writes about war by writing about something else, and, paradoxically in so doing, she extends what it means to write the "real" war, just as she moves poetry from the Transcendental ideal of Emerson to a new realism that is both psychological and social.

The idea of Dickinson as a realistic war poet seems absurd. Almost every critic studying her has confirmed that she took no interest in the war. Moreover, critics of war poetry generally agree that realism in war poetry is rooted in the experience of war, in the concrete or the literal. Thus Walt Whitman, although he wrote of only one battle, can be considered a war poet because he was there; Dickinson cannot be a war poet because she was not there. This appeal to literal experience is age-old and compelling; but as recent critics of women war poets have argued, it is also dangerous because it restricts war experience to the soldier's as if that were the only "real" experience. Such thinking has prevented recognition of other war experiences and the poetry that details them, as Susan Schweik argues, in placing Emily Dickinson in the context of other women writers on war such as Marianne Moore in "In Distrust of Merits," Edith Sitwell in "Still Falls the Rain," and H.D. in *Trilogy*. Discussing Moore in the context of the poetry of World War II, Schweik notes: "In American forties war poetry, for instance, 'experience of war' was generally taken to comprehend the experience of the soldier but not generally, during the war itself, the experience of the Holocaust victim, the Japanese American in an internment camp, or a woman working in a defense plant."[11] Here Schweik is making a case for writing war poetry like a woman, citing Moore's "In Distrust of Merit," in which obviously stylized and didactic literary techniques signal from the start their literariness and political and philosophical techniques; but, she argues, "a more narrative war poem which refers more openly to real experience may not recognize the limits of what constitutes the 'real' within it."

American women writers, from the colonial captivity narratives on, have worked to expand an understanding of the "real" war experience to include not only the actual battlefield but a full range of experiences, including the psychological dislocation that Dickinson expressed in writing, "War feels to me an oblique place." Strangely enough, Moore too, in talking about the Vietnam War to Grace Schulman in 1967, expressed the same sense, claiming, "I don't dare face it, actually."[12] Removed from the actual war, these women are not refusing to respond to it; rather, they express such a keen awareness of its reality that it becomes something they cannot face directly any more than some combatants can, than some war novelists will. Dickinson's poetry of the Civil War period indicates just how deep her understanding of it was.

It is not necessary to argue an understanding of her interests that the poet herself nowhere admitted. She herself saw her poetry as relevant to war. Responding immediately to that "oblique place" to which, she discovered, her friend and confidant Higginson had departed, Dickinson sent him a poem that employs the rhetorical device of hysteron proteron. It was not a poem written for the occasion since she had made copies of it two years before she sent its last stanza to Higginson in 1863, but it is a poem which she clearly identifies with the war.[13] The entire poem reads:

That after Horror — that 'twas *us* —
That passed the mouldering Pier —
Just as the Granite Crumb let go —
Our Saviour, by a Hair —

A second more, had dropped too deep
For Fisherman to plumb —
The very profile of the Thought
Puts Recollection numb —

> The possibility—to pass
> Without a Moment's Bell
> Into Conjecture's presence—
> Is like a Face of Steel—
> That suddenly looks into ours
> With a metallic grin—
> The Cordiality of Death—
> Who drills his Welcome in—(286)

This poem, acknowledging the borderline between life and death as delicate and unannounced, recovers the sense, expressed in her first letter to Higginson, of how quickly he himself had disappeared into the war: "I found you were gone, by accident, as I find Systems are, or Seasons of the year, and obtain no cause—but suppose it a treason of Progress—that dissolves as it goes" (L 280). Moreover, it equates war and death as states almost synonymous for her, and she goes on, "Perhaps Death—gave me awe for friends—striking sharp and early, for I held them since—in a brittle love—of more alarm, than peace" (L 280). Although, as Cynthia Griffin Wolff points out, this poem, as well as her letters to Higginson, cluster around some of the most troubling elements of the New Testament, the poem is set deliberately in wartime, figuring death as gunfire in its "face of Steel," "metallic grin," and drilling its welcome in.[14]

Later writing to Higginson after she learned that he had been wounded and left the army, Dickinson again condenses his war experience with other news of death as if the two subjects were inseparable in her mind ("I did not know that you were hurt. Will you tell me more? Mr. Hawthorne died.") and again includes a poem, the first stanza of Poem 827, in the letter:

> The Only News I know
> Is Bulletins all Day
> From Immortality.

Even when she takes up her correspondence with Higginson eighteen months later, her news is again of death: "Carlo died— / E. Dickinson/ Would you instruct me now?" (L 314).

So, however distant from the war she was, Dickinson seemed immersed in its "news" of death. If her fascination with living death might have grown out of her domestic life quite distinct from the military, her anguished awareness of the ferocious speed of death in war derives from the war itself, as she notifies her Norcross cousins that Frazer Stearns, son of the president of Amherst College, was shot in the heart by a "minie ball," "lived ten minutes in a soldier's arms, asked twice for water — murmured just, 'My God!' and passed!" (L 255). Dickinson reports that even her brother was "chilled — by Frazer's murder — He says — his Brain keeps saying over 'Frazer is killed' — 'Frazer is killed,' just as Father told it — to him" (L 256). The speed of Stearns's death contrasts with the length of her brother Austin's absorption of the shocking fact in that odd expansion and contraction of time that crises effect. Speed figures too in Poem 596, where Dickinson writes:

> When I was small, a Woman died —
> Today — her Only Boy
> Went up from the Potomac —
> His face all Victory
>
> To look at her — How slowly
> The Season must have turned
> Till Bullets clipt an Angle
> And He passed quickly round —

But the speedy bullet was not the only death on the battlefield that Dickinson details; death there could come, too, slowly after much suffering and torment, as in the gradual decay of "the mouldering Pier —" earlier in "That after Horror" or the broken "Plank in Reason" (280) or, in a later poem, "Crumbling is not an instant's Act" (997). In poem after poem, Dickinson probed death's infinite variety.[15]

Dickinson seemed also oddly cognizant of how the felled soldier might feel, writing, "The Doomed — regard the Sunrise / With different Delight" (294) or "Death sets a Thing significant / The Eye had hurried by" (360) or "Victory comes late — / And is held low to freezing lips —" (690). The "Doomed" is identified as a man in battle:

> The Man — to die — tomorrow —
> Harks for the Meadow Bird —
> Because its music stirs the Axe
> That clamors for his head — (294)

Although these poems are not pointedly military, the "perished Creature" in Poem 360 is a male friend now gone, as if in war, and fondly remembered. And the late victory would appear to come to someone abandoned, perhaps on a battlefield, his lips "rapt with frost."

Keenly attentive to the moment of death in poems about dying at home such as "I heard a Fly buzz—when I died" (465), Dickinson could also transfer that interest to the battlefield, writing:

> Tell that the Worse, is easy in a Moment—
> Dread but the Whizzing, before the Ball—
> When the Ball enters, enters Silence—
> Dying—annuls the power to kill. (358) [16]

Or, again, speaking of herself, she writes of the limits of suffering: "No Rack can torture me— / My Soul—at Liberty—" (384). Or, of a speaker impatient for death, she writes, "They cannot take me—any more! / Dungeons can call—and Guns implore" (277).

She could also admit her distance from war, taking up the mourner's hopeless desire for knowledge of the death of a loved one:

> To know just how He suffered—would be dear—
> To know if any Human eyes were near
> To whom He could entrust His wavering gaze—
> Until it settled broad—on Paradise—(622)

Yet nothing could be more remote from "dear" than knowing how the soldiers died in the Civil War, as her account of Frazer Stearns's death suggests. She herself could also imagine a death so meaningless as to be without consolation despite the false comfort of faith she tacks on at the end of the poem:

> They dropped like Flakes—
> They dropped like Stars—
> Like Petals from a Rose—
> When suddenly across the June
> A wind with fingers—goes—
>
> They perished in the Seamless Grass—
> No eye could find the place—
> But God can summon every face
> On his Repealless—List. (409)

At other points, she could express the woman's traditional guilt as the survivor:

> It feels a shame to be Alive—
> When Men so brave—are dead—
> One envies the Distinguished Dust—
> Permitted—such a Head—(444)

But she refused to be consoled by the conventional wisdom "that 'Time assuages,'" claiming rather, "Time never did assuage— / An actual suffering strengthens / As Sinews do, with age" (686).

And in the middle of the war, she could express the feeling of a war-weary population:

I many times thought Peace had come
When Peace was far away—
As Wrecked Men—deem they sight the Land—
At Centre of the Sea—

And struggle slacker—but to prove
As hopelessly as I—
How many the fictitious Shores—
Before the Harbor be—(739)

In these and many other poems, Dickinson reveals an extreme awareness of the national crisis of the Civil War as a lived experience. At the same time, she was writing at the height of her powers as if the war had unlocked in her some creative spring quite distant from the war's devastation and horror.[17] In this respect, Dickinson is not unique among women poets writing during war. Virginia Woolf felt that her art had been subtly strengthened and strangely inspired by the deaths and defeats of World War I. In their study of World War I and women writers, Sandra Gilbert and Susan Gubar claim that war acted as a muse not only to Woolf but to Katherine Mansfield, H.D., and Edith Wharton, as well.[18] And in 1944, Louise Bogan could argue that the reason might or might not have been war, but "the fact is an unusually large number of books written by women have appeared at the beginning of this fall season."[19] And so the productivity of women writers during times of war moved into the World War II era and beyond, as women poets, such as Denise Levertov and Adrienne Rich, for example, responded to the Vietnam War and even the Gulf War with poems as well as protests.

Dickinson belongs to this long tradition of women driven to writing during a time of war. Still, the frenzy of her creativity during the years of the Civil War— in which she was inspired not just to write of war, as in the poems discussed above, but simply to write—sets her apart from any number of her contemporaries—Hawthorne, Emerson, Lydia Maria Child, for example, who found their creative energies exhausted by the war. Even Whitman, writing from the front, felt imaginatively inadequate to it, claiming:

These Hospitals, so different from all others—these thousands, and tens and twenties of thousands of American young men, badly wounded, all sorts of wounds, operated on, pallid with diarrhea, languishing, dying with fever, pneumonia, &. open a new world somehow to me, giving closer insights, new things, exploring deeper mines than any yet, showing our humanity . . . tried by terrible, fearfulest tests, probed deepest, the living soul's the body's tragedies, bursting the petty bounds of art. To these, what are your dramas and poems, even the oldest and the tearfulest?[20]

Although he could promise, "My idea is a book of the time, worthy the time," in fact the Civil War ended his most creative years.[21] What, then, did it set off in Dickinson's imagination? What is the connection between the national carnage and this poet's creativity? The Civil War opened a new world to her not just by providing a reality that taxed her imagination to express but also by rescuing her from the sentimental religion of romance, the gospel of love, and her own and the century's particular art of dying, or rather by revealing within these conventions a starker reality that allowed her to deepen their conventional purposes.[22] In this, she resembles those American fiction writers studied by Limon who inverted the lessons of their contemporary wars. Substituting the funeral for the military ceremony, Dickinson can nonetheless keep the soldiers hovering over the civilian ritual, their "Service, like a Drum — / Kept beating — beating" as they "creak" "With those same Boots of Lead" (280). Or inverting warfare into romance, she could write of lovers as prisoners of war:

> They took away our Eyes —
> They thwarted Us with Guns —
> "I See Thee" each responded straight
> Through Telegraphic Signs —
>
> With Dungeons — they devised —
> But through their thickest skill —
> And their opaquest Adamant —
> Our Souls saw — just as well — (474)

Dickinson's use of "Telegraphic Signs" indicates not only a substitution of the romantic plot for a war narrative but a choice of language shaped and sharpened by experiences of war because telegrams announced the war dead.[23]

Again, in the "Master" letter written about 1861, Dickinson writes a love letter as if to one absent in the war, pleading, "If it had been God's will that I might breathe where you breathed — and find the place — myself — at night — if I (can) never forget that I am not with you — and that sorrow and frost are nearer than I — if I wish with a might I cannot repress — that mine were the Queen's place — the love of the Plantagenet is my only apology —" (L, II, 233).

The dead is imagined as murdered in a poem that recalls Austin Dickinson's response to Stearns's death in the war:

It don't sound so terrible — quite — as it did —
I run it over — "Dead," Brain, "Dead."
Put it in Latin — left of my school —
Seems it don't shriek so — under rule.

. . . .

It's shrewder then
Put the Thought in advance — a Year —
How like "a fit" — then —
Murder — wear! (426)

Even in her poems of extreme psychic experience, as in "'Twas like a Maelstrom, with a notch" (414), she could substitute the warlike experience of capture, torture, and then release for the experience, asking, "Which Anguish was the utterest — then — / To perish, or to live?"

The war that, in Whitman's words, burst "the petty bounds of art" also elicited from Dickinson an acknowledgment of the limitations of language to express not just such an ineffable catastrophe but the very idea of it. "I found the words to every thought / I ever had — but One —" (581) or "A Thought went up my mind today — / That I have had before —" (701) are two of the many poems in which Dickinson claims to be haunted by memories that transcend her ability to express them, even to know them. Conversely, conventional signs do not serve, as Dickinson writes, "What care the Dead, for Chanticleer —" (592). Choosing an image of male prowess in uncanny anticipation of Elizabeth Bishop's war poem "Roosters," Dickinson goes on to locate her poem in the dead of winter and in the geography of the Civil War where to the dead, "As soon the South — Her Breeze / / Of Sycamore — or Cinnamon — / Deposit in a Stone."

Thus directly and indirectly Dickinson wrote poetry that detailed the psychological reality of the war years in which her imagination worked so fervently. She was not alone among women writing during the Civil War, and if her work is to center the new literary history of the American nineteenth century, it will have to be placed in the context of those writers and not those only but male writers of the war. In this company, Dickinson's poems seem to take on some of the shades of the war experience reported directly by eyewitnesses such as Louisa May Alcott, whose first book, *Hospital Sketches* (1863), derives from her brief experience as a nurse in the war. She writes of a dying soldier:

> The strong body rebelled against death, and fought every inch of the way, forcing him to draw each breath with a spasm, and clench his hands with an imploring look, as if he asked, "How long must I endure this, and be still!" For hours he suffered dumbly, without a moment's respite, or a moment's murmuring; his limbs grew cold, his face damp, his lips white, and again and again, he tore the covering off his breast, as if the lightest weight added to his agony; yet through it all, his eyes never lost their perfect serenity, and the man's soul seemed to sit therein, undaunted by the ills that vexed his flesh.[24]

The narrative might have inspired Dickinson's "'Twas Crisis—All the length had passed" (948).

At other points, Dickinson stands out from contemporaries such as Harriet Beecher Stowe, who, writing in *Atlantic Monthly* in January 1865, offered this wisdom:

> There is a certain amount of suffering which must follow the rending of the great chords of life, suffering which is natural and inevitable; it cannot be argued down; it cannot be stilled; it can no more be soothed by any effort of faith and reason than the pain of a fractured limb, or the agony of fire on the living flesh. All that we can do is brace ourselves to bear it, calling on God, as the martyrs did in the fire, and resigning ourselves to let it burn out.[25]

Stowe consoles, "Time heals all things at last" against Dickinson's warning, "Time never did assuage" (686). Stowe's active interest in both the Union cause and female moral authority sets her apart from Dickinson, as does Lydia Maria Child's obsession with the fate of the slave and emancipation. Although she claimed that she could not write unless her mind were free, Child worked tirelessly during the war for the freedom of the slaves and urged John Greenleaf Whittier to write war poetry, claiming:

> Nothing on earth has such effect on the popular heart as Songs, which the soldiers would take up with enthusiasm, and which it would thereby become the fashion to whistle and sing at the street-corners....
>
> Ballads, too, told in your pictorial fascinating style, would do a great work at this crisis. If you see returned soldiers, you will have plenty of subjects suggested.[26]

If Dickinson's war poetry could never have served Child's patriotic purposes and if she herself could not share Child's enthusiasm for the war, neither did she share Emerson's conviction, expressed in his *Journal*, "The War is a great teacher, still opening our eyes wider to some larger consideration. It is a great reconciler, too, forgetting our petty quarrels as ridiculous."[27] But Emerson, like Child and Stowe, did not enjoy Dickinson's imaginative productivity during the war, as he wrote to Thomas Carlyle, "Here we read no books. The war is our sole & doleful instructor."[28] Even Hawthorne agreed with Emerson, who, he noted, "is breathing slaughter, like the rest of us" that "If the war only lasts long enough (and not too long) it will have done us infinite good."[29] These sentiments of writers she knew found no echo in Dickinson's Civil War writing. Much closer to her feelings was Higginson's comment in "Regular and Volunteer Officers," published in *Atlantic Monthly* on September 14, 1864, "What is called military glory is a fitful and uncertain thing."[30]

Considered with those writers who wrote poetry of the Civil War—Melville and Whitman—Dickinson would, of course, stand out as a woman, and yet would she? She was no less involved in the war experience than Melville, who, in a headnote to *Battle-Pieces and Aspects of the War* (1866), acknowledges that he writes from inspiration alone: "Yielding instinctively, one after another, to feelings not inspired from any one source exclusively, and unmindful, without purposing to be, of consistency, I seem, in most of these verses, to have but placed a harp in a window, and noted the contrasted airs which wayward winds have playing upon the strings."[31] Even Whitman's experience of war was that of nurse, not combatant, tending as Alcott did the wounded and suffering.

If their experiences of war were those of the attendant, the maternal nurturer, the passive receiver of news much like Dickinson's experience, Melville and Whitman depart from her in their poetry of the war, fastening on actual events of battle such as the call to arms, the wounded, marches, bivouacs, the death watch, the martyrdom of soldiers, for example. And yet behind these subjects, although Whitman could cry, "No dainty rhymes or sentimental love verses for you terrible war,"[32] he actually wrote poems of great sentimentality—"Come up from the Field Father," "Vigil Strange I Kept on the Field One Night," "Adieu to a Soldier." And Melville, providing a chronological treatment of the war in *Battle-Pieces*, was still confused by its impact, writing in "Commemorative of a Naval Victory," "But seldom the laurel wreath is seen / Unmixed with pensive pansies dark." In the paradoxes, ironies, and multiple perspectives of his Civil War poems, Melville expresses his own doubts and fears for the nation that are not unlike Dickinson's.

The war acted on these poets' imaginations differently. Whitman wrote little during its first two years, and then, inspired by his nursing experience, he started to write poetry, which, despite its patriotic fervor, never rose to the triumphant celebration of self and nation with which his career had started. The Civil War was the death knell not only to his hopes for democracy but to his own poetry. By contrast, Melville had appeared to exhaust his artistic energies in the decade before the Civil War and was inspired by the war to start writing poetry. But his poetry was not well received, and eventually he gave up trying to publish it.

Perhaps it is not fair to compare Dickinson at the height of her powers to these writers at the end of theirs, and yet the comparison does suggest that, for her, the Civil War was a more formative influence. Melville and Whitman, Emerson and Hawthorne all were at the end of their greatest work when the war intervened. Dickinson alone had productive years ahead; but because she had lived through the war during an important period of her writing, it touched all that she wrote, deepening it and splitting it off from the pre–Civil War pieties of both sentimental and reform literature. It made her into a modern — and, in some ways, a modernist — writer. And it can be no coincidence that the generation that was to write the next war found Dickinson their contemporary.

If Dickinson's writings during the Civil War are to be placed at the center of nineteenth-century American literary history, the so-called American Renaissance could be renamed something more appropriate (perhaps American Nature Writing) and pushed back to 1830–55. Dickinson's work might serve as the beginning of a reconsidered American realism that would feature the women novelists as well and run through the last half of the nineteenth century.

NOTES

I have been instructed in the course of writing this paper by my colleague Douglas Anderson and my graduate student Leigh-Anne Urbanowicz Marcellin, and I am grateful to both of them.

1. *The Complete Poems of Emily Dickinson*, ed. Thomas Johnson (Boston: Little, Brown, 1960), poem number 508. Hereafter the poem numbers will be cited in parentheses in the text.

2. Betsy Erkkila, *The Wicked Sisters: Women Poets, Literary History and Discord* (New York: Oxford University Press, 1992). Hereafter cited in parentheses in the text.

3. Wendy Martin, "Emily Dickinson," *Columbia Literary History of the United States* (New York: Columbia University Press, 1988), 609.

4. Cynthia Griffin Wolff, "Emily Dickinson," *The Columbia History of American Poetry*, ed. Jay Parini and Brett Millier (New York: Columbia University Press, 1993), 146.

5. Elsewhere, I have argued that Dickinson does not fit into the American Renaissance as it has been conventionally construed. See "Reperiodization: The Example of Emily Dickinson," *College English* 52 (April 1990): 397–409.

6. Shira Wolosky, *Emily Dickinson: A Voice of War* (New Haven: Yale University Press, 1984), 35. Hereafter cited in parentheses in the text.

7. Acknowledging that Dickinson's most driven years as an artist were precisely the period of the Civil War, Vivian Pollak states nonetheless that "she has almost nothing to say about its precipitating causes, its events, or its consequences. Instead, she flaunts a schismatic style which announces that she has seceded from 'their story' into hers" (*Dickinson: The Anxiety of Gender* [Ithaca: Cornell University Press, 1984], 18). Pollak, too, may be mistaking "ceded" for "seceded," but here she expresses the conventional view of Dickinson's interest in the Civil War.

8. John Limon, *Writing After War: American War Fiction from Realism to Postmodernism* (New York: Oxford University Press, 1994), 159. By contrast, Erkkila's comment on Dickinson's death poems seems off the mark: "Moreover, for all the nay-saying power of Dickinson's poetic revolution, her attempt to challenge the logocentric order of the Word as God the Father was not finally successful. Despite her satanic and pagan identification with the bloom of female creation, that bloom was always under arrest by the absolute power of Death, which Dickinson consistently represented as a male figure whose tyrannical power is associated with the 'marauding Hand' of a punishing and at times sadistic God" (53).

9. *The Letters of Emily Dickinson*, ed. Thomas H. Johnson, vols. 2 and 3 (Cambridge, Mass.: Harvard University Press, 1958), 280. Hereafter the letter numbers will be cited in parentheses in the text as L.

10. Limon, *Writing After War*, 7. Disagreeing with Harold Bloom that feminism posed the first radical challenge to literary history because it would establish a pedigree that does not descend from Homer, Limon views Louisa May Alcott, Margaret Mitchell, Willa Cather, Edith Wharton, Bobbie Ann Mason, and Maxine Hong Kingston as important in that pedigree, as committed as male writers to discovering techniques that would allow them in the presence of war *not* to write about it.

11. Susan Schweik, "*A Gulf So Deeply Cut*": *American Women Poets and the Second World War* (Madison: University of Wisconsin Press, 1991), 51.

12. Grace Schulman, *Marianne Moore: The Poetry of Engagement* (New York: Paragon House, 1986), 68.

13. Sending this poem to Higginson, Dickinson must have wished to draw a connection between her poems and the Civil War that surrounded them. Thus she seems to contradict David Porter's assertion that "there was no way for these poems of pure style and screened eye to see or to take in the historical world" (*Dickinson: The Modern Idiom* [Cambridge, Mass.: Harvard University Press, 1981], 183).

14. Cynthia Griffin Wolff, *Emily Dickinson* (New York: Knopf, 1986), 265. Griffin Wolff's reading of the New Testament references in this poem might not be the only interpretation of "Savior" and "Fisherman." It is possible that "Our Saviour" refers to the "mouldering Pier" that did not give way until after they passed, and the "Fisherman" would be that person who might have had to rescue them had they "dropped too deep." Thus the poem would be about escaping death just barely, and its final stanza would be an appropriate reminder of the peril of his station to one in battle.

15. Limon notes that the final stanza of poem 997 is quoted in *Gravity's Rainbow* (*Writing After War*, 149).

16. In her reading of "My Life had stood—a loaded Gun—" (754), Wolosky links this last line with the enigmatic final stanza of that poem with its central tension and contradiction that the Creator is destructive; but it seems to me that the early annulment in death of the "power to kill" is quite different from the unrelenting rage of "My Life had stood—a loaded Gun—" where the speaker claims to have no "power to die."

17. In a letter to her Norcross cousins about the war late in its progress, Dickinson seems to be aware of her curious ability to write despite her sense that

> sorrow seems more general than it did, and not the estate of a few persons, since the war began; and if the anguish of others helped one with one's own, now would be many medicines.
>
> 'Tis dangerous to value, for only the precious can alarm. I noticed that Robert Browning had made another poem, and was astonished—till I remembered that I, myself, in my smaller way, sang off charnel steps. Every day life feels mightier, and what we have the power to be, more stupendous. (L 298)

18. Sandra Gilbert and Susan Gubar, *No Man's Land: The Place of the Woman Writer in the Twentieth Century*, vol. 2 (New Haven: Yale University Press, 1989), 307–8.

19. Quoted in Schweik, "A Gulf So Deeply Cut," 3.

20. Quoted in Louis P. Masur, ed., *The Real War Will Never Get in the Books: Selections from Writers During the Civil War* (New York: Oxford University Press, 1993), 263.

21. Ibid.

22. See Barton Levi St. Armand's *Emily Dickinson and Her Culture: The Soul's Society* (Cambridge, Eng.: Cambridge University Press, 1984), 9–114, for a reading that places her completely within these conventions.

23. See Dickinson's announcement, "Mrs. Adams had news of the death of her boy today, from a wound at Annapolis. Telegram signed by Frazer Stearns." (L 245) I am grateful to Douglas Anderson for pointing out the way Dickinson's imagination was fired by the technological facts of war.

24. Quoted in Masur, ed., *Real War*, 35–36.

25. Ibid., 249.

26. Ibid., 45–46.

27. Ibid., 125.

28. Ibid., 137.

29. Ibid., 167.

30. Ibid., 187.

31. Ibid., 199.

32. Ibid., 203.

MARÍA AMPARO RUIZ DE BURTON NEGOTIATES AMERICAN LITERARY POLITICS AND CULTURE

Amelia María de la Luz Montes

La inaguracion de Mr. Lincoln ha pasado sin novedad, y ha dado su primera "public reception" sin q. lo hayan asesinado como amenazaban. El estado del pais continua en agitacion y el peligro de guerra todabia hace temblar á los infelices q., como yo, tanto tendrian q. arriesgar. . . . No deje de venir, y yo quiero tener el placer de presentarlo á Mr. y Mrs. Lincoln . . . yo sé muy bien q. si yo lo presento será muy bien recibido.

[Mr. Lincoln's inauguration has occurred without incident, and he has given his first "public reception" without having been assassinated as they had threatened. The state of the country continues in alarm and the threat of war makes those unfortunate ones tremble because they, like me, would have much to place at risk. . . . Do not forget to come, and I want to have the pleasure of presenting you to Mr. and Mrs. Lincoln . . . I know very well that if I present you, you will be well received.]

—María Amparo Ruiz de Burton to Mariano Guadalupe Vallejo, March 8, 1860[1] [1]

"LET ME PRESENT YOU": OPENING PREESTABLISHED BOUNDARIES

Of all the racial and cultural impressions people imagine of nineteenth-century Americans, it is doubtful they envision a learned Mexican American woman who writes from Washington, converses with the Lincolns, and reports on the Civil War.[2] Mexicans, like novelist María Amparo Ruiz de Burton, who became American after 1848 were recreated into stereotypes or dismissed as writers.[3] During and after the Mexican-American War, Mexican women were described in western popular books and newspapers as loose and undisciplined while the men were portrayed as sleepy dons or drunken bandidos.[4] Such stereotypes made it difficult for emerging Mexican American voices to establish themselves in American literary circles. Even today, American canonical literature figures nineteenth-century Americans of Mexican descent as decaying curiosities: ghostly exotica haunting the wheat fields and missions up and down the West Coast. By the late 1800s, traditional American literature depicted Mexican presence in the West as nonexistent. A good example is Frank Norris's turn-of-the-century novel *The Octopus*. Norris's California is a backdrop for what he felt would be a new American work, or more specifically a great American epic of the West.[5] In the novel, Norris's old Mexican ranch is named Los Muertos (the dead), and he describes the Spanish-Mexicans as "relics of a former generation."[6] What happens in the first half of the novel is a fascinating metaphor for Anglo-western canon formation, a metafictional construction in which Norris's western literary space creates an American literary history to privilege an Anglo-American experience. Presley says he wants to be a poet "of the west, that world's frontier of Romance, where a new race, a new people— hardy, brave, and passionate—were building an empire . . . but its poet had not yet arisen" (9). Yet there is a poet present before Presley's arrival: the dark and brooding Vanamee, whose symbol is romantic and whose heritage is not quite Indian and not quite Mexican, making him a mestizo of uncertain origin. Presley describes him as a shattered "half-real, half-legendary" person. Norris's Latin naming of Vanamee is no accident. *Vannus* or *vanus* connotes "someone born in a bacchus festival; empty and void . . . whose actions are without consequence (vain)."[7] *Vannus* coupled with *amee* or *ame* meaning "soul" underlines Norris's intent to pronounce romanticism at its end and announce the arrival of realism, but he does so at the expense of a Mexican American literary presence in California. Presley the new poet is youthful, vigorous, and determined, in contrast to the "centenarian [Mexican] of the town, decrepit beyond belief" (20). The Mexican American presence and literary voice in Norris's novel is without soul, without meaning, and worse yet, without truth. There is no room in this literary landscape for multiple voices of color.

How can such a historical literary landscape accommodate the vibrant existence of a Mexican American woman's novels which focus on California as well as New England and reveal modes of realism and naturalism thirty years before Norris? It cannot. The focus of my work, then, concerns revisiting traditional American periodization not to delete its literary contents but to complicate what is there by including Ruiz de Burton's works, which help us further understand the emergence of realism, naturalism, and muckraking.[8] Ruiz de Burton's novels, *Who Would Have Thought It?* (1872) and *The Squatter and the Don* (1885), provide an opportunity to see American literary history in a more sophisticated manner because these works broaden racial and cultural perspectives.[9] Still, there is much work to do in this area. Today when people ask me about the writings of Ruiz de Burton, I find myself repeating more than once that she was an American, wrote her novels in English, did not need the services of a translator, and wrote primarily for Anglo-American audiences because she wanted them to understand her Mexican perspective on American soil.[10] Students and acquaintances tell me that when they finally sit down to read her novels, they are at first incredulous and then they want to know more. They become fascinated suddenly to find a western literary history they never read about in previous classrooms. It is no wonder, then, that historian Susan Johnson tells us that "The dominant popular culture suggests that [nineteenth-century] . . . women of color were temptresses or drudges, and men of color were foils for the inevitable white male hero."[11] It is an irony in itself to introduce Ruiz de Burton's nineteenth-century novels to a contemporary American audience when in her lifetime, as the letter fragment quoted in the epigraph to this essay reveals, she was in a position to present Abraham and Mary Lincoln to any of her acquaintances—to us if we had been there and known her.

Two important factors in Ruiz de Burton's personal life affected her lifelong struggle to create a literary space for the Mexican American woman in the emerging United States. First, she grew up in California when it was still under Mexican rule. Second, she experienced American colonization. Her personal, cultural, and political transformations from a Mexican to a Mexican American woman are significant. These complex events continually challenged her and are predominant themes in her writing. When she said in 1860 that "the definitive topic of two races is a grand theme" and that "the scenes [of her novel *The Squatter and the Don*] should be set in California," she was not erasing Anglo-American presence but creating a space in which to observe and negotiate both cultures within a literary landscape.[12] Norris's vision is in keeping with American efforts to colonize and establish an Anglo-American voice. His work figuratively displaces the Mexican literary landscape and replaces it with an Anglo-American vision. Unlike Norris's work, Ruiz de Burton's fiction reveals a heterogeneous perspective in both vision and form. While Ruiz de Burton's work is categorized as historical romance, it also reveals experiments with realism and naturalism: modes that are classified much later in traditional literary periodization. Her literary inheritance is not solely British but also Mexican, Spanish, and French. All of these variables add to the difficulty of fitting Ruiz de Burton's works into any preestablished periods or traditions because the establishment of such periods never considered writers of varying ethnicities or classes. Ruiz de Burton is not the only writer with such multitudinous aspects.

Sarah Winnemucca Hopkins's *Life Among the Piutes* presents interesting perspectives, as does Elizabeth Keckley's *Behind the Scenes or Thirty Years a Slave and Four Years in the White House*.[13] Rebecca Harding Davis's *Life in the Iron Mills* is key to analyzing early mastery of realism and muckraking modes. To enter a discussion of these works with already established writings would, as Annette Kolodny has said, "free American literary history from the persistent theories of continuity that have made it virtually impossible to treat frontier materials as other than marginalia or cultural mythology."[14] I seek not to draw new demarcations of literary periods but instead, through an analysis of Ruiz de Burton's personal and public writings, I work toward collapsing borderlines and time lines, leaving open literary frontiers from the Pacific shores to the eastern seaboard. In this way, Ruiz de Burton's writings and those of Sarah Winnemucca Hopkins, Rebecca Harding Davis, Elizabeth Keckley, and a multitude of others can enliven and enrich discussions of our American literary heritage.

"CONCERNING BOOKS AND FORMER CONVERSATIONS": RUIZ DE BURTON, THE WESTERN NOVELIST

Yo no quiero ilusiones opticas; prefería verlos — (á u. y mi prima) — con mis propios ojos y no con imaginaria telescopio desde aquí á Chicago! Tampoco quiero verlo de prisa. No señor. Quiero q. nos sentemos en paz, muy quietos y sin apurre, y comensemos nuestras antiguas platicas pasando en revista todo. Hombres, mujeres, cuentos, hechos, cosas, teorias, libros, autores, política, religion x x y á propos de todo esto ¿que piensa u. del pronunciamento de [padre] Hyacinthe contra el papa? . . . Y á leido u. el último cháchara político de Victor Hugo titulado *L'homme qui rit*[?] [Que] le parece? [Y] á propos de libros — ¿Como vá el de u., su historia de Calif*a*?

[I do not want optical illusions; I prefer to see you — (you and my cousin) — with my own eyes and not with an imaginary telescope from here to Chicago! I also do not want to see you in a hurry. No sir. I want us to sit down peacefully, patiently, without hurry, and in this way we may begin our former conversations reviewing everything: men, women, stories, exploits, concerns, theories, books, authors, politics, religion x x. And in respect to all of this, what do you think of Father Hyacinthe's statement against the Pope? . . . And have you read the latest political chatter of Victor Hugo's entitled *L'homme qui rit*? What do you think? and referring to books — how goes yours, your history of California?] (October 11, 1869).

Think of how the following phrases have been illustrated in twentieth-century textbooks: bustin' broncos, ridin' the range, and diggin' for gold in the West. These are not unfamiliar but instead are popular literary scenes drawn and painted in our memories. More unusual is visualizing a nineteenth-century Mexican American woman who shuns "optical illusions" and prefers realism to fantasy. Remarkable still is contemplating Ruiz de Burton speaking with authority about men, women, literature, theories, politics, and religion. In the above letter fragment addressed to the prominent Californio Mariano Guadalupe Vallejo, Ruiz de Burton encapsulates her wide-ranging interests. Vallejo also shared these interests.[15] For Ruiz de Burton, Vallejo was an important reader and adviser. Her epistolary communication with him reveals a direct link to the writing of her novels. A second look at the fragment above reveals one of her literary influences: Victor Hugo.

Victor Hugo does not figure in the contemporary imagination of the nineteenth-century California West, but for many reasons he was quite present in discursive form up and down the Pacific Coast. The Gold Rush had attracted many Europeans and South Americans. Among these racial groups were the French who settled on California lands. The Gold Rush also encouraged Louisiana's French to venture westward. One important historical event, however, that furthered the popularity of writers such as Hugo was the French capture of Mexico City in 1863. French occupation in Mexico during the nineteenth century is another vague concept in contemporary popular imagination. The irony is that many of today's American cities hold parades and celebrations on Cinco de Mayo (Fifth of May) without fully understanding the Mexican historical event that took place in 1862. They view Cinco de Mayo as a celebration of Mexican music, food, and dancing when in reality it is a recognition of Mexican subaltern strength over French military troops in a tremendous battle from Orizaba to the borders of Puebla led by General Ignacio Zaragoza.

Weeks before the battle, the Mexican people had organized a grassroots campaign to raise funds against France. Even the Gran Teatro Nacional held a benefit for the military hospitals by hosting a production of Verdi's opera *La Traviata*. A year later, however, France captured Mexico City and proclaimed Archduke Maximilian of Austria and his wife, Carlota, the emperor and empress of Mexico. Their four-year occupation of Mexico is the stuff of romantic legend today as well as realistic scorn by some Mexican historians.[16] French immigration and the influence of arts and letters outlasted the mere four years of actual physical occupation. Victor Hugo, Alexandre Dumas, and Maximilian's fondness for Spanish theater (José Zorrilla, Tirso de Molina, Cervantes) resulting in the establishment of the Royal Theater in Mexico, all infiltrated Mexican culture and moved up the coast to California.[17] Ruiz de Burton, never having been south of La Paz, caught the romantic imagination of French royalty instead of its realistic consequences. She took in the influence of French arts and letters enthusiastically.

As a result, Ruiz de Burton was realistic in her attitude toward Anglo-American political matters in California but a fierce romantic when contemplating the Mexican birthplace of her cultural beginnings. In her novel *The Squatter and the Don*, a French maid plays nurse to the youthful romantic heroine, the Mexican Mercedes. In a complex twist of power relations, Mexicans figure as the superiors over the French. Madam Halier is called upon when Mercedes faints or when she twists her ankle. Even the Alamar house, with its appointed French windows, architecturally belies French influence. When Carlota, namesake of the empress no doubt, notes that Mercedes is engrossed in a book, she says to Madam Halier, "Mercedes' French novel must be very interesting." Halier answers, "It is not a novel — it is French History." [18] The Alamar house, then, does not reveal itself solely as coming from a Spanish Mexican heritage but also a French one. Interestingly, Halier's subaltern position as nurse accentuates Ruiz de Burton's own complicity in power relations: her continual insistence on Mexican Spanish superiority. But there are always contradictions to Ruiz de Burton which make her personal and public self all the more interesting. The fact that Mercedes, the daughter of the don, could also pass for French weaves a familial thread into the French/Mexican complex relation of power. Mercedes is the epitome of romance in Ruiz de Burton's novel: a *sleeping beauty* with "little curls ... like golden threads ... white throat ... delicate wrist ... a child's hand, so dimpled and white and soft" (151).[19] Whereas Frank Norris's *Octopus* plows the literary landscape clean of everything except the Anglo-American voice, Ruiz de Burton embodies and embraces — fuses other cultures into her own brand of what contemporary Chicana scholars have now termed "mestizaje." [20] This she does under the mode of romance. She experiments with realism within the historical scenes of California.

In *The Squatter and the Don*, she begins some of her chapters with quotations from Dickens, Emerson, and Carlyle in order to foreground her perspective surrounding the political events in California. "'The one great principle of English law ... is to make business for itself,'" she quotes Dickens. Then she adds:

> The one great principle of American law is very much the same; our lawgivers keep giving us laws and then enacting others to explain them. The lawyers find plenty of occupation, but what becomes of the laity?
> "No. 189. An Act to ascertain and settle the private land claims in the State of California," says the book.

> And by a sad subversion of purposes, all the private land titles became unsettled. It ought to have been said, "An Act to unsettle land titles, and to upset the rights of the Spanish population of the State of California." (88)

The book she refers to is the Land Act of 1851. To protect Californio lands, the United States government had formed the Land Commission, a tribunal requiring Californios to prepare legal documents which outlined proof of territorial ownership. Squatters had already hoped the government would simply declare all California lands free for the taking. When the government refused, squatters created a form of filibustering by electing themselves to the commission or overwhelming sitting judges with threatening letters if hearings continued or if Mexican claims were confirmed.[21] Ironically, the lawyers, defenders of Californio rights, were the ones who fared well in the end. They were called upon to translate titles, write up legal documents, and litigate in court for many of the Californios. The process was laborious, and Ruiz de Burton experienced each costly step. At one point, Ruiz de Burton personally drew up her own legal documents and litigated in court because she could no longer afford the costs. She fought for roughly ten years before she finally lost everything. By the time court hearings took place and claims were either rejected or confirmed, the Californios were bankrupt and in many instances, the lawyers were recipients of lands they had won for their clients as payment for their "business." "Thus the government," wrote Ruiz de Burton, "washes its hands clean, liberally providing plenty of tribunals, plenty of crooked turnings through which to scourge the wretched land-owners" (88–89). The first part of this chapter, which describes these political situations, is certainly not a swashbuckling western scene or even a typical mode of popular romance. Ruiz de Burton's writing reveals multiple levels of genre (realism, naturalism) which later writers would develop: William Dean Howells, Upton Sinclair, Theodore Dreiser. In addition, her settings are multifarious and widely placed. She does not necessarily stay in the West but, as in *Who Would Have Thought It?* brings the West to New England. Rare are the nineteenth-century novels that formulate perspectives of eastern culture and thought from the vantage point of western sensibility—especially Mexican American sensibilities. Ruiz de Burton's writings also evoke those writers not well known who are being recovered of late. Rebecca Harding Davis is one who, like Ruiz de Burton, develops well-known motifs that create realistic, harsh views of American life.

In Davis's novel *Life in the Iron Mills*, "a dirty canary chirps desolately in a cage beside me. Its dream of green fields and sunshine is a very old dream,—

almost worn out."[22] The narrator observes not Whitman's uplifting line, "I see my soul reflected in nature . . . as I see through a mist, one with inexpressible completeness and beauty,"[23] but instead a world "clotted and black."[24] Sharon Harris, author of *Rebecca Harding Davis and American Realism*, notes that Davis's use of the caged bird is a "leitmotif throughout turn-of-the-century naturalism" and the "'dream' that has outworn its usefulness becomes in Davis's literature the symbol of Emersonian transcendentalism, a philosophy she rebukes for its potentially corrupting influence on American life."[25] Ruiz de Burton also uses the motif but to a different end. Instead of one solitary bird, there are many in one New England cage. In a twist of perspectives, the Mexican American girl Lola is the observer and dominant voice in the scene. This scene occurs in Ruiz de Burton's novel *Who Would Have Thought It?*[26] Lavinia, a homely spinster, finally makes the decision to leave the domestic sphere and become a military nurse for the Civil War soldiers. But she must make a decision about her charges: a cageful of canaries. She decides to kill them with chloroform, put them to sleep. "If I leave you, you will die of hunger, or some miserable cat might devour you, one by one" (85–86). When the last bird escapes, she chases after it and bumps into the cunning Reverend Hackwell. Lavinia faints. Reverend Hackwell proceeds to take advantage of her by fondling her breasts and kissing her. Lola sees everything, interrupts the lascivious Hackwell, and saves the bird from death by chloroform. Lavinia, in the end, is the caged bird who leaves the domestic sphere but becomes victim of the corrupting influences of the American "dream"—material wealth. She thinks she can participate equally with men now that she has entered the public sphere as a nurse but finds otherwise. After attempting to speak with officials in Washington, she says: "What a miserable, powerless thing woman is, even in this our country of glorious equality! Here I have been sitting up at night, toiling, and tending disgusting sickness, and dressing loathsome wounds, all for the love of our dear country, and now, the first time I come to ask a favor—a favor, do I say? No. I come to demand a right—see how I am received!" (106).

Ruiz de Burton's satirical and comic edge, however, departs from Davis's spare dark prose. There is no room for frivolity when Davis's stark realism is at its height:

> The hands of each mill are divided into watches that relieve each other as regularly as the sentinels of an army. By night and day the work goes on, the unsleeping engines groan and shriek, the fiery pools of metal boil and surge. Only for a day in the week, in half-courtesy to public censure, the fires are

partially veiled; but as soon as the clock strikes midnight, the great furnaces break forth with renewed fury, the clamor begins with fresh, breathless vigor, the engines sob and shriek like "gods in pain." (19)

When Ruiz de Burton breaks the narrative and speaks directly to the reader, the realism in her novels parallels Davis's sharp rhetoric. Toward the end of *The Squatter and the Don*, Lizzie observes that California has become a land of wealthy entrepreneurs who exploit and stereotype the Mexican as lazy and shiftless. What has disappeared in California is the Spanish Mexican familial community. Lizzie grieves for Gabriel:

> But if Gabriel had never complained, the eloquence of facts had said all that was to be said. In that hod full of bricks not only his own sad experience was represented, but the entire history of the native Californians of Spanish descent was epitomized. Yes, Gabriel carrying his hod full of bricks up a steep ladder, was a symbolical representation of his race. The natives, of Spanish origin, having lost all their property, must henceforth be hod carriers.
>
> Unjust laws despoiled them, but what of this? Poor they are, but who is to care, or investigate the cause of their poverty? The thriving American says that the native Spaniards are lazy and stupid and thriftless, and as the prosperous know it all, and are almost infallible, the fiat has gone forth, and the Spaniards of California are not only despoiled of all their earthly possessions, but must also be bereft of sympathy, because the world says they do not deserve it. (352)

Like Davis, Ruiz de Burton's keen descriptions, her political protests, and her awareness of human limitations (including her own and those of the Californios) are preliminary sketches of these various genres. Contemporary critics as well as textbook publishers have attributed realism and naturalism to later novels and novelists, categorizing each genre into separate headings and chronological ordering. Writers such as Davis and Ruiz de Burton published more than thirty years before William Dean Howells, Frank Norris, or Stephen Crane. Their works move in and out of realism, naturalism, and romance. Because Ruiz de Burton's letters are linked within the construction of these genres, we can further trace and investigate her stylistic development. From epistolary prose to structured scenes, her style consistently breaks fictional narrative for various reasons: to achieve a direct authorial voice, to provide realistic focus, to create a mood. In addition, Ruiz de Burton's works also contain literary aspects attributed to the later American group of writers known as the muckrakers.

When learning about the writers leading the muckraking movement, we are often guided to turn-of-the-century writers such as Upton Sinclair. Theodore Dreiser and Frank Norris are also placed under the category of naturalism. All of these writers are indeed significant. But contemporary readers are at a disadvantage without having access to cross-class, multiracial literature from nineteenth-century authors who became Americans or were born in the United States and who experimented with a myriad of genres.

Ruiz de Burton's first chapter of *The Squatter and the Don* may be compared with chapter 9 of Harriet Beecher Stowe's *Uncle Tom's Cabin*. Ruiz de Burton creates the scene in the home of a New England family. The wife is admonishing her husband for being a squatter and taking land that legally is not his but that of the Alamar Californio family: "I beg of you, do not go on a Mexican grant unless you buy the land from the owner. This I beg of you specially, and must *insist upon it*" (57). The scene also mirrors Ruiz de Burton's letters to Vallejo that urge him to follow her advice. Chapter 9 in *Uncle Tom's Cabin* also begins within the home. Senator John Bird, a member of Ohio's legislature, and his wife, Mary, are sitting at the table. From this domestic sphere, Mary admonishes the senator after he tells her he supports "a law forbidding people to help off the slaves that come over from Kentucky . . . I never could have thought it of you, John. . . . You ought to be ashamed."[27] At the conclusion of both novels, the discursive structure changes from what began as a romance to a realistic mode which seeks specific ends toward reform. Stowe calls for an end to slavery and delineates how legislation is violating human rights. Ruiz de Burton calls for an end to harassment of Californios and outlines ways the Treaty of Guadalupe Hidalgo has not been honored. She calls for new legislation. Both Stowe and Burton defend their views with copious quotations from published legislation, treaties, and political figures of the time. Ruiz de Burton ends her novel by pointing out: "Our representatives in Congress, and in the State Legislature, knowing full well the will of the people, ought to legislate accordingly. If they do not, then we shall—as Channing said 'kiss the foot that tramples us!' and 'in anguish of spirit' must wait and pray for a Redeemer who will emancipate the . . . slaves of California" (372). Twenty-one years after Ruiz de Burton's book appeared, Upton Sinclair's 1906 publication of *The Jungle* ends: "The rallying of the outraged workingmen of Chicago . . . we shall organize them, we shall drill them, we shall marshal them for the victory! We shall bear down the opposition, we shall sweep it before us—and Chicago will be ours."[28]

Sentimentalism is a mode that has designs on the world. If writing has an ideological (and historical) base (and I look to Mikhail Bakhtin's theory of dialogisms here as well as nineteenth-century constructions/reviews of fiction), then we must look at the ways discourse shapes the ranges of perspectives.[29] In this case, what ends does the realism and naturalism mode seek to achieve upon the larger world? What kind of textual work does it try to achieve? When Ruiz de Burton writes, "I slander no one but speak the truth" (364), she parallels Theodore Dreiser when he writes in *Sister Carrie*, "The needle of understanding will yet point steadfast and unwavering to the distant pole of truth."[30] Ruiz de Burton and Dreiser rupture fictional narrative to appropriate a more direct authority. Their intentions or "truths" may differ, but to investigate such considerations broadens the discussion of literature and literary history.

I would argue that my examples reveal an attempt at a restructuring of American literature which has unlimited possibilities in the number and kind of text and genre. These examples untie the stringent, exiguous textbook lists that have kept readers in unnecessary corsetry. As Jane Tompkins points out, "'Literature' is not a stable entity, but a category whose outlines and contents are variable."[31] Other critics, including Paul Lauter, Henry Louis Gates Jr., William Spengemann, Toni Morrison, and Ramón Saldívar, have also called for reconsiderations of American literary history. I return to Annette Kolodny's appeal for a new kind of American literary canon which "frees American literary history from the persistent theories" that "treat frontier materials" as "marginalia or cultural mythology."[32] Ruiz de Burton's marginalization was not solely a literary one but one of personal identity. After the Treaty of Guadalupe Hidalgo was signed, and especially after her husband died, Ruiz de Burton fought a daily battle against becoming an exotic or mythologized figure in Californio history.

"REMEMBER WHO I AM AND WHO I WANT TO BE": IDENTITIES IN CRISIS

Acuerdese q. soy mujer . . . y Mejicana . . . con el alma enserrada en una jaula de fierro, pues así nos encierra "la Sosiedad" luego q. nacimos, como los Chinos los pies de sus mujeres.

[Remember that I am a woman . . . and Mexican . . . with my soul enclosed in an iron cage. This is the manner in which *Society* confines us as soon as we are born, like the Chinese and the feet of their women.]
(August 12, 1869)

The caged bird motif in Ruiz de Burton's epistolary writing underlines her sudden status as a widow and her realization that she must fight to defend her personal and literary presence in a public arena: the United States. This is no easy task for a Californiana who is alive but supposedly dying or dead in Anglo-American literary fiction. In 1869, Californianas such as Ruiz de Burton were being appropriated by Anglo-American writers. Publishers and book collectors such as Hubert H. Bancroft would send their clerks to Californio households to gather their testimonials. Such appropriations helped further the disappearing voice of the Mexicano. Bancroft was one of the most active in these endeavors.

Bancroft began as an enterprising young bookseller who was most interested in what Rosaura Sánchez describes as the "reproduction of cultural technologies." During his lifetime, he would amass "sixty thousand volumes" on "the Americas (especially Mexico and Central America)." The volumes included testimonials he collected from various Californios such as Dorotea Valdez, Fermina Espinoza, and the once powerful Mariano Guadalupe Vallejo. Sánchez writes:

> A number of writers, none of them historians by training, would be hired to use the materials in Bancroft's collection for the writing of these volumes in what resembled a literary assembly line with its strict division of labor and mass production techniques. All of the works, however, would be published under Bancroft's name; he assumed that because he was paying for the writers' labor he could lay claim to their work as his own.[33]

In one particular "history," titled "Forty Years of Mexican History," one of Bancroft's many unnamed historians writes, "'There is a revolution in Mexico every ten minutes' is a saying we Americans take great delight in, partly because of the implied superior stability of our own political institutions."[34] And in another historical account named "The Land of the Aztecs," the historian writes, "The masses of the people of Mexico have no more voice in the government of their country, nor do they seem to care to have, than the Chinese have in governing California."[35] Descriptions like these, which generalized and marginalized all minorities as well as the Mexicans and the Californios, were commonplace. Ruiz de Burton and her fellow Californio Vallejo were aware of such power. At one point, Vallejo told Bancroft, "Your work will be accepted by the world . . . as a reliable and complete history of my native land."[36] He knew as well as Ruiz de Burton did that the Californio stories would be in Bancroft's complete control.

But Bancroft was not the only one who took the main stage in appropriating the Californio/Mexican American identity. "Thomas Jefferson Farnham's *Travels in the Californias and Scenes in the Pacific Ocean*, published in 1844, was sensationalistic and vituperative," says historian Adelaida Del Castillo. She describes Farnham as "a lawyer, [who] came to California from Illinois by way of Oregon. In his words, 'the Californios are an imbecile, pusillanimous race of men, and unfit to control the destinies of that beautiful country. . . . The ladies, dear creatures, I wish they were whiter, and that their cheekbones did not in their great condescension assimilate their manners and customs so remarkably to their Indian neighbors . . . a pity it is . . . that they have not stay and corset makers' signs among them, for they allow their waists to grow as God designed they should, like Venus de Medici, that ill-bred statue that had no kind mother to lash its vitals into delicate form."[37]

These are just some of the voices with which Ruiz de Burton had to contend. If one looks through the *San Francisco Argonaut* of 1885, one will not find Ruiz de Burton's books mentioned. The now established canonical writers are present: Henry James and William Dean Howells. Helen Hunt Jackson is also mentioned numerous times as the official writer of the Indian and Mexican romance. On September 12, 1885, under "Literary Notes" in the *San Francisco Argonaut*, a notation reads: "Mrs. Helen Hunt Jackson's novel, *Ramona*, has now reached its eighteenth thousand." All of the above writers were in one way or another supported monetarily and professionally by Hubert H. Bancroft. He offered to romanticize Ruiz de Burton into another history, his romance which he called *California Pastoral*. His biography of Ruiz de Burton was just as sensationalized as the aforementioned accounts of Mexico. Making Ruiz de Burton a passive character whom he called "The Maid of Monterey" helped the public forget that she was a serious writer. A ballad was written about her which was inspired from the brief insurrection at La Paz in the 1840s. Ruiz de Burton would have been a teenager at this time. It had been documented that she had worked in a nearby hospital, caring for the sick. The ballad reads:

> The moon shone but dimly
> Beyond the battle plain
> A gentle breeze fanned softly
> O'er the features of the slain
> The guns had hushed their thunder
> The guns in silence lay
> Then came the señorita
> The Maid of Monterey.
>
> She cast a look of anguish
> On the dying and the dead
> And made her lap a pillow
> For those who mourned and bled
> Now here's to that bright beauty
> Who drives death's pangs away
> The meek-eyed señorita
> The Maid of Monterey.

As late as the 1930s, the romanticization of Ruiz de Burton continued. Her biographer Winifred Davidson wrote: "Those who used to know her remember her lovely, small feet with their high curved arches and her grace that was perfection itself in the dance. Her good nature overcame her native hauteur."[38]

Had Ruiz de Burton not been marginalized and had her works been widely read, a different view of the Californio would have been established. I would not say a definitive view of the Californio would have been established because Ruiz de Burton could never speak for all Californios. She brings to both our present Chicano literary history as well as Anglo-American literary history a contributing voice that complicates the definition of what it means to be an American in this country. Her writings bring to the literary community another side to the prism of history. The historian Hayden White says that "narrative in general, from the folktale to the novel, from the annals to the fully realized 'history,' has to do with the topics of law, legality, legitimacy, or, more generally, authority."[39] To give Ruiz de Burton full "authority" would have been to allow a pluralistic perspective in American literary history. Today we are finally recovering such perspectives, which now leads me to a consideration of Ruiz de Burton as precursor to Chicana writing.

Rosaura Sánchez, Mexican American scholar and editor of Ruiz de Burton's *The Squatter and the Don*, understands the need to recover and investigate nineteenth-century Mexican American writing. She says: "This period also marks the beginning of our [Mexican American] production as a marginal ethnic group. If we hope to prepare for the future, as well as to grasp the present better, we will have to understand the past. But even more importantly, if we hope to make ourselves heard, we will have to enable previously silenced voices to speak."[40]

Ruiz de Burton, who reveals the inequities of women in American society in her novels and letters, becomes, for Chicana writers today, a prophetic voice from the nineteenth century. I place her in this context with caution because of her failure to recognize the Indígena, the brown skin, as her own. Ruiz de Burton does not hide her upper-class origins. In a personal letter of 1855, she reveals her class-conscious identity when she includes her workers in a gracious and familial manner. She is careful to place the family and workers in order of importance. She says: "Todos estamos buenos . . . empezando por el Capitan, mi mamá, yo, Federico, Nelly, Harry, los indios en el rancho, las bacas, beceros [etc.]" [We are all fine . . . beginning with the Captain, my mother, myself, Federico, Nelly, Harry, the indians in the ranch, the cows, calves, [etc.] — 3 November 1855]. Indians are not only written in the lower case, but they are placed on the ranch next to the animals. In *The Squatter and the Don*, when Don Alamar tells the squatters that they might be better off raising cattle, Mathews replies, "What do I know about whirling a lariat?" (94). Alamar answers him, "You can hire an Indian boy to do that part" (94). Hired help for Ruiz de Burton is cheap labor—reserved for a marginalized class. Ruiz de Burton's cultural ambivalence and adherence to a class structure produce a body of writing full of complexities. I support an exploration of these contradictions because they resist what American literary canons and nineteenth-century constructions of the Mexicans have been doing—marginalizing, stereotyping, creating a one-dimensional caricature of the Mexican, thereby erasing her.

Our complex relationships to power cross ethnic, gender, and racial borderlines. By conceptually unraveling these intricate relationships to power, such as Ruiz de Burton's writings as well as those of others from various cultures and positions (Margaret Fuller, Elizabeth Keckley, the canonical writers—Hawthorne, Emerson, Whitman), we take the necessary step of confronting the very systems in which we participate in the twentieth century. In all literature and public discourse, we cannot think or imagine ourselves out of being implicated in power, and a good example is our twentieth-century ability or inability to discuss conflicts within the Anglo community, the Chicano community, and other communities concerning class issues, sexism, gender or sexual orientation. Even as Chicanas, we are situated differently in more than one position concerning identity.

To read texts that dare to reveal and portray the complexities of power relations is to bring us face to face with our own implications in power structures today. Such readings encourage public conversations about how we are all embedded in these relations, which then help to develop a consciousness of power relations with a goal of making concrete change. This is why someone like Ruiz de Burton is useful to read and discuss: she was trying to contribute to public conversations about different kinds of power, and she was self-consciously trying to contribute to the kinds of power she recognized. What is equally interesting about her is how she reveals (unwittingly) her own complicity in power relations.

Many critics have recoiled at the anti-Indian sentiment in her work, but I argue that it is important to study this in order to look at how we still perpetuate such sentiments in the twentieth century. To survive, to assimilate, to continue her upper-class patriarchal upbringing may be reasons for Ruiz de Burton's relations of power, which reveal her elitism. Those aspects inherent in her works must not be ignored but fully discussed. To dwell solely on this area, however, dismisses the complexity of our Chicana heritage at a most critical time in history. To dismiss and exclude her as a precursor to Chicana/o literature would be, as scholar Tey Diana Rebolledo has also pointed out, to dismiss voices of

Hispanic nineteenth-century women who, because of their economic privilege, had the means to speak and create for themselves a literary space in a primarily male Mexican and American literary landscape.[41] Critic and scholar Erlinda Gonzalez-Berry notes that Ruiz de Burton's "posture toward las clases populares is offensive yet therein lies her position in the matrix of 'difference.'"[42] In her book *The Last Generation*, Cherríe Moraga faces the fact that her Chicana heritage is not only one of the "Indígena" but also of the "Conquistador." She has inherited both the colonized and the colonizer. "Most Mexicans can claim the same," Moraga says, "but my claim is more 'explorer' than not. And yes, most days I am deathly ashamed."[43] From this shameful heritage, Moraga recognizes that to grow and imagine a new world, "we must open the wound to make it heal, purify ourselves with the prick of Maguey thorns."[44] To look Ruiz de Burton full in the face is to understand the humanness inherent in her body of work and to gain an understanding of yet another aspect of a heritage from which Chicana writers have come. What we learn from reading Ruiz de Burton is a recognition that American literature is rich with voices, rich with a multifaceted history. Ruiz de Burton is just one among a large group of silenced writers whose works provide the opportunity to expand our understanding of American and Chicana literary history. She brings to both our present Chicano literary history and to Anglo-American literary history a voice that complicates the definition of what it means to be an American. Her writings bring to the literary community another side to the prism of history. To give Ruiz de Burton's writings a space for discussion and criticism in the twentieth century is to contribute to a much larger project of creating a pluralistic perspective of American literary history. "¡Mucho hay que ver!" ["There is much to see"], says Ruiz de Burton in her letter dated 1860[1]. It is up to us today to take up this larger project and see ourselves within it—not apart from it.

NOTES

I would like to thank Noelle Arrangoiz, Mary Kelley, Luis Leal, María Herrera-Sobek, Tey Diana Rebolledo, Chela Sandoval, Susan Johnson, Barbara Schulman, José Aranda, Anne E. Goldman, J. Alemán, and Rik Knablein for their comments on drafts of this essay. I am also grateful to the Santa Barbara Mission Archive Library and the Huntington Library for their support of this research and for permission to quote from the De La Guerra Collection.

1. María Amparo Ruiz de Burton to Mariano Guadalupe Vallejo, March 8, 1860[1], De La Guerra Collection, Huntington Library and Santa Barbara Mission Archive Library. This letter fragment as well as subsequent excerpts from Ruiz de Burton's letters

are cited parenthetically by dates. It is my opinion that the date Ruiz de Burton used for this letter (1860) is incorrect. This letter and that of another (June 23, 1860) describe events that could only pertain to the year 1861: the inauguration and receptions on behalf of President Lincoln. To remain true to her letters, however, I have added a [1] next to her date. Currently, I am finishing a translation and interpretation of Ruiz de Burton's letters, which cover roughly thirty-five years of her life: 1851–87. All of these letters are correspondence to Mariano Guadalupe Vallejo (1808–90), prominent Californio and founder of Sonoma. Vallejo served in the Mexican military and was commander of San Francisco between 1831 and 1834. During the Mexican-American War, Vallejo sought to befriend the Americans yet was arrested by the Bear Flaggers in 1846. He cooperated with Hubert Howe Bancroft in gathering Californio testimonials for Bancroft's *History of California* but in the end was not pleased with many of the descriptions of his people. Ruiz de Burton's letters reveal a political and cultural kinship with Vallejo (see note 15 below). She relied on him for advice and solace, and the letters also uncover Ruiz de Burton's need to be on an equal standing with Vallejo.

2. Ruiz de Burton lived in several eastern cities, including New York, Washington, D.C., and Richmond, Virginia, because of her marital connection to General Henry Stanton Burton. Burton hailed from a prominent New England family who had connections to legislators and prominent politicians in Washington, D.C. Burton, whose father was a West Point graduate, followed in his father's footsteps and graduated from West Point in 1839. He met Ruiz de Burton when he was lieutenant colonel during the Mexican-American War. In 1847, he was ordered to invade La Paz, Ruiz de Burton's hometown. Historian Frederick Bryant Oden notes that the invasion was a peaceful one. He writes: "On July 3, 1847, a total of 115 men under Lieutenant Colonel Henry S. Burton left for lower California. They would land in María Ruiz's hometown of La Paz about three weeks later. The Mexicans there offered little resistance, and Lieutenant Colonel Burton reinstated the civil government on the condition that it remain loyal to the United States" (Frederick Bryant Oden, "The Maid of Monterrey: The Life of María Amparo Ruiz de Burton, 1832–1895," M.A. thesis, University of San Diego, 1992), 14. At some point during this year, Henry Burton met the young María Amparo Ruiz and after the war helped her family as well as other Californio families move north. This assistance was possible because many La Paz families had aligned themselves with the United States and were certain that Mexico would cede Baja California. After the Treaty of Guadalupe Hidalgo was signed, however, La Paz remained part of Mexico. The families, fearing reprisal from Mexico, decided to flee La Paz. By the time they reached Monterrey, Burton was courting María Amparo Ruiz, and they married shortly thereafter. Throughout their marriage they traveled because of Burton's military orders. She lived mostly in the East during the Civil War years. While in Virginia, Ruiz de Burton became acquainted with U.S. political structures. She attended Senate hearings and speeches, and the Burtons were invited to political balls, including President Lincoln's inauguration festivities. The characters she develops in *Who Would Have Thought It?* are loosely based on actual people she knew in New England. Toward the end of the Civil War, Burton contracted malaria and died on April 4, 1869. His death severed her

ties with East Coast upper-class society, which shows the influence her husband had and the powerlessness of a widow in the nineteenth century. It is to Ruiz de Burton's credit that she sought publication so her voice could be heard.

It is also important to note that there are many terms for the California Mexican ranch owners during the nineteenth century. Most often they called themselves Californios (an "o" instead of an "a" as in California). Other terms show up in manuscripts (letters, documents) and in Ruiz de Burton's novels and personal writings. She uses the following names interchangeably: *Spanish Mexicans, Spaniards, Mexicans, Californiana(s)*. All these terms refer to Mexicans living on California lands before the Mexican-American war and who chose to remain on those lands and become American after the signing of the Treaty of Guadalupe Hidalgo. It is important not to confuse Spanish Mexicans with recent immigrants from Spain. These ranch owners had been native to Mexico for generations. To refer to oneself as *Spanish* was simply to identify oneself as part of the upper elite within the stringent class structure still present in Mexico.

3. To establish itself politically, economically, and socially, the United States launched a massive print campaign to erase or stereotype both the Mexican and the Indian. Published books, pamphlets, travel materials, newspapers, and newsletters all had strongly biased Anglo-American patriotic and political perspectives. The idea of Manifest Destiny figures prominently in this print phenomenon for much of the material describes Anglo-American peoples who must "save" or "redeem" or "cleanse" the West of its lesser-human inhabitants. Antonia I. Castañeda's article "The Political Economy of Nineteenth Century Stereotypes of Californianas," in *Between Borders: Essays on Mexicana/Chicana History*, ed. Adelaida R. Del Castillo (Encino, Calif.: Floricanto Press, 1990) illustrates how these ideas were disseminated: "The literature of the period was generally written by middle class, Anglo males who interpreted women's experience from their own gender and class perspective of women's proper roles. In this way, these authors created sexist and unidimensional portrayals of women ... stereotyped into four sexually defined roles: gentle tamers, sunbonneted helpmates, hell-raisers and bad women" (213–14). Also see the following: Susan Lee Johnson, "Bulls, Bears, and Dancing Boys: Race, Gender, and Leisure in the California Gold Rush," *Radical History Review* 60 (Fall 1994): 4–37. Johnson's essay focuses on Anglo writers' sensationalist accounts of the Mexican as well as other peoples of color in California during the Gold Rush period.

4. Hubert Howe Bancroft was the most influential book collector in California and methodically organized a statewide campaign to collect testimonials from the Californios. His methods were unreliable because he sent amateur clerks to record testimonials. If a testimonial were incomplete or vague, Bancroft would sensationalize it and create his own narrative connections. His histories of California and Mexico romanticize the environment and depict its peoples as complacent, passive individuals. See Bancroft's *History of California*, 7 vols. (San Francisco: History Company, 1884–89) and *Pastoral California* (San Francisco: History Company, 1888). See also Thomas Jefferson Farnham's *Travels in the Californias and Scenes in the Pacific Ocean* (1844; rpt. Oakland: Biobooks, 1947). Farnham portrays the Mexican in negative, at times bestial, terms.

5. See Frank Norris, "The Great American Novelist," *Literary Criticism* (January 19,

1903): 123–24. Norris states that a great American novelist cannot exist because of the country's expansive and varying environments. He argues for great American regional novelists such as Howells (East), Cable (far South), Eggleston (Middle West). He believes that "the Great Novelist" "shall also be an American." In *The Octopus*, Norris is seeking to be the great novelist of the West without taking into account Californio writers who were present before he was. Although the Californios were legally American after 1848 (in accordance with the Treaty of Guadalupe Hidalgo), they were not recognized as such.

6. Frank Norris, *The Octopus* (New York: Penguin Books, 1986), 20. Subsequent quotations from the novel are cited in parentheses.

7. J. R. V. Marchan and Joseph F. Charles, eds., *Cassell's Latin Dictionary* (New York: Funk and Wagnalls, 1956), 605.

8. The term "muckraking" did not exist during Ruiz de Burton's literary lifetime. Yet I mention muckraking here because the term (coined by President Theodore Roosevelt) originates from John Bunyan's allegory, *Pilgrim's Progress: From This World to That Which Is to Come*, published in 1678 and 1684 (parts I and II respectively). Christian, Bunyan's main character, must flee his city, which is to be burned. Ruiz de Burton's California in *The Squatter and The Don* experiences colonization — a burning that dislocates and melds the Alamar family into hod carriers and an inevitable invisibility. Her writing is no allegory because of the naturalist and realist modes she incorporates in the novel, but her intent is similar to that of the later muckraking writers. Theodore Roosevelt used this term to demean American writers whose aim was to expose business, city, state, and national corruption. Ruiz de Burton's work could easily be placed in this category.

9. Ruiz de Burton's novels were out of print for over one hundred years. Thanks to the efforts of Rosaura Sánchez and Beatrice Pita, Ruiz de Burton's works are now in print. *The Squatter and the Don*, originally published in San Francisco in 1885, was republished in 1992, with a new edition in 1997. *Who Would Have Thought It?*, originally published in Philadelphia in 1872, was republished in 1995.

10. I am asked about Ruiz de Burton both in the classroom and at academic conferences, which makes me realize the amount of education that still needs to be conducted about histories of the West as well as the history of the Mexican-American War. It is not often that I see the Mexican-American War or California in the nineteenth century (before and after 1848) as the focal topic in secondary or university curricula or course syllabi. And if there were such courses, I would hope they would include a focus on the peoples who were present in California during the nineteenth century: the Indians, Mexicans, Chinese, South Americans, Australians. An excellent reference is Susan Lee Johnson's dissertation, "'The Gold She Gathered': Difference, Domination, and California's Southern Mines, 1848–1853" (Yale University, 1993). Johnson's forthcoming book, *Roaring Camp: The Social World of the California Gold Rush* (New York: W. W. Norton, 2000), is based on "'The Gold She Gathered.'"

11. Susan Lee Johnson. "'A Memory Sweet to Soldiers': The Significance of Gender

in the History of the 'American West,'" *Western Historical Quarterly* 24 (November 1993): 495–517.

12. In this letter, Ruiz de Burton is not looking at the American as an enemy but proposing the writing of a novel as a way to understand the coexistence of two races. She said, "Realmente para apreciar bien una cosa es necesario mirar bien otra. Creo q. lo mejor q. yo pueda hacer es escribir un libro" [In reality to truly appreciate one thing it is necessary to look well at another. I think the best that I can do is to write a book] (June 23, 1860). This is an interesting rationale for writing a novel in contrast to Norris's desire to be the great western regional writer who privileges an Anglo-American perspective.

13. These two works present contrasting perspectives of the nineteenth-century voice from both the West and the East. Both works parallel Ruiz de Burton's adherence to a class structure as well as her nonapologetic racist attitudes toward other peoples of color. Because these authors reveal their varying participation in power relations, their writing becomes unconventional and differs greatly from nineteenth-century Anglo-western writings, which tend toward uncomplicated stereotypes of other races and of women.

14. Annette Kolodny, "Letting Go Our Grand Obsessions: Notes Toward a New Literary History of the American Frontiers," in *Subjects and Citizens*, ed. Cathy N. Davidson and Michael Moon (Durham: Duke University Press, 1995), 12.

15. Mariano Guadalupe Vallejo had an extensive library on his ranch in Alta California. Ruiz de Burton made use of it and even at one time borrowed all forty-four volumes of Alexandre Dumas's works. She also shared her favorite books with Vallejo, as well as her love of writing. Vallejo was not a novelist but a historian. He wanted to preserve the history of the Californios and spent years gathering testimonials of his fellow Californios and recounting his early memories of California in a book he named "Recuerdos" (see Mariano Guadalupe Vallejo, "Recuerdos Históricos y Personales Tocante a la Alta California," 5 vols., 1875, MS, Bancroft Library, University of California, Berkeley). Vallejo's work was also an effort to fight the Anglo-American social and print campaign which sought to depict false or simplistic descriptions of the Californio. See Genaro M. Padilla, *My History, Not Yours: The Formation of Mexican American Autobiography* (Madison: University of Wisconsin Press, 1993). Padilla describes Vallejo as a careful and critical historian: "Vexed by the social and discursive ill-treatment his people were receiving, he elaborately counterpositioned examples of early Californio social manners against what he regarded as Yankee-induced moral and political corruption throughout California. And rather than just rail against the past, he documents his opposition to pervasive nineteenth-century representations of the Californios as illiterate, culturally backward, socially and morally degenerate inhabitants of a progressive, right-minded, visionary American society. As early as the second volume, while describing the work of the Deputación Provincial, the governing body of California, he pointedly compares the integrity of the members and proceedings of the Mexican assembly with the corrupt dealings of the American assembly in 1874, where corruption went all the way up to President Ulysses S. Grant" (98). Unfortunately, Hubert Howe Bancroft would take Vallejo's "*Recuerdos*" and re-work them—culling from the history what seemed fit to him and disre-

garding the rest. In the end, Vallejo's work remained on Bancroft's archive shelves. Because of Bancroft's well-known tendency to alter Californio writings, Ruiz de Burton did not ask for Bancroft's full support for her novels. Instead, she used most of her own money to finance her publications.

16. In the introduction to his book *El teatro en México durante el Segundo Imperio, 1862–1867* (Mexico City: Imprenta Universitaria, 1959), Luis Reyes de la Maza describes the Mexican popular culture idealizing and revering the French occupation as romantic royal fantasy. For Reyes de la Maza, Carlota and Maximilian were simply political pawns. They had no idea how to govern a country (9). He argues for a more realistic view of the French monarchy in Mexico. Although his work is almost forty years old, it is easy to compare it with contemporary American idealizations of and preoccupations with the British royal family.

17. See note 16 above.

18. María Amparo Ruiz de Burton, *The Squatter and the Don*, ed. Rosaura Sánchez and Beatrice Pita (Houston: Arte Público Press, 1992), 120. Subsequent quotations from the novel are cited in parentheses.

19. Mercedes looks Anglo, but she is signaled as French with a Mexican last name. While the Alamar family speaks and acts against the impending squatter invasion, Mercedes becomes the unconscious offering toward complete Mexican erasure. Mercedes assimilates by losing her name to the Darrell family, and her French "whiteness" becomes easily subsumed. How, then, does Ruiz de Burton's book differ from Frank Norris's, who privileges an Anglo-American perspective? After all, aside from Presley, Norris's characters (Annixter, Harran, Broderson, Osterman) are not Anglo but recent immigrants. They are what St. John de Crèvecoeur describes as "individuals of all nations [who] are melted into a new race of men" (see J. Hector St. John de Crèvecoeur, *Letters from an American Farmer and Sketches of Eighteenth-Century America*, ed. Albert E. Stone [New York: Penguin Books, 1986], 70). Frank Norris's novel seeks to reveal railroad monopoly corruptions but also, through Presley, to colonize a new epic American writer. The new European-American immigrants die and Presley is left to tell their story—to write his epic American poem. Ruiz de Burton seeks to write an obituary of remembrance.

20. First, I want to point out how Latin-American definitions of "mestizaje" and contemporary Chicana feminist theories of "mestizaje" differ. I recognize those critics who insist on the historicity of "mestizaje" coming from the Ibero-Hispano, peninsular, Hispano-American countries. The Venezuelan scholar Arturo Uslar Pietri, for example, sees the formation of the mestizo as a historical cultural process. The mestizo is a collective (the Spanish, Indian, and black) forming a consciousness, an identity called "mestizaje." Pietri also points out that this mestizo collective passed "a América y en ella han empezado a caminar tropezando hacia nuevas formas de mestizaje universal" [to America, and there, has begun walking, stumbling upon new forms of a universal mestizaje] ("Otra Historia," *De una a otra Venezuela* [Caracas: Monte Avila Editores, 1992], 121–25). Pietri's historical look at the evolution of "mestizaje" is important because it serves as a counterpoint for Chicana feminist theorists. Writers such as Gloria Anzaldúa and Chela Sandoval write of a resistant mestizaje: one that rejects a universal consciousness

(see Chela Sandoval, "New Sciences: Cyborg Feminism and the Methodology of the Oppressed," in *The Cyborg Handbook*, ed. Chris Hables Gray [New York: Routledge, 1995], 407–21). Pietri's universal mestizaje does not take into consideration North American historical racial inheritances, which are political and not solely cultural. The Chicano, as scholar Lora Romero pointed out, "is the result of over a century of political organizing in response to an even longer history of social, economic, and cultural violence. The word 'Chicano' does not refer to race in any simple sense—which is why most progressives use 'Chicano' in place of 'Mexican-American'" ("'When Something Goes Queer': Familiarity, Formalism, and Minority Intellectuals in the 1980s," *Yale Journal of Criticism* 6 [1993]: 121).

To read Ruiz de Burton, keeping these definitions in mind, is to be aware of the complex racial and political history Chicanas/Chicanos inherit in the United States. Ruiz de Burton's body of work (private letters and public writings) reveals a writer who infused Anglo, French, black, and Indian as well as Californio Mexican in her literary landscape. The way she portrays these cultures makes for an interesting, complex, infuriating, and therefore important literary voice. I see Ruiz de Burton as an ancestor to our contemporary Chicana identity. In *Borderlands/La Frontera: The New Mestiza* (San Francisco: Aunt Lute Books, 1987), Gloria Anzaldúa calls for the mestiza to understand from where she comes so she can transcend the borders that limit her identity and her potential. Anzaldúa says, "Her [la mestiza] first step is to take inventory. Despojando, desgranando, quitando paja. Just what did she inherit from her ancestors? This weight on her back—which is the baggage from the Indian mother, which the baggage from the Spanish father, which the baggage from the Anglo?" (82). In many ways, Anzaldúa's words encourage us to understand Ruiz de Burton as our ancestor—from the Spanish father. In her own time, Ruiz de Burton's inheritance was an upper-class military elite background that disregarded the Indian. She was complicit in power relations that subordinated the position of the Indígena/o, and yet culturally she comes from an Indígena inheritance. Her inheritances are also historical. Ruiz de Burton comes to us with the following. First, she experienced the Mexican-American War, which in its aftermath transformed her into a subordinate in an Anglo-American society. Second, her inheritance involves France's imperial occupation in Mexico for four years. She was also swept into an American society in the throes of establishing its nationhood, which compelled her to decide where her loyalties lay. Finally, during the Civil War, the question of slavery and black prejudice were also her inheritance. Anzaldúa writes of the mestiza:

> The future will belong to the mestiza. Because the future depends on the breaking down of paradigms, it depends on the straddling of two or more cultures. By creating a new mythos—that is a change in the way we perceive reality, the way we see ourselves, and the ways we behave—*la mestiza* creates a new consciousness.(80)

The ways Ruiz de Burton battled her own marginalization brought her to a new consciousness that she was able to articulate in her two novels. No, she is not what we would hope our ancestor to be like: a voice for the indigenous peoples. She cannot speak to us from that vantage point. But she provides a new look into our mestizaje which makes us conscious of power relations and how we are embedded within them because we inherit them. If we read Ruiz de Burton, we become conscious of the ways our progenitors complied within power structures. By reading and understanding Ruiz de Burton (and other previously silenced writers) we can hope to reach a future mestizaje.

21. The lawyer Henry Wagner Halleck represented Californios during the Land Commission hearings. His job was to protect and defend a majority of Californio lands, which included the De La Guerra properties. He wrote De La Guerra daily during the court sessions. These letters reveal the corruption inherent in the government structure. See Henry Wagner Halleck, letter to Pablo de la Guerra, November 22, 1853, De la Guerra Collection, Santa Barbara Mission Archive Library. Halleck wrote to Pablo de La Guerra of the frustrations in working with the Land Commission board: "I have no further confidence in this Board, & I am fully satisfied that they are — or at least 2 of them are — *Squatters*, and were appointed by squatters. I should now not be surprised if all your fathers titles were rejected on the plea that the boundaries described in the title are indefinite. And yet they may confirm them all. We have argued them as strongly as we could; and yet we can have no confidence in the result. The decisions are so variable that no one can calculate with any certainty whether the decision will be favorable or unfavorable."

22. Rebecca Harding Davis, *Life in the Iron Mills and Other Stories*, ed. Tillie Olson (New York: Feminist Press, 1985), 12.

23. Walt Whitman, *Leaves of Grass* (New York: Penguin Books, 1986), 120.

24. Davis, *Life in the Iron Mills*, 12

25. Sharon M. Harris, *Rebecca Harding Davis and American Realism* (Philadelphia: University of Pennsylvania Press, 1991), 29–30.

26. María Amparo Ruiz de Burton, *Who Would Have Thought It?*, ed. Rosaura Sánchez and Beatrice Pita (Houston: Arte Público Press, 1995). Subsequent quotations from the novel are cited in parentheses.

27. Harriet Beecher Stowe, *Uncle Tom's Cabin, or, Life Among the Lowly*, ed. Ann Douglas (New York: Penguin Books, 1983), 142–44.

28. Upton Sinclair, *The Jungle* (New York: Bantam Books, 1981), 346.

29. See Jane Tompkins, *Sensational Designs: The Cultural Work of American Fiction, 1790–1860* (New York: Oxford University Press, 1985). Tompkins says, "When one sets aside modernist demands . . . and attends to the way a text offers a blueprint for survival under a specific set of political, economic, social, or religious conditions, an entirely new story begins to unfold, and one's sense of the formal exigencies of narrative alters accordingly, producing a different conception of what constitutes successful characters and plots" (xvii–xviii). In this sense, the romance (as formal canons call this literature) offers us (or one could say, "designs" for us) a way to see and discuss narrative on a multiplicity of levels or dialogisms (see M. M. Bakhtin, *The Dialogic Imagination: Four Essays*, ed. Michael Holquist [Austin: University of Texas Press, 1994], 259–82). Tompkins also points out that throughout the years, anthologies have repeatedly reorganized and restructured standards of aesthetics in an effort to codify a method of literary analysis: "Evidence of the anthologies demonstrates not only that works of art are not selected

according to any unalterable standard, but that their very essence is always changing in accordance with the systems of description and evaluation that are in force. Even when the 'same' text keeps turning up in collection after collection, it is not really the same text at all" (196).

30. Theodore Dreiser, *Sister Carrie*, ed. Donald Pizer, 2d ed. (New York: Norton, 1991), 57.

31. Tompkins, *Sensational Designs*, 190.

32. Kolodny, "Letting Go Our Grand Obsessions," 10.

33. Rosaura Sánchez, *Telling Identities: The California Testimonios* (Minneapolis: University of Minnesota Press, 1995), 17.

34. *San Francisco Argonaut* 16, no. 6 (February 7, 1885), 10.

35. Ibid., 3.

36. Sánchez, *Telling Identities*, 17.

37. Adelaida R. Del Castillo, ed. *Between Borders: Essays on Mexicana/Chicana History* (Encino, Calif.: Floricanto Press, 1990), 216. See also Thomas Jefferson Farnham, *Travelers in California and Scenes in the Pacific Ocean* (1844; rpt. Oakland: Biobooks, 1947).

38. I acquired the song from the following article: Kathleen Crawford, "María Amparo Ruiz Burton: The General's Lady," *Journal of San Diego History* 30 (Spring 1984): 198–211; Winifred Davidson, "Enemy Lovers," *The Los Angeles Times Sunday Magazine*, October 16, 1932, p. 5:1. Davidson was another writer who perpetuated the Ruiz de Burton stereotype into the twentieth century. Her depictions of Ruiz de Burton as well as of other nineteenth-century Californios gave new life to these old myths.

39. Hayden White, *The Content of the Form: Narrative Discourse and Historical Representation* (Baltimore: Johns Hopkins University Press, 1992), 13.

40. Rosaura Sánchez, "Nineteenth-Century Californio Narratives: The Hubert H. Bancroft Collection," in *Recovering the U.S. Hispanic Literary Heritage*, ed. Ramón Gutiérrez and Genaro Padilla (Houston: Arte Público Press, 1993), 291.

41. Tey Diana Rebolledo, *Women Singing in the Snow: A Cultural Analysis of Chicana Literature* (Tucson: University of Arizona Press, 1995). Not only does Rebolledo note Ruiz de Burton's elite status, which gave her the means to write, but she also reminds readers that Ruiz de Burton "explores and documents the clash of two different legal systems, two different ways of doing business, two different cultures" (126). I will take her words further by adding that within each system, there are other cultures influencing the systems of thought. It is important to explore them as well, such as the French influence in Mexico during the Maximilian era.

42. Erlinda Gonzalez-Berry, "Two Texts for a New Canon: Vicente Bernal's Las Primicias and Felipe Maximiliano Chacón's Poesía y Prosa," in *Recovering the U.S. Hispanic Literary Heritage*, ed. Gutiérrez and Padilla, 130.

43. Cherríe Moraga, *The Last Generation: Prose and Poetry* (Boston: South End Press, 1993), 122.

44. Ibid., 192.

EDITH WHARTON'S IRONIC REALISM

Carol J. Singley

Despite her achievements, Edith Wharton's place in literary history is far from secure.[1] Early critics considered her a minor writer, using labels such as "grande dame," "disciple of Henry James," and "novelist of manners" to describe her.[2] They neglected her roots in the nineteenth-century tradition of female domestic fiction, compared her negatively with male practitioners of realism, and virtually ignored modernist aspects of her writing, which put her in the company of a dynamic, experimental, and largely male group of writers. Critics still have difficulty placing Wharton in a single literary tradition or movement, and they often disagree on the stature and significance of her work. Since the 1970s, however, her reputation has risen, especially in critical studies that examine her work from feminist and increasingly diverse critical perspectives.[3] The recent Wharton revival—marked by reprintings of her lesser-known novels, editions of her letters and nonfiction, film adaptations of *Ethan Frome* and *The Age of Innocence*, and numerous book-length critical studies—all suggest that Wharton is now receiving her proper due. Yet she still is not, as Linda Wagner-Martin writes, "a truly canonized writer" in the sense that Walt Whitman and Ernest Hemingway are; her stories and novels are taught less frequently than those by other realists such as Twain or James; and the range of Wharton scholarship remains relatively limited.[4]

One way we might better understand Wharton's work is to view it in relation to sentimentalism, realism, and naturalism—modes of writing current in her time—and to examine this work through the lens of irony, a technique she employed frequently and artfully. Wharton created a distinctive body of fiction with a quality that I will call "ironic realism." Like the sentimental writers who preceded her, she often focuses on domestic subjects and on women in particular. Like other realists, she describes individuals in relation to society and details everyday experience—whether of the New York aristocracy or the New England poor. And like the naturalists, she infuses her fiction with Darwinian principles, demonstrating the power of biology and environment in shaping character and events. And yet she is neither a romantic nor an objective observer. Rather,

Wharton is a subtle but forceful social and moral critic of the world she depicts. Irony is the means by which she both exposes her characters' foibles and deals debilitating blows to their value systems. Wharton demonstrates a full range of ironic techniques in her fiction, from the wry ("Genius is of small use to the woman who does not know how to do her hair"[5]) to the dramatic (in *The House of Mirth*, Lawrence Selden arrives with avowals of love after Lily Bart is dead),[6] to the brutally comic (in *The Age of Innocence*, Newland Archer spends a lifetime defending values he barely believes in, only to find them obsolete).[7]

In his study of irony, Wayne Booth describes the process by which a reader decides that a given piece of literature is ironic. Such an identification, he maintains, is a "communal achievement" requiring shared values between reader and writer; both must have "confidence that they are moving together in identical patterns."[8] Wharton's readers are privileged to know intimate details of her aristocratic world, but we also stand outside this group, just as Wharton herself did. We become the "select few"—as she called the circle of intellectuals, artists, and philosophers who were her closest friends—enjoying her texts all the more because of a shared sense of irony. Wharton, however, never allows this sense of inclusion to lapse into complacency. Her irony extends beyond social convention to larger issues of moral and universal significance. She wrestles with timeless questions of right and wrong as well as questions of religious and spiritual meaning that occupied writers of her period. Wharton's commitment to scientific method and logical positivism followed from her extensive reading in science, philosophy, and intellectual history. She upheld the need for absolute values, but unlike the previous generations of writers who had not yet assimilated the effects of Darwinian science, she was skeptical of Christian pieties and doctrines of salvation. This moral idealism stems as much from classical sources as from Christian ones, as much from her readings in Greek philosophy and religion as from the Scriptures.

Wharton's characters often suffer the bitter disappointment of shattered dreams—losses resulting not so much from God's disfavor as from seemingly random acts of fate or chance. Indeed, many of her stories unfold with a sense of inevitable doom. Wharton describes these disappointments with an ironic detachment we associate with modernism, reserving derision for characters who bathe in self-pity and esteem for those who face adversity with humor, grace, or stoic forbearance. Despite these judgments, Wharton does not lack sympathy for her characters. When we laugh at them, we risk ridiculing ourselves because we, too, are vulnerable to the same confused values that plague her characters. Wharton writes with just enough tragic impact to remind us that her characters' fates may well be our own.

We can appreciate Wharton's use of irony by looking first at her life and career and then at her critical and literary responses to three modes of writing. These include her relationship to the sentimental tradition of writing, her range of ironic techniques in her realistic novels, and her distinct combination of moralism and naturalism.

Irony is particularly suited to Wharton's fictional purposes and style, allowing her to express strong views about her subjects — especially women's roles — indirectly, with a minimum of personal exposure. Irony is an especially appropriate technique for a female writer whose very accomplishments defied expectations of family and society. The irony of Wharton's life is that upper-class wealth and privilege — normally liberating qualities — worked against her aspiration to be a writer. Her elite society discouraged serious art, with the result that Wharton experienced Old New York as deprivation rather than empowerment.[9] She suggests the poverty of such affluence in her exquisitely detailed descriptions of aristocratic manners. Whether she describes the name of the china, the breed of a roasted bird, or the position of a knife at a New York dinner party, she conveys the arbitrary, even foolish, standards by which a smug, anti-intellectual society establishes its most sacred values. Wharton found this New York world stifling and ultimately had to turn to friends and colleagues in Europe to find support for her work. One such friend was Henry James, whom Wharton described in terms of their shared sense of irony: "The real marriage of true minds is for any two people to possess a sense of humour or irony pitched in exactly the same key. . . . In that sense Henry James was perhaps the most intimate friend I ever had."[10]

Irony allows Wharton to draw attention away from her intelligence at the same time that she points readers toward it. It thus serves as the perfect vehicle for a woman who felt the need to camouflage her talents and whose genteel manners belied the ferocity with which she criticizes social conventions in her fiction. Wharton's road to authorship was long and difficult, and her early attempts at writing were marked by a profound ambivalence toward her own literary achievement — which elsewhere Susan Elizabeth Sweeney and I have identified as "anxious power."[11] As her work earned royalties and favorable reviews, her confidence grew. Despite great success as a professional writer, however, she never fully abandoned the role of "lady novelist." Publicity photographs capture these contrasts: they show her sitting at her desk, draped in furs and pearls, looking more as is if she were pouring tea than writing a novel. Wharton kept the roles of lady and writer in tension throughout her life, never openly defiant of the rules she constantly broke.

All the while that Wharton maintained an image of herself as Victorian grande dame, she developed a decidedly critical stance toward sentimental fiction, as Amy Kaplan notes.[12] Wharton follows historically from this feminine tradition of sentimentality, and she is linked to it by the fact of her gender in ways that other realists such as William Dean Howells, Mark Twain, and Henry James are not. For example, when Howells offers a scathing critique of sentimental notions of love and war in a short story such as "Editha"[13] and Twain ruthlessly mocks sentimentality in his portrayal of Emmeline Grangerford in *The Adventures of Huckleberry Finn*,[14] they do so with a sense of amused distance that Wharton does not enjoy. As female, she is automatically implicated in the sentimental conventions she wishes to criticize.

Wharton did share some ideological assumptions with her sentimental predecessors. She wanted a social system that honored feminine as well as masculine values. However, she feared that nineteenth-century sentimental virtues worked against the free, open development of critical intelligence which she viewed as women's best opportunity to achieve parity with men.[15] She did not accept assumptions about sentimentality and Christianity, which as Susan Harris notes, were "the two most prevalent culturally based codes in midcentury women's novels,"[16] and she rejected sentimental views that women's most hallowed roles were those of wife and mother. She thus publicly distanced herself from her female predecessors, decrying sentimental codes of female passivity, piety, and submissiveness, which she considered outmoded in an aggressively capitalistic and secularized culture. She renounced "the rose-and-lavender pages" of New England local colorists such as Sarah Orne Jewett and Mary Wilkins Freeman and the "laxities of the great Louisa [Alcott],"[17] aligning her work instead with the fiction of Nathaniel Hawthorne. Her challenge was how to protest women's restrictive roles without relinquishing her own femaleness, that is, without being charged with thinking like a man — a complaint originally leveled against her by Percy Lubbock and made even today.[18]

Irony was sometimes Wharton's best vehicle for voicing concern about women's roles and opportunities, as she demonstrates in several early fictions. In one autobiographical tale, "The Mission of Jane" (1902), a wealthy couple is distressed by their adopted daughter's precociousness. Jane's adoption in the story alludes to the rumor that Wharton, so different from the rest of her family, was the offspring of her brothers' tutor, not George Jones;[19] and Jane's marriage to a pompous, doting suitor resembles Wharton's conventional marriage to Edward (Teddy) Wharton. Jane's erudition, like Wharton's, scares away suitors, so much so that her parents feel only "relief" when Jane finally weds.[20] No doubt when Wharton wrote this story early in her career, insecurity about her own mental abilities led to the satiric portrait of her protagonist. Although she describes Jane as "extraordinarily intelligent," she adds that "Jane's ideas did not increase with her acquisitions. Her young mind remained a mere receptacle for facts: a kind of cold storage from which anything . . . could be taken out at a moment's notice, intact but congealed."[21]

The larger irony of the story, however, is that Jane may very well possess a major intelligence that none of the characters in the story appreciates. We learn about her only through the perspective of her adoptive father, who has little regard for female intellect. His mockery of Jane's erudition confirms what Wharton knew about her society: smart women must subordinate their brilliance to domestic niceties. In fact, Wharton provides clues that Jane has an impressive scientific intelligence that society permits her to express only in trivial ways:

> She proved to [her father] by statistics that he smoked too much, and that it was injurious to the optic nerve to read in bed. . . . She instructed Mrs. Lethbury in an improved way of making beef stock, and called her attention to the unhygienic qualities of carpets. She poured out distracting facts about bacilli and vegetable mold, and demonstrated that curtains and picture frames are a hotbed of animal organisms. She learned by heart the nutritive ingredients of the principal articles of diet, and revolutionized the cuisine by an attempt to establish a scientific average between starch and phosphates. Four cooks left during this experiment.[22]

As the title of the story indicates, Jane has a particular "mission." Wharton suggests that under different circumstances, she may have wished to become a scientist. As it is, her aspirations are limited to the feminine geography of home. Jane's mission is ultimately fulfilled, not by cultivating her mental gifts but by drawing her aristocratic parents together by her marriage.

Wharton pursues this theme of female intelligence in another story, "The Pelican" (1898). A widowed mother begins lecturing on evolution to support herself and her young son. People attend in droves, the narrator tells us, because they feel sorry for her. In keeping with sentimental standards of feminine modesty and piety, Mrs. Amyot apologizes for taking on masculine, rational, and controversial subjects like science—"the growing demand for evolution was what most troubled her. Her grandfather had been a pillar of the Presbyterian ministry, and the idea of her lecturing on Darwin or Herbert Spencer was deeply shocking to her mother and aunts"[23]—but she continues to lecture. She is still lecturing—and still using her son as an excuse—long after the boy has grown up. We first perceive Mrs. Amyot as foolish, noting the irony of a woman using her grown son as a pretext for working. But then we realize that this impression is created by the male narrator, who exhibits an outmoded, sentimental bias: "I don't think nature had meant her to be 'intellectual', but what can a poor thing do, whose husband has died of drink when her baby is hardly six months old." The narrator repeatedly comments on Mrs. Amyot's appearance— "she was very pretty"[24]—and criticizes her lack of humor—Wharton's clues that he judges her more as an ornament than as a thinking human being. The only way to stop her lectures, he suggests, is to find someone to marry her.

In fact, Mrs. Amyot is a bright woman who cannot openly acknowledge her ambition and creativity. She is forced into acting the part of the intellectual, a role that she actually may be well suited for. Mrs. Amyot comes from a line of intelligent, accomplished women: a celebrated poet-mother, an aunt who was dean of a "girls' college," and another aunt who translated Euripides.[25] The narrator, however, discounts all of these accomplishments as well as Mrs. Amyot's knowledge of diverse subjects such as Greek language and art, Shakespeare, Gothic architecture, and Schopenhauer. Wharton's sympathy for her character is apparent in her title, an allusion to Psalm 102, which is a cry of the afflicted: "I am like a pelican of the wilderness: mine enemies reproach me all the day; and they that are mad against me are sworn against me." The irony is not that Mrs. Amyot uses motherhood as an excuse well beyond its time but that society rewards only acts of maternal sacrifice, not other real accomplishments by women. Wharton also reveals that the son for whom Mrs. Amyot has made her "sacrifice" is not worth the effort. The now-grown man "exhibits a self-importance out of keeping with the humdrum nature of his story, as though a breeze engaged in shaking out a tablecloth should have fancied itself inflating a banner."[26] Maternal self-sacrifice, whether sincere or feigned, fails to make the son a better human being.

"The Angel at the Grave" (1901), a story Wharton published three years after "The Pelican," also shows the danger of maternal service.[27] Pauline Anson devotes her life to preserving the memory of her deceased grandfather, Orestes Anson, a famous Transcendentalist reminiscent of Emerson. But she is disappointed to find the house and the papers she curates overrun by intellectual tourists and trend-setters. She despairs of accomplishing a higher good until one day a visitor discovers that Anson has made a monumental contribution—not to Transcendentalism, however, but to the theory of evolution. Although Pauline's years of selfless service have not been in vain, the ideas she thought she was defending are insignificant. Ironically, it takes a male scholar trained in science to recognize the genius that Pauline so mindlessly serves.

Misplaced maternal energy is also the theme of Wharton's early novella *Sanctuary* (1903).[28] Kate Orme futilely sacrifices herself for the sake of her child, who, despite her teachings, lacks moral fortitude. Although she finally convinces her son not to steal another's architectural designs, her life of service remains hollow because the young man does not internalize his mother's lessons. Most likely, he will appropriate another's work again so as to succeed in his career. Writers of sentimental fiction hoped that women, repositories of moral virtue, could slow if not halt capitalism's march. They resisted the pressures of an increasingly industrialized and commercialized culture and sought to extend the model of home as haven into the larger world. Wharton, however, considered society's corruption by materialistic values a fait accompli. Consequently, there is little romantic wishfulness in her fiction.[29] Convinced of commercialism's pervasive, insidious power, she describes the increasingly materialistic and impersonal mechanisms by which even the most intimate human relations are organized. Unlike her forebears, she does not locate the solution to such problems in feminine virtue.

The success of Wharton's irony in "The Mission of Jane," "The Pelican," "The Angel at the Grave," and *Sanctuary* depends on her readers' shared sense of the indignities and injustices of women's experience. Restricted to roles of wife and mother, Wharton argues, women lose the chance to develop their intellectual gifts. At the time she was writing, however, Wharton felt she must be cautious, even circumspect, in her depictions of these bright, frustrated women. Indeed, her critiques of sentimentalism are so artfully designed that some readers miss her irony altogether.[30]

Wharton's ironic technique develops in her later novels, where the focus of her irony expands beyond women's roles. If realism is understood as the representation of bourgeois values, Wharton's portraits are ironic commentaries on the falseness and futility of family and social life. Community, loyalty, even simple friendship are singularly lacking in Wharton's fiction. Whether her characters are shunned insiders like Lily Bart; inarticulate New Englanders like Ethan, Mattie, and Zeena in *Ethan Frome*; audacious social climbers like Undine Spragg in *The Custom of the Country* (1913); or old-fashioned sentimentalists like Kate Clephane in *The Mother's Recompense* (1925), they find themselves alienated from the very people who should offer them comfort. Amid the busyness of daily life; despite innovations in technology, travel, and communication; and regardless of financial means, Wharton's characters are often alone, plagued with an emptiness that material amenities cannot alleviate. In this regard, Wharton's fiction differs not only from that of her sentimental predecessors but from that of other realists such as Howells. Whereas Howells develops his characters in family and community settings, Wharton emphasizes characters' isolation, especially in domestic settings. Brief discussions of three novels—*The*

House of Mirth, Ethan Frome, and *The Age of Innocence*—demonstrate the range of Wharton's ironic techniques and her broad knowledge of irony's development over time.

The House of Mirth (1905) demonstrates Wharton's skill as a dramatic, or tragic, ironist. This form of irony originated in Aristotle's *Poetics* and emerged strongly in nineteenth-century literature. Commonly defined as a discrepancy between what is said or done and what actually exists, irony is "double-layered," as D. C. Muecke notes. He suggests three key elements that distinguish it from other forms of indirect discourse such as sarcasm, metaphor, or lies.[31] First, at the lower level is a situation as it appears to the victim of irony or as it is deceptively presented by an ironist—in the case of fiction, by an ironic narrator. At the upper level is a situation as it appears to the observer or ironist. This upper level of meaning may be evoked or implied rather than stated. Second, there is an opposition between the two levels. There may even be a further opposition between two elements at the lower level, what William Empson refers to as "double irony."[32] Third, irony involves an element of innocence or naiveté in which the victim remains unaware of other, higher levels of meaning. In its simplest form irony is corrective, suggesting need for social or moral reform; in its more complex form, it is philosophical about the difficulty of solving problems of human nature.

In Wharton's novel of love and marriage in high society, the beautiful and charming Lily Bart seems the most marriageable of all young women; but this portrait is deceptive, a representation at the lower level of meaning, to use Muecke's term. Lily's situation gradually changes, however, until she eventually dies in a shabby boardinghouse, friendless and poverty-stricken. The detached, ironic narrator offers no explanation for why the most attractive, talented, and sensitive character of the novel should die thus, but Wharton's tragic intent can be inferred from the text. It is certainly clear from her comments about the novel in her memoir, *A Backward Glance.* Lily, Wharton says, lives in a materialistic, morally depleted society "whose power lies in debasing people and ideals." Such a "frivolous society can acquire dramatic significance only through what its frivolity destroys"—Lily Bart.[33] Lily falls victim to a culture that trains women to be little more than beautiful objects and then ironically discards them as mere commodities. Somewhat unreflective and optimistic even when such optimism is unwarranted, Lily is the innocent victim that Muecke finds essential to irony.

The irony of the novel is intensified, or doubled, by the fact that Lily is doomed whether or not she plays according to society's rules. When she decides, for example, to do what is expected of her and pursue the wealthy but boring Percy Gryce, her instinctual need for love — exemplified through her attraction to Lawrence Selden and his "republic of the spirit" — sabotages her efforts to snare her prey. On the other hand, when she rebels against society's materialism by refusing to blackmail Bertha Dorset and by rejecting Simon Rosedale's offer of marriage as good business, her moral actions further estrange her from others. Ironically, Lily is too scrupulous to succeed in a callous society and too socially conditioned to reject such a society. Endowed with sentimental values no longer valid in the twentieth century, she is caught in a cultural bind. This tension between nineteenth- and twentieth-century codes appears in Wharton's ironic use of "house" in her title and in her representation of homes throughout the novel — Lily becomes literally homeless by the end of the narrative. Female friends and relatives who might nurture Lily — from her aunt Peniston and cousin Stepney to her traitorous friend Bertha — all reject her. Well-meaning women such as Gerty Farish and Nettie Struthers lack the means to offer her more than temporary relief.

Wharton's extensive use of irony helps to explain why at the end of the novel we feel that something should have been done to help Lily, but at the same time we understand that her fate is inevitable. Too much is required to correct the system in which Lily lives. Widespread social and moral reform, not to mention revisions of elements of chance, would be necessary to halt Lily's downward spiral. Readers of the novel, who can foresee the outcome of Lily's actions, may even fault her for sabotaging herself. More likely, however, we sympathize with the unfairness of her victimization. In Muecke's words, Lily exhibits "a certain unwarranted trust in the impossibility of impossible situations, an assumption . . . that society ought not to have been so unjustly organized."[34] We share this sense of an "unjustly organized" society.

In her New England novel, *Ethan Frome* (1911), Wharton expands on the sense of fate that drives characters' lives.[35] The dramatic irony of the novel is obvious: Ethan Frome and Mattie Silver, lovers who dream of running away together, decide instead on suicide. When the suicide fails, they end up maimed, crippled, and trapped in a dreary household with Ethan's wronged wife, Zeena. In this novel, Wharton moves beyond issues of social injustice to a sense of cosmic unfairness. Her characters suffer in a world governed by a cynical or uncaring and distant God. Although consumed by feelings of desire, they are unable to articulate their needs or control the outcome of their actions. In this most moody of all Wharton's novels, we see romantic as well as dramatic irony. Romantic irony emerged in the nineteenth century through the work of Friedrich Schlegel. It is an irony of cosmic or philosophical dimensions that begins, as René Wellek explains, with "recognition of the fact that the world in its essence is paradoxical."[36] Romantic irony emphasizes the incongruity of human aspiration and accomplishment; it contrasts the ideal and real, in which "man is a tiny flash of light in 'the great cold the great dark.'"[37] The role of the artist is to dignify the reaches of human will and, if possible, to transcend limitation through art. Indeed, for the romantic ironist, art is the medium through which a profound and poignant sense of human suffering and joy can be expressed.

Wharton was not easily given to romantic indulgences, although she often mused about the aesthetic qualities of her writing and its effect on readers. Prescient about future critics' dismissal of her work, she even once lamented to a friend, Daisy Chanler, in 1925: "As my work reaches its close, I feel so sure that it is either nothing, or far more than they know. . . . And I wonder, a little desolately, which?"[38] Of all her novels, *Ethan Frome* was the one Wharton valued most for its technical accomplishment. Although the subject matter is bleak—indeed, among the bleakest in all of American literature—the composition of this novel brought Wharton "the greatest joy and the fullest ease" of anything she wrote. Reviewers criticized the novel's narrative frame structure, but Wharton defended herself from attack, reveling in the fact that when writing *Ethan Frome*, she "felt the artisan's full control of his implements."[39] She was sure that the novel's construction was not its weak point. The irony that Wharton expresses in this novel is that a subject of terrible human failure could become such a beautiful work of art.

In *The Age of Innocence* (1920), Wharton engages in a form of irony that stems from the classical period. Irony's long history in Western literature can be traced to Socrates, who in Plato's *Republic* feigned ignorance when he addressed interlocutors in his pursuit of philosophical truths. Wharton, who taught herself Greek and read widely in classical literature, history, and philosophy, certainly knew of irony's origins in the Greek comic character *eiron*, who hid his intelligence. The *eiron* was a "dissembler who spoke in understatement and deliberately pretended to be less intelligent than he was yet triumphed over the *alazon*—the self-deceiving and stupid braggart."[40] Wharton portrays just such a Socratic questioner in her heroine, Ellen Olenska.

Having returned home after a long stay in Europe, Ellen questions Newland Archer about Old New York's habits of thought and behavior. Announcing her intention to settle in this society—which she calls "heaven" and praises for its "straight-up-and-downness, and the big honest labels on everything"—she claims Archer as her teacher and guide. "You'll tell me all I ought to know," she tells him, apparently innocent of the social machinery already in place to send her back to Europe.[41] In fact, no one is more sensitive than Ellen to the jealousy and spite that surround her, and in the end no one is more prepared than she to leave New York behind. Archer mouths platitudes that "women ought to be free — as free as we are"[42] but ties himself more tightly to the conventional May Welland at every turn. His decision to advise Ellen against divorce prevents him from having what he most wants: a chance to love her freely. Trapped by May's announcement of their coming child, he can only contemplate escape in foreign travel, while Ellen, deprived of Old New York's protection, thrives in an atmosphere of Parisian art and culture. At the end of the novel, Wharton shows that the rules for which Archer has renounced happiness no longer apply to his son's generation. Archer has the unenviable task of justifying a way of life in which even he has lost faith. In the final scene, which Wharton treats both ironically and sympathetically, Archer has the chance to reunite with Ellen, but he declines this opportunity. His sense of loss is tempered by an almost comic and good-willed resignation. Although he has missed the flower of life, he has been a decent husband, father, and citizen. Perhaps life cannot be expected to yield more.

Wharton's practice of subjecting her characters to coincidence, "fate," or other forces beyond their control has led some critics to describe her as a naturalist, in the same literary school with Stephen Crane, Frank Norris, and Theodore Dreiser.[43] The irony of naturalism is that the struggle for survival — a struggle humans wish to elevate to heroic proportions — only exposes their vulnerability and powerlessness before forces of biology and environment. The comparison of Wharton and Dreiser is particularly apt since she, like him, incorporates and reworks sentimental codes.[44] Whereas one might debate the extent to which Dreiser endorses sentimentality in his first novel, *Sister Carrie*, Wharton takes a critical, ironic stance toward sentimental principles in her first bestseller, *The House of Mirth*. Qualities such as compassion, care, generosity — hallmarks of domestic fiction — are no match for the harsh realities of the marriage market. Although Lily Bart appears to make decisions freely, she can do no better than her background and environment allow.

Wharton, like the other naturalists, draws on Darwin to explain her characters' defeats, but she does not do so dispassionately. Instead, she indicts social and moral values that lead to an exploitation of evolutionary theories, especially with respect to women. Wharton finds irony in the fact that science, ostensibly objective, is employed with such partiality. First, Wharton registers concern with the spiritual displacement of women that resulted from Darwinian science. In the sentimental tradition, women played vital roles in the spiritual life of the family and society. What remained to them after Darwinism, as Lily Bart's plight makes clear, is a merely decorative or ornamental function, a monetary rather than spiritual value. When Wharton describes the links of Lily Bart's expensive bracelet as "manacles chaining her to her fate,"[45] she conveys her heroine's uselessness and commodification with an image that is simultaneously Darwinian and unsentimentalist.

Second, Wharton laments that women who accept the new scientific rationalism can find no acceptable ethical codes to take the place of faith. In her story "The Quicksand" (1902), for example, a young woman feels hurt when the man she loves refuses to stop his unethical business practices. The irony of the story is that had the woman less critical intelligence, she would have been more, rather than less, satisfied with their relationship. As the narrator comments, "You can make a religious woman believe almost anything.... But when a girl's faith in the Deluge has been shaken, it's very hard to inspire her with confidence."[46] Wharton's protagonist faces a dilemma. Discouraged from entering the business world because she embraces traditionally feminine values but lacking a framework for exercising those values, she feels herself sinking, as if in "quicksand." Although the modern loss of faith affected society in general, it presented special challenges to women. As this story, "The Pelican," and "The Angel at the Grave" suggest, with their Darwinian references, women had to think rationally if they were to be taken seriously, but when they displayed their knowledge, they were charged with being less feminine.

The scope of Wharton's naturalism—and realism—becomes clearer if examined in relation to two figures: Hippolyte Taine, an intellectual historian whose theories provided Wharton and others with a blueprint for literary realism,[47] and George Eliot, whom Wharton admired for her realistic, moral literature. Wharton, an astute reader of theories of evolutionary science and logical positivism, was especially impressed with Taine. She referred to him in a letter to Sara Norton as "one of the formative influences of my youth" and followed debates about his ideas.[48] Taine believed that all knowledge derived from experience. He replaced the abstract intellectual and emotional qualities associated with romanticism with those of the physical world and viewed humans as subject to an inflexible determinism. In an essay on Balzac, for example, Taine describes the naturalist as one who views the human subject "not [as] a reasoning creature who is independent, superior, healthy in himself ... but a simple force, of the same order as other creatures." The naturalist "understands and handles forces ... he does not say: what a fine sight! but what a fine subject!" Following Darwin and Taine, Wharton depicts characters such as Lily Bart, Ethan Frome, and Newland Archer, who rise no higher than their biologies and circumstances allow. But she does not follow Taine's dictum of moral neutrality. For him, the naturalist "has scarcely any concern for purity and grace: to his eyes a toad is as important as a butterfly; a bat interests him as much as a nightingale."[49] For Wharton, aesthetic concerns were not only linked to, but dependent on, moral ones.

Neither is Wharton a moral realist in the sense that George Eliot is. Although she shares Eliot's desire, expressed in *Adam Bede*, to portray "men and things as they have mirrored themselves," she finds no "light of heaven" shining on the commonplace subjects that make up realistic fiction. Eliot can find beauty and moral worth even in the coarse and vulgar: in "those old women scraping carrots with their work-worn hands" or "those heavy clowns taking holiday in a dingy pot-house."[50] Wharton, in contrast, is repelled by physical ugliness and rarely finds it morally uplifting. For example, in an autobiographical fragment, *Life and I*, she describes her intense "suffering from ugliness" when, as a young girl, she entered certain unappealing rooms in London and in an aunt's house.[51] In all of her writing, Wharton maintains a standard of transcendent beauty and truth that is based in aesthetic *and* moral principles. In *The House of Mirth*, for example, Mrs. Peniston's and Gerty Farish's rooms oppress Lily not only because they are "dingy" but because their dinginess corresponds to a lack of spiritual or creative energy. Similarly in *The Age of Innocence*, Ellen Olenska combines beauty, taste, intelligence, and passion, qualities which New York society finds threatening but which Archer recognizes as his only source of aesthetic and moral, as well as romantic, idealism. In these novels and others, Wharton is not strictly a naturalist because she measures her characters according to their achievement of an aesthetic and moral ideal. The irony of holding them to this ideal, however, is that they will surely fail to meet it.

There is no ready term to capture the precise quality of Wharton's writing. Lionel Trilling uses the term "moral realism" to describe Henry James's fiction — and, by implication, Wharton's.[52] Although this term captures the genteel sensibility of her writing, it is inadequate to describe its intensity and irony. It also neglects the sources of Wharton's moral vision as well as the techniques she employs to achieve it. Wharton read voraciously in religion, science, and philosophy; her library contained more volumes on religion than on any other subject.[53] These religious and philosophical interests are evident throughout her writing: in her titles (*The Valley of Decision*, drawn from Joel; *The House of Mirth*, from Ecclesiastes; *The Fruit of the Tree*, from Genesis; and *The Descent of Man*, from Darwin); in her fictional representations of various creeds — from Episcopalianism to Calvinism, Transcendentalism, and Catholicism — and in her use of classical allusion.[54] Throughout her career, Wharton sought answers to questions of moral meaning, hoping to find alternatives — whether Christian or classical — to the rampant materialism, relativism, and self-centeredness she saw around her. Wharton's sensibility is thus more philosophical than Trilling's term "moral realism," with its connotations of social convention and genteel culture, implies.

Finally, to the extent that realism is thought of as literature of compromise or even as vestigial romanticism, Wharton presents a special case. In the fiction of William Dean Howells, for example, characters unable to reach their loftiest ambitions settle for less but still harbor romantic notions of a future rise or compensation. In *The Rise of Silas Lapham*, Lapham experiences financial ruin, but at the end of the novel he begins dreaming about how to remake his fortune.[55] Wharton's fiction exhibits none of this romantic optimism. Her outlook is bleaker than most realists', and this bleakness has made her somewhat unpopular with American readers, who, as Wharton observed, want "a tragedy with a happy ending."[56] There are few happy, or even marginally happy, endings in Wharton's fiction. Indeed, her pervasive, sometimes comic, sense of irony suggests modernism as much as realism.

The school of high modernism, dominated by figures such as Ezra Pound and T. S. Eliot, traditionally excludes female writers.[57] Because of Wharton's domestic subjects and rather conventional writing style — she deplored James Joyce's experimental prose, which she called "drivel"[58] — critics have overlooked the modernist dimensions of her fiction. Like the modernists, however, Wharton favored classical rather than Victorian models and incorporated themes of futility, dislocation, and despair in her work. Indeed, in some of her writing, she demonstrates skill as a modernist innovator. In *Ethan Frome*, for example, Wharton uses spare, economical language, emphasizes the psychological dimensions of Ethan's failures, and tells the story through a subjective narrator. Her New England landscapes are no less emotionally and morally desolate than those found in Eliot's *Waste Land*; her characters, stripped of elegant settings, no less defeated and unconscious than those in Hemingway's novels. Although she sought absolute standards, Wharton could not be sure that a caring God was in charge of the universe. This uncertainty led to portrayals of spiritual emptiness more modernist than realistic.

Wharton insists on harsh reality to counter romantic fantasy. Unlike her modernist contemporaries, Hemingway and Fitzgerald, whose characters escape themselves and their world through bullfights and alcoholic binges, Wharton's characters confront the fact that there is no such escape. She leads us to the unhappy knowledge that we cannot have it all — and in some cases, we can have very little. Her message is the same as that of another modernist and moral regionalist, Robert Frost, who presents the haunting image of "the road not taken" and asks, in "The Oven Bird," "What to make of a diminished thing?"[59] Wharton's fiction, with its emphasis on sacrifice and renunciation — on passion denied or paid for at great cost—teaches neither avoidance nor acceptance (which might imply salvation) but forbearance. Wharton combines realistic reportage with modernist irony, which she sees in life itself as well as in her characters' particular circumstances. Indeed, her main subject is ironic: a privileged class's struggle to survive in an age that has already made it obsolete. More poignant, however, is the larger irony that despite their best efforts, her characters remain trapped in situations of their own or others' making.

Wharton is a realist, then, whose fiction pushes against the boundaries of realism. Yet critics have persistently missed the nuances in her work, with the result that her place in literary history remains uncertain. She is a singular figure poised between periods and centuries, between manners and morals, and doubly marginalized—as a woman writing in a predominantly male tradition and as a woman writing differently from her female predecessors. Even recent volumes such as the *Columbia Literary History of the United States* discuss Wharton primarily in terms of her popularity and naturalism but not as a "Major Voice."[60] Indeed, Wharton's very use of irony might put her at critical risk. As Linda Hutcheon observes, irony is essentially political. It is a discursive practice whose meaning is impossible to predict or fix because it relies as much on the interpreter as on the creator of the text. There is always a risk that irony's "edge" will be misread or misunderstood.[61] Wharton, who engages so extensively in irony, constantly puts herself at such risk.

In his essay on the function of an author, Michel Foucault outlines four criteria for achieving a "name." Wharton demonstrates three of these criteria: she maintains a high level of quality in her texts, exhibits thematic coherence, and writes in a unified style. She does not (yet) meet Foucault's fourth and most important criterion: that of becoming a historical figure in whom a series of events converge.[62] According to this measure, Wharton's work is still inferior to that of other realists.

It is interesting that despite biases against her, Wharton asserted her right not only to create fiction but to discuss it in terms of literary history and theory. In her book *The Writing of Fiction*, she sets forth her standards for greatness, and in the process, she implies her own success in meeting them. "Abundance," she writes, alluding to her prolific career, "almost always marks the great creative artist."[63] She also praises the achievements of various writers, implicitly ranking her own work with theirs. For example, she credits Madame de La Fayette with beginning "modern fiction" in the seventeenth century when she transferred the action of the novel "from the street to the soul." Her *La Princesse de Clèves* is a remarkable story "of hopeless love and mute renunciation in which the stately tenor of the lives depicted is hardly ruffled by the exultations and agonies succeeding each other below the surface." In praising La Fayette's use of irony, Wharton also validates her own narrative poetics. The great realist Balzac, she continues, corrected the faults of his romantic predecessor Scott, who "became conventional and hypocritical when he touched on love and women," "substituting sentimentality for passion." Here we find Wharton's critique of her own romantic predecessors, the sentimental novelists. Stendhal as well as Balzac were distinguished, Wharton writes, by "refinement of soul analysis"; that is, they were able both to individualize their characters *and* show them as "product[s] of particular material and social conditions."[64] In short, Wharton's analysis of French writers shows her preference for realism that is material, ironic, and moral. Unfortunately, her choice to align herself with European writers makes it easy for critics to overlook her importance in an American literary tradition.

Despite her efforts in *The Writing of Fiction* to secure her place in literary history, Wharton was not successful in shaping critical response to her work. Misunderstood as a sentimentalist at early stages of her career; as an aloof aristocrat when her fame peaked; and as a shrill, old-fashioned expatriate as her career waned, she struggled all her life with negative labels. Gender and genre also conspired against her. Readers expected a female writer as elegantly attired and mannered as she to treat domestic subjects sympathetically and felt betrayed when she dared to speak from her head as well as her heart. The novel form itself posed problems. Critics debate the extent to which the woman's romance is conservative, replicating with its marriage plot the very choices and conventions it purports to subvert.[65] By practicing an art form that is open to charges of repetitiveness and redundancy, Wharton risked reinscribing herself in the conservative tradition of women's writing that she wished to challenge. Her ironic treatment of women's roles, her plots of mute longing, and her endings of renunciation show her tacit acknowledgment of this risk and her conscious separation from all that is pejoratively termed "women's fiction."

Wharton relentlessly criticizes sentimental excess, careless thought, and empty convention. Like Emily Dickinson, a proto-modernist who also makes dark, brilliant art out of sentimental materials, Wharton delivers a strong "no" to the world. "Dont you know that 'No' is the wildest word we consign to Language?" Dickinson once asked.[66] She hid most of her over seventeen hundred poems in a bureau drawer, sensing that society was not ready to hear her truth. Wharton was too polite to state her "no" loudly, even if, unlike Dickinson, she did publish her work widely; but if we consider Wharton in a tradition of American dissenters like Dickinson, we can better understand her ironic, moral vision. It is true that Wharton delivers her critique of individuals and society without setting forth a positive alternative; her ironic realism is cautionary rather than constructive or visionary. But its value is precisely in this caveat. Wharton's readers note the eloquence and irony with which she portrays her characters' failures and realize the need for change, without necessarily believing in its likelihood.

NOTES

1. Wharton did not begin to write seriously until she was nearly forty; but once her career was under way, she turned out, on average, one book a year. She published eighty-six short stories and twenty-five novels, including the Pulitzer Prize–winning *The Age of Innocence*; books of poetry; travel and war literature; guides to interior design and gardening; an autobiography; and a book on the theory of fiction. Earning critical as well as popular acclaim, she was at one point the highest paid living novelist in the United States.

2. In Robert E. Spiller's view, essentially unchanged in editions from 1948 on, Wharton is a satirist of high society, which she portrays "in its narrowest sense," a late regionalist, and a follower of James (*Literary History of the United States*, 3 vols. [New York: Macmillan, 1948], 1197, 1209–11). Alfred Kazin similarly finds her limited, with "no conception of America as a unified and dynamic economy, or even as a single culture" (*On Native Grounds: An Interpretation of Modern American Prose Literature* [New York: Reynal, 1942], 82). Other early critics who disparage Wharton's work while ostensibly praising it include Percy Lubbock, *Portrait of Edith Wharton* (New York: Appleton-Century-Crofts, 1947); Irving Howe, ed. and intro., *Edith Wharton: A Collection of Critical Essays* (Englewood Cliffs, N.J.: Prentice-Hall, 1962), 1–18; Vernon Parrington, "Our Literary Aristocrat," ibid., 151–54; and Edmund Wilson, "Justice to Edith Wharton," ibid., 199–31.

3. R. W. B. Lewis's Pulitzer Prize–winning biography inspired a Wharton reevaluation (*Edith Wharton: A Biography* [New York: Harper, 1975]). Cynthia Griffin Wolff followed with a psychological study of her development as a female artist (*A Feast of Words: The Triumph of Edith Wharton* [1978; rpt. and expanded, New York: Addison Wesley, 1995]). Richard H. Lawson offers a balanced discussion of Wharton as a novelist of manners (*Edith Wharton* [New York: Ungar, 1977]), and Elizabeth Ammons explores Wharton's feminism (*Edith Wharton's Argument with America* [Athens: University of Georgia Press, 1980]).

More recently, Shari Benstock's biography positions Wharton as a modernist and self-fashioned professional (*No Gifts from Chance: A Biography of Edith Wharton* [New York: Scribner's, 1994]); Eleanor Dwight's illustrated biography focuses on travel, homes, and gardens (*Edith Wharton, An Extraordinary Life: An Illustrated Biography* [New York: Harry N. Abrams, 1994]). Susan Goodman discusses Wharton's personal and literary relationships in *Edith Wharton's Inner Circle* (Austin: University of Texas Press, 1994); Dale

Bauer places Wharton in the context of philosophical and social issues such as reproduction and eugenics in *Edith Wharton's Brave New Politics* (Madison: University of Wisconsin Press, 1994); Carol J. Singley analyzes her work in relation to religion and philosophy in *Edith Wharton: Matters of Mind and Spirit* (New York: Cambridge University Press, 1995). Gothic fiction is the subject of Kathy Fedorko's *Gender and the Gothic in the Fiction of Edith Wharton* (Tuscaloosa: University of Alabama Press, 1995); Helen Killoran discusses literary allusion in *Edith Wharton: Art and Allusion* (Tuscaloosa: University of Alabama Press, 1996). *The Cambridge Companion to Edith Wharton*, ed. Millicent Bell (New York: Cambridge University Press, 1995), provides a welcome new collection of essays. Alan Price analyzes Wharton's relief efforts in *The End of the Age of Innocence: Edith Wharton and the First World War* (New York: St. Martin's, 1996); Sarah Bird Wright discusses travel in *Edith Wharton's Travel Writing: The Making of a Connoisseur* (New York: St. Martin's, 1997); and Maureen E. Montgomery analyzes social ritual and ceremony in *Displaying Women: Spectacles of Leisure in Edith Wharton's New York* (New York: Routledge, 1998). Recent comparative studies include Elsa Nettels's *Language and Gender in American Fiction: Howells, James, Wharton, and Cather* (Charlottesville: University Press of Virginia, 1997); and Janet Beer's *Kate Chopin, Edith Wharton and Charlotte Perkins Gilman: Studies in Short Fiction* (New York: St. Martin's, 1997).

4. Linda Wagner-Martin notes that "criticism of Wharton and her work tends to plateau, to halt in pools of agreement," and "to reify past criticism." She calls for volumes of retrospective critical essays; collections of her letters (to supplement R. W. B. Lewis and Nancy Lewis, eds., *The Letters of Edith Wharton* [New York: Random House, 1988], which includes only 10 percent of Wharton's extant correspondence); collections of her reviews and nonfiction (now available in Frederick Wegener's *Edith Wharton: The Uncollected Critical Writings* [Princeton: Princeton University Press, 1996]); and more print and on-line catalogs for her manuscript and correspondence collections ("Prospects for the Study of Edith Wharton," *Resources for American Literary Study* 22 [1996]: 3–5).

5. Edith Wharton, *The Touchstone* (New York: Scribner's, 1900), 55.

6. Edith Wharton, *The House of Mirth* (1905; rpt., New York: Penguin, 1985).

7. Edith Wharton, *The Age of Innocence* (1920; rpt., New York: Scribner's, 1970).

8. Wayne C. Booth, *A Rhetoric of Irony* (Chicago: University of Chicago Press, 1974), 13.

9. Wharton reached high levels of literary achievement with no formal education. Her parents considered serious learning unladylike; instead, she eavesdropped on her brothers' lessons in her father's library. Her mother, in particular, forbade novel-reading. Wharton explains that because she was given no writing paper, she "was driven to begging for the wrappings of the parcels delivered at the house," and she complains that her childhood and youth were spent "in complete intellectual isolation" (*A Backward Glance* [New York: Scribner's, 1933], 65, 73, 169).

10. Ibid., 173. The irony of Wharton's friendship with James was that it helped encourage the view of her as "disciple" of the "great master." In fact, James and Wharton de-

veloped divergent writing styles and themes. James favored an introspective narrative technique that, according to Wharton, "tended to sacrifice ... the spontaneity which is the life of fiction" (ibid., 190); she found his refined late style virtually unreadable, observing that he "talks, thank heaven, more lucidly than he writes" (quoted in Lewis, *Edith Wharton*, 124). Whereas James is interested in the subtle nuances of inner experience—"A felt life," as he writes in his preface to *The Portrait of a Lady* (New York: Penguin, 1984), 45—Wharton subjects her characters more directly to the vicissitudes of passion. Indeed, Cecelia Tichi finds that for Wharton, sex "is central to woman's personal and social power" ("Women Writers and the New Woman," in *Columbia Literary History of the United States*, gen. ed. Emory Elliott [New York: Columbia University Press, 1988], 604). See Susan Elizabeth Sweeney's comparison of Wharton's "Roman Fever" and James's *Daisy Miller*: "Whereas James preserves a woman's innocence even in death, Wharton calculates the price that women must pay for gaining forbidden knowledge" ("Edith Wharton's Case of *Roman* Fever," in *Wretched Exotic: Essays on Edith Wharton in Europe*, ed. Katherine Joslin and Alan Price [New York: Lang, 1993], 319). Wharton's characters often take risks with love and marriage that James's only contemplate, and they suffer real consequences of these risks.

11. Carol J. Singley and Susan Elizabeth Sweeney, eds., *Anxious Power: Reading, Writing, and Ambivalence in Narrative by Women* (Albany: State University of New York Press, 1993), xiii–xxvi.

12. Amy Kaplan, *The Social Construction of American Realism* (Chicago: University of Chicago Press, 1988).

13. William Dean Howells, "Editha," in *Between the Dark and the Daylight; Romances* (New York: Harper, 1907), 125–43.

14. Mark Twain, *The Adventures of Huckleberry Finn*, 2d Norton Critical ed. (1884; rpt., New York: Norton, 1977).

15. Wharton criticizes sentimental views of women's intelligence in her novel *The Touchstone*: "If man is at times indirectly flattered by the moral superiority of woman, her mental ascendancy is extenuated by no such oblique tribute to his powers. The attitude of looking up is a strain on the muscles" (New York: HarperCollins, 1991), 54.

16. Susan K. Harris, *Nineteenth-Century American Women's Novels* (New York: Cambridge University Press, 1990), 79.

17. Wharton, *Backward*, 293–94, 51. Wharton employs sentimental conventions in some of her early stories—for example, in "Friends" (1900), a Freeman-like story about a New England schoolteacher who accepts diminished opportunities, and "April Showers" (1900), an autobiographical tale of a young fiction writer who lacks a publisher but receives encouragement from her father. These stories, however, are not her strongest. Wharton herself noted a discrepancy in tone between her writing and the sentimentalists', commenting about her depiction of the protagonist in "Friends": "The contrast is too violent between her 'schwarmerei' [rapture] in pink satin & the ensuing squalor" (Lewis and Lewis, eds., *Letters of Edith Wharton*, 32).

18. Lubbock, *Portrait*, 11, 54. See Wagner-Martin, "Readings are still dominated by the

view that Wharton was as good a writer as she was largely because she *was* one of the boys. . . . [One] view discounts the issue of whether or not she was influenced by Henry James by contending that in some ways she *was* Henry James" ("Prospects," 7).

19. Lewis, *Edith Wharton*, 254, 535–39; Benstock, *No Gifts*, 7–11.

20. Edith Wharton, "The Mission of Jane," in *The Collected Short Stories of Edith Wharton*, ed. R. W. B. Lewis, 2 vols. (New York: Scribner's, 1968), 1:379.

21. Ibid., 372. Wharton may have been parodying a backhanded compliment that Paul Bourget paid her in his 1893 book *Outre-Mer*. She certainly would not have been entirely pleased by his portrayal: She "has read everything, understood everything, not superficially, but really, with an energy of culture that could put to shame the whole Parisian fraternity of letters. . . . Only she does not distinguish between [ideas]. She has not an idea that is not exact, yet she gives you a strange impression as if she had none. One would say that she has ordered her intellect somewhere, as we would order a piece of furniture, to measure, and with as many compartments as there are branches of human knowledge. She acquires them only that she may put them into these drawers" (quoted in Louis Auchincloss, *Edith Wharton: A Woman in Her Time* [New York: Viking, 1971], 53–55).

22. Wharton, *Collected Stories*, 1:372–73.

23. Ibid., 95.

24. Ibid., 88.

25. Ibid.

26. Ibid., 97.

27. Ibid., 245–58.

28. Edith Wharton, *Sanctuary, Madame de Treymes and Others: Four Novelettes* (New York; Scribner's, 1970), 85–162.

29. Here I depart from critics such as Eric Sundquist, who finds that realism, like the literature that preceded it, "kept spilling out into the 'neutral territory' of romance that Hawthorne had made emblematic of American literature" (ed., *American Realism: New Essays* [Baltimore: Johns Hopkins University Press, 1982], 7) and Joan Lidoff, who reads *The House of Mirth* as a "romance of identity" informed by the Narcissus myth ("Another Sleeping Beauty: Narcissism in *The House of Mirth*," *American Quarterly* 32 [1980]: 519–39, rpt. in Sundquist, ed., *American Realism*, 239).

30. This is true, for example, of Lewis, who refers to Mrs. Amyot in "The Pelican" as simply "a rattlebrained woman" (*Edith Wharton*, 81), and of Lawson, who calls her "rather simpleminded," with a memory "far from good" (*Edith Wharton*, 79). Wolff, however, notes the deeper irony of Wharton's story: "No one had ever understood the fierceness of her need to *do something*; society had given her nothing to do unless it could be done in the name of maternal sacrifice (*Feast*, 97); as does Benstock: the story "exposes the false compromises women with professional desires were forced to make in a society that privileged marriage and motherhood" (*No Gifts*, 89).

31. D. C. Muecke, *The Compass of Irony* (London: Methuen, 1969), 19–22.

32. William Empson, *Seven Types of Ambiguity* (London: Chatto and Windus, 1930).

33. Wharton, *Backward*, 207.
34. Muecke, *Compass of Irony*, 28.
35. Edith Wharton, *Ethan Frome* (1911; rpt. New York: Scribner's, 1933).
36. René Wellek, *A History of Modern Criticism, 1750–1950*, vol. 2, *The Romantic Age* (1955; rpt. New Haven: Yale University Press, 1961), 14.
37. Friedrich Schlegel, *Literary Notebooks, 1797–1801*, ed. Hans Eichner (Toronto: University of Toronto Press, 1957), quoted in Muecke, *Compass of Irony*, 191.
38. Lewis and Lewis, eds., *Letters of Edith Wharton*, 483, ellipsis in original.
39. Wharton, *Backward*, 293, 209.
40. M. H. Abrams, *A Glossary of Literary Terms*, 4th. ed. (New York: Holt, 1981), 89.
41. Wharton, *Age of Innocence*, 76–78.
42. Ibid., 42.
43. See, for example, Katherine Joslin, *Edith Wharton*, Women Writers Series (New York: St. Martin's Press, 1991), 38–43, and Blake Nevius, *Edith Wharton: A Study of Her Fiction* (Berkeley: University of California Press, 1953), 58–59.
44. Kaplan, *Social Construction*, 140–41.
45. Wharton, *House of Mirth*, 7.
46. Wharton, *Collected Stories*, 1:398.
47. George J. Becker, *Documents of Modern Literary Realism* (Princeton: Princeton University Press, 1963), 105.
48. Lewis and Lewis, eds., *Letters of Edith Wharton*, 136, 177.
49. Hippolyte Taine, "Balzac," in *Nouveau Essais de culture et de l'histoire* (Paris: Hachette, n.d.), 1–94, quoted in Becker, *Documents*, 106–7.
50. George Eliot, *Adam Bede* (1859; rpt. New York: Airmont, 1966), 140, 142.
51. Edith Wharton, "Life and I," in *Edith Wharton: Novellas and Other Writings*, ed. Cynthia Griffin Wolff, Library of America Series (New York: Literary Classics of the United States, 1990), 1072.
52. Lionel Trilling describes a kind of writing that is morally inquisitive rather than righteous, whose purpose is to "raise questions in our minds not only about conditions but about ourselves . . . to lead us to refine our motives" ("Manners, Morals, and the Novel," in *The Liberal Imagination: Essays on Literature and Society* [New York: Viking, 1950], 219–20).
53. Lewis, *Edith Wharton: A Biography*, 510.
54. See Singley, *Edith Wharton*, and Killoran, *Edith Wharton*.
55. William Dean Howells, *The Rise of Silas Lapham* (1885; rpt., ed. Don L. Cook, Norton Critical Editions, New York: Norton, 1980).
56. Edith Wharton, *The Writing of Fiction* (New York: Scribner's, 1925), 360.
57. See, for example, Shari Benstock, whose study of female artists on the Paris Left Bank, including Wharton, "illuminate[s] heretofore overlooked aspects of the cultural setting in which Modernism developed" (*Women of the Left Bank: Paris, 1900–1940* [Austin: University of Texas Press, 1986], 3).
58. Lewis and Lewis, eds., *Letters of Edith Wharton*, 461.

59. Robert Frost, "The Road Not Taken" and "The Oven Bird," *Selected Poems of Robert Frost*, intro. Robert Graves (New York: Holt, 1963), 71–72, 76, line 14.

60. *Columbia Literary History of the United States*, gen. ed. Elliott, 478, 533, 597.

61. Linda Hutcheon, *Irony's Edge: The Theory and Politics of Irony* (London: Routledge, 1994), 10–16.

62. Michel Foucault, "What Is an Author?" in *Twentieth-Century Literary Theory: An Introductory Anthology*, ed. Vassilis Lambropoulos and David Neal Miller (Albany: State University of New York Press, 1987), 132–33.

63. Wharton, *Writing of Fiction*, 77.

64. Ibid., 3–7.

65. Joanne S. Frye observes that the realist novel "gave women access to literary voice . . . but it also constrained their notions—and ours—of women's lives within the assumptions and values of a decidedly patriarchal society. Its conventions were both those by which women gained access to literary expression and those by which we have come to see women's lives defined as primarily domestic and relational" (*Living Stories, Telling Lies: Women and the Novel in Contemporary Experience* [Ann Arbor: University of Michigan Press, 1986], 35–36).

66. Millicent Todd Bingham, ed., *Emily Dickinson: A Revelation* (New York: Harper, 1954), 82.

THE "FOUNDING MOTHER":
Gertrude Stein and the Cubist Phenomenon

Jacqueline Vaught Brogan

> our knowledge is historical, flowing, and flown
>
> —Elizabeth Bishop
>
> She wanted a "flow"
>
> —Kathleen Fraser

But they called it a "flaw."[1] In fact, while our historical knowledge of Gertrude Stein, both as a person and as an artist, has certainly improved in recent years, and some recent critics have gone so far as to see Stein as the first modernist writer or as a quintessentially feminist writer, and now most recently as a proto-postmodernist writer, our appreciation of Stein as an individual artist as well as her place in the artistic movement she helped to inaugurate, particularly for American authors, remains deeply flawed. As Michael J. Hoffman noted in 1986, in his introduction to a collection of essays and reviews that represent all those various responses to Stein (and others), "Twenty years ago I was able to claim that nothing in Stein scholarship was comparable to the burgeoning 'Joyce industry.' That claim can no longer be made."[2] And certainly, in the intervening decade, critics have given more and more attention to Stein, particularly a Stein that is experimental, particularly in an "antipatriarchal" way, or a Stein that is psychoanalytical in a somewhat "French feminist" way, or a Stein whose meditations on love, war, and place are manifestations of encoded lesbian love and desire in much the way that they are for other contemporary lesbian writers.[3] In other words, part of the recent surge of interest in Stein stems from the legitimate ways her work in the first part of the century can be seen to anticipate numerous developments in poetic practice at the end of this century.

I am less interested in tracing our critical responses to Stein over time, however, than I am in seriously placing Stein back in her "period"—that somewhat contradictory but certainly exciting period we have traditionally called "modernism." It is not merely that reinserting Stein back into the artistic movements of which she was so clearly a seminal figure moves the dates of "modernism" back by a decade (a point already made by Ellen Friedman and Miriam Fuchs), or that doing so reaffirms the importance of women writers as a constitutive force in that period (a point made by the same critics, as well as by Margaret Dickie and Linda Wagner-Martin, to name only a few), but that her writing—and the subsequent aesthetic response of other writers—dismantles the very notions of modernism and postmodernism themselves in ways that allow us to appreciate anew and more accurately Stein's self-proclaimed genius.[4] Such a dismantling also forces us to reevaluate such canonized works as Eliot's "The Waste Land," James Joyce's *Ulysses*, and Virginia Woolf's *The Waves* and such less well known works as Mina Loy's *Songs to Joannes*, Parker Tyler's "Sonnet," and Jean Toomer's *Cane* as all being part of the same aesthetic climate—essentially the "cubist moment," or (as I am redefining it here) the "cubist phenomenon."[5] In other words, putting Stein seriously back into her own time revises our notion of that period of modernism to the point that the term evaporates. If Stein, rather than Eliot or Pound or Joyce, is seen as the ironically charged matrix of the literary activity of the time, our inherited vision of modernism as a (largely male) nostalgia for an order no longer available shifts to a focus on the remarkable breakthroughs (including most particularly the possibility of multiplicity of perspectives) that characterized virtually all the major writings—and paintings—of the time. It is notably that aspect of the cubist aesthetic, of which Stein was both a proponent and a creator in the realm of literature, which is its most important legacy in the experimental writings at the end of the century.

In this regard, my argument that Stein reveals "her period" as actually an explosion of a wider cubist phenomenon at the time makes one gigantic swerve away from Marianne DeKoven's otherwise excellent and groundbreaking discussions of Stein. Although subsequent critics such as Margaret Dickie and Lisa Ruddick have convincingly shown that thematically, Stein was often writing from very specific gendered concerns, DeKoven's insistence that Stein's writing should be called "experimental"—when by the term, DeKoven specifically means "antipatriarchal modes of signification"—distorts both the aesthetic animating Stein's best verse, as well as that animating the writings of many of the men around her and the actual company she chose to keep in her real life.[6] DeKoven specifically dismisses the importance of cubism in understanding

Stein's work in favor of an "alternative mode of signification" that is "antipatriarchal and antilogocentric."[7] And yet as Dickie rightly points out, despite the subversions of various parts of such a poem as "Patriarchal Poetry," in other sections of that same poem Stein is clearly "attempting to find a place for herself in the tradition of patriarchal poetry"—as were T. S. Eliot and Ezra Pound, other writers who were also writing a new kind of poetry in response to the cubist aesthetic dominating the times.[8] It is not that cubism, with its privileging of multiple perspectives in particular, is not open to feminist or poststructuralist concerns. It is. But it is not necessarily or exclusively antipatriarchal—either in the hands of Stein or other male writers of a literary time or period she both shared in and largely inaugurated.

The preceding is not meant to suggest that in her lifetime or that in subsequently written literary histories Stein has gone unrecognized. From various serious and popularized parodies of her work, to such appellations as the "Mother Goose of Montparnasse," the "Mama of Dada," or more recently (following her own lead) the "Mother of Us All," Stein's presence—and the importance of that presence—in the artistic scene of the early twentieth century has remained generally acknowledged, even if undervalued. But as I am arguing, more important, her presence and importance have been misinterpreted. For although Stein could well have been called with more reverence the "Mother of Modernism," she should be called, with far more accuracy, the "founding mother" of American cubist literature.[9] It is not merely that Stein's experimental writing was already in print years before T. S. Eliot's "Love Song of J. Alfred Prufrock" ushered in (at least for Ezra Pound) modern verse, but that her experiments allow us to see that particular poem—with its multiple voices, repetitions, and collage-like scenes—as well as "The Waste Land" as essentially cubist poems. Thus reinserting Stein into the literary scene of which she was so much a critical part forces us well beyond a mere reevaluation of her work in that period, or a mere reassessment of the dates of that period, into a critical reinterpretation of precisely what the "period" following the turn of the century, in literary arts as well as the visual arts, really was. Doing so helps to explain why, at the end of the century, literary critics are everywhere finding in supposedly "modernist" writers—especially female modernist writers—precursors to postmodernist prose, poetry, and generically noncategorizable literary blends.[10]

Perhaps the most obvious works to consider when reevaluating Stein's own work and its importance to other contemporaneous writers are *Three Lives* (composed around 1905 but not published until 1909) or the more famous *Tender Buttons* (composed between 1911 and 1913 and published in 1914). Certainly, in the choice of subject matter, in the refusal of both works to follow normally prescribed generic or narrative lines, and in the experimental manipulation of the language, we find ample evidence to support seeing Stein as a radically advanced modernist author, feminist protester, and postmodernist experimenter from stream-of-conscious techniques to resistance to linear closure. The real importance of these works, however, is far more discernible in her less well known publications of 1912—the generically slippery portraits of "Matisse" and "Picasso" (composed in 1911) that appeared not in a literary magazine but in the American photographic journal *Camera Work*, edited by Alfred Stieglitz.[11]

Although it is not my purpose here to repeat a history I have elsewhere documented at length, the importance of this particular issue of *Camera Work* lies in Stieglitz's combined effort to introduce cubist paintings (via photographic reproductions) to a relatively hostile American audience and, simultaneously, to justify this introduction of a suspect aesthetic movement with two literary texts by Gertrude Stein, which in their own time (and now in retrospect) can certainly be regarded as a defense or apologia for cubism.[12] Responding to the perhaps somewhat surprising rejection of Picasso's exhibition of cubist paintings at the Photo-Secession in 1911, Stieglitz printed a special issue of *Camera Work* with two verbal portraits by Stein ("Matisse" and "Picasso"), several "representative" paintings and sculptures by these artists, and an introductory editorial that perhaps not ingenuously insists that "the fact is" that it is Stein's verbal pieces ("articles," he calls them) and "not either the subject with which they deal or the illustrations that accompany them" that "are the true *raison d'être* of this special issue."

Although the entire issue, with its photographic reproductions of various works by Matisse and Picasso, is clearly a deliberate "apology" for what Stieglitz calls "Post-Impressionism," its importance here is that he finds in Stein's writing, "whose raw material is words," precisely the same "spirit" as that which is conveyed in the visual works he is reproducing. He goes so far as to say that "it is precisely because, in these articles by Miss Stein, the Post-Impressionist spirit is found expressing itself in literary form that we thus lay them before the readers of CAMERA WORK." More important, he then adds that in what Stein is doing with the "medium" of words, readers of *Camera Work* can find a "decipherable clew [sic] to that intellectual and esthetic attitude which underlies and inspires the movement upon one phase of which they are comments and of the extending development of which they are themselves an integral part."

Thus, with the publication of Stein's portraits, we find the possibility of what we might now call cubist literature (rather than "Post-Impressionist" literature) being introduced self-consciously as an "integral" part of the visual aesthetic they were both responding to and extending. Given how very difficult it has proven for subsequent readers and critics to recognize just what the writing of Gertrude Stein was introducing on the American scene, as well as continuing in Europe, it is somewhat amusing to find Stieglitz glibly assuming that what was difficult to comprehend initially in the visual medium would be transparently clear in the verbal medium.[13] Discussing the difficulty of comprehending the new visual movement, "which, with a merely chronological appropriateness, has been christened Post-Impressionism," he concludes that if the "expression" of that movement "came through an art with the raw materials and rough practice of which we were ourselves familiar—let us say through the art of literature, whose raw material is words—even an unpiloted navigator of the unknown might feel his way into the harbor of comprehension." And while many subsequent critics have tried to discount the possibility of an aesthetic convergence between arts of different media (here, the visual and the verbal), Stieglitz introduces Stein's verbal portraits specifically as "a Rosetta stone of comparison" for understanding the radically new works of Matisse and Picasso.

For understanding Stein's own radically new works, the 1912 publication of "Matisse" and "Picasso" clarifies the sharp break Stein had already made between the retrospectively normalized writing of *Three Lives* (however different from nineteenth-century writings that text can well be seen to be) and the far more radicalized writing of *Tender Buttons* (which would inaugurate the tendency of others to write, both seriously and parodically, "Steinese"). At the same time, "Matisse" and "Picasso" furnish the perspective we need to see the degree to which in *Three Lives* Stein was already turning away from simple stream-of-consciousness (that form of writing she had supposedly become interested in from studying psychology with William James) to a concern with language as a self-consciously reflective medium, a concern that would be characteristic of the majority of her works through the rest of her career.[14]

Although it may well be true that *Three Lives* represents a distinct break from her previously written (although posthumously published) *Q.E.D.*, compared with the generically puzzling verbal portraits of Matisse and Picasso, each of the *Three Lives* (which Stein first called "histories") seems almost traditional in its reliance on relatively normal linear narration and conservative grammatical structure.[15] Consider, for example, the opening and closing paragraphs of "Matisse":

> One was quite certain that for a long part of his being one being living he had been trying to be certain that he was wrong in doing what he was doing and then when he could not come to be certain that he had been wrong in doing what he had been doing, when he had completely convinced himself

that he would not come to be certain that he had been wrong in doing what he had been doing he was really certain then that he was a great one and he certainly was a great one. Certainly every one could be certain of this thing that this one is a great one. (SWGS, 329)

Some were certainly wanting to be doing what this one was doing that is were wanting to be ones clearly expressing something. Some of such of them did not go on in being ones wanting to be doing what this one was doing that is in being ones clearly expressing something. Some went on being ones wanting to be doing what this one was doing that is, being ones clearly expressing something. Certainly this one was one who was a great man. Any one could be certain of this thing. Every one would come to be certain of this thing. This one was one certainly clearly expressing something. Any one could come to be certain of this thing. Every one would come to be certain of this thing. This one was one, some were quite certain, one greatly expressing something being struggling. This one was one, some were quite certain, one not greatly expressing something being struggling. (SWGS, 332–33)

Although there does appear to be an implicit narrative story about Matisse's aesthetic development configured in these words (and in the words between the opening and closing paragraphs, which deliberately repeat many of these words "again and again"), the effect of this writing is largely to undermine any real linear development on Matisse's part and to make us, however ironically, slowly change our predicted perspective on and veneration of Matisse to something closer to amused skepticism. Through the simple device of repetition and variation, we come to feel that Matisse himself is perhaps repetitive or derivative. (This, I should clarify, is in complete contrast to the accompanying portrait of "Picasso," which—again through devices of repetition and variation—manages to suggest that others are repeating and being derivative of Picasso and that Picasso is genuinely "working," presumably like Stein herself.)[16] Far more important, however, such cognitive judgments are clearly a tertiary consequence to the writing of the portraits. Rather, the obvious verbal repetitions Stein employs, as well as the subtle variations on her theme, acutely remind us that her writing is specifically a construction made of a verbal medium, open to similar self-referentiality and to multiplicity of perspectives characteristic of the works of Picasso reproduced in Stieglitz's issue, if not that of Matisse.[17] Thus, though nominally "about" Matisse, Stein's verbal portrait exhibits two of the most important characteristics of cubist writing—multiplicity of perspectives and self-referentiality.

So, too, does her verbal portrait of "Picasso," which (while it may well be more laudatory of its nominal subject than "Matisse") is far more concerned with repeating—or translating—a visual cubist aesthetic into a verbal medium than in suggesting any modernist, feminist, or postmodernist perspective on artistic productivity:[18] "One whom some were certainly following was one who was completely charming. One whom some were certainly following was one who was charming. One whom some were following was one who was completely charming. One whom some were following was one who was certainly completely charming" (SWGW, 333). In fact, and in contrast to "Matisse," Stein introduces the actual "subject" of cubism in a somewhat unexpected paragraph in "Picasso" that seems to describe, almost exactly, not only the cubist development in the visual arts but also the critical reactions—both positive and negative—that were already accompanying the exhibitions of cubist work to which, in turn, this special issue of *Camera Work* was responding. As if quickly tracing Picasso's movement through various "periods" of his own making to cubism (and the almost instantaneous "cubist school" that more or less rose up around him and Georges Braque), Stein writes:

> This one always had something being coming out of this one. This one was working. This one always had been working. This one was always having something that was coming out of this one that was a solid thing, a charming thing, a lovely thing, a perplexing thing, a disconcerting thing, a simple thing, a clear thing, a complicated thing, an interesting thing, a disturbing thing, a repellant thing, a very pretty thing. This one was one certainly being one having something coming out of him. This one was one whom some were following. This one was one who was working. (SWGS, 334)

It is not accidental, I believe, but quite to the point that when Stein would reprint these portraits many years later (1934), they would be preceded by an additional "portrait" of Cezanne, that painter whose attention to form and self-referentiality in both paint and canvas provided the initial impetus for cubism.[19]

Something of these concerns can be found in *Three Lives*, but they had become overt in *Tender Buttons* (a work that has been variously described as "cubist," "dada-ist," "feminist," and "poststructuralist"). Compared to her portraits in *Camera Work*, each of the "three lives" has a far more normalized linear development, even if their tendency toward repetition and their frustrating of climactic closure marks them as inherently different from earlier prose compositions. Nonetheless, something of Stein's heightened consciousness of the verbal medium as such (as opposed to mere stream-of-consciousness) surfaces from time to time in *Three Lives*, as in the following quotation from "Melanctha": "He was silent, and this struggle lay there, strong, between them. It was a struggle, sure to be going on always between them. It was a struggle that was sure always to be going on between them, as their minds and hearts always were to have different ways of working" (SWGW, 392–93). The similarity in and self-consciousness about language to that of "Matisse" and "Picasso" seems obvious. In the next paragraph of "Melanctha," however, Stein writes, "At last Melanctha took his hand, leaned over him and kissed him" (SWGS, 393) — a form of writing quite foreign to her subsequently written portraits or to her famous *Tender Buttons*, as well as to much later writings. Here, for example, is the opening of the second section of *Tender Buttons*: "In the inside there is sleeping, in the outside there is reddening, in the morning there is meaning, in the evening there is feeling. In the evening there is feeling. In feeling anything is resting, in feeling anything is mounting, in feeling there is resignation, in feeling there is recognition, in feeling there is recurrence and entirely mistaken there is pinching" (SWGS, 477). Again, the similarity to her 1911 portraits in the manipulation of her verbal medium seems apparent. In contrast to a basically simple use of repetition and variation for narrative purpose (a technique Hemingway would clearly borrow from Stein), in both the portraits and *Tender Buttons* repetition and variation become the purpose of the writing as well as the process, thus marking them as essentially cubist productions.

I should clarify here that precisely what constitutes the nature of cubist writing is, and has been, a subject open to much heated debate. While some critics would limit the possibility of cubist literature to works published in France between 1912 and 1919, and others would deny the possibility of cubist literature altogether, I would argue that cubist writing was — and arguably still is — the most important literary development of the twentieth century.[20] Given the wide range of visual possibilities that the difference between analytic cubist paintings (largely focused on static forms) and synthetic cubist paintings (implying a dynamic temporality) engenders, it is certainly possible to find an equally diverse number of "cubist" possibilities in literature. Thus, in my schema, Stein's "Matisse" and "Picasso," like certain well-known poems by William Carlos Williams ("The Red Wheelbarrow," for example) may be described as analytic cubist writing, whereas *Tender Buttons* or Williams's *Paterson* may be more accurately described as synthetic cubist writing. Similarly, Wallace Stevens's "Thirteen Ways of Looking at a Blackbird" could be considered analytic cubist literature, James Joyce's *Ulysses* could be considered synthetic cubist literature, with both Virginia Woolf's *The Waves* and *The Years* on the continuum of the transition between. Thus, though cubist literature may cover an enormous range of possibilities — as in the difference between Picasso's *Three Women* of 1908–9 and his 1921 *Three Musicians* — cubist literature is likely to be marked by concern with visual form (ranging from cubelike structures to radical experimentation on the printed page); by a distortion of normal word, line, or sentence boundaries; by a thematic concern with its own modernism (not "modernism," when that erroneously means a nostalgia for order and traditions) and intense preoccupation with perception; by narrative and temporal disjunctions that, in a collage-like fashion, employ multiple voices, sections, and textual fragments; and finally by a heightened sense of textuality, which self-consciously questions the very nature of presentation and representation. If we add to this deliberate textual play various self-consciously imposed ethical and political protests, we are but one remove from defining certain contemporary feminist and postmodernist writings that were, in fact, more than anticipated by various writers, including Gertrude Stein in such works as "Patriarchal Poetry" or "Have They Attacked Mary, He Giggled," in the early part of this century.

Consequently, the preceding emphasis on that cubist nature of Stein's and others' writing is not to say that *Tender Buttons* can be considered only from a cubist perspective or that Stein's other works can be regarded only in this manner. Although I personally can find no "feminist" intent in "Matisse" or "Picasso," it is clearly present in *Tender Buttons* and overt in later publications, such as "Patriarchal Poetry," which alternates the injunction to "Let her try" with the ambiguous challenge or complaint—"Never to be what he said." While some of *Tender Buttons* may well be read as a "tender" veneration of the supposedly female domains of houses and cooking, some of the "buttons" are hardly "tender," but rather fairly startling exposés or complaints—as in one of the last entries in the section called "Objects":

PEELED PENCIL, CHOKE
Rub her coke. (SWGS, 476)

In this and other similar instances, it might be fair to say that in Stein at least it is precisely the mixture of a cubist aesthetic and a feminist intent that gives us something like "postmodernism."[21] What this insight also tells us is that postmodernism itself is not a different category from what we have been calling modernism—rather, both may be simply different facets of cubism, in the way that analytic and synthetic cubist works are different facets of cubism in the visual arts. It should come as no surprise, for example, that what we could now legitimately call the major extended collages of such male writers as Eliot or Pound should bear something of a nostalgia for a tradition lost by the multiple perspectives of twentieth-century aesthetics and politics, or that similar aesthetic strategies in the hands of women writers and, to some extent, minority writers such as Langston Hughes, might have more of a sense of defiance or liberation toward abandoning that "tradition."

It is perhaps, then, no accident that Stein would also write in the "Roastbeef" entry of *Tender Buttons*, "In kind, in a control, *in a period*" (emphasis added), "the length of leaning a strong thing outside . . . does not mean that there is overtaking, this means nothing precious, this means clearly that the chance to exercise is a social success" (SWGS, 478–79). There is, then, aligned with Stein's aesthetics a social consciousness and purpose that is akin to much of the cubist literature that would follow (although, depending on the side of the Atlantic on which that literature was produced, the various "politics" that conjoined with this new poetics would range from a tendency toward anarchist destruction to what was even then called a "democracy of feeling").[22] It is precisely the more destructive possibility of the cubist aesthetic that would lead Williams, however ironically, given his obvious similarities to Stein and Joyce, to dismiss both authors as "disintegrationists" when trying to create a new and democratic poetics from/for the American soil.[23] And, indeed, given various similar polarizations that have occurred in the world of criticism and theory since the advent of deconstruction (a theoretical development I see as the progeny of cubism in the critical arts), it is fitting that Gertrude Stein herself may have coined the term "deconstruction."[24]

Something of a more politically pointed purpose is already indicated in Stein's "Portrait of Mabel Dodge at the Villa Curona," which was published in *Camera Work* the year after "Matisse" and "Picasso," with Picasso's well-known portrait of Gertrude Stein (thus doubling the complexity created by Stein's verbal portrait) and his well-known *Woman with Mandolin*. In "Portrait of Mabel Dodge," Stein suggestively writes, "Abandon a garden and the house is bigger," "In burying that game there is not a change of name. There is not perplexing and co-ordination. The toy that is not round has to be found and looking is not straining such relation. There can be that company," and finally, "Praying has intention and relieving that situation is not solemn. There comes that way" (SWGS, 529–30). Given the compelling personage of Mabel Dodge, or that it was this portrait which first introduced the work of Gertrude Stein to Carl Van Vechten, who would in turn contribute to the growing "infinite regress" of verbal portraits about paintings about portraits, the political charge of this piece has gone largely unnoticed. As she also says in the same piece, "So much breathing has not the same place when there is that much beginning. So much breathing has not the same place when the ending is lessening" (SWGS, 527) — remarks that seem to correspond well to Williams's well-known desire to "clear the ground" or to our current preoccupations with various political as well as poetic dismantlings.

Certainly by the time Stein produced "Composition as Explanation" (1926), a text that repeats exactly many of the linguistic strategies of her early "portraits," a concern with temporality and a concern with an intensely political climate aligned with temporal awareness have been infused into this important and self-consciously theoretical manifesto. As she "says" of these early works in "Composition as Explanation," "In the meantime to naturally begin I commenced making portraits of anybody and anything. In making these portraits I naturally made a continuous present as including everything and a beginning again and again within a very small thing. That started me into composing anything into one thing" (SWGS, 518–19). This I regard as a similarly "analytic" demonstration of her earlier practice. As she goes on to clarify, however, the advent of the war presented a transformative urgency to this aesthetic, of which the larger "Composition" is an example in praxis:

> So then I as a contemporary creating the composition in the beginning was groping toward a continuous present.... This then was the period that brings me to the period of the beginning of 1914.... And so the art creation of the contemporary composition which would have been outlawed normally outlawed several generations more behind even than war, war having been brought so to speak up to date art so to speak was allowed not completely to be up to date, but nearly up to date, in other words we who created the expression of the modern composition were to be recognized before we were dead. (SWGS, 520–21)

The "modern composition" of which she is giving expression here is, I believe, cubist literature, a phenomenon I have elsewhere argued is largely bracketed by the two world wars—at least in American poetry—but which I suggest was equally prevalent in prose and mixed genres and which is now, after a post–World War II reentrenchment into tradition, resurfacing with perhaps even greater energy today. In this sense, I totally concur with Marianne DeKoven's conclusion that had Stein lived, "one can imagine her emerging as a leader of the avant-garde's resurgence in the late fifties, the sixties, and the seventies, when 'postmodernists' began to do what she, almost alone, had done fifty years before."[25] I would simply add that the recent resurgence of feminist issues in our culture might well have seen a revisiting of Stein's poetic practices to an aesthetic that animated her earliest verse in ways that might not have been revisited in the same way by some of her male peers during the "cubist phenomenon," in which she was hardly alone.

That Stein was a forerunner in giving expression to this "modern composition"—and not a causal agent—is something I should stress. The cubist phenomenon, which virtually exploded in various artistic media (including sculpture, architecture, and cinematography) after World War I, was clearly alive and well in the hands of several writers and editors of small journals such as *Broom* and *transition* across Europe, as well as in America. It is clearly following Stein's first "portraits" and subsequent experiments that Mina Loy's typographically self-conscious and feminist verse would appear in *Camera Work* and *Others*, that Stevens's brief dalliance with cubism would also appear in *Others* and elsewhere, that Williams would begin his sustained interaction with analytic and synthetic cubist poetry, that Parker Tyler's or Henri Ford's cubist poetry would appear in *Blues* (along with later poems by Stein herself), or that E. E. Cummings—arguably the most parodic while equally talented practitioner of this aesthetic—would erupt in journals all over the country. Similarly, we find that it would be well after Stein's first publications that James Joyce would change the style of writing characterizing *Dubliners* to that of *Ulysses* and *Finnegan's Wake*; that William Faulkner would produce the essentially cubist novels *The Sound and the Fury* and *Absalom, Absalom!*; or that Virginia Woolf would compose *The Waves* rather than the far more normalized (however "modern") *To the Lighthouse*. These are but a handful of the important instances of cubist literature that would arrive on the scene between the two world wars—in addition to the myriad of hybrid-generic works such as Jean Toomer's *Cane* (a text equally indebted to cubism and to Sherwood Anderson).

I would like to suggest that Gertrude Stein's experimentation with cubist literature and then her (temporary) abandonment of that aesthetic has a curious parallel to—and significant difference from—that of other writers, ironically such as Wallace Stevens, during the first half of the century. As I argued at some length in *Part of the Climate*, for numerous American writers at least, the sheer magnitude of chaos that the pressure of a second world war meant for people of the time had the understandable consequence of a number of writers abandoning the potentially chaotic experiments of cubist literature and committing themselves more earnestly to traditional and normalized forms of writing. So, too, did Gertrude Stein, whose more accessible works such as *Wars I Have Seen* (1945) seem clearly motivated by the war—in content and aesthetic response—than by a reaction to the Great Depression or other concerns of the 1930s.[26] Nonetheless, in late works such as some of her plays and operas or *How Writing Is Written*, Stein proved far more willing than other writers who had abandoned the literary aesthetic during World War II to resume a cubist—and admittedly feminist, postmodernist—experimentation with language. Such a willing return to the play and politics of the cubist aesthetics in the verbal medium makes her the understandable precursor to the second wave of the cubist phenomenon in contemporary writing (most notably, perhaps, in any number of L=A=N=G=U=A=G=E poets, from John Cage to David Atkin, or more particularly from Susan Howe to Lyn Hejinian, as well as in the highly creative criticism of such uncategorizable authors as Rachel Blau DuPlessis).[27]

I should conclude, however, by stressing that Stein's importance as an author and influence is not limited to the impact of cubism on the literature of her time. Her profound influence on Ernest Hemingway, who in most instances could not be called a cubist writer (*In Our Time* being a notable exception if one regards it, as I do, as a "cubist anatomy" rather than as a collection of short stories) is illimitable, as it is on others.[28] For example, although her influence on Hemingway is given distinctly different versions in *The Autobiography of Alice B. Toklas* and Hemingway's *Moveable Feast*, her stylistic presence (and occasionally vestigial personal presence) is clear from his first successful short stories throughout his novels. Repetition of simple sentence structures and the use of indeterminant pronouns that continually change in reference are not only the hallmark of Stein but also of Hemingway from "Hills Like White Elephants" to his posthumously published *Garden of Eden*. In fact, both a parody of Stein as a stylist and as a person and an incorporation of the basic theme of "Composition as Explanation" are central to one of his most famous novels, *For Whom the Bell Tolls*.[29]

As should be clear, however, reinserting Stein into "her own time" challenges our very notion of what that "time" was, as well as subsequent times or periods, and shows how seminal (the word is intentional) she was to a cubist phenomenon of which we are still a part. It is perhaps fitting, then, that Sherwood Anderson well anticipated the genuine importance of Gertrude Stein in this century: "Would it not be a lovely and charmingly ironic gesture of the gods," he asks, "if, in the end, the work of this artist were to prove the most lasting and important of all the word slingers of our generation."[30] Or, as Stein herself wrote in "Composition as Explanation" with perhaps more prescience—in an uncanny remark that summarizes this entire essay—"Nothing changes from generation to generation except the thing seen and that makes a composition." What changes here when we seriously place Stein back into her not-so-lost generation is the entire notion of "modernism" itself that suddenly transforms, as if through a kaleidescope, into a "cubist phenomenon" that is still, as it was at the beginning of this century, expanding as we approach the next century. Indeed, our literary and historical knowledge, however "flawed" or "flown," is still "flowing."

NOTES

1. The word "flaw" is the obvious interpolation to be made from Kathleen Fraser's epigraph, cited in the text above. As she goes on to say of this desired "flow" in "this. notes. new year." from *Each Next* (Berkeley: Figures, 1980) — "in the translation it was corrected, displacing the *o* and substituting *a*" (11). Such a "correction," which is indeed

a mark of denigration, neatly encapsulates an entire tradition of dealing with women, whether in terms of their desire for a writer's flow or the fact of monthly flows. In fact, their supposed "flaw" is much to the point of this book, of which this essay is merely a part. In addition, although I do find an important affinity between experimental female writers of the end of this century and Gertrude Stein at the beginning of the century, I would like to emphasize in this essay what is gained by putting Stein seriously back into her actual "period," however much her work may legitimately be said to anticipate certain contemporary poetic strategies.

2. Michael J. Hoffman, Introduction to *Critical Essays on Gertrude Stein*, ed. Hoffman (Boston: G. K. Hall, 1986), 3, citing his *The Development of Abstractionism in the Writings of Gertrude Stein* (Philadelphia: University of Pennsylvania Press, 1965), 18.

3. See, respectively, Marianne DeKoven, *A Different Language: Gertrude Stein's Experimental Writing* (Madison: University of Wisconsin Press, 1983); Lisa Ruddick, *Reading Gertrude Stein: Body, Text, Gnosis* (Ithaca: Cornell University Press, 1990); and Margaret Dickie, *Stein, Bishop, and Rich: Lyrics of Love, War, and Place* (Chapel Hill: University of North Carolina Press, 1997).

4. The most obvious instance of Stein's identifying herself as a "genius" is in *The Autobiography of Alice B. Toklas*, where, in addition to identifying herself, repeatedly, as a genius, she specifically aligns herself in that regard with Pablo Picasso and Alfred Whitehead. In "Context and Continuities," the introduction to *Breaking the Sequence: Women's Experimental Fiction* (Princeton: Princeton University Press, 1989), Ellen G. Friedman and Miriam Fuchs make the point that "the tradition of experimental women writers"—including Gertrude Stein, among others—"alters received ideas of the beginning of modernism in fiction" (8). I am not simply extending this insight to include poetry as well but am challenging the very notion of "modernism." Nonetheless, Friedman and Fuchs are right in asserting that women are a central, not secondary, force in the literary developments of the early part of this century. In this regard, see also Margaret Dickie, "Women Poets and the Emergence of Modernism," *The Columbia History of American Poetry*, ed. Jay Parini (New York: Columbia University Press, 1993), 233–59; Linda Wagner-Martin, "Notes from a Women's Biographer" (an excerpt from her longer biography of Stein and family), in *Narrative* 1 (October 1993): 265–72; and any number of other Stein critics, from Marianne DeKoven and Michael Hoffman to Lisa Ruddick and Margaret Norris.

5. In *Part of the Climate: American Cubist Poetry* (Berkeley: University of California Press, 1991), I called the period roughly corresponding to that between the two world wars the "cubist moment." I am more inclined now to call it the "cubist phenomenon," implying that both the aesthetics and the politics of this artistic movement have continued to be felt with variously decreasing and increasing intensity in the creative work as well as the criticism of the latter part of this century. I should add that whether "canonical" or not, the various works listed in the text above are all readily available in print, with the exception of Parker Tyler's extraordinary "Sonnet," which first appeared in the March 1929 issue of *Blues* and is reprinted in *Part of the Climate*, 166–67.

6. The phrase in quotations is taken from DeKoven, *A Different Language*, 70, though

her sense that Stein's "experimental" writing is "anti-patriarchal" informs the entire book. As she notes in the conclusion, "This historical-political context enables us to see Stein's experimental writing as a location of her literary rebellion, against the patriarchal structures which excluded her, in language itself rather than in thematic content" (149–50).

7. Although DeKoven dismisses the importance of cubism in A *Different Language* (70), she is most overt in "Gertrude Stein and Modern Painting: Beyond Literary Criticism," *Contemporary Literature* 22 (1981): 81–95; rpt. in Hoffman, ed., *Critical Essays*, 171–83: "Useful as these analyses of Stein's writing as literary cubism have been in helping us approach her work, we should not overrate their reliability in accounting for its specific linguistic shapes" (171).

8. Dickie, *Stein, Bishop, and Rich*, 1. Dickie goes on to argue, convincingly, "Read in the light of its connection to 'Lifting Belly,' then, the sonnet ['Patriarchal Poetry'] celebrates a love that coincides with both the values of the patriarchy and with Stein's own, and it forces a reconsideration of Stein's attitudes toward the patriarchy. Moreover, if, as she writes, patriarchal poetry is the same as patriotic poetry, we should remember that Stein herself spent the decade between 'Lifting Belly' and 'Patriarchal Poetry' writing war poetry that was patriotic. This poetry also places Stein in a more cordial relationship to patriarchal/patriotic poetry than we might have first imagined" (38–39).

9. Although I emphasized Stein's importance in introducing a cubist aesthetic to American poetry in *Part of the Climate*, calling her the "'founding mother' of American cubist poetry" (8), I would like to stress here her equal, if not even larger, importance to the aesthetic experiments in prose during her lifetime, both in America and in Europe. Michael J. Hoffman gives an excellent overview of Stein's critical reception, including the various skilled and not-so-skilled parodies of her work, in the introduction to *Critical Essays on Gertrude Stein*, 1–24.

10. In particular, the relatively new hybrid of the "prose-poem" became current in both America and Europe during the first half of this century—a direct consequence of the breaking of traditional perspectives and rules that the cubist aesthetic encouraged. This particular aspect of literary development is to be found in Stein's work itself: as Dickie has pointed out, Stein's work "is not easily separated into genres; she worked to overthrow the conventions of genre, to mix prose and poetry, and to question the idea of a continuous work" ("Women Poets and the Emergence of Modernism," 238)—which helps to account for Stein's continued appeal to certain contemporary writers who also break generic confines such as Susan Howe and Lyn Hejinian. Although I concur with Dickie in this regard, I should note that, following Randa Dubnick, Hoffman suggests that Stein herself did distinguish between "poetry" and "prose" (see Hoffman, "Introduction," 20–21).

11. I shall be citing Stein's portraits, as well as Stieglitz's "Editorial," from the 1912 issue of *Camera Work*. (The subsequent reference in the text to Stein's "Portrait of Mabel Dodge at the Villa Curona" cites the Special Number of *Camera Work* of June 1913). All these are reprinted in *Selected Writings of Gertrude Stein*, ed. Carl Van Vechten (1962;

rpt. Vintage, 1990), the text I shall use for the remaining quotations from Stein; hereafter abbreviated as SWGS. In A *Different Language*, Marianne DeKoven specifically avoids Stein's "famous portraits," saying that they do not constitute a "'work,' in the way we normally understand that word: a coherent literary unit, separate and distinguishable from any other" (*Different Language*, xv). I see at least the two portraits I discuss in the text, however, not only as fine literary works of the cubist aesthetic in literature but as absolutely central to understanding both Stein and the larger time she both represents and introduces.

12. I have given a brief overview of several critical responses to this Picasso exhibition in *Part of the Climate*, 12–16. The following response by James Huneker, though somewhat extreme, captures the almost alarmed rejection of cubism when it first appeared in the United States: implying that Picasso is speaking for a new "generation," Huneker concludes that "his is not the cult of the ugly for the sake of ugliness, but the search after the expressive in the heart of ugliness. A new aesthetic? No, a very old one revivified, and perhaps because of its modern rebirth all the uglier, and as yet a mere diabolic not divine, stammering" (*Camera Work*, October 1911, 54).

13. Although various individual works by Stein that are elsewhere described as "postmodernist" or "feminist" have been called "cubist," Stein herself has not been typically identified as a cubist writer in general. As I clarify in the text above, the possibility of cubist literature has itself been rejected by several theorists during this century. From the particular publications of Guillaume Apollinaire in France to the popularized presumption of cubist literature when Dorothy Sayers introduces a "cubist poet" in *Lord Peter Views the Body* (1928), the actual presence of cubist literature has remained, for some, a fact beyond doubt—even if "young cubists" were open to parody (see Marsden Hartley, who ridicules their "over-dressing" in "Farewell, Charles [Demuth]," *The New Caravan of 1936*, ed. Alfred Kreymborg, Lewis Mumford, and Paul Rosenfeld [New York: Norton, 1937], 553).

14. Both DeKoven and Ruddick, in their books, note at length a similar change in Stein's style during this period, though they variously attribute the change to a larger antipatriarchal or feminist concern. Although I agree that there is certainly a strong feminist element in many of Stein's works, these early portraits—particularly the veneration of Picasso that I will subsequently discuss—seem essentially cubist in aesthetic and not antipatriarchal or feminist in intent.

15. See Ulla E. Dydo, "To Have the Winning Language: Texts and Contexts of Gertrude Stein," in *Coming to Light: American Women Poets in the Twentieth Century*, ed. Diane Wood Middlebrook and Marilyn Yalom (Ann Arbor: University of Michigan Press, 1985), 58; Dydo discusses the departure of *Three Lives* from Stein's earlier, more autobiographical work, whereas I am calling attention to the somewhat traditional sentence structures of *Three Lives* when compared to her "portraits" and to *Tender Buttons*.

16. As suggested above, Stein specifically aligns herself with Picasso in *The Autobiography of Alice B. Toklas*. But because Stein is attempting a verbal equivalent to Picasso's new visual aesthetic in her "portraits," it is possible to deduce from the portraits that she

is aligning herself with Picasso as someone seriously working. In this regard, it is important to distinguish several different "he's" in the last paragraph of "Picasso," as if Stein were pointing around the room — or around a picture of several artists together — distinguishing the he "who was working" and "whom some were certainly following" (Picasso) from a "he" or "this one" who "was not one completely working" (possibly Matisse or even Braque). See the complete "Picasso" reprinted in SWGS.

17. Although this comment may seem out of line with assessments of Matisse's admitted craft and talent, the particular works of Matisse reproduced in this issue of *Camera Work* are far more lyrical, even romantic, than those of Picasso. In particular, the artistic medium fades to transparency — it gives way to the "subject" — whereas the artistic medium of the work by Picasso, like that of Stein's portraits, is itself the "subject." A similar distinction might be made between the difference in Ezra Pound's imagistic poem "In a Station of the Metro" and William Carlos Williams's more cubist "Red Wheelbarrow." Whereas the interest in the former lies almost exclusively in the mental perception created by the images or words, in the latter the mental perception involved rapidly becomes an interest in plural perceptions, while equal interest is focused on the material construction of the poem itself.

18. Here I disagree with Dickie's otherwise excellent discussion of Stein in "Women Poets and the Emergence of Modernism." There Dickie interprets the repeated line from "Picasso," "This one was one having always something being coming out of him," as having to do with the "metaphor of childbearing for the creative act" (238). While there is certainly within Western culture a deeply embedded connection between the labor of women in childbearing and other forms of masculine labor, Stein's repeated emphasis on Picasso's genuinely "working" and the somewhat secondary emphasis on "something coming out of him" could equally refer to a similarly embedded connection between artistic production and that of seminal fluid. Whatever the precise metaphor that underlies Stein's phrase really is (and I think it indeterminant in her text), the emphasis does seem to me on a strictly masculine production.

19. In "To Have a Winning Language," Dydo goes so far to suggest that what allowed "Stein to initiate an entirely new approach to composition" (one she is defining in relation to *Three Lives*) is "above all her encounter with the work of Cezanne, 'the master of realization of the object itself'" (60). I generally agree, although I am shifting the emphasis from "master of realization" to the implicit cubist perception operative in many of Cezanne's works.

20. A more thorough discussion of the problematic reception of the term "cubist literature" — as well as its consistent use since the early part of this century — can be found in my "Cubism" entry, in *The Princeton Encyclopedia of Poetry and Poetics*, 3d ed., ed. Alex Preminger and T. V. F. Brogan (Princeton: Princeton University Press, 1993). For a discussion of whether cubism in literature is possible, see *Cubisme et litterature*, Special Issue of *Europe: Revue litteraire mensuelle* 638–39 (1982), especially Michel Decaudin, "Petite histoire d'une appellation: 'Cubisme litteraire,'" 7–25.

21. In her discussion of *Tender Buttons*, Ruddick gives an excellent account of the

many—and contradictory—possibilities of meaning in the two lines above (see *Reading Gertrude Stein*, 210–13). That some of the possibilities include an uncensored male perspective and others various female perspectives only reinforces my contention that the cubist aesthetic aligned with feminist concerns gives us something like what we have come to call "postmodernism" at the end of this century.

22. While the political ramifications of the cubist aesthetic are very much at the heart of *Part of the Climate*, the conclusion in particular discusses the potential for cubism to lean toward a democracy or multiplicity and, variously, to lean toward destruction or anarchy.

23. See *Selected Letters of William Carlos Williams* (New York: McDowell, Obolensky, 1957), 131. Despite this disparagement, it is useful to remember that Williams composed an essay titled "The Work of Gertrude Stein," which was originally conceived as a "Manifesto: in the form of a criticism of the works of Gertrude Stein"—or, as the aesthetic explanation and justification for a new literary magazine in 1930 titled *Pagany*. The more negative possibility of writing simply as a "disintegrationist" remains as a negative criticism of Stein: although using different terms (specifically antihumanist), Laura Riding Jackson indicted Stein's writing as "denial of meaning," including all values, even human value. See "The Word-Play of Gertrude Stein," in Hoffman, ed. *Critical Essays*, 240–60.

24. It should go without saying that a similar divisiveness toward "deconstruction" as that which characterized the initial responses to cubism has been characteristic of the latter part of this century. Carolyn Burke first fortuitously pointed out that Stein may have coined the term "deconstruction"; see "The New Poetry and the New Woman," in *Coming to Light*, ed. Middlebrook and Yalom, n. 39.

25. DeKoven, *Different Language*, 151.

26. In her entry "Modernism" in *The Oxford Companion to Women's Writing in the United States*, ed. Cathy N. Davidson and Linda Wagner-Martin (New York: Oxford University Press, 1995), Wagner-Martin identifies the structural and typographical changes of "modernism" that occurred during the 1930s as the consequence of the subject of human "loss and waste" as having become "itself sufficient" to contribute to modernist awareness (574). This insight may well be true, but I find the particular structural conservatism—or abandonment of overt experimentation—in the late 1930s to be prompted by the growing pressure of the coming world war.

27. With regard to the connection between Lyn Hejinian and Gertrude Stein, see Hejinian's "Two Stein Talks," *Temblor: Contemporary Poets* 3 (1986): 128–39. The connection between the two writers is admirably discussed in Craig Douglas Dworkin's "Penelope Reworking the Twill," *Contemporary Literature* 36 (1995): 58–81. With regard to DuPlessis's noncategorizable creative criticism, see *The Pink Guitar: Writing as Feminist Practice* (New York: Routledge, 1990), a text equally, however variously, indebted to Wallace Stevens and Gertrude Stein. In a far more normalized critical text, DuPlessis discusses the connections between Stein and Virginia Woolf in "Woolfenstein," *Breaking the Sequence*, ed. Friedman and Fuchs, 99–114.

28. See my "Hemingway's *In Our Time* as a Cubist Anatomy," *Hemingway Review* 17, (Spring 1998): 31–46.

29. As Hoffman has pointed out ("Introduction," 22), the simplest parody of Stein and Steinese occurs in Hemingway's text when he has Robert Jordan think "a stone is a stein is a rock is a boulder is a pebble" (see Hemingway, *For Whom the Bell Tolls* 1940; rpt. New York: Scribner, 1987), 289. Joseph Waldmeir, however, has pointed out that Stein is the specific provocation for the complicated character of Pilar in the novel ("Chapter Numbering and Meaning in *For Whom the Bell Tolls*," *Hemingway Review* 8, [Spring 1989]: 43–45). I would add that in the second and final love scene between Jordan and Maria, Hemingway incorporates Stein's "continuous present," a change in temporal awareness necessitated by war, as she explains in "Composition as Explanation," as part of the actual substance and style of the famous chapter 37. As I have argued elsewhere, Hemingway's emphasis on the "forever now" that includes "what had been and now and whatever was to come" is not merely a liturgical revision or allusion but a specific response to Stein's description of the "time of the composition" and the "continuous present" as "at times a present thing . . . at times a past thing . . . at times a future thing"—as well as a notably "natural thing." See "Parody or Parity?: A Brief Note on Gertrude Stein and *For Whom the Bell Tolls*," *Hemingway Review* 15 (Spring 1996): 89–95.

30. Sherwood Anderson, "The Work of Gertrude Stein," rpt. in Hoffman, ed., *Critical Essays*, 39–41.

THE SELF-CATEGORIZATION, SELF-CANONIZATION, AND SELF-PERIODIZATION OF ADRIENNE RICH

Sylvia Henneberg

Since 1951, when her first collection of poetry, *A Change of World*, appeared, Adrienne Rich has been a constant and influential presence in the literary world. Only twice has she taken more than three years to publish a major collection of poetry or prose; more often than not, a new book has appeared within two or three years, and sometimes, as in 1976 and in 1986, two works came out in a single year. Rich has sustained this pace for almost fifty years.

Critics unanimously agree that Rich's style and subject matter have undergone significant changes since 1951, when, in his foreword to *A Change of World*, W. H. Auden was charmed by poems that "speak quietly but do not mumble, respect their elders but are not cowed by them, and do not tell fibs."[1] Granting that these by now notorious comments may apply to Rich's very early work, critics who deal with her later writings claim to discover new and ever-changing tendencies and, giving their studies such titles as "From Patriarchy to Female Principle," "The Radicalization of Adrienne Rich," "The Moment of Change," and "Beginning Again," they repeatedly focus on the evolution of Rich's career.[2] In his book chapter "Poetry and Process: The Shape of Adrienne Rich's Career," Craig Werner describes Rich's oeuvre as a "multileveled process since the mid-1950s" and assures us that few critics disagree with his assessment.[3]

Rich is well aware of the evolving nature of her career. The word "change" emerges again and again in her writing, and she always emphasizes that her work is "a process still going on," "a continuing exploration," "a struggle to keep moving."[4] In her volume of essays *Blood, Bread, and Poetry*, she lets her readers know that by 1956, she had begun dating her poems because "I was finished with the idea of a poem as a single, encapsulated event, a work of art complete in itself; I knew my life was changing, my work was changing, and I needed to indicate to readers my sense of being engaged in a long, continuing process."[5]

The ever-shifting nature of this process seems to thwart all possibility of determining the canonization, categorization, and periodization of Rich's work. As Cary Nelson suggests, we tend to read any of Rich's writings as a commentary on her previous writings, which can "blunt the impact of her work, since we are implicitly urged to delay coming to terms with any given poem."[6] Such consciousness of Rich's propensity for change has, however, hardly kept her from being canonized, categorized, and periodized. Assessing the quantity and examining the quality of response she has received over time reveals that critics' and other canon-shapers' recognition of Rich as a major poet began in the 1970s and 1980s. Her prominence coincides with and may in large part be attributed to the appearance of her radical lesbian-feminist prose in those two decades. Since the publication of such essays as "When We Dead Awaken: Writing as Re-Vision" (1971), "Compulsory Heterosexuality and Lesbian Existence" (1980), and, above all, such volumes of highly politicized prose as *Of Woman Born: Motherhood as Experience and Institution* (1976), *On Lies, Secrets, and Silence* (1979), and *Blood, Bread, and Poetry* (1986) the quantity and quality of response to her poetry have established her as one of the leading poetic figures of the twentieth century in the United States.

Emphasizing the importance of the connection between poetry and politics, calling for "the affirmation of an organic relation between poetry and social transformation,"[7] Rich's political essays have provided helpful and convenient shortcuts toward understanding her poetry. They have led to an increased response to all of her work and, more important, they have seduced critics into approaching Rich's poetry on the poet's rather than our own terms. Channeling most of our comments on her poetry through her prose, we have tended to focus our attention on the poet's radical prose voice of the 1970s and 1980s, generating a one-sided image of her poetry which, despite all efforts, ultimately fails to reflect the complexity and changeability of her poetry and also fails to give Rich, in Willard Spiegelman's words, "the *literary* criticism she most deserves."[8] Through the publication of her radical political prose works, Rich has thus significantly influenced and, to some extent, limited the periodization, canonization, and categorization of her poetry.

Before 1970, Rich was not at the center of critical debate, although she had already published six volumes of poetry.[9] More than forty of her poems had been anthologized once or several times between 1950 and 1969,[10] and she had received over forty reviews, more than ten awards, and an honorary doctorate, but there were nonetheless only one article and no book-length studies.[11] During these two decades, critics often perpetuated Auden's condescension: in 1956 Randall Jarrell perceived her as "an enchanting poet," "a sort of princess in a fairy tale"; in 1963, Philip Booth praised her for being reticent and "quiet," a term he employed three times in his first paragraph; and in 1966 John Ashbery was glad to see that "she ha[d] made progress since those schoolgirlish days" of *A Change of World*.[12] Reviewers were either benevolent or mildly critical but generally failed to convey strong feelings about Rich's work.[13] When in 1969 Richard Tillinghast wrote, "Adrienne Rich has developed slowly and unspectacularly to become one of the best poets in America," his was perhaps the most committed and passionate commentary published to that point.[14]

In the 1970s, critical commentary became much less aloof and much more abundant. Response to her poetry in the form of reviews, anthology entries, book chapters, articles, awards, and prizes increased exponentially once Rich's first essays and especially her first two collections of prose were published. Between 1970 and 1989, she received more than three times as many reviews as in the previous two decades although she published less than twice as many books of poetry.[15] The volumes *Diving into the Wreck* (1973) and *The Dream of a Common Language* (1978) alone were reviewed more often than all six books Rich had published in the 1950s and 1960s.[16] In these twenty years, her work was anthologized in more than sixty collections, often in several editions.[17] Such mainstream anthologies as *The American Tradition in Literature*, which had existed long before the 1970s, gradually incorporated more of her poetry; major anthologies that first appeared in that decade, such as the McMichael *Anthology of American Literature*, *The Norton Anthology of American Literature*, and *The Norton Anthology of Poetry*, included a large or steadily growing number of selections.[18] Between 1973, when the first edition of *The Norton Anthology of Modern Poetry* was published, and 1988, when its second and last edition appeared, the editors Richard Ellmann and Robert O'Clair doubled the number of Rich's poems, reaching a total of fourteen. Classic textbooks such as Cleanth Brooks and Robert Penn Warren's *Understanding Poetry* included Rich's poetry for the first time, and textbooks that were to become classics such as X. J. Kennedy's *Literature: An Introduction to Fiction, Poetry, and Drama* incorporated a steadily increasing number of her poems.[19] Hundreds of critical articles on and five book-length studies of her poetry were published.[20] As many have pointed out, the only *Norton Critical Edition* that concentrates on the works of a living poet is *Adrienne Rich's Poetry*, first published in 1975.[21] Rich received more and far more prestigious awards in these two decades; two of them were the National Book Award in 1974 and the Ruth Lilly Poetry Prize in 1982.[22] She was awarded three more honorary doctorates.[23]

It is perhaps only natural for an extremely talented and prolific poet to receive more and more attention as time goes by and more material is published. But it is not only the numbers that changed as Rich's prose began to appear. The nature of Rich's critical reception, too, underwent a transformation, and the detached attitude of many critics gave way to either unconditional enthusiasm or categorical rejection. Albert Gelpi concluded his 1974 essay assuring us of "the centrality of Adrienne Rich's work in the contemporary scene."[24] Two years later Margaret Atwood stated that "Adrienne Rich is not just one of America's best feminist poets or one of America's best woman poets, she is one of America's best poets."[25] In 1986, Paula Bennett wrote, "In recent years [Rich] has emerged as the spokeswoman for an entire new generation of women poets."[26]

At the same time, passionately critical voices came to the fore. In 1973 Robert Boyers declared Rich "neither a radical innovator nor the voice of an age." He lamented the lack of intelligence in her then recent poetry, calling it "nauseous propaganda of the avance-guard [sic] cultural radicals." Boyers pessimistically concluded, "I don't know that we may hope for very much from her verse beyond striking fragments."[27] Six years later, Carol Muske wrote: "Rich's tendency to generalize, to aggrandize the truth she spends so much time tracking, is disturbing.... She indulges in a brand of self-heroics which congratulates itself on the page." And in 1981, Helen Vendler complained that Rich could conceive of a topic only autobiographically and that she was producing "propaganda poetry" that generated "a counterproductive aesthetic result."[28]

Those who had a vested interest in her feminist politics and looked to her as an important shaper and product of the women's movement saw Rich as the most significant poet of the twentieth century; those who did not, who were offended by what Alicia Ostriker once called Rich's totalitarian "Lesbian Imperative,"[29] or who felt excluded by what soon came to be understood as the blatant essentialism underlying much of Rich's feminism of the time generally undertook a wholesale dismissal of her poetry. As Spiegelman commented during this period, Rich's "defenders usually take a feminist line, discussing and approving her poetry mostly in terms of its political content or in relation to her prose explorations, and her hostile critics simply adjust their sights in the same way but with an aim to destroy rather than to praise." At least in part because of her prose, which Bonnie Zimmerman has tellingly called "a feminist version of an eighteenth- or nineteenth-century book of sermons," Rich developed into not only one of the most widely read but also one of the most widely resisted woman poets of the century.[30]

If, as a more detailed investigation reveals, some of the most influential canon-shapers—literary historians, anthologists, scholars, and critics—have welcomed the politics set forth in Rich's prose as a means to assess and label her poetry, then one must conclude that they have, to some extent, abdicated their role to

Rich, allowing her to prescribe the canonization and categorization of her own poetry. Rich's attempt to shape the way her career is perceived, as Charles Molesworth has described it, might thus be safely called successful.[31]

The representation of Rich in literary histories, to begin with one example, clearly reflects the impact of her prose on the canonization, categorization, and, by extension, the periodization of her poetry. An examination of literary histories of the 1970s and 1980s, however, does not yield the most valuable insights because the time lag involved in producing and publishing such studies automatically shifts their focus to Rich's early career, a time when her prose could not yet have been an influence.[32] One must instead look to more recent literary histories to obtain a sense of how the reception of Rich's poetry has been affected by the emergence of her prose. In *The Columbia History of American Poetry*, published in 1993, Gregory Orr stresses the importance of such "postconfessional" poems as "After Dark" and "From a Survivor" from the 1970s and adds: "Certainly her strongest and most sustained work in this [postconfessional] mode is in the 1978 book, *The Dream of a Common Language*." Orr sees Rich's poetry as "important expansions of autobiographical subject matter" because "her goal is never to arrive at the self but always to connect outward from self to other in a social and political context."[33]

Orr's observations are insightful but hardly original since they are clearly colored by Rich's insistence on the link between the public and the private throughout her entire prose oeuvre. More specifically, Orr's words on Rich's poetry closely echo the assertions she makes in "When We Dead Awaken." Being a good writer and an autonomous individual, Rich states in that essay, does not mean having a "devouring ego." "There must be ways . . . in which the energy of creation and the energy of relation can be united."[34] Of course one need not conclude that *The Columbia History of American Poetry* is more accurately a history of American prose, but it begins to become clear that Rich's essays play a significant role in determining which poetry is represented and how that poetry is read and understood.

Betsy Erkkila proves similarly reliant on Rich's essays in her 1992 book *The Wicked Sisters: Women Poets, Literary History, and Discord*. Erkkila believes that Rich's works of the 1970s "placed Rich and feminist poetry at the very center of the feminist movement in the United States." Establishing numerous parallels between the poet and such literary foremothers as Emily Dickinson, parallels which Rich herself has drawn in numerous essays, Erkkila concludes that Rich's verse represents a "poetics of female bonding."[35] Since it depends heavily on the information Rich provides in her famous essay "Vesuvius at Home: The

Power of Emily Dickinson" (1975), such a conclusion is necessarily unoriginal and points to the fact that in a literary history on women *poets*, it is above all Rich's *prose* that provides substance and support for Erkkila's argument. The two genres are treated as one, and we are not offered any perspectives on Rich's poetry that have not already been laid out previously in her prose.

Unlike Orr and Erkkila, Robert von Hallberg, in *The Cambridge History of American Literature* (1996), largely resists reading Rich's poetry through the lens of her prose, perhaps because he strongly prefers and concentrates on her early poetry, which was unaccompanied by prose. He sees Rich's verse since 1968 as marked by a systematic subordination of the private self to the "political-ideological work to be done." Von Hallberg is not opposed to "distinguished political poetry [which] challenges the political opinions of its audience," but he perceives Rich's post-1968 political verse as limited to what fits her personal ideological allegiances and consequently judges it as "hopelessly corny and self-satisfied" and, more important, as insufficiently intellectual and ethical. Despite his conclusion that there is good reason to doubt the value of Rich's politics to poetry, however, he cannot but acknowledge the power and influence of her political prose in general and on her poetry in particular. By employing the genre of "a poet's social criticism," he explains, Rich has successfully redirected her career, reaching large publics since 1975 and satisfying their "appetite for sages," for poet-critics who are vested with the authority of the poet but who are also willing to write in the more accessible genre of prose. Influential as it has become, her prose, then, plays no small part in promoting the tremendous sales not just of her prose but also her poetry, and it has contributed to securing Rich's position as, in von Hallberg's words, "the most popular political poet writing in America."[36]

Like literary histories, major anthologies are an important source for establishing how a writer has been and will be received. *The Norton Anthology of American Literature* is a good example because it has been a significant influence on the literary canon in the United States over a long period of time and because, as the longtime publisher of both Rich's poetry and her prose, Norton has, unlike some, made an effort to trace significant developments in Rich's life and career.[37] The number of poems included does not grow from the first edition (1979) to the fourth (1994), but several changes are made in the fifteen or so selections per edition, the most important being the addition of four of the *Twenty-One Love Poems* in the second edition (1985). The introduction to Rich in the first edition focuses on her "increasing commitment to feminism" and identifies her as "radical"; the next edition adds the dimension of Rich's protest against "American participation in the Vietnam war and our government's support of the corrupt South Vietnam regime."[38] In the third edition, Rich is seen in yet a different light; during the 1970s and 1980s, the editors argue, "the feminist movement made many poets aware of the need for a poetic language to explore the experiences of women hitherto silenced or unrepresented in literature. Among these was Adrienne Rich, whose significantly titled collections *Diving into the Wreck* and *The Dream of a Common Language* suggest the necessity to probe what lies beneath the surface and to forge a language of shared experience."[39] Clearly Rich has received frequent updating and special attention in *The Norton Anthology of American Literature*.

Nevertheless, the editors' attempt at doing justice to Rich's development has remained one-sided. Although they have frequently chosen not to collect any of Rich's prose,[40] they have just as frequently effaced the full breadth and implications of her poetry by writing introductions in which they allow striking fragments from her prose of the 1970s and 1980s to serve as labels for her poetry from all periods. In these introductions, topics such as feminism, lesbianism, Jewish identity, the fusion of the personal and political, and compulsory heterosexuality are evoked in conjunction with such prose works as *Of Woman Born*, *On Lies, Secrets, and Silence*, and *Blood, Bread, and Poetry*. But since no prose follows these introductions, they function as introductions to and descriptions of the succeeding poetry selections, negatively affecting the literary complexity of Rich's verse. Even in the most recent (fifth) edition of *The Norton Anthology of American Literature* (1998), which contains an impressive selection of poems from Rich's volume *An Atlas of the Difficult World* from 1991, the editors continue to introduce her poetry as a natural extension of her prose of the 1980s, writing:

> In other important later poems she has carried out a dialogue with lives similar to and different from her own, and in the generous and powerful title poem of her collection *An Atlas of the Difficult World*, she unites self-examination with an imaginative apprehension of lives separated from her own by history or by social circumstance. As she writes in *Blood, Bread, and Poetry*, in her development as a poet she came to feel "more and more urgently the dynamic between poetry as language and poetry as a kind of action, probing, burning, stripping, placing itself in dialogue with others."[41]

The editors of *The Norton Anthology* appear to be aware of the influence of Rich's essays since they acknowledge that "Rich's collections of prose ... provide an important context for her poems,"[42] but they may not realize that in the end, not they but Rich and her prose determine the canonization, categorization, and periodization of her poems.

Finally, the tendency to let Rich determine her own reception by using her prose as a gloss on her poetry was, consciously or unconsciously, also perpetuated by critics and scholars publishing in the 1970s and 1980s. In 1973, when Erica Jong wrote her essay "Visionary Anger," there were only a few essays by Rich that could have affected the tenet of Jong's commentary.[43] One was "The Anti-Feminist Woman" (1972), an essay from which Jong quotes and which she employs to make the point that the overarching theme in Rich's verse is the relationship between poetry and patriarchy. More important, however, Jong makes implicit but extensive use of "When We Dead Awaken." This essay makes much of female anger and warns us that unless man hands over some of his power to woman, he too will degenerate and perish. Rich closes her essay by writing, "The creative energy of patriarchy is fast running out; what remains is its self-generating energy for destruction. As women, we have our work cut out for us."[44] Jong borrows these ideas, along with some of Rich's terms, to draw her own conclusions about Rich's poems. She writes, "But her main point seems to be that after too many centuries of uncontested phallic power, we need to right the balance. Women may have to take over for a while to save men from their own self-destructiveness."[45] Jong's comments on several volumes of Rich's poetry thus all too neatly parallel Rich's essay and the politics she lays out in it.

In her influential article "Private Lives/Public Images," published in 1983, Marjorie Perloff is similarly affected by Rich's essays. The critic objects to a contradiction she sees between Rich's prose and poetry: although the poet calls for free play of the mind and for the imaginative transformation of reality in her essay "When We Dead Awaken," Perloff argues, she fails to pursue these goals ten years later in her book of poems *A Wild Patience Has Taken Me This Far* (1981). Instead, Perloff continues, Rich uses "a rhetoric indistinguishable from that of the Male Oppressor" and follows in the footsteps of Sylvia Plath by "having to write a poetry that would win the approval of the judges." Seemingly baffled, the critic asks, "How does it happen that a poet as committed to radical feminism as is Adrienne Rich should cast her poems, perhaps quite unwittingly, in the very masculine modes she professes to scorn?"[46] Perloff clearly recognizes a discrepancy between Rich's poetry and prose, yet she can hardly overcome her expectations of finding the one confirming and matching the other. Rich's prose has dictated the label "radical feminism," and if a collection of poetry does not suit this label, it is, to Perloff, necessarily flawed.

In 1984, Adrian Oktenberg voiced the necessity of reading *Twenty-One Love Poems* in the context of Rich's entire oeuvre, "both poetry and prose." The critic sees Rich's work as highly "self-referential" and bases her argument that in

Twenty-One Love Poems Rich "pronounces herself, more explicitly than ever, disloyal to [civilization]," on a number of essays collected in *On Lies, Secrets, and Silence*. Similarly, "the reference to midwives' hands, eschewing forceps in the delivery of a child [in the fifth of the *Love Poems*] finds an explanation in *Of Woman Born*," as does the mention of the Eleusinian cave in love poem VI. Moreover, the line "Every peak is a crater. This is the law of the volcanoes," of poem XI, directly recalls Rich's essay on Emily Dickinson, "Vesuvius at Home." According to Oktenberg, then, the essays inspire the poems; Rich's politics as manifested in her prose become the foundation of the poems. Although Oktenberg emphasizes that "Rich has never been a particularly personal, certainly not a confessional, poet" and that "it is important to recognize that the 'Twenty-One Love Poems' are not an anomaly in her work," she does believe that the personal experiences and convictions described in Rich's prose works significantly affect and shape individual poems.[47]

Given the tendency among critics and the makers of canons to allow Rich to canonize, categorize, and periodize herself, it was fairly predictable that they would immediately begin to see much of her poetry as pervaded by lesbian-separatist elements when she came out in 1976 and proceeded to call attention to and solidify that decision by writing a long, powerful essay titled "Compulsory Heterosexuality and Lesbian Existence" (1980).[48] That essay, more than any other piece of prose, enabled Rich to shape her critics' perception and categorization of her poetry.

It is in "Compulsory Heterosexuality" that Rich introduces her famous "lesbian continuum" along which we as women can choose to place ourselves, "whether we identify ourselves as lesbian or not."[49] Rich scholarship proceeded to generate a myriad of lesbian readings of her subsequent and previous poetry. One example is Joanne Feit Diehl's "'Cartographies of Silence': Rich's *Common Language* and the Woman Poet." In her discussion of *Twenty-One Love Poems*, Diehl argues, "What these poems seek to accomplish is to combine a self-consciousness associated with starting an alternative poetic ground based on a lesbian relationship, a world without men." Rich employs "exclusionary tactics," Diehl continues, which may "provide an untainted source of female power." In these and other poems, Rich "creates experiences which exclude men; she envisions a world of women, a kind of love in which men play no part."[50]

Diehl, along with numerous other critics, anthology editors, and literary historians, read the poems on Rich's terms, and when they didn't, Rich did not hesitate to criticize them publicly and correct the undesired response. Her reaction to heterosexual readers who enjoyed and identified with *Twenty-One*

Love Poems was the surprisingly intolerant gesture of publicly rectifying what she saw as a gross misappropriation of her work. In an interview with Elly Bulkin she thus stated and published: "I found myself angered, and when I asked myself why, I realized that it was anger at having my work essentially assimilated and stripped of its meaning, 'integrated' into heterosexual romance. That kind of 'acceptance' of the book seems to me a refusal of its deepest implications.... I see that as a denial, a kind of resistance, a refusal to read and hear what I've actually written, to acknowledge what I am."[51] Feeling wronged and misunderstood, Rich essentially told her readers to consider the identity politics laid out in her prose before they made any attempt at approaching her poetry. As the late Frank Kalstone recognized a long time ago, Rich makes "the explicit demand ... not only to understand but to be understood."[52]

As this incident and the body of scholarship—anthologies, literary histories, articles, reviews, books—show, Adrienne Rich's reception in the 1970s and 1980s relied perhaps not so much on periodization, categorization, and canonization imposed by the literary establishment as on the concepts and labels she provided in her prose writings. She shaped her career according to her own terms and was soon, as Zimmerman puts it, "in hot demand for words, both poetry and prose."[53] Many canon-formation theorists fail to acknowledge the possibility of such intervention on the part of the artist; they frequently tell us that periodization, categorization, and canonization are beyond the control of the artist and instead depend on the preferences, tastes, and evaluations of the readers. Both Jerome McGann and Frank Kermode believe that critics who are in a position to shape the canon found their judgments on more or less pure self-interest.[54] Some critics, such as James E. G. Zetzel, Winthrop Wetherbee, and Michael Fiend, do emphasize the living artist's contribution to forming canons, but the effect, they hold, is necessarily delayed. Rather than promoting themselves, living artists can only canonize artists from previous eras by letting their forerunners' work resonate throughout their own writing.[55] Neither model, however, fully describes Rich's prominence, for it is first and foremost Rich herself who, in the 1970s and 1980s, secured her position as a major poet in the canon of American literature.

The price Adrienne Rich pays for such self-canonization, categorization, and periodization is high. Criticism of her work is to this day suspiciously uniform and predictable; many readings of her poetry appear to be collective shortcuts through her strongly politicized prose of the 1970s and 1980s, ultimately compromising her art. Her prose of the previous two decades, however important to the women's movement and valuable in its own right, cannot do justice to the complexity and ever-changing nature of her poetic oeuvre and certainly fails to cast sufficient light and attention on her more recent as well as her earlier poetry. It seems that while Rich has clearly succeeded in canonizing her politics and prose, she has, in the process, run the risk of colonizing her poetry.

One can only speculate why Rich has chosen such a compromise. Perhaps it was never her intention to turn her political prose into a reader's manual for her poetry; after all, with the exception of one striking instance, she has rarely gone so far as to explicate specific poems in her prose.[56] Supposing that she did intend the results she has achieved, her reason is perhaps simply a desire for self-aggrandizement, for which various critics have faulted her.[57] Perhaps, as readers have often complained, she cannot reach beyond her didacticism and moralism, thus privileging politics and preaching over her art.[58]

I believe that Rich had different reasons when she first wrote and published her prose. She consciously manipulated the periodization, categorization, and canonization of her poetry by means of her essays because she much preferred the risk of limiting her poetry's scope *herself* to exposing it to the arbitrariness and restrictions of what she perceived and continues to perceive as a sexist and homophobic literary establishment. She resisted dependence on the self-interest of the canon makers whom McGann and Kermode evoke and refused to rely on the favor of future artists who, as Zetzel, Wetherbee, and Fiend have it, may or may not validate her feminist poetics in the near and far future. As she voices in her essay "Toward a More Feminist Criticism" (1981), she feels threatened by what she calls "dominant lit. crit." and the "academic/intellectual game" that is research. To Rich, the "so ultra-cool, so bright, so spruce and polished" language of much of what she reads, even within feminist criticism, "talk[s] through or over" the poet, never addresses her directly, and is not rooted in the "real world."[59] Deeply mistrustful of the shapers of canons, Rich decided to determine her position and period in literary history and to regulate the canonization and categorization of her poetry herself. Her prose of the previous two decades was instrumental in allowing her to do so, but the effect, I believe, has been limiting and all too lasting.

Rich's poetry, then—not the early pieces, as so many have argued, but her more mature poems—can, at least in some sense, be seen as a continuation of the modernist endeavor: she, like Pound and Eliot, is her own greatest promoter; her prose, like theirs, incites readers to grapple with her poetry, to go about it immediately, and to do so in a certain way—her way.

NOTES

1. W. H. Auden, "Foreword to *A Change of World*," rpt. in *Reading Adrienne Rich: Reviews and Re-Visions*, ed. Jane Roberta Cooper (Ann Arbor: University of Michigan Press, 1984), 211.

2. Wendy Martin, "From Patriarchy to Female Principle: A Chronological Reading of Adrienne Rich's Poems," in *Adrienne Rich's Poetry, a Norton Critical Edition: Texts of the Poems, the Poet on Her Work, Reviews and Criticism*, ed. Barbara Charlesworth Gelpi and Albert Gelpi (New York: Norton, 1975), 175–89; Gale Flynn, "The Radicalization of Adrienne Rich," *Hollins Critic* 11 (October 1974): 1–15; Susan Morris, "The Moment of Change," special section on Adrienne Rich in *Anonymous: A Journal for the Woman Writer* (Fresno, Calif.) 2 (1975): 5–9; Jane Vanderbosch, "Beginning Again," in *Reading Adrienne Rich*, ed. Cooper, 111–39.

3. Craig Werner, *Adrienne Rich: The Poet and Her Critics* (Chicago: American Library Association, 1988), 1.

4. Adrienne Rich, *Poems, Selected and New, 1950–1974* (New York: Norton, 1975), xv; Adrienne Rich, *Blood, Bread, and Poetry: Selected Prose, 1979–1985* (New York: Norton, 1986), xii, 211.

5. Rich, *Blood, Bread, and Poetry*, 180.

6. Cary Nelson, *Our First Last Poets: Vision and History in Contemporary American Poetry* (Urbana: University of Illinois Press, 1981), 150.

7. Rich, *Blood, Bread, and Poetry*, 184.

8. Willard Spiegelman, *The Didactic Muse: Scenes of Instruction in Contemporary American Poetry* (Princeton: Princeton University Press, 1989), 147.

9. Rich, *Necessities of Life, Poems, 1962–1965* (New York: Norton, 1966), *Leaflets* (New York: Norton, 1969), and, above all, *Snapshots of a Daughter-in-Law* (New York: Norton, 1963) received a great deal of response several years after their publication. *Snapshots of a Daughter-in-Law* is now often considered Rich's first transitional work and is routinely privileged as such in overviews of Rich's oeuvre.

10. *Granger's Index to Poetry* (Supplement to the 4th ed., ed. Raymond J. Dixon; 5th ed. rev., ed. William F. Bernhardt; supplement to the 5th ed., eds. William F. Bernhardt and Kathryn W. Sewny; 6th ed. rev., ed. William James Smith [New York: Columbia University Press, 1957, 1962, 1967, 1973]) and Kirby Congdon's *Contemporary Poets in American Anthologies, 1960–1977* (Metuchen, N.J.: Scarecrow Press, 1978) indicate that in the 1950s, Rich's poetry was anthologized in three different collections of poetry. "For the Conjunction of Two Planets" appeared in *Imagination's Other Place: Poems of Science and Mathematics*, comp. Helen Plotz (New York: Thomas Y. Crowell, 1955); "New Year's Eve in Troy" was included in *Untune the Sky: Poems of Music and Dance*, comp. Helen Plotz (New York: Thomas Y. Crowell, 1957); "At a Bach Concert," "Orient Wheat," "Versailles," "The Celebration in the Plaza," "Bears," "Epilogue for a Masque of Purcell," "Living in Sin," "A Walk by the Charles," and "Love in the Museum" were published in *New Poets of England and America*, ed. Donald Hall, Robert Pack, and Louis Simpson (New York: Meridian Books, 1957). In the 1960s, Rich's work was represented in eleven anthologies. A few examples: *New Poets of England and America: Second Selection*, ed. Donald Hall and Robert Pack (Cleveland: World, 1962) contains seven of Rich's poems; *A Controversy of Poets: An Anthology of Contemporary American Poetry*, ed. Paris Leary and Robert Kelly (New York: Doubleday, 1965), includes six; and *Poems*

of Our Moment, ed. John Hollander (New York: Pegasus, 1968), anthologizes ten poems. According to the above index sources, a given poem was generally anthologized once between 1950 and 1969, and very few poems appeared more than three times. Altogether, more than fifty different poems were collected in American anthologies over this twenty-year span.

11. For what I have found to be an exhaustive list of American reviews from 1950 to 1981, see *Reading Adrienne Rich*, ed. Cooper. My count disregards the British book reviews Cooper lists. The awards include the Yale Younger Poets Award (1951), two Guggenheim Fellowships (1952–53 and 1961–62), the Ridgely Torrence Memorial Award (1955), the National Institute of Arts and Letters Award for Poetry (1960), a Bollingen Foundation grant (1962), an Amy Lowell traveling fellowship (1962–63), and the Eunice Tietjens Memorial Prize of *Poetry* magazine (1968). The honorary doctorate was awarded by Wheaton College (1969). According to Cooper, Rich received only two reference guide entries, one in *The Oxford Companion to American Literature*, 4th ed., ed. James D. Hart (New York: Oxford University Press, 1965) and one in *Modern American Literature: A Library of Literary Criticism*, 4th ed., ed. Dorothy Nyren Curley, Maurice Kramer, and Elaine Fialka Kramer (New York: Frederick Ungar, 1969). The former contains a forty-four-word biographical entry on Rich; the latter presents extracts of seven book reviews. The article is Richard Howard's "Adrienne Rich: 'What Lends Us Anchor But the Mutable?'" in his *Alone with America: Essays on the Art of Poetry in the United States Since 1950* (New York: Atheneum, 1969), 423–41.

12. Randall Jarrell, review of *The Diamond Cutters*, by Adrienne Rich, *Yale Review* 46 (Autumn 1956): 100–103; Philip Booth, "Rethinking the World," *Christian Science Monitor*, January 3, 1963, 15; John Ashbery, "Tradition and Talent," *New York Herald Tribune Book Week*, September 4, 1966, 2.

13. Critics reacted harshly to *Snapshots of a Daughter-in-Law*. That reaction, however, does not seem to have become apparent until a good decade after its publication in 1963. The American reviews Rich received for *Snapshots of a Daughter-in-Law* in the 1960s do not generally reflect strong dissatisfaction or extraordinary praise.

14. Richard Tillinghast, review of *Necessities of Life*, by Adrienne Rich, *Southern Review* 5 (April 1969): 583.

15. The count includes her two volumes of selected poetry (*Poems, Selected and New, 1950–1974* [New York: Norton, 1975]; *The Fact of a Doorframe, Poems Selected and New* [New York: Norton, 1984]) and her two chapbooks (*Twenty-One Love Poems* [Emeryville, Calif., 1976]; *Sources* [Woodside, Calif.: Heyeck Press, 1983]).

16. In my count of reviews, I again rely on Cooper as well as on *The Index to Book Reviews and Scholarly Journals* (1980–90 cumulations) and the *Book Review Digest* (1980–90).

17. The figures are based on *Granger's Index to Poetry*, 7th ed., ed. William James Smith and William F. Bernhardt; 8th ed. rev., ed. William F. Bernhardt (New York: Columbia University Press, 1982, 1986), on *The Columbia Granger's Index to Poetry*, 9th ed. rev., ed. Edith P. Hazen and Deborah J. Fryer; 10th ed. rev., ed. Edith P. Hazen (New

York: Columbia University Press, 1990, 1994), on Congdon's *Contemporary Poets in American Anthologies*, and on the *Poetry Index Annual*, 1982–91, prepared by the Editorial Board, Granger Book Co., (Great Neck, N.Y.: Poetry Index Press, 1983–91]). There were, of course, many more anthologies published during this twenty-year span which include Rich's poetry, and the figures give only a tentative idea.

18. *The American Tradition in Literature*, edited by Sculley Bradley et al., included four of Rich's poems in the third regular edition, vol. 2 (New York: Grosset & Dunlap, 1967) and three in the shorter 1967 edition. In the sixth editions (1985), regular (vol. 2) and shorter, a total of six poems appeared. The *Anthology of American Literature: Vol. 2, Realism to the Present*, ed. George L. McMichael et al. (New York: Macmillan), collected six poems in 1974, ten in 1980, and eleven in 1989. The *Concise Anthology of American Literature*, also ed. McMichael et al., included four in 1974 and five in 1985. The *Norton Anthology of American Literature*, ed. Nina Baym et al., selected thirteen poems in the 1979 regular edition (vol. 2), twenty in 1985, and fifteen in 1989. (The shorter editions contained eight poems in 1980, eleven in 1986, and eleven in 1989. The *Norton Anthology of Poetry* selected six poems for the first edition (ed. Arthur M. Eastman et al., 1970), none for the second (ed. Alexander W. Allison et al., 1975), and eleven for the third (ed. Alexander W. Allison et al., 1983). The shorter editions included six poems in 1970 (1st ed.), two in 1975 (2d ed.), and seven in 1983 (3d ed.).

19. While no poems by Rich can be found in first, second, and third editions of *Understanding Poetry*, "Living in Sin" appears in the first edition of the 1970s (4th ed. [New York: Holt, Rinehart and Winston, 1976]). X. J. Kennedy includes "The Insusceptibles" in the 1976 edition of *Literature: An Introduction to Fiction, Poetry, and Drama* (Boston: Little, Brown). "Diving into the Wreck" appears in the 1979 (2d) edition, "Aunt Jennifer's Tigers" and "Diving into the Wreck" in the 1983 (3d) edition, and "Aunt Jennifer's Tigers," "Diving into the Wreck," and "Song" in the 1987 (4th) edition.

20. The estimate of articles is largely based on the MLA bibliography and gives only a very tentative idea of how many American publications are available. The books are *Adrienne Rich's Poetry*, ed. Gelpi and Gelpi, *Reading Adrienne Rich*, ed. Cooper, Myriam Díaz-Diocaretz's *Translating Poetic Discourse: Questions on Feminist Strategies in Adrienne Rich* (Amsterdam: John Benjamins, 1985), Claire Keyes's *The Aesthetics of Power: The Poetry of Adrienne Rich* (Athens: University of Georgia Press, 1986), and Craig Werner's *Adrienne Rich*. In the 1970s and 1980s the critics David Kalstone, *Five Temperaments: Elizabeth Bishop, Robert Lowell, James Merrill, Adrienne Rich, and John Ashbery* (New York: Oxford University Press, 1977); Wendy Martin, *An American Triptych: Anne Bradstreet, Emily Dickinson, Adrienne Rich* (Chapel Hill: University of North Carolina Press, 1984); and Paula Bennett, *My Life a Loaded Gun: Female Creativity and Feminist Poetics* (Boston: Beacon Press, 1986), also wrote substantial though not book-length studies of Rich's poetry.

21. In 1993, Gelpi and Gelpi even edited a second *Norton Critical Edition of Adrienne Rich's Poetry and Prose* (New York: Norton).

22. Rich rejected the National Book Award as an individual but consented to accept

it jointly with the other nominees, Audre Lorde and Alice Walker, in the name of all women.

23. The honorary doctorates were awarded by Smith College (1979), the College of Wooster, Ohio (1987), and Brandeis University (1987).

24. "Adrienne Rich: The Poetics of Change," in *Adrienne Rich's Poetry*, ed. Gelpi and Gelpi, 148.

25. Margaret Atwood, "Adrienne Rich: 'Of Woman Born,'" rpt. in her *Second Words: Selected Critical Prose* (Toronto: House of Anansi Press, 1982), 254.

26. Bennett, *My Life*, 9.

27. Robert Boyers, "On Adrienne Rich: Intelligence and Will," rpt. in *Adrienne Rich's Poetry*, ed. Gelpi and Gelpi, 157, 156, 160.

28. Carol Muske, "Backward into the Future," *Parnassus: Poetry in Review* 7 (Spring–Summer 1979): 84–85; Helen Vendler, "All Too Real," *New York Review of Books*, December 17, 1981, 33.

29. Alicia Ostriker, *Writing Like a Woman* (Ann Arbor: University of Michigan Press, 1983), 121.

30. Spiegelman, *Didactic Muse*, 147; Bonnie Zimmerman, "Disobedient Daughter," *Women's Review of Books* 4 (April 1987): 5.

31. Charles Molesworth, "'Backward-spreading brightness': Career's End in Contemporary American Poetry," *LIT* 1 (March 1990): 186.

32. David Perkins's study *A History of Modern Poetry: Modernism and After* (Cambridge, Mass.: Belknap Press of Harvard University Press, 1987), serves as an example. Perkins includes Rich's poetry in his section titled "Postmodernism." By "postmodernism," Perkins does not, however, mean the movement characterized by such groundbreaking postmodernist writings as Roland Barthes's *S/Z* (1970) and Jacques Derrida's *Glas* (1974), along with their translations into English in subsequent years. Perkins instead refers to the confessional poetry of the 1960s. Accordingly, he calls Rich a "confessional" poet and groups her together with Sylvia Plath and Anne Sexton in a single chapter. Perkins seems uninfluenced by Rich's prose, and it seems likely that he terminated and published his study before he came into contact with it.

33. Gregory Orr, *The Columbia History of American Poetry*, ed. Jay Parini (New York: Columbia University Press, 1993), 661–62.

34. Adrienne Rich, *On Lies, Secrets, and Silence, Selected Prose, 1966–1978* (New York: Norton, 1979), 43.

35. Betsy Erkkila, *The Wicked Sisters: Women Poets, Literary History, and Discord* (New York: Oxford University Press, 1992), 169, 174.

36. Robert von Hallberg, *The Cambridge History of American Literature: Vol. 8, Poetry and Criticism, 1940–1995*, ed. Sacvan Bercovitch (Cambridge: Cambridge University Press, 1996), 26, 37–38, 201–2, 33.

37. Anthologists who fail to update, expand, and modify their entries and commentaries produce collections which are more or less useless for any examination of a writer's reception over time. The McMichael *Anthology of American Literature*, for instance,

appears particularly uncommitted to tracing developments in Rich's life and work. In the first edition (1974), the editors do not mention the existence of any prose writings in their introduction. The second edition (1980) changes almost nothing except for a brief mention of her essay volume *On Lies, Secrets, and Silence*. Here, the editors completely disregard her book of prose *Of Woman Born* (1976), *Twenty-One Love Poems* (1976), and her arguably most famous collection of poetry, *The Dream of a Common Language* (1978). The third edition (1985) has nothing more to say, continues to neglect the prose, and additionally fails to mention her long poem *Sources* (1983) and *The Fact of a Doorframe: Poems Selected and New, 1950–1984* (1984). In 1989, the fourth edition was issued, and the editors content themselves with adding a reference to *The Fact of a Doorframe*.

It is forgivable that the editors mistake the title of her 1984 collection for *"The Fact of a Door,"* but that it should take them till the fifth edition in 1993 to mention the word "feminist" in connection with Rich (the term "lesbian" is not to be found in any edition up to that point) and that their vague phrasing intended to explain her political commitment should remain virtually unchanged throughout fifteen years makes the McMichael anthology untrustworthy, at least as far as the evaluation of Rich's poetry in the first four editions is concerned. Whatever the reasons, George McMichael and his coeditors do not do justice to Rich's career.

38. *Norton Anthology*, ed. Baym et al. (1979), 2255–56; *Norton Anthology*, ed. Baym et al. (1985), 2250.

39. *Norton Anthology*, ed. Baym et al. (1989), 2377.

40. Both the 1985 and 1996 editions of *The Norton Anthology of Literature by Women: The Traditions in English*, ed. Sandra H. Gilbert and Susan Gubar (New York: Norton) do contain one essay by Rich.

41. *Norton Anthology*, ed. Baym et. al. (1998), 2712.

42. *Norton Anthology*, ed. Baym et al. (1989), 2691–92, ibid. (1994), 2703, ibid. (1998), 2713.

43. Erica Jong, "Visionary Anger," rpt. in *Adrienne Rich's Poetry*, ed. Gelpi and Gelpi, 171–74.

44. Rich, *On Lies, Secrets, and Silence*, 49.

45. Jong, "Visionary Anger," 172.

46. Marjorie Perloff, "Private Lives/Public Images," *Michigan Quarterly Review* 22 (Winter 1983): 132, 136.

47. Adrian Oktenberg, "'Disloyal to Civilization': The *Twenty-One Love Poems* of Adrienne Rich," in *Reading Adrienne Rich*, ed. Cooper, 83, 72.

48. Although Rich felt the necessity to defend herself against being labeled "lesbian separatist," her objections, for a long time, clearly centered around the word choice and did not regard the practical and emotional implications of lesbian separatism. In her "Foreword" to *Blood, Bread, and Poetry*, she writes, "At no time have I ever defined myself as, or considered myself, a lesbian separatist. I have worked with self-defined separatists and have recognized the importance of separatism as grounding and strategy. I have opposed it as a pressure to conformity and where it seemed to derive from biological

determinism. The necessity for autonomous women's groups still seems obvious to me" (viii, n. 1)

49. Ibid., 54.

50. Joanne Feit Diehl, "'Cartographies of Silence': Rich's *Common Language* and the Woman Poet," in *Reading Adrienne Rich*, ed. Cooper, 91–110, 99, 100, 101, 105.

51. Rich, "An Interview with Adrienne Rich," by Elly Bulkin, part 2, *Conditions* 2 (1977): 58.

52. Kalstone, *Five Temperaments*, 142.

53. Zimmerman, "Disobedient Daughter," 5.

54. See Jerome McGann's "The Meaning of The Ancient Mariner," *Critical Inquiry* 8 (1981): 35–67 and Frank Kermode's "Institutional Control of Interpretation," *Salmagundi* 43 (1979): 72–86. Both essays were called to my attention by Charles Altieri in his influential and often reprinted essay "An Idea and Ideal of Literary Canon," *Canons and Consequences: Reflections on the Ethical Force of Imaginative Ideals* (Evanston: Northwestern University Press, 1990), 21–47.

55. James E. G. Zetzel, "Re-creating the Canon: Augustan Poetry and the Alexandrian Past," 107–29; Winthrop Wetherbee, "*Poeta che mi guidi*: Dante, Lucan, and Virgil," 131–48; Michael Fiend, "Painting Memories: On the Containment of the Past in Baudelaire and Manet," 227–59, all in *Canons*, ed. Robert von Hallberg (1983; rpt. Chicago: University of Chicago Press, 1984).

56. In her essay "The Genesis of 'Yom Kippur 1984'" (1987), Rich explicated her poem in some detail. See *Adrienne Rich's Poetry and Prose*, ed. Gelpi and Gelpi (1993), 252–58.

57. For examples, see Muske's essay "Backward into the Future" and von Hallberg's section on Rich in *The Cambridge History of American Literature*.

58. This is a recurrent point of criticism in Helen Vendler's reviews of Rich's poetry.

59. Rich, *Blood, Bread, and Poetry*, 99, 92, 93; Rich, "An Interview with Adrienne Rich," by Elly Bulkin, 61.

CONTRIBUTORS

Jacqueline Vaught Brogan is a professor of English and American literature at the University of Notre Dame. Her publications include *Stevens and Simile: A Theory of Language; Part of the Climate: American Cubist Poetry;* and *Women Poets of the Americas: Toward a Pan-Hellenic Gathering,* coedited with Cordelia Candelaria.

Margaret Dickie was Helen S. Lanier Distinguished Professor of English at the University of Georgia until her death in January 1999. Her most recent book is *Stein, Bishop, and Rich: Lyrics of Love, War, and Place* (1997). She has written several books on American poetry, including *Lyric Contingencies: Emily Dickinson and Wallace Stevens* (1991) and *On the Modernist Long Poem* (1987).

Josephine Donovan is a professor of English at the University of Maine. Her publications include *Sarah Orne Jewett; New England Local Color Literature: A Women's Tradition;* and *Feminist Theory: The Intellectual Traditions of American Literature.* Her most recent work is a book on early modern women writers, *Women and the Rise of the Novel, 1405–1726* (1998).

Shirley Geok-lin Lim, professor of English and Women's Studies at the University of California, Santa Barbara, and currently Chair Professor of English at the University of Hong Kong, has published four books of poetry, three collections of stories, and two critical books. She received the Commonwealth Poetry Prize for her first book of poems, *Crossing the Peninsula* (1980), and the American Book Award for her memoir, *Among the White Moon Faces* (1996). *The Forbidden Stitch: An Asian American Women's Anthology,* which she coedited, received the American Book Award in 1990. She is currently writing a study of Asian American literature.

Sylvia Henneberg is an assistant professor in American literature at Morehead State University. She specializes in poetry and has published on such writers as Emily Dickinson, Adrienne Rich, and Judy Grahn.

Mary Loeffelholz is a member of the English Department at Northeastern University, the author of *Dickinson and the Boundaries of Feminist Theory* (1991), and the editor of *Studies in American Fiction.*

Crystal J. Lucky teaches in the English Department at Villanova University. She has published essays on Harlem Renaissance writers and on Robert Graves in *Focus on Robert Graves and His Contemporaries.*

Susan McCabe is an assistant professor in modern and contemporary American poetry at the University of Southern California at Los Angeles. Her book *Elizabeth Bishop: Her Poetics of Loss* appeared in 1994. She has published essays in *Antioch Review* and *Denver Quarterly*, and has forthcoming work in the *Wallace Stevens Journal* and in a collection of essays, *Women Poets of the Americas*. Her poems have appeared in *Colorado Review*, *Volt*, and *Hayden's Ferry Review*.

Amelia María de la Luz Montes teaches nineteenth-century American literature and Chicana/o literature in the Departments of Chicano Studies and Women's Studies at the University of California, Santa Barbara. Among her publications are "'Es Necesario Mirar Bien': The Letters of María Amparo Ruiz de Burton" in *Recovering the U.S. Hispanic Literary Heritage*, vol. 3, and "Theory by Any Other Name Is Still Theory" in *California English*.

Carla L. Peterson is a professor in the Department of English and the Comparative Literature Program at the University of Maryland and affiliate faculty of both the Women's Studies and the American Studies Departments. Her major publications include *"Doers of the Word": African-American Women Speakers and Writers in the North (1830–1880)* (1995) and essays in *Feminist Studies*; *Criticism and the Color Line: Race and Revisionism in American Literary Studies*, ed. Harry Wonham (1996); *Listening to Silences: New Essays in Feminist Criticism*, ed. Shelley Fisher Fishkin and Elaine Hedges (1994); and *Famous Last Words: Women Against Novelistic Endings*, ed. Alison Booth (1993).

Carol J. Singley is associate professor of English at Rutgers University, Camden. She is the author of *Edith Wharton: Matters of Mind and Spirit* (1995) and the coeditor of two collections of essays: *Anxious Power: Reading, Writing, and Ambivalence in Narrative by Women* (1993) and *The Calvinist Roots of the Modern Era* (1997). She has published articles on nineteenth-century American writers, feminist theory, and rhetoric. She is presently writing a book on representations of adoption in American literature and culture.

Teresa A. Toulouse is an associate professor of English at Tulane University. Her publications include *The Art of Prophesying: New England Sermons and the Shaping of Belief* (1987); *The Complete Sermons of R. W. Emerson*, vol. 2, coedited with Andrew Delbanco (1990); and articles in *American Literature*, *Early American Literature*, and *Studies in Puritan Spirituality*.

Joyce W. Warren is a member of the English Department at Queens College, CUNY. Her publications include *The American Narcissus: Individualism and Women in Nineteenth-Century American Fiction* (1984); *Fanny Fern: An Independent Woman* (1992); *Ruth Hall and Other Writings* by Fanny Fern, edited (1986); and *The (Other) American Traditions: Nineteenth-Century Women Writers*, edited (1993). She is currently working on a book on women and economics, *Women, Money, and the Law: Nineteenth-Century Gender Identities in American Literature and Culture*.

INDEX

abolition and abolitionists, 14, 15, 47, 50, 54
Absalom, Absalom! 259
Adam Bede, 238
Adams, Henry, 186
"After Dark," 271
Age of Innocence, The, 226, 227, 233, 235–36, 238, 242
"Alcedama Sparks," 29
Alcott, Louisa May, 39, 196, 229
Althusser, Louis, 20
"American Literature," 172
American Novel and Its Tradition, The, 7, 22
American Renaissance, ix, xvii, 27, 36, 37, 39, 159, 161, 162, 164, 165, 169, 172, 173, 178, 199
American Renaissance, The, 186
American Tragedy, An, 8
Ammons, Elizabeth, 22
Anderson, Benedict, 41
Anderson, Jervis, 97
Anderson, Sherwood, 260
"Angel at the Grave, The," 231, 232, 237
"Anticipation," 70
"Anti-Feminist Woman, The," 274
Antin, Mary, 130
Anzaldua, Gloria, 132, 222–23
Apollinaire, Guillaume, 263
"April Showers," 244
Apthorp, Elaine Sargent, 23
Aristotle, 29, 233
Armstrong, Nancy, 142, 149–55, 156, 158
Arthur, T. S., 48
Ashbery, John, 269
At Home and Abroad, 166
Atkin, David, 259
Atlas of the Difficult World, An, 273
Atwood, Margaret, 270
Auden, W. H., 267, 268
Autobiography of Alice B. Toklas, The, 260, 261, 263
Autumn Love Cycle, An, 99

Backward Glance, A, 233
Baker, Houston, 108
Bakhtin, Mikhail, xi, 211, 224
Balzac, Honoré de, 19, 237, 241
Bambara, Toni Cade, 93
Bancroft, Hubert H., 213, 218, 219, 221–22
Baraka, Amiri Imamu, 108
"Bargain of 1877," 46
Barthes, Roland, 281
"Basket, The," 69–70
"Bath," 69, 73
Battle-Pieces and Aspects of the War, 198
Baudelaire, Pierre Charles, 66, 69, 70, 83
Baym, Nina, xxi, 22, 28, 121, 182
Beginnings of Critical Realism in America, 1860–1920, The, 7
Behind the Scenes, 204
Bell, Elise, 22
Bell, Michael Davitt, 18–19
Bennett, Gwendolyn, 97
Bennett, Paula, 270
Benstock, Shari, 87, 245, 246
Berssenbrugge, Mei, 110
"Bettine Brentano and Her Friend Gunderode," xx, 177, 178
Beyond Manzanar, 117
Bishop, Elizabeth, 248
Black Codes, 40
Black Power in America, 97
Blauner, Robert, 122
Blood, Bread, and Poetry, 267, 268, 273, 282
Bloom, Harold, 88, 108, 200
Bloomer, Amelia, 168
Bogan, Louise, 194
Booth, Philip, 269
Booth, Wayne, 227
Borderlands/La Frontera, 132, 223
Boumelha, Penny, 20
Bourget, Paul, 245
Boyers, Robert, 270
Braque, Georges, 254

Bread Givers, 130
Breitwieser, Mitchell, 142–46, 148, 150, 152, 156
Brodhead, Richard, 39, 52
Brogan, Jacqueline, xviii
Brooks, Cleanth, 269
Brooks, Gwendolyn, 93
Brooks, Van Wyck, 7
Brown, Sterling, 108
Brown, William Wells, 42
Bryher (Annie Winifred Ellerman), 67, 82
Buell, Lawrence, 27, 37, 113, 172–73, 178
Bulkin, Elly, 276
Bunyan, John, 220
Burke, Carolyn, 265
Burton, Henry Stanton, 218–19
Butler, Johnnella, 107
Butler, Judith, xxii, 6
Byron, Lord (George Gordon), 65

Cable, George Washington, 56
Cage, John, 259
Calvinism, 32, 238
Camera Work, 251, 254, 257, 259, 262
Cane, 249, 259
canon, American literary, ix, xiii, xviii, 5, 7, 21, 26, 27, 28, 29, 36, 63, 64, 85, 88, 92, 93, 94, 103, 108, 109, 121, 122, 123, 138, 162, 173, 178, 181, 184, 202, 203, 214, 216, 268, 270, 271, 272, 273, 276, 277
"Captured Goddess, The," 78, 80
Carafiol, Peter, 161, 162, 179–80
Carby, Hazel, 25, 108
Carlyle, Thomas, 198, 207
Carter, Everett, 21
Cary, Alice, 9
Castañeda, Antonia I., 219
Cather, Willa, 5, 29
Cezanne, Paul, 254, 264
Cha, Theresa Hak-Kyung, 120
Chan, Jeffrey Paul, 122
Chang, Diana, 123
Change of World, A, 267, 269
Chanler, Daisy, 235
Chase, Richard, 7, 22
Chateaubriand, François René de, 11
Chaucer, Geoffrey, 3
Chesnutt, Charles, 39–40, 42, 59
Cheung, King-Kok, 110, 126
Chevigny, Bell Gale, 159–60, 179, 183
Child, Lydia Maria, 194, 197, 198

Chin, Frank, 110, 111, 112, 122, 130
China Men, 109, 125
Christian, Barbara, 24, 127
"Christmas Jenny," 29
Cinco de Mayo, 206
Civil War (American), xvii, 3, 41, 42, 45, 47, 50, 51, 53, 162, 185, 186, 189, 190, 193, 194, 195, 196, 198, 199, 202, 209, 218, 223
Cixous, Hélène, xxi
"Clary's Trial," 29
class, social, x, xii, xv, xvii, xviii, 4, 6, 9, 13, 14, 16, 17, 18, 27, 31, 43, 52, 53, 57, 58, 107, 113, 114–15, 116, 121, 123, 126, 127, 160, 173, 177, 215, 228, 240
Clay Walls, 115–16, 117, 119
Clifford, James, xxiii
Coffin Tree, 125
Colacurcio, Michael, 159, 161
Coleman, Anita Scott, 94, 100–101, 103
Coleridge, Samuel Taylor, 50
"*Common Language* and the Woman Poet," 275
Communism, xi
"Composition as Explanation," 257, 258, 260, 266
"Compulsory Heterosexuality and Lesbian Existence," 268, 275
Cook, Blanche Wiesen, 86–87
Cooke, Rose Terry, xv, 6, 9, 26, 29, 32–34, 52
Copway, George (Ojibwa), 165
Council of Jamnia, 27–28
Country of the Pointed Firs, 29
"Courting of Sister Wisby, The," 29
Cowdery, Mae V., 103
Crane, Stephen, 3, 8, 23, 210, 236
Crèvecoeur, J. Hector St. John de, 222
Crossings, 125
cubism, xviii, 248–66
Cummings, E. E., 259
Custom of the Country, The, 232

Dante, 32
Darwin, Charles, 226, 227, 230, 236, 237
Davidson, Winifred, 215
Davis, Rebecca Harding, 6, 9, 205, 208–9
Dearborn, Mary V., 130
"Decade," 71
deconstruction theory, xi, xii, 20, 257, 264
DeKoven, Marianne, 249, 258, 262, 263
Del Castillo, Adelaida, 213
democracy, xi, xx, 40, 43, 257

INDEX : **289**

Demos, John, 149
Derounian, Kathryn Zabelle, 153
Derrida, Jacques, xx, 20, 281
Descent of Man, The, 238
Dial, The, 165
"Dialogue, A," xx, 177, 178
Dickens, Charles, 32, 207
Dickie, Margaret, xvii, xx, 85, 249, 261, 262, 264
Dickinson, Blanche Taylor, 103
Dickinson, Emily, ix–x, xvii, 162, 171, 177, 182, 185–201, 241, 271, 275
Dictee, 120
Diehl, Joanne Feit, 275
"Dinner-Party, The," 89
Divakaruni, Chitra, 122
Diving into the Wreck, 269, 273
Dix, Dorothea, 168
Dogeaters, 120
Dome of Many-Coloured Glass, A, 72
Donovan, Josephine, xv
Doolittle, Hilda. See H. D.
Douglas, Ann, 159, 184
Douglass, Frederick, 24, 43, 51, 165, 187
Dream of a Common Language, The, 269, 271, 273
Dreiser, Theodore, 3, 8, 23, 208, 211, 212, 236
Dubliners, 259
Dubnick, Randa, 262
Du Bois, W. E. B., 59, 95
Dumas, Alexandre, 206, 221
DuPlessis, Rachel Blau, 259
Duse, Eleanor, 67
Dydo, Ulla E., 263, 264

écriture féminine, xii, 119
"Editha," 229
Edwards, Jonathan, 141
Eggleston, George Cary, 56
Eliot, George, 237, 238
Eliot, T. S., xx, 32, 43, 65, 66, 67, 70, 72, 77, 83, 239, 249, 250, 277
Ellison, Julie, 162, 173, 174, 175, 176, 178
Ellmann, Mary, xxi
Ellmann, Richard, 87–88, 269
Ellrodt, Robert, xiv
Emerson, Ralph Waldo, ix, 12, 159, 164, 165, 168, 172, 174, 175, 189, 194, 198, 207, 209, 216
"Emp Lace," 82
Empson, William, 233

Erckmann-Chatrian, Thérèse, 50
Erkkila, Betsy, 185, 188, 200, 271–72
Ethan Frome, 226, 232, 233, 234–35, 239
ethnicity, x, xvi, xvii, 52, 107, 108, 109, 110, 112, 113, 114, 115, 116, 117, 118, 119, 121, 122, 123, 124, 126, 129, 136, 177, 180
"Eurydice," 75
Exclusion Acts, 123, 128
Eysteinsson, Astradur, 87

"Fancy Etchings," 43
Farewell to Manzanar, 115, 117, 119, 125, 130
Farnham, Thomas Jefferson, 213
fascism, xi
Faulkner, William, 259
Fauset, Jessie Redmon, 94, 95, 97
Feidelson, Charles, Jr., 87–88
Felski, Rita, 85–86
Fern, Fanny, xv, 6, 9, 12–14, 23–24, 166
Fetterley, Judith, xxi
Fields, James T., 6, 51, 54
Fiend, Michael, 276, 277
Fifth Chinese Daughter, 115, 117
Finnegan's Wake, 259
Fitzgerald, F. Scott, 189, 239
Fitzhugh, George, 15
Fitzpatrick, Tara, 142, 146–48, 151, 152, 156
Flaubert, Gustave, 22
"Flight of Betsey Lane, The," 29
Foner, Eric, 40
Foote, Shelby, 30, 36
Ford, Henri, 259
"Foreigner, The," 29
Foreman, P. Gabrielle, 25
Forest Life, 9, 10, 11
Forten, Charlotte, xv–xvi, 40–42, 50–59
For Whom the Bell Tolls, 260, 266
Foucault, Michel, xi, xx, 20, 152, 155, 171, 182, 240
Fraser, Kathleen, 248, 260
Freedmen's Bureau, 40
"Freedom Wheeler's Controversy with Providence," 29, 32–34
Freeman, Mary E. Wilkins, xv, 19, 26, 35–36, 229
Freud, Sigmund, xii
Friedman, Ellen, 248, 261
Friedman, Susan, 67, 72, 90
"Friends," 244
"From a Survivor," 271
Frontiers of Love, The, 123

Frost, Robert, 239
Fruit of the Tree, The, 238
Frye, Joanne S., 247
Fuchs, Miriam, 249, 261
Fuller, Margaret, xvii, xix, xx, 159–84, 186, 216

Gadamer, Hans-Georg, xxii–xxiii
"Garden," 74
"Garden by Moonlight, The," 78
Garden of Eden, The, 260
Garrison, William Lloyd, 54, 57
Garvey, Marcus, 96–97
Garvey and Garveyism, 97
Gates, Henry Louis, Jr., 24, 108, 212
"Geisha, the Good Wife, and Me, The," 117
Gelpi, Albert, 270
gender, x, xii, xv, xvi, xvii, xviii, xxii, 3, 4, 6, 7, 8, 9, 11, 13, 14, 16, 17, 18, 62, 63, 64, 65, 69, 70, 71, 93, 94, 107, 108, 111, 112, 113, 114, 115, 116, 119, 120, 121, 124, 125, 127, 137, 142, 144, 148, 149, 151, 152, 156, 159, 162, 165, 170, 171, 173, 174, 175, 177, 178, 183, 241
Gender, Fantasy, and Realism in American Literature, 17
"Gift, The," 74
Gilbert, Sandra, 121, 194
Gilliard, Professor, 46
Gilligan, Carol, 113
Glas, 281
Goethe, Johann von, 175
Gonzalez-Berry, Erlinda, 217
Gordon, Deborah A., 121
Gough, John, 48
Gould, Jean, 90
Graham, Ottie Beatrice, 94, 101–2, 103
Grant, Ulysses S., 221
Grazia, Margreta de, 142
"Great Lawsuit, The," 166, 172, 182
Greenblatt, Stephen, xxii
Gregg, Frances, 67
Grimké, Charlotte Forten. *See* Forten, Charlotte
Grimké, Francis, 41
Grosz, Elizabeth, 71, 80, 83
"Growing Up Asian in America," 112
Gubar, Susan, 87, 121, 194

Habegger, Alfred, 7, 8
Hagedorn, Jessica, 120, 122
Hallberg, Robert von, 272
Halleck, Henry Wagner, 224
Hamburg Massacre, 46
Harding, Sandra, 121
Harlem Renaissance, x, vi, 91, 92, 94, 96, 100, 103, 104
Harper, Frances, xv–xvi, 16, 40–50, 52, 55, 58, 59
Harris, Joel Chandler, 56
Harris, Sharon, 209
Harris, Susan, 229
Harrison, Daphne Duval, 91
Hartman, Geoffrey, 108
"Hatred," 99–100
"Have They Attacked Mary, He Giggled," 256
Hawthorne, Nathaniel, 164, 165, 184, 194, 198, 216, 229, 245
Hayes, Rutherford B., 46
Hayslip, Le Ly, 124
Hazard of New Fortunes, A, 8, 189
H. D., xvi, 62, 63, 64, 65, 66, 67, 68, 69, 71, 72–75, 77, 78, 79, 80–82, 84, 85, 90, 183, 189
Heart of a Woman, The, 99
Hedges, Elaine, xiv, 138
Heine, Heinrich, 32
Hejinian, Lyn, 259, 262, 265
Hemingway, Ernest, 8, 30, 189, 226, 239, 255, 260, 266
Henneberg, Sylvia, xviii
Henry, William A., 3d, 26–27
hermeneutics, xii
"Hermione," 81
Higginson, Thomas Wentworth, 50, 51, 55, 56, 188, 190, 191, 198
Hilda's Book, 74
"Hills Like White Elephants," 260
Hoffman, Michael J., 248, 262, 266
Honey, Maureen, 91
Hopkins, Sarah Winnemucca, 204, 205
Hospital Sketches, 196–97
House of Mirth, The, 227, 233–34, 236, 238, 245
Houston, James, 115, 130
Houston, Jeanne Wakatsuki, 115, 117, 125, 130
"How Celia Changed Her Mind," 29
Howe, Susan, 259, 262
Howells, William Dean, 3, 5, 8, 32, 51, 52, 55, 189, 208, 210, 214, 229, 232, 239
Howitt, William, 56
How Writing Is Written, 259

Hua, Chuang, 125
Huckleberry Finn, 29, 30, 229
Hughes, Langston, 256
Hugo, Victor, 32, 205, 206
Hulme, T. E., 65, 72
Huneker, James, 263
"Huntress, The," 80, 82
Hurston, Zora Neale, 93, 97, 105
Hutcheon, Linda, 240
Hwang, David, 122, 125

"If Sartre Was a Whore," 118
imagism, 62–90
"In a Station of the Metro," 67, 264
"In Excelsis," 80
In Our Time, 260
"In the Cliff Temple," 74
Iola Leroy, 16, 59
Irigaray, Luce, xxi, 75
Iser, Wolfgang, xxi
Is Literary History Possible? xiii, xiv
"I Want to Die While You Love Me," 99

Jackson, Helen Hunt, 214
Jacobs, Harriet, 9, 165
Jacques-Garvey, Amy Euphemia, 96–97
James, Henry, 3, 5, 21, 22, 52, 186, 214, 226, 228, 229, 238, 243–45
James, William, 252
Jameson, Fredric, 139–40, 142, 144, 146, 148, 152, 153
Jarrell, Randall, 268
Jen, Gish, 122
Jewett, Sarah Orne, xv, 19, 26, 29, 34–35, 39, 52, 229
Johnson, Andrew, 40, 49
Johnson, Charles S., 92
Johnson, Georgia Douglas, 94, 97, 98–100, 105
Johnson, Helene, 104
Johnson, Samuel, 23
Johnson, Susan, 204, 220
Johnson, Thomas, 141–42, 143, 150
Johnson-Odim, Cheryl, 121
Jones, James, 188
Jong, Erica, 274
Joyce, James, 239, 248, 249, 257, 259
Jungle, The, 211

Kadohata, Cynthia, 122
Kalstone, Frank, 276

Kamani, Ginu, 124
Kant, Immanuel, 76
Kaplan, Amy, 20, 22, 229
Kazin, Alfred, 242
Keckley, Elizabeth, 204, 205, 216
Kelly, Joan, xiii, 26, 137, 161, 173, 174
Kennedy, X. J., 269
Kenner, Hugh, 86
Kerber, Linda, 163
Kermode, Frank, 276, 277
Kim, Elaine H., 111, 117
Kim, Tommy S., 129
Kimball, Roger, 26
King, Edward, 56
King Philip's War, 143
Kingston, Maxine Hong, 109, 112, 122, 123, 125
Kirkland, Caroline, xv, 9, 13, 23, 165
Knopf, Marcy, 94
Kolodny, Annette, xiii–xiv, 19, 127–28, 138, 174, 205, 212
Kutzinski, Vera, 172–73, 178, 183

Lacan, Jacques, 108
Lafayette, Marquis de, 240
Land Act of 1851, 208
Larsen, Nella, 93
Last Generation, The, 217
Lauretis, Teresa de, 85
Lauter, Paul, 93, 212
Law-Yone, Wendy, 124, 125
lesbianism, x, xii, xvi, xxii, 62–90, 176, 177, 248, 268, 270, 273, 275–76, 282–83
"Lest," 70
Levertov, Denise, 194
Lewis, R. W. B., 245
Lewis, Wyndham, 66, 77, 88
Lidoff, Joan, 245
Life among the Piutes, 204
Life in the Iron Mills, 205, 208–10
"Life on the Sea Islands," 50, 51, 52–55, 56
"Lifting Belly," 69, 81, 262
Lim, Genny, 117–18, 119
Lim, Shirley Geok-lin, x, xvi, 122
Limon, John, 188–89, 200
Lincoln, Abraham, 202, 204, 218
Lincoln, Mary Todd, 202, 204
Ling, Amy, 126
local color, xix, xviii, 26, 27, 29, 36, 37, 52, 54, 55, 56, 229. *See also* regionalism
Locke, Alain, xvi, 91, 94–95, 96

Loeffelholz, Mary, xvii, xx
London, Jack, 8
Longfellow, Henry Wadsworth, 164
"Lotus Blossoms Don't Bleed," 112
Lovell, Terry, 4, 20
"Love Song of J. Alfred Prufrock, The," 250
Loving in the War Years, 177
Lowell, Amy, xvi, 62–63, 64, 65, 66, 67, 68–72, 73, 74, 75, 77, 78–80, 81, 82, 84, 85, 86, 87, 89, 90
Lowell, James Russell, 51
Loy, Mina, 249, 259
Lubbock, Percy, 229
Lucky, Crystal, x, xvi, 105

McCabe, Susan, x, xvi
McCarthy, Joseph, xi
McDowell, Deborah, xxi
McGann, Jerome, 276, 277
"Madonna of the Evening Flowers," 79
Maggie, A Girl of the Streets, 8
"Maid of Monterey, The," 214
Margret Howth, 6
Marshall, Paule, 93
"Martha's Lady," 29
Marxism, xv, 4, 20, 122, 139
Mather, Cotton, 147
"Matisse," 251, 252, 253–54, 255, 257
Matisse, Henri, 251, 252, 253–54, 264
Matthiessen, F. O., ix, xvii, xx, 164, 186, 187, 188
Maximilian, Archduke, 206, 222
Mazumdar, Sucheta, 113, 114, 128
M. Butterfly, 122, 125
Melville, Herman, 164, 169, 198, 199
Messer-Davidow, Ellen, 108, 127
Metacomet, 143
"Mid-day," 72
"Midwifs," 118
Miller, Elise, 21
Miller, James, 164
Miller, Kelly, 95
Miller, Perry, xvii, 141–42, 143, 145, 148, 150
Millett, Kate, xxi
Minh-ha, Trinh T., 120
Minister's Wooing, The, 29
Minnie's Sacrifice, 43, 44, 45, 46–48, 49–50
"Miscast," 90
"Mission of Jane, The," 229–30, 232
"Miss Lucinda," 29
"Miss Tempy's Watchers," 29, 34–35

Mitford, Mary Russell, 56
Moby-Dick, 169
modernism, x, xvi, xviii, 4, 35, 63–68, 72, 74, 83–84, 86, 87–90, 183, 226, 227, 239, 240, 241, 248, 249, 250, 256, 264
Mohanty, Chandra, 121
Molesworth, Charles, 271
Montes, Amelia M. de la Luz, x, xvii–xviii
Moore, Marianne, 189, 190
Moraga, Cherríe, 177, 178, 217
Morrison, Toni, 93, 212
Mother's Recompense, The, 232
Moveable Feast, A, 260
"Mr. Savage's Sermon, 'The Problem of the Hour,'" 58
"Mrs. Flint's Married Experience," 29
Muecke, D. C., 233
Mukherjee, Bharati, 122, 124
Mulberry and Peach, 125
Murphy, Beatrice, 97–98, 103
Muske, Carol, 270

Native American Indians, xii, xiv, 34, 140, 141, 144, 145, 146, 148, 149, 173, 215, 216, 217, 219
Nature, 174, 175
Nelson, Cary, 268
New Criticism, xi, xii, xv, 4
"New England Nun, A," 29
new historicism, ix, xii, xxii
New Home, Who'll Follow?, A, 9–12, 23
New Negro, The, xvi, 91, 95
Newsome, Mary Effie Lee, 103
Nicholls, Peter, 66, 77
Nieh, Hua Ling, 125
Noda, Kesaya E., 112
Norris, Frank, 3, 5, 203, 204, 210, 211, 219–20, 222, 236
Norton, Sara, 237
Notes on Thought and Vision, 63

O'Clair, Robert, 269
Octopus, The, 203, 220
Oden, Frederick Bryant, 218
Of Woman Born, 268, 273, 275
Ojibwa (George Copway), 165
Okihiro, Gary, 122, 126
Oktenberg, Adrian, 274–75
Oldtown Folks, 29
"Old Woman Magoun," 29
Omi, Michael, 122

"One Phase of the Race Question," 51
On Lies, Secrets, and Silence, 268, 273, 275
"Only Rose, The," 29
"Orchard," 74
"Oread," 72, 73
"Orion Dead," 74
Orr, Gregory, 271, 272
Ostriker, Alicia, 270
Others, 259
Our Nig, 14–18
"Outlaw," 84
"Oven Bird, The," 239
Owen, Chandler, 96
Owens, Maude Irwin, 94

Padillo, Genaro M., 221
Page, Thomas Nelson, 56
Paint It Today, 67
Pamela, 150, 152
Papers on Literature and Art, 177
Parker, Mark, 156
Parrington, Vernon Louis, 7, 20, 22, 181
"Parting, The," 97–98
Part of the Climate, 259, 261, 262, 263
Parton, Sara Payson Willis. *See* Fern, Fanny
Paterson, 255
"Patriarchal Poetry," 250, 256, 262
"Patterns," 89
"Pear Tree," 81
"Pelican, The," 230–31, 232, 237, 245
Pendleton, Leila Amos, 94
Penn, I. Garland, 42
performativity, xxii, 3, 6, 9, 13, 14, 17
periodization, ix–xxiv, 26, 64, 92, 109, 124, 126, 137–55, 156, 159, 161, 162, 163, 164, 165, 169, 174, 175, 176, 177, 178, 204, 205, 249, 250, 260, 268, 271, 273, 276, 277
Perkins, David, xiii, xiv, 86, 281
Perloff, Marjorie, 274
Perry, Donna, 127
Peterson, Carla, xv, 61
Petry, Ann, 93
Phelps, Elizabeth Stuart, 22
Phillips, Wendell, 57
Philosophy and Opinions of Marcus Garvey, The, 97
"Picasso," 251, 252, 253–54, 255–56, 257, 261, 263, 264
Picasso, Pablo, 251, 252, 253–54, 255, 257, 263–64
Pietri, Arturo Uslar, 222–23

Pilgrim's Progress, 220
Pink Melon Joy, 78
Plath, Sylvia, 244, 281
Plato, 235
Pocahontas's Daughter, 130
Poe, Edgar Allan, 164
"Poetess, A," 29
Poetics, 233
Pollak, Vivian, 200
Popel, Esther, 103
"Portrait of Mabel Dodge at the Villa Curona," 257
postcolonialism, 109, 120, 121, 122, 124, 125, 126
postmodernism, xiii, xvi, 4, 8, 125–26, 188, 248, 249, 250, 256, 258, 259, 263, 281
poststructuralism, xi, xv, 4
Pound, Ezra, x, 63, 65, 66, 67, 68, 72, 73, 74, 77, 86, 183, 239, 249, 250, 264, 281
Princesse de Clèves, La, 240
"Procne's Song: The Task of Feminist Literary Criticism," 127
Promised Land, 130
Puritanism and Puritans, American, xvii, 141, 142, 143, 144, 145, 146, 147, 148, 149, 155
"Pursuit," 80

queer theory, xxii
"Quicksand, The," 237

race, x, xii, xv, xvi, xxi–xxii, 4, 6, 14, 15, 16, 17, 18, 27, 31, 39–59, 91–106, 107, 111, 112, 114–115, 116, 121, 122, 123, 125, 127, 138, 149, 160, 173, 177, 180, 202, 204, 206, 223
Randolph, A. Philip, 95–96
Randolph, Ruth Elizabeth, 94
realism, x, xv, xviii, xx, 3–25, 26, 29, 31, 37, 39, 204, 205, 206, 207, 208, 209, 210, 226, 232, 237, 238, 239, 240, 241, 245
Reason for Singing, 100
Rebolledo, Tey Diana, 216, 225
Reckless Eyeballing, 130
Reconstruction, 39, 40, 41, 43, 45, 46, 55, 58, 59
"Red Wheelbarrow, The," 264
Reed, Ishmael, 110, 130
regionalism, xv, 19. *See also* local color
Republic, 235
Reyes de la Maza, Luis, 222
Reynolds, David, 186
Rich, Adrienne, xviii, 194, 267–83

Richardson, Samuel, 150
Rise of Silas Lapham, The, 239
romanticism, 7, 8, 9, 10, 11, 12, 14, 65, 66, 168, 169, 175, 181, 184, 203, 206, 207, 214, 237
Romero, Lora, 223
Ronyoung, Kim, 115–16
Roosevelt, Theodore, 220
Roses, Lorraine Elena, 94
Rowlandson, Mary White, xvi, 137–58
Ruddick, Lisa, 249
Ruiz de Burton, María Amparo, xvii–xviii, xix, 202–25
Russell, Ada, 67, 72, 79, 80, 85, 88–89, 90
Ruth Hall, 12, 13, 14

Said, Edward, xxiii
Saldívar, Ramón, 212
Sánchez, Rosaura, 213, 215
Sanctuary, 231–32
Sand, George, 32
Sandoval, Chela, 222–23
Sappho, 62, 64, 78, 80
Sartre, Jean-Paul, 118
Sayers, Dorothy, 263
Scarlet Letter, The, 29
Schlegel, Friedrich, 234
Schockley, Ann Allen, 106
Schulman, Grace, 190
Schussele, Christian, 169, 170
Schweik, Susan, 189–90
Scott, Bonnie Kime, 84, 86
Scott, Joan, 22–23, 104, 139–40, 142, 144, 145, 146, 148, 152, 153
Scruggs, Lawson, 41
Sea Garden, 67, 68, 72, 80, 82
"Sea Gods," 80
"Sea Lily," 75
"Sea Rose," 72, 75
"Sea Violet," 75
Sedgwick, Eve Kosofsky, xxii, 7, 178
sentimentalism, 5, 175, 184, 195, 199, 211, 226, 228, 229, 236, 237, 241
Sexton, Anne, 281
sexuality, x, xii, 5, 6, 13, 27, 63, 64, 65, 66, 67, 68, 70, 71, 75, 76, 77, 81, 87, 89, 96, 111, 118, 119, 123, 168, 170, 171, 176, 177, 178, 273
Shakespeare, William, 3
Shelley, Percy Bysshe, 65
"Sheltered Garden," 73, 75, 82

Showalter, Elaine, xxi
"Shrine, The," 81
Sidhwa, Bhapsi, 124
Silber, Nina, 56
Simpson, David, 183
Sinclair, Upton, 208, 211
Singing Bells, The, 100
Singley, Carol, x, xviii
Sister Carrie, 212, 236
"Sister Liddy," 29, 35–36
"Sisters, The," 62
Sitwell, Edith, 189
"Slackened Caprice," 101–2
slavery, 30–31, 42, 44, 45, 47, 53, 54, 55, 57, 58, 100, 101, 223
Sleeper Wakes, The, 94
Smiley, Jane, 29
Smith, Barbara, xxi
Smith-Rosenberg, Carroll, 176
Snapshots of a Daughter-in-Law, 279
Social Darwinism, 8
"Some Account of Thomas Tucker," 29
Some Imagist Poets, 89
Songs to Joannes, 249
Sound and the Fury, The, 259
Sowell, Thomas, 131
Sowing and Reaping, 43, 44, 45, 46, 48–49, 50
Spencer, Herbert, 230
Spengemann, William, 212
Spiegelman, Williard, 268, 270
Spiller, Robert, 141, 142, 145, 150, 242
Spillers, Hortense, xiv
"Sprig of Rosemary, A," 79
Spring Day, 69
Squatter and the Don, The, 203, 204, 207–8, 210, 211, 215–16
Stanton, Elizabeth Cady, 166, 168
Stearns, Frazer, 191–92, 193
Stein, Gertrude, x, xvi, xviii, 62, 63, 64, 65, 66, 67, 68, 69, 71, 75–77, 81, 82–83, 84, 85, 87, 89–90, 248–66
Steinbeck, John, 3
Stendhal (Henri Beyle), 9, 241
Stevens, Wallace, 65, 259
Stewart, Mother, 45
Stieglitz, Alfred, 251, 252, 253, 254
Stimpson, Catherine, 67
Stone, Lucy, 168
Story of Avis, The, 22

Stowe, Harriet Beecher, xv, 9, 26, 29–32, 52, 186, 187, 197, 198, 211
Suleiman, Susan Rubin, 119
Suleri, Sara, 124
Summer on the Lakes, 174, 175
Sundquist, Eric, 245
Sweeney, Susan Elizabeth, 228, 244
Swinburne, Charles Algernon, 66
Sword Blades and Poppy Seed, 67, 68, 72
S/Z, 281

Taine, Hippolyte, 237
Tanner, Benjamin, 42
"Task of Negro Womanhood, The," 96
Tendencies in Modern American Poetry, 69, 77, 85
Tender Buttons, 67, 75, 76, 89, 250, 252, 254, 255, 256, 257
Tennenhouse, Leonard, 142, 149–55, 156, 158
Ten Nights in a Bar-Room, 48
Theory of Literature, xi
Thompson, Eloise Bibb, 94
Thoreau, Henry David, 164
"Three Dogs and a Rabbit," 100–101
Three Lives, 250, 252, 254–55
Tichi, Cecelia, 244
Tillinghast, Richard, 269
"To a Wild Rose," 101
Toklas, Alice B., 63, 67, 78, 85, 88
Tolstoy, Leo, 32
Tompkins, Jane, 212, 224–25
Toomer, Jean, 249, 259
To the Lighthouse, 259
Touchstone, The, 244
Toulouse, Teresa, xvii
Toussaint L'Ouverture, Pierre Dominique, 55
"Toward a More Feminist Criticism," 277
Treaty of Guadalupe Hidalgo, 211, 212, 219, 220
Trial and Triumph, 43
Trilling, Lionel, 19, 238, 246
Tripmaster Monkey, 112, 122
Turgenev, Ivan, 32
Twain, Mark, 186, 226, 229
Twenty-One Love Poems, 272, 274–75, 276
Tyler, Parker, 249, 259

Ulysses, 249, 259
Umemoto, Ann, 131
Uncle Tom's Cabin, 29–32, 211
Untermeyer, Louis, 68

Vallejo, Mariano Guadalupe, 206, 211, 217–18, 221–22
Valley of Decision, The, 238
Vechten, Carl Van, 257
Vendler, Helen, 270
"Vesuvius at Home," 271, 275
Vietnam War, xi, 190, 194, 272–73
"Vintage," 71
"Visit to the Birthplace of Whittier, A," 50, 56

Wagner-Martin, Linda, 226, 243, 244–45, 249, 265
Waldmeir, Joseph, 266
Walker, Alice, 93
Wall, Cheryl, 91, 105
Warner, Charles Dudley, 5
Warner, Susan, 9
Warren, Austin, xi
Warren, Joyce, xv, xx, 22, 23–24
Warren, Robert Penn, 269
Wars I Have Seen, 259
Washington, Mary Helen, 93, 103
Waste Land, The, 239, 249, 250
Waves, The, 249, 255, 259
"Wayfaring Couple, A," 29
Weiss, Andrea, 87
Weisstein, Naomi, xxii
Wellek, René, xi, 234
Werner, Craig, 267
West, Dorothy, 93, 94, 104
Wetherbee, Winthrop, 276, 277
Wharton, Edith, xviii, xix, 5, 226–47
"When We Dead Awaken," 268, 271, 274
"Whisper to Romantic Young Ladies, A," 12
White, Barbara, 24
Whitehead, Alfred, 261
"White Heron, A," 29
Whitman, Walt, 170, 171, 177, 189, 194, 198, 208, 216
Whittier, John Greenleaf, 50, 51, 54, 55, 56–57, 197
Who Would Have Thought It? 203, 208, 209–10, 218
Wicked Sisters, The, 271
Wilde, Oscar, 177
Wild Patience Has Taken Me This Far, A, 274

Willard, Frances, 49
Williams, Lucy Ariel, 103
Williams, William Carlos, 255, 257, 259, 263, 264, 265
Wilson, Harriet, xv, 9, 14–18
Wolff, Cynthia Griffin, 186, 191
Wolosky, Shira, 187–88, 201
Woman Warrior, The, 109, 112, 114, 123
Women's Christian Temperance Union (WCTU), 46, 49
Wong, Jade Snow, 115, 117
Wong, Shawn, 110, 130
Wood, Mary, 173, 176, 177
Woolf, Virginia, 194, 249, 255, 259
World War I, 63, 258
World War II, 258, 259
Writing of Fiction, The, 240, 241

Yamada, Mitsuye, 116
Yamamoto, Hisaye, 110
Yamashita, Karen Tei, 118, 119
Yamauchi, Wakako, 110
Years, The, 255
Yeats, William Butler, 66
Yezierska, Anzia, 130
Yogi, Stan, 110

Zaragoza, Ignacio, 206
Zarco, Cyn., 110
Zavella, Patricia, 127
Zetzel, James E. G., 276, 277
Zimmerman, Bonnie, xxii, 64–65, 85, 87, 276
Zwarg, Christina, 173–74, 175, 177, 179